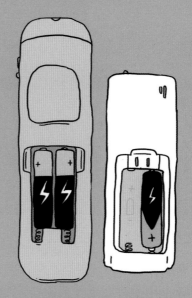

I'M A MESS:

A GUIDE TO A MESSY LIFE

EINAT TSARFATI

Translated from Hebrew by Annette Appel

Written & Illustrated by Einat Tsarfati
Translated by Annette Appel
English language layout by Noa Mishkin
Additional lettering by Micah Meyers
Maverick Senior Editor: Lauren Hitzhusen
Graphic Design by Keren & Golan

English translation rights arranged through S.B.Rights Agency by Stephanie Barrouillet

I'm a Mess: a Guide to a Messy Life published by Mad Cave Studios, LLC. 8838 SW 129th St. Miami, FL 33176.

First Printing. Printed in China.
ISBN:978-1-5458-0086-7

One of the mysterious things I learned while working on this book is that almost all human beings think of themselves as messy people. Yes, even the ones who keep an organized home, a neat weekly calendar—and even the ones who have had the same spare house key for years and put all of their cereal in airtight containers for freshness.

As an inherently messy person, that surprised me. After all, those people have it all together—they've got a special container for their cereal! But I can't argue with their feelings (and there's no doubt that, sometimes, the people who look the most organized are the messiest ones of all (but more on that in chapter 2)).

It's possible that the feelings of mess that accompany each of us are rooted in the basic human desire for stability and order. But, the truth is, no one can promise us that. Then again, it's also possible that the people I talked to were just trying to make me feel better about myself.

While I was working on this book, it got lost twice (once during the sketching stage and again on the computer's hard drive). You could say that, in general, organizing this information about messiness was a bit of a mess!

There are many sides to a mess. Sometimes, it can be petty and redundant—while other times a mess can be abstract and larger than life. I can't promise that all the data in this book is 100% correct—or that, from time to time, I didn't lose myself in the pettiness of it all. Sometimes, I may have even been carried away by its chaos.

This guidebook isn't really to make you less of a mess, nor is it to explain every subject in an orderly manner. But maybe this book will help you realize that you're not the only messy person in the world.

Einat

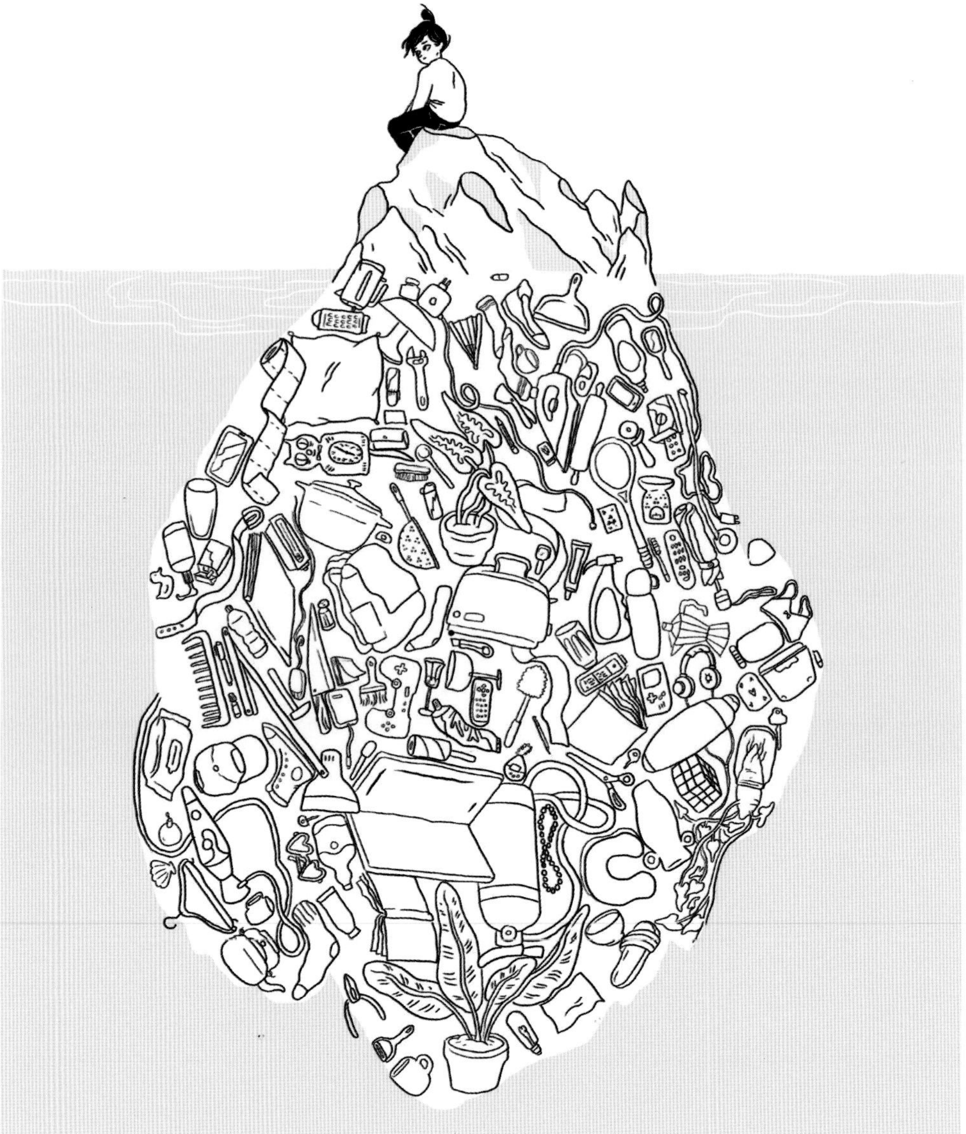

Contents

Chapter 1

WHY IS BEING MESSY
A PROBLEM?

Chapter 2

ARE YOU MESSY?

Chapter 3

WHAT CONSTITUTES
A MESS?

Chapter 4

HOW TO DEAL WITH THE MESS
or:
WHAT ARE YOU UP AGAINST?

Chapter 5

HOW TO ORGANIZE
WITHOUT GETTING ORGA-
NIZED

Chapter 6

THE ORGANIZED ONES

Chapter 7

THE EVOLUTIONAL ADVAN-
TAGES OF
BEING MESSY

Chapter 8

WHEN DO I NEED
TO GIVE IN

Chapter 9

SALVATION

WHY IS BEING MESSY A PROBLEM?

People are born messy

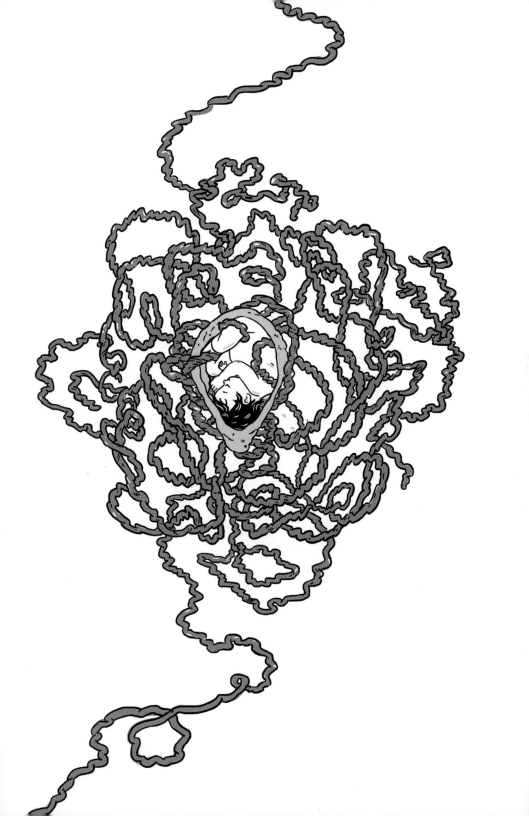

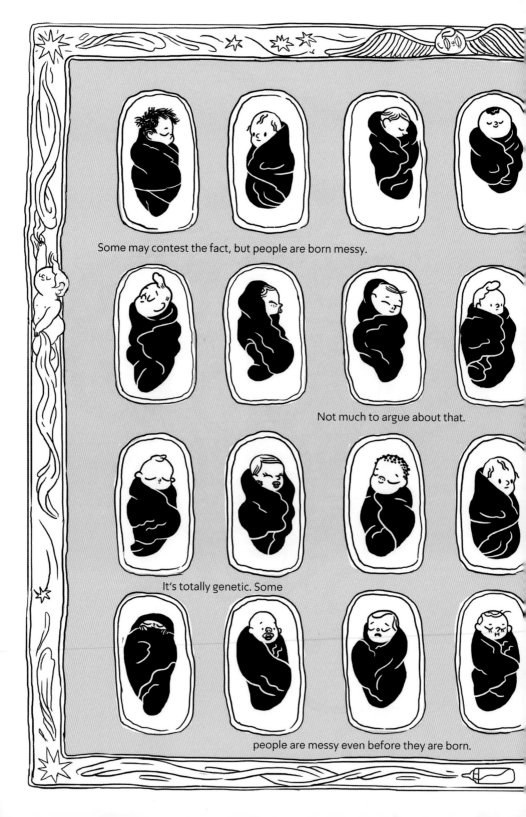

Some may contest the fact, but people are born messy.

Not much to argue about that.

It's totally genetic. Some

people are messy even before they are born.

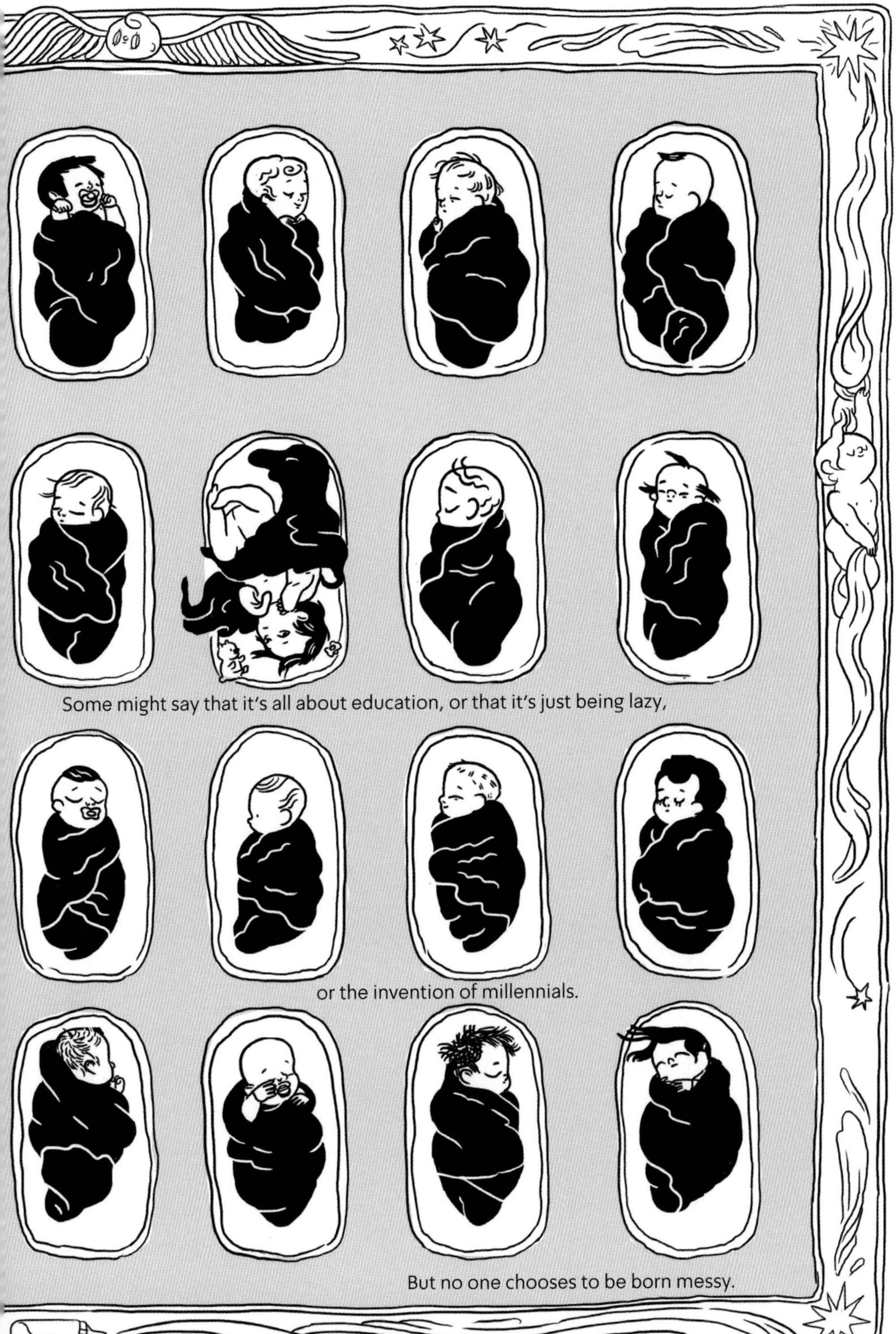
Some might say that it's all about education, or that it's just being lazy,
or the invention of millennials.
But no one chooses to be born messy.

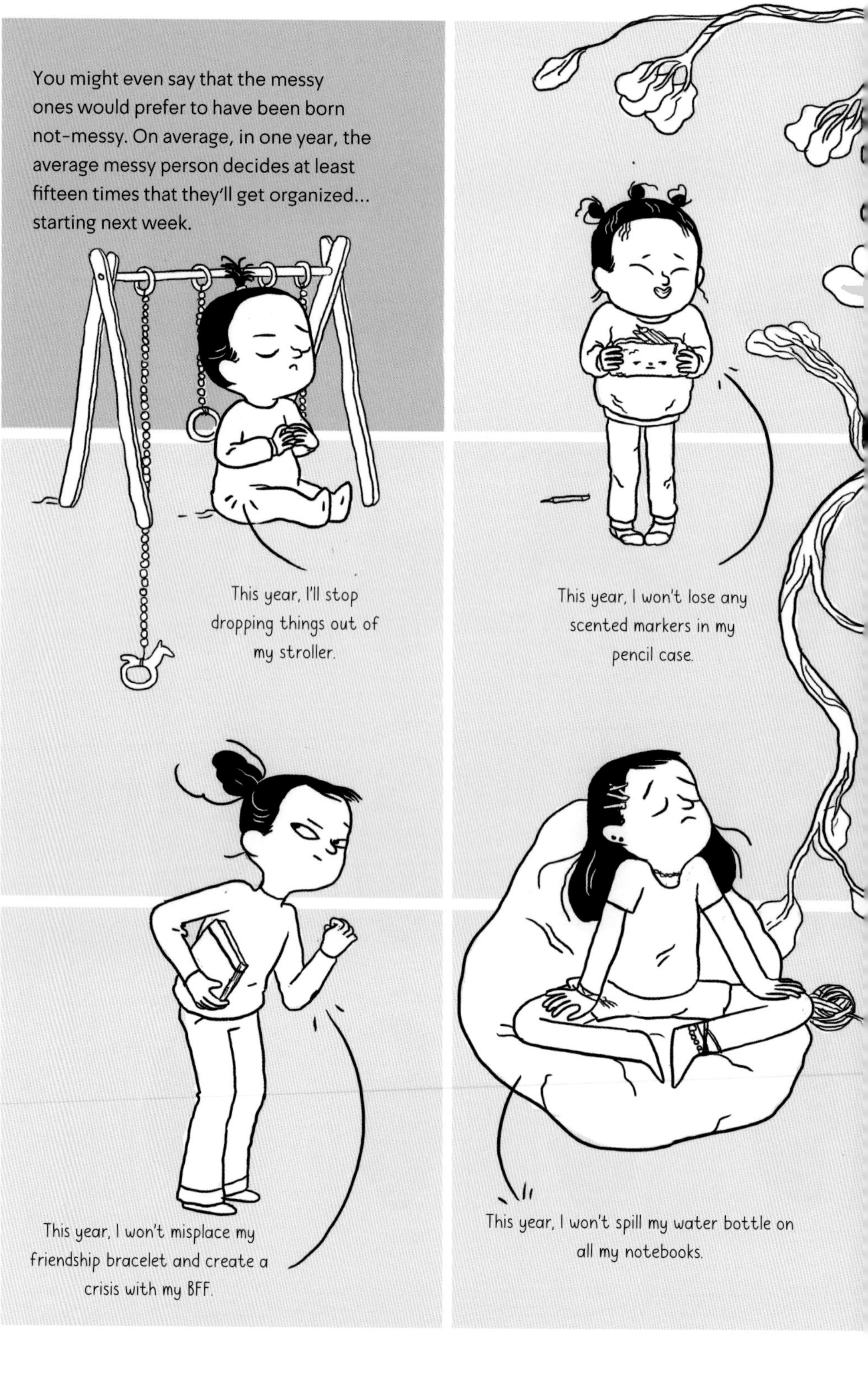
You might even say that the messy ones would prefer to have been born not-messy. On average, in one year, the average messy person decides at least fifteen times that they'll get organized... starting next week.
This year, I'll stop dropping things out of my stroller.
This year, I won't lose any scented markers in my pencil case.
This year, I won't misplace my friendship bracelet and create a crisis with my BFF.
This year, I won't spill my water bottle on all my notebooks.

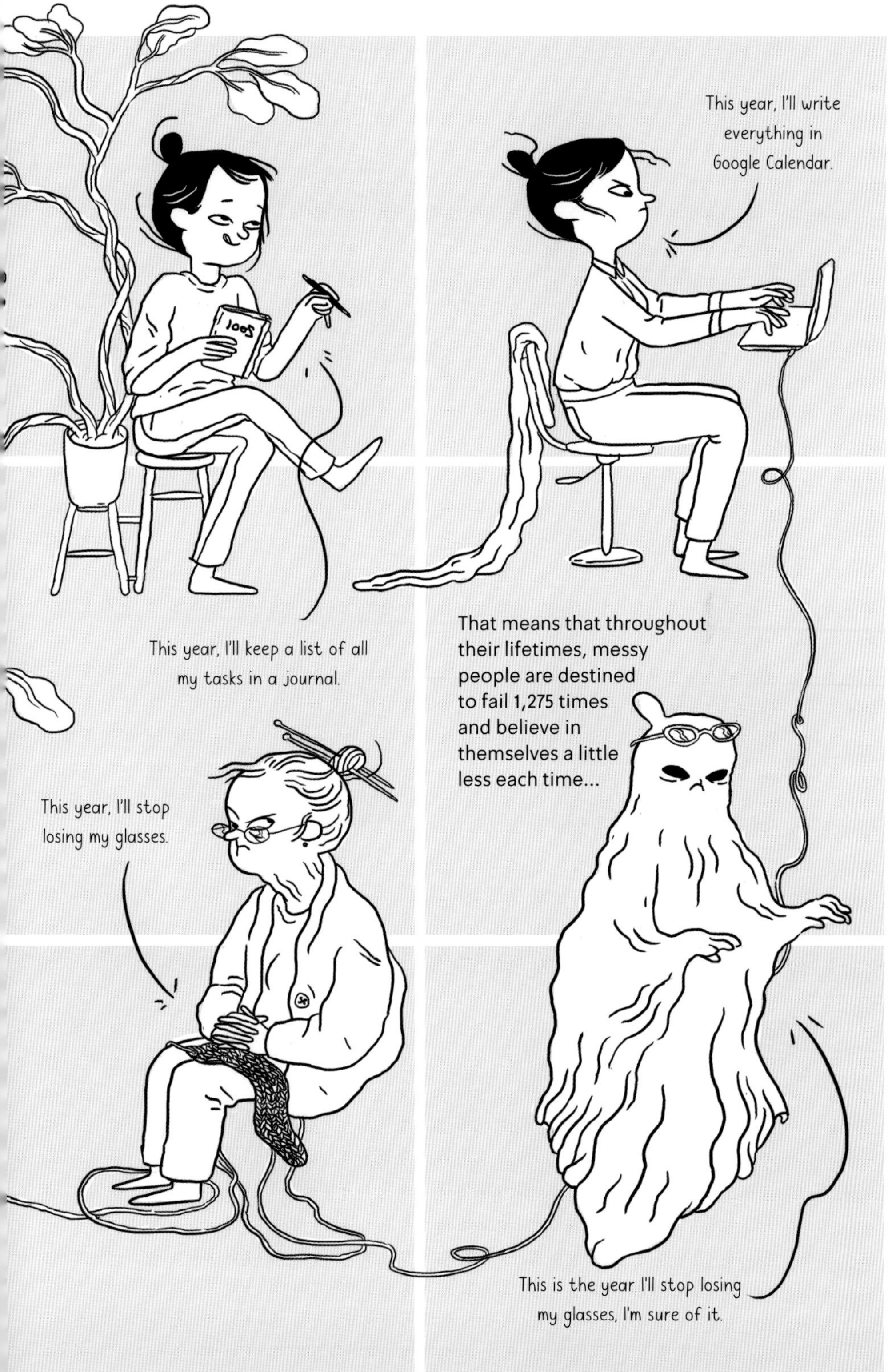
This year, I'll keep a list of all my tasks in a journal.
This year, I'll write everything in Google Calendar.
This year, I'll stop losing my glasses.
That means that throughout their lifetimes, messy people are destined to fail 1,275 times and believe in themselves a little less each time...
This is the year I'll stop losing my glasses, I'm sure of it.

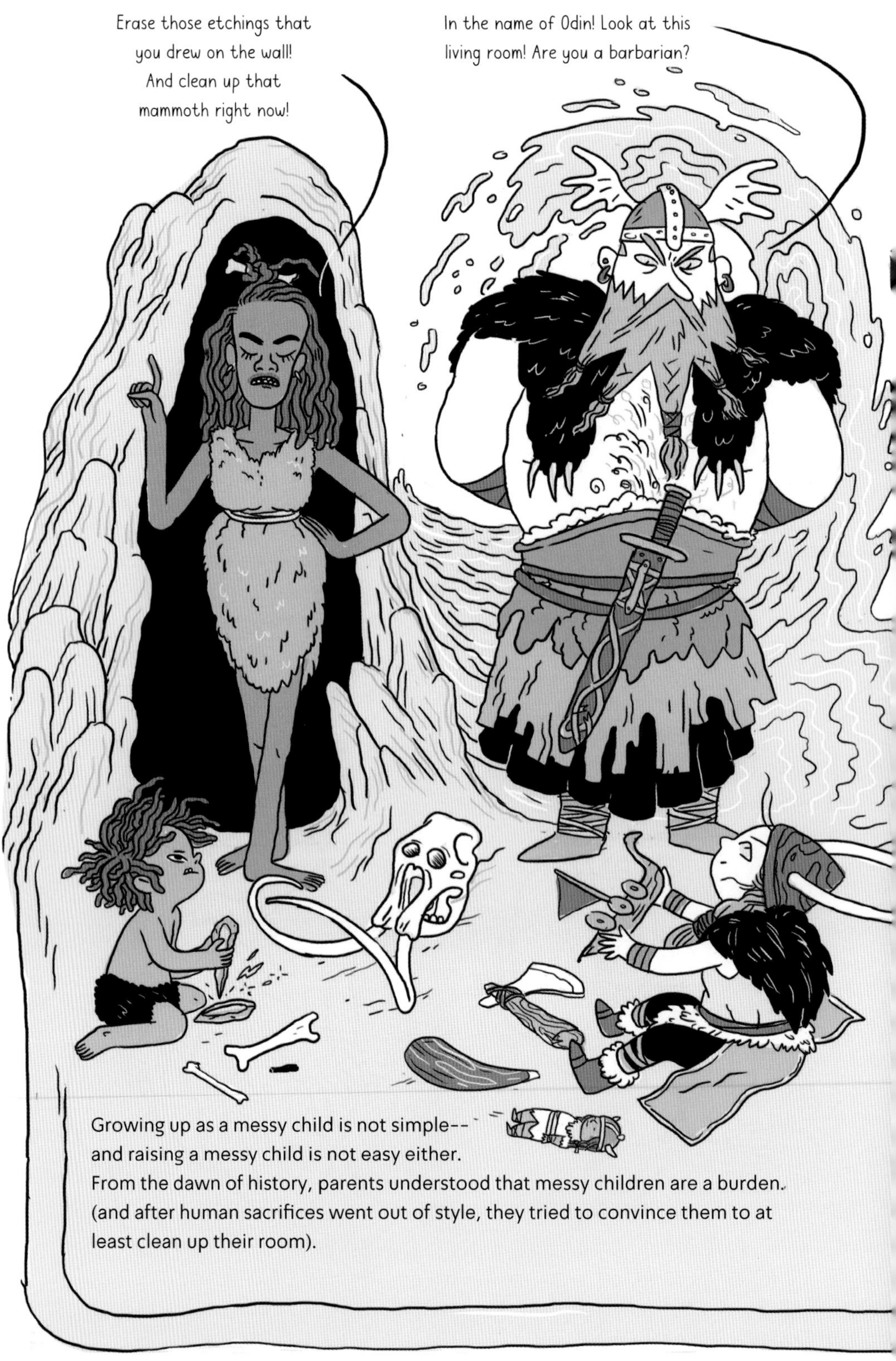
Erase those etchings that you drew on the wall! And clean up that mammoth right now!
In the name of Odin! Look at this living room! Are you a barbarian?
Growing up as a messy child is not simple--
and raising a messy child is not easy either.
From the dawn of history, parents understood that messy children are a burden.
(and after human sacrifices went out of style, they tried to convince them to at least clean up their room).

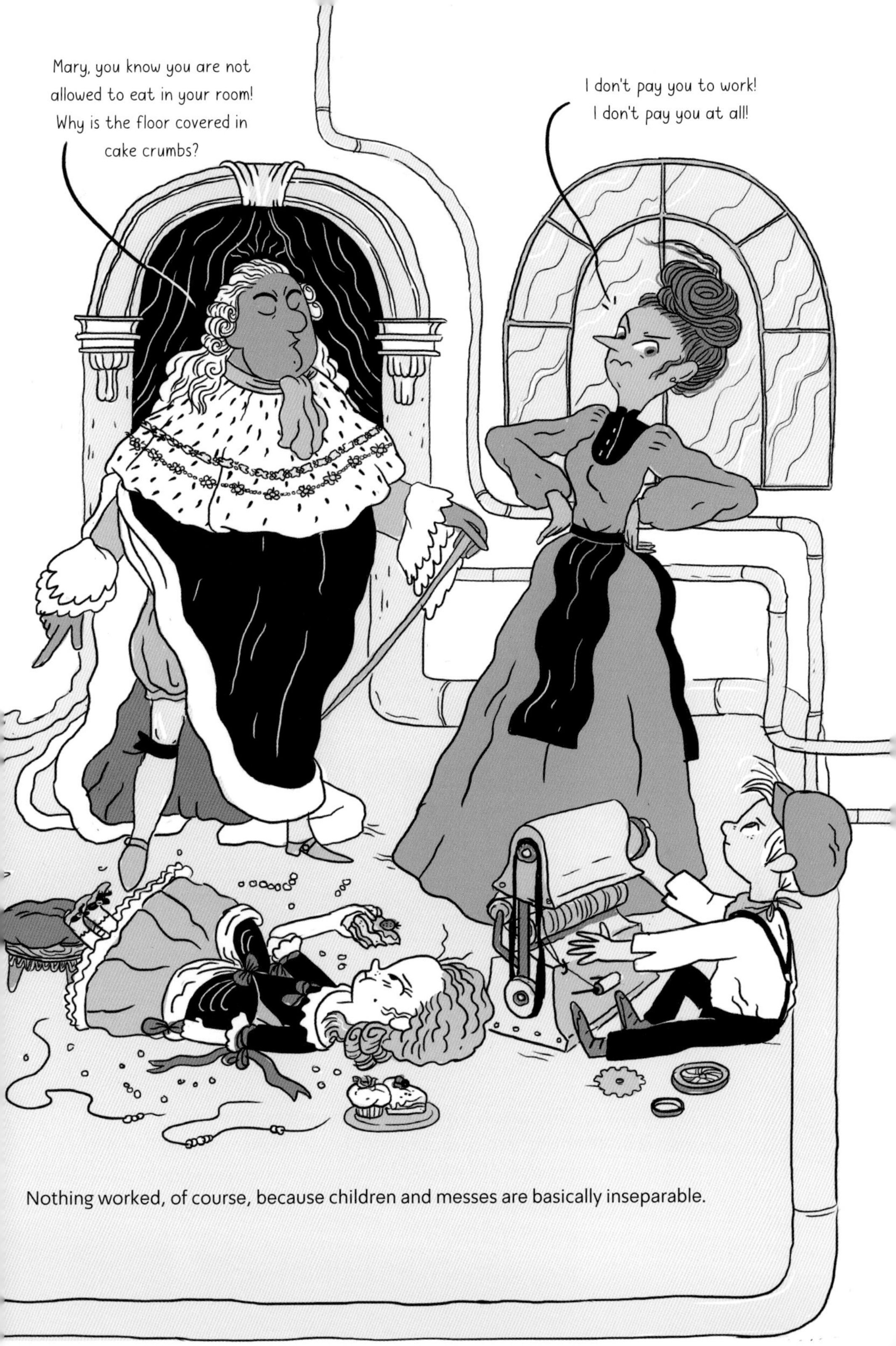
Mary, you know you are not allowed to eat in your room! Why is the floor covered in cake crumbs?
I don't pay you to work! I don't pay you at all!

Nothing worked, of course, because children and messes are basically inseparable.

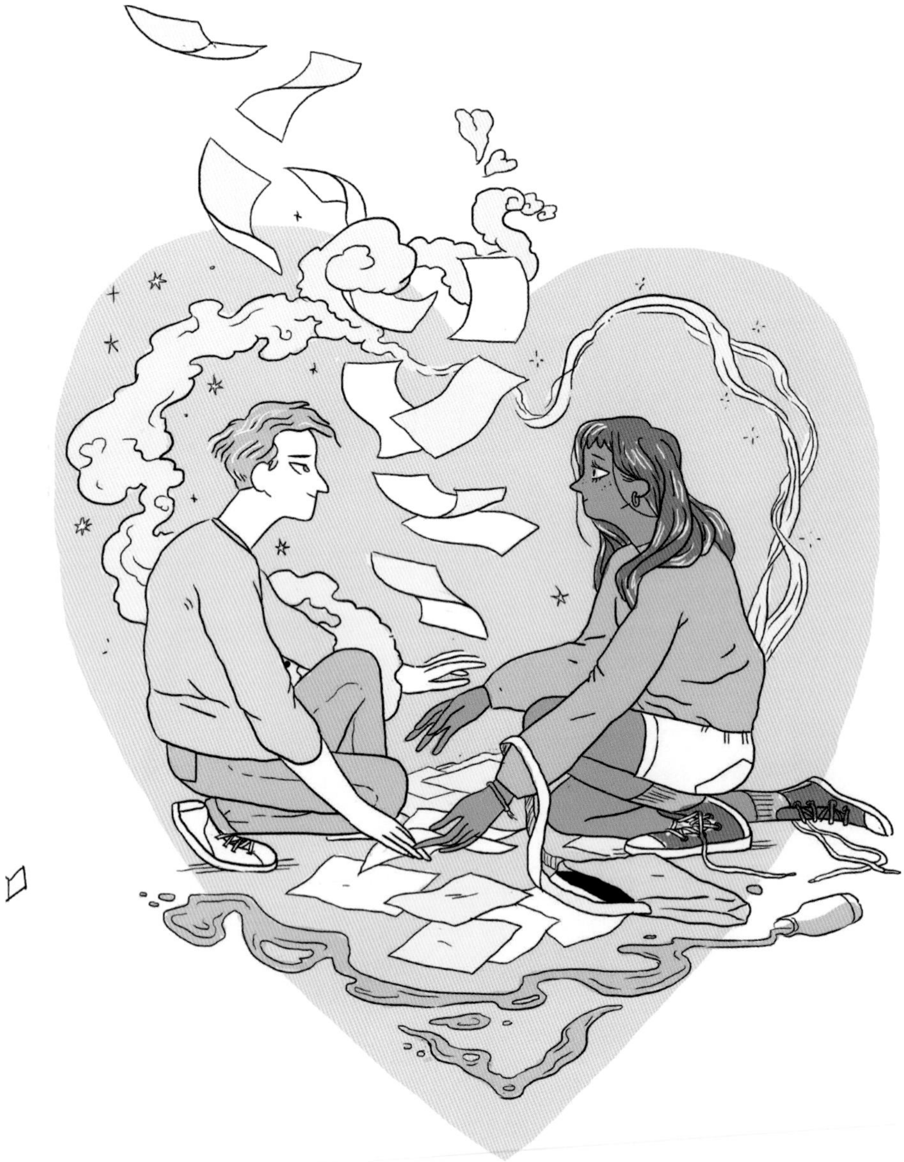

You could say that--aside from romantic comedies, when the messy-but-charming heroine drops her sloppy-but-charming bag on the floor and everything falls out and that's how she meets her soulmate--being messy has never helped anyone in any way.

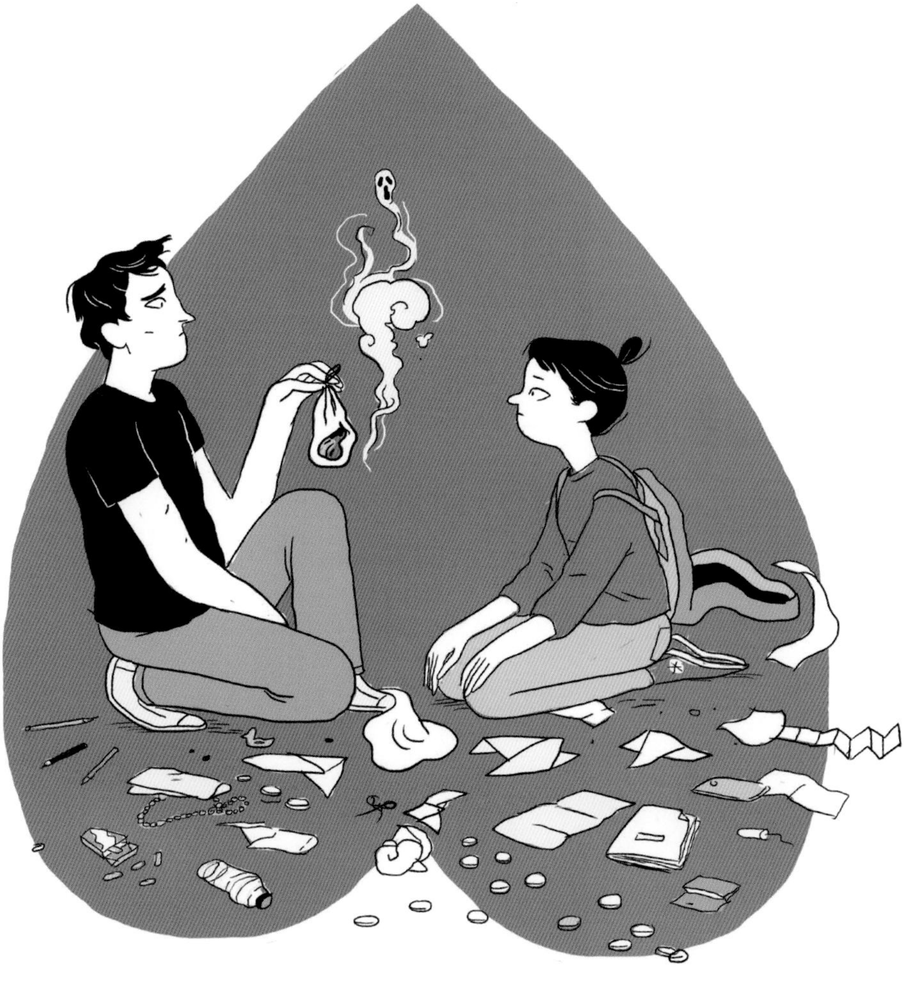

I'm pretty sure that if I had a bag and it spilled out onto the floor, no one in my immediate radius would want to connect his fate to mine. I'm pretty sure it would be just the opposite. It's not that I want to be organized. It's more like I'm tired of being a mess. I've been a mess for so many years and I can say from experience, that it's a nightmare.

First of all, there's the
material aspect.
Messy people don't have many
opportunities to accumulate
anything. They're always busy
losing stuff, or forgetting where
they put it, or leaving in on a bus.

These are the things that an average person loses during an average year:

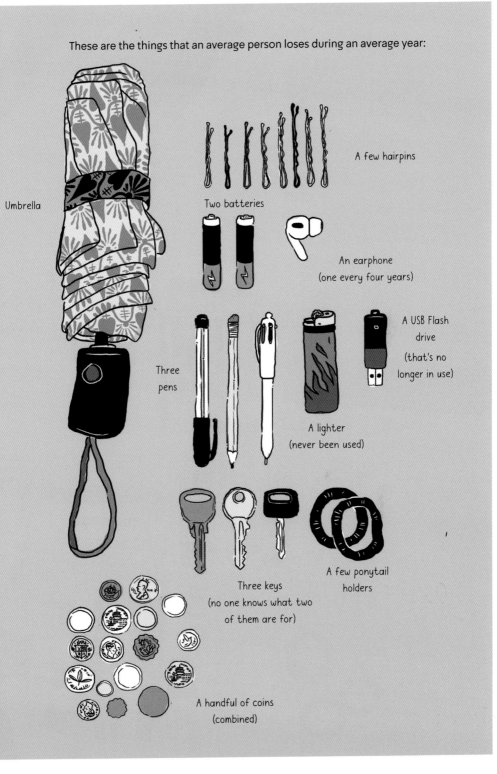

Umbrella

A few hairpins

Two batteries

An earphone
(one every four years)

Three
pens

A lighter
(never been used)

A USB Flash
drive
(that's no
longer in use)

Three keys
(no one knows what two
of them are for)

A few ponytail
holders

A handful of coins
(combined)

And these are the things that a messy person loses in two months:

Two chargers, a diamond ring, a kid's sandal, a purse, three wallets, two credit cards (not including those in the wallets – see above.) one stuffed in a coat pocket and one stored in a mobile phone case, because it seemed like a good idea at the time, two mobile phones (not the one with the credit card. that's a different story), two right foot socks, three left foot socks, (but not the ones that match the missing right foot ones), a tweezer, keys to a bike, keys to a journal, math notebook, five umbrellas, 1,000 hairpins, three earbuds (but not from the same set), a few ponytail holders, usb (in use), $400 in coins, a lighter (in use), twelve batteries.

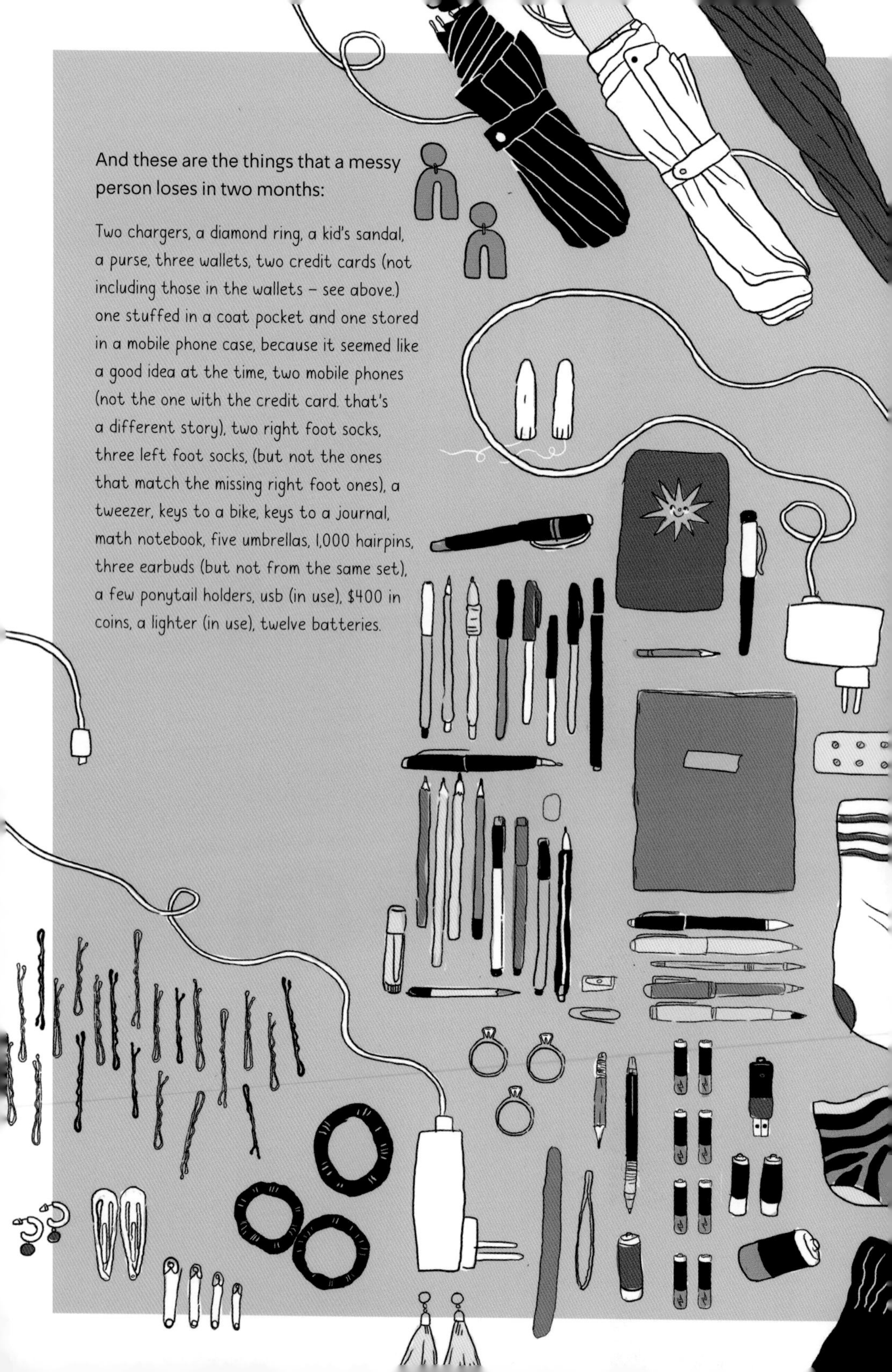

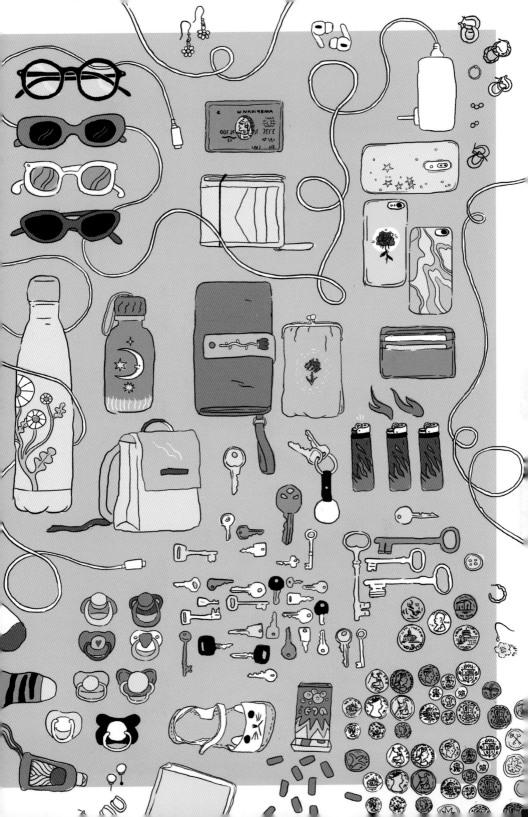

Now, let's take a minute to talk about **the waste of time**. Messy people spend an average of five years of their lives searching for house keys.

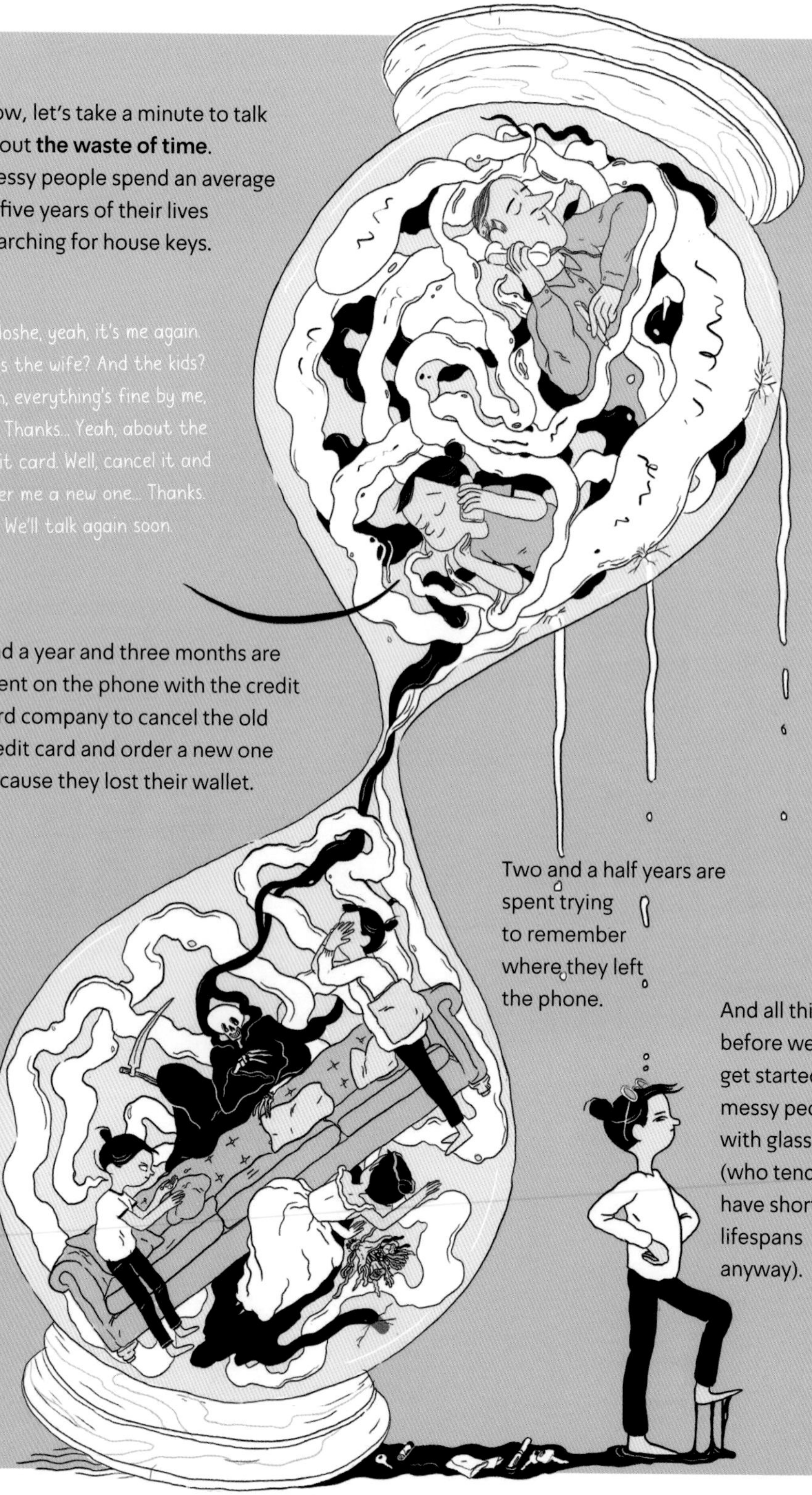
Hi Moshe, yeah, it's me again. How's the wife? And the kids? Yeah, everything's fine by me, too. Thanks... Yeah, about the credit card. Well, cancel it and order me a new one... Thanks. We'll talk again soon.

And a year and three months are spent on the phone with the credit card company to cancel the old credit card and order a new one because they lost their wallet.

Two and a half years are spent trying to remember where they left the phone.

And all this is before we even get started on messy people with glasses (who tend to have short lifespans anyway).

Of course, not all messy people are alike.
Oh, all of them lose important items all the time
(wallets, mobile phones, glasses, and keys).
Nevertheless, it is important to note that messy people
have different techniques to look for their misplaced items:

Messy People Techniques for Finding Keys:

The laidback technique: used by those who believe that if they stay calm and play hard-to-get, the key will come to find them.

The physical technique: used by those who are certain that gestures full of pathos and a dramatic enactment of the search will hasten the finding of the key.

The metaphysical technique: implies that it's all about karma and if the item is summoned by positive energies, the universe will find a way to send it back to its owner.

The exaggerators: They approach the search as if they were hunting down a wild animal in the jungle, throwing themselves flat on the floor at the slightest noise. If they want to check if the key might be hiding under an object, they'll always do so quickly with an element of surprise, as if the object could run away.

Of course, none of these techniques were actually proven to be effective.

But the truth is, the worst part is the constant feeling of insecurity that makes being a messy person a real downer. All the mess means that while you're trying to find your way in this world, you're going to have to live with the feeling that even if you manage to find your way home, chances are that you forgot to take the key and so you'll inevitably get stuck outside.

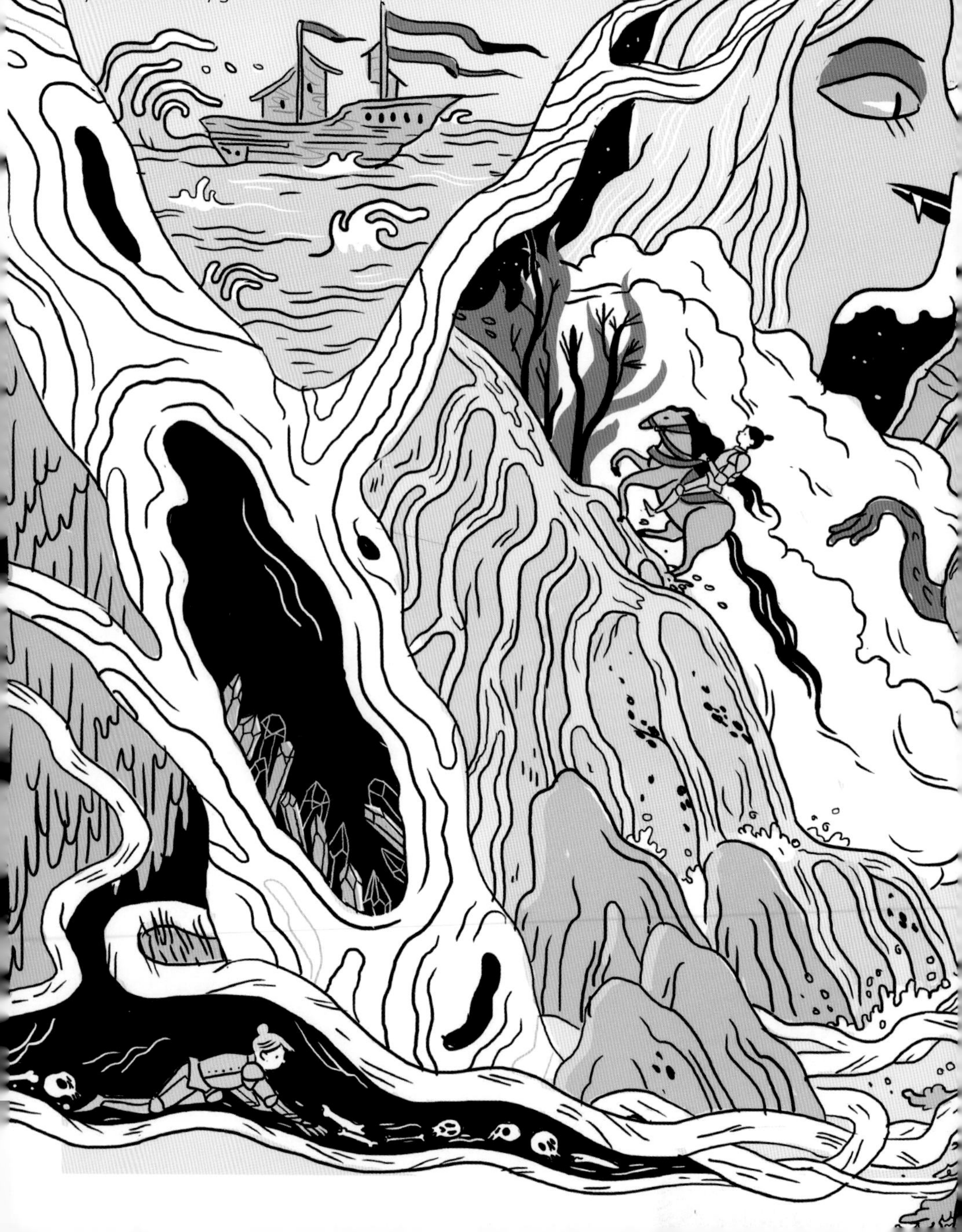

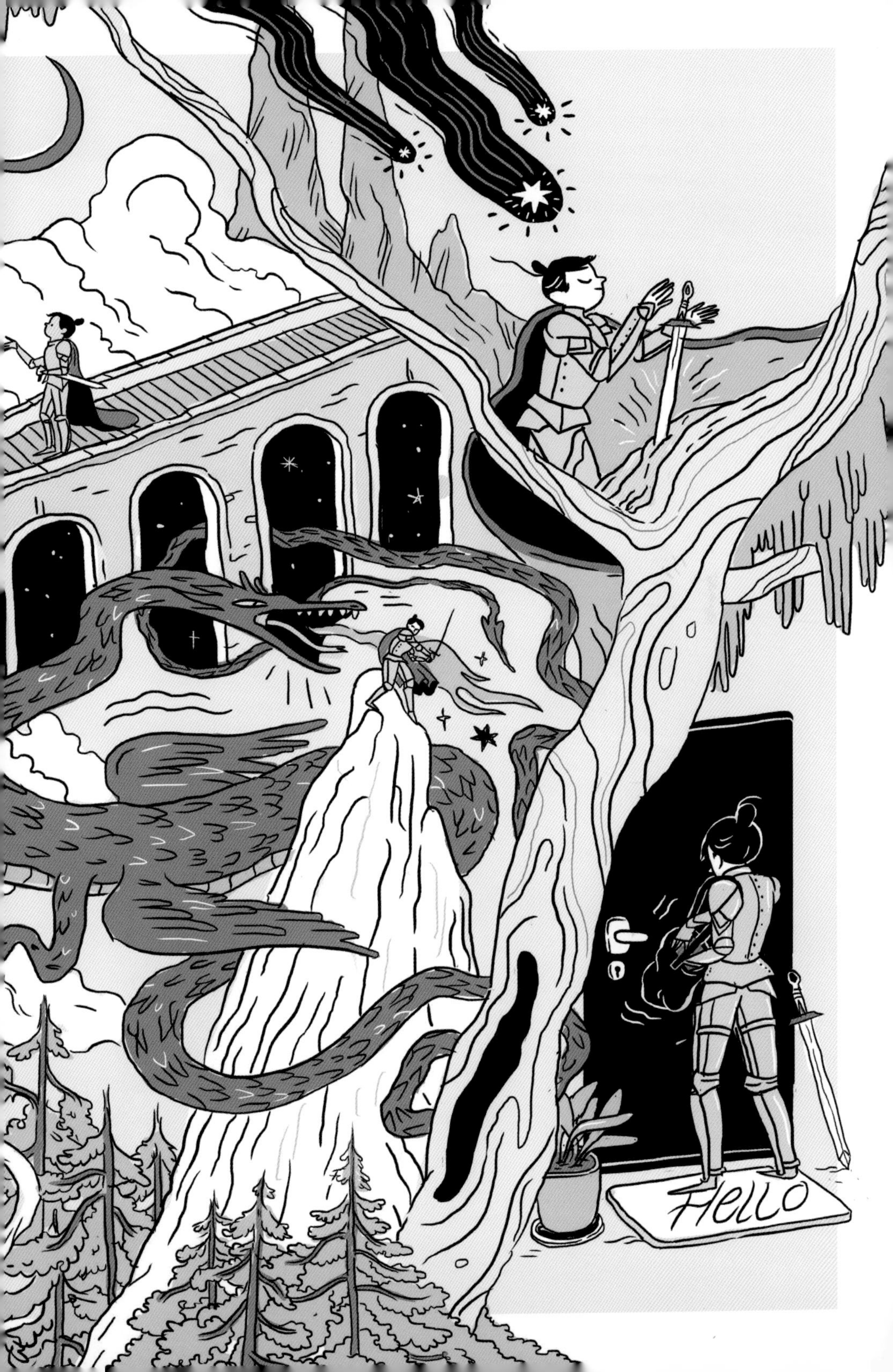
Hello

As a young messy person, one of the things
I feared most was organizing my backpack.
Even as an adult messy person, I still hate it.
(That's why I have a lot of handbags.)
Because a handbag is a mini-cosmos with straps
that holds the entire world of the messy person.
It is the mirror of the messy person, inside and out.

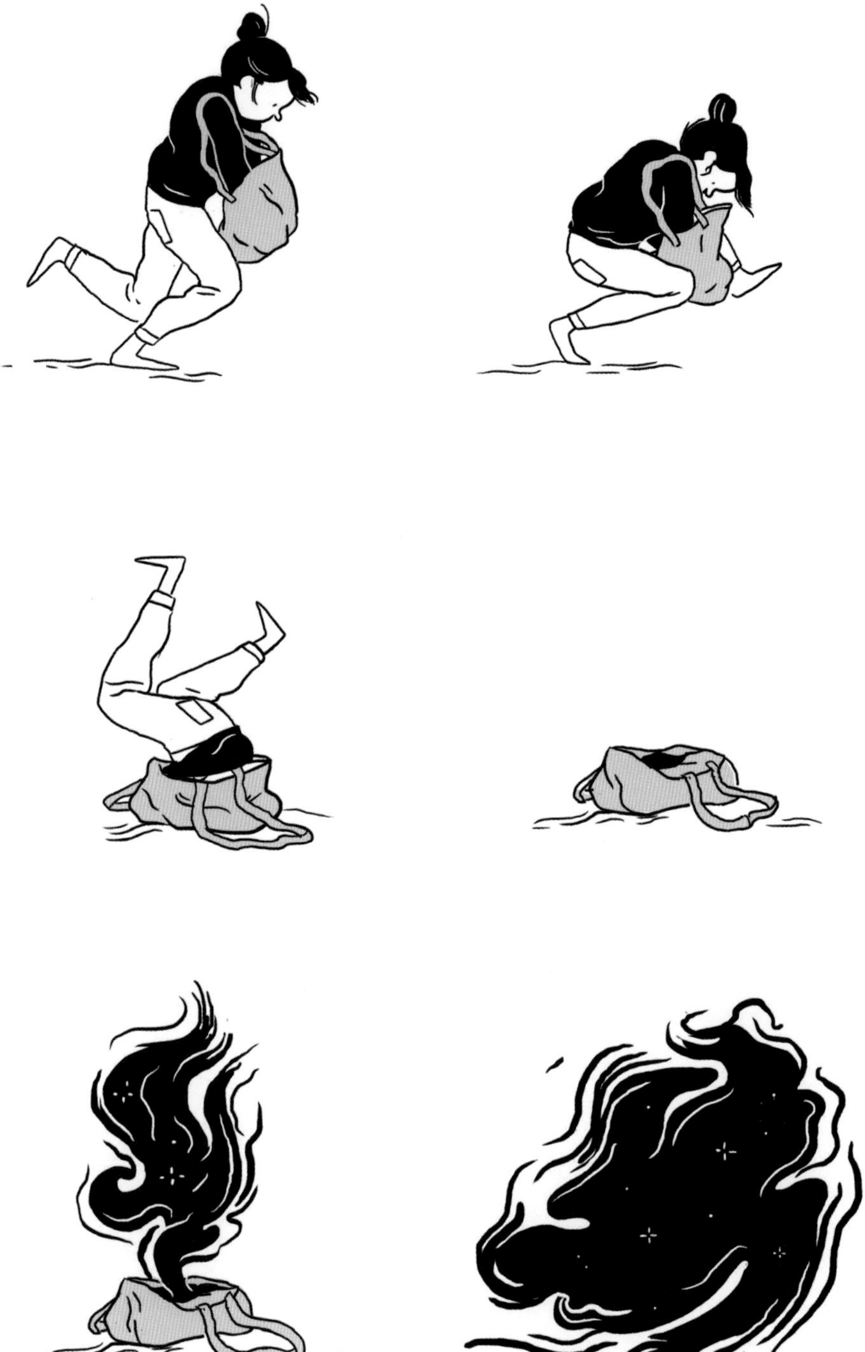

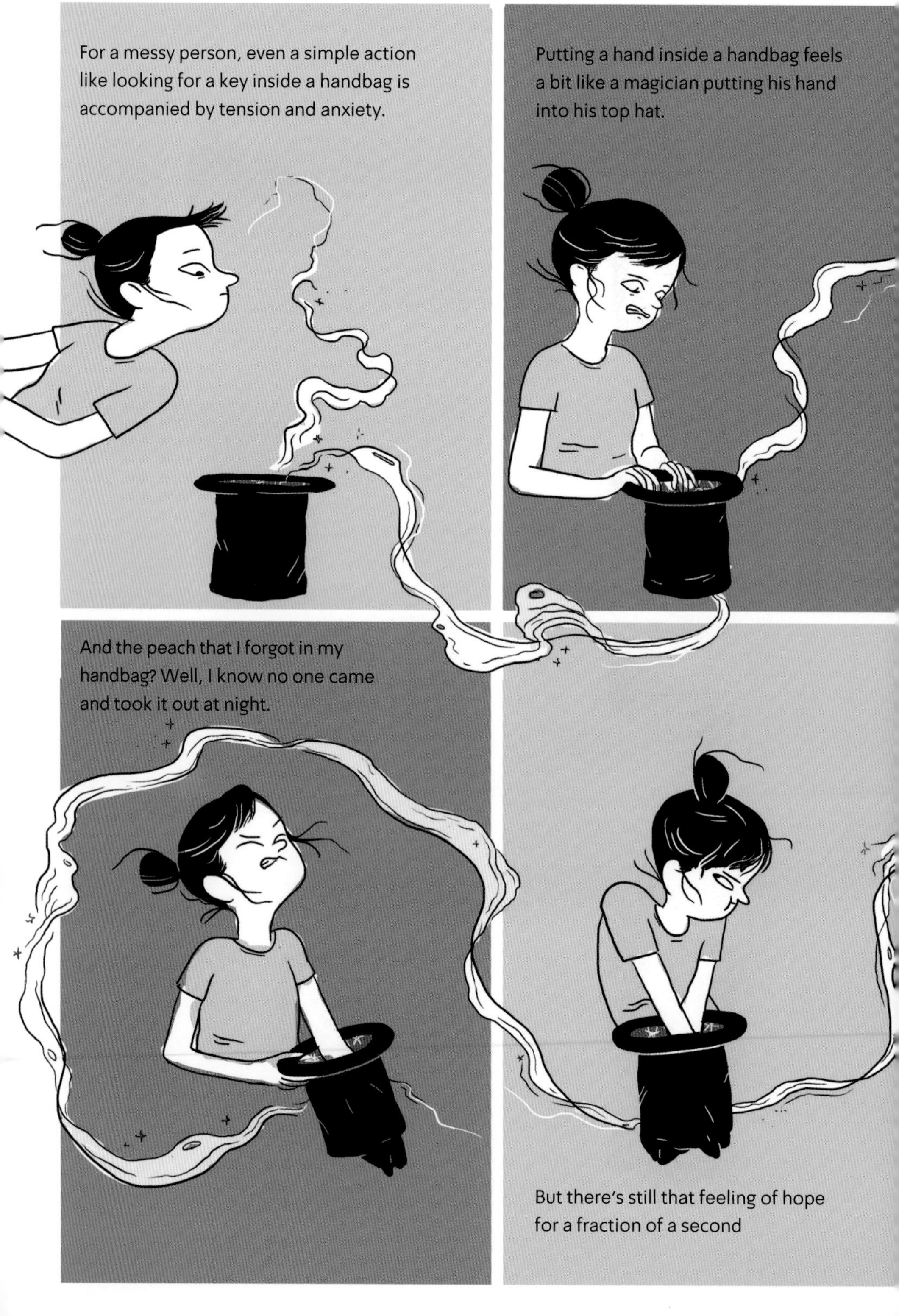
For a messy person, even a simple action like looking for a key inside a handbag is accompanied by tension and anxiety.
Putting a hand inside a handbag feels a bit like a magician putting his hand into his top hat.
And the peach that I forgot in my handbag? Well, I know no one came and took it out at night.
But there's still that feeling of hope for a fraction of a second

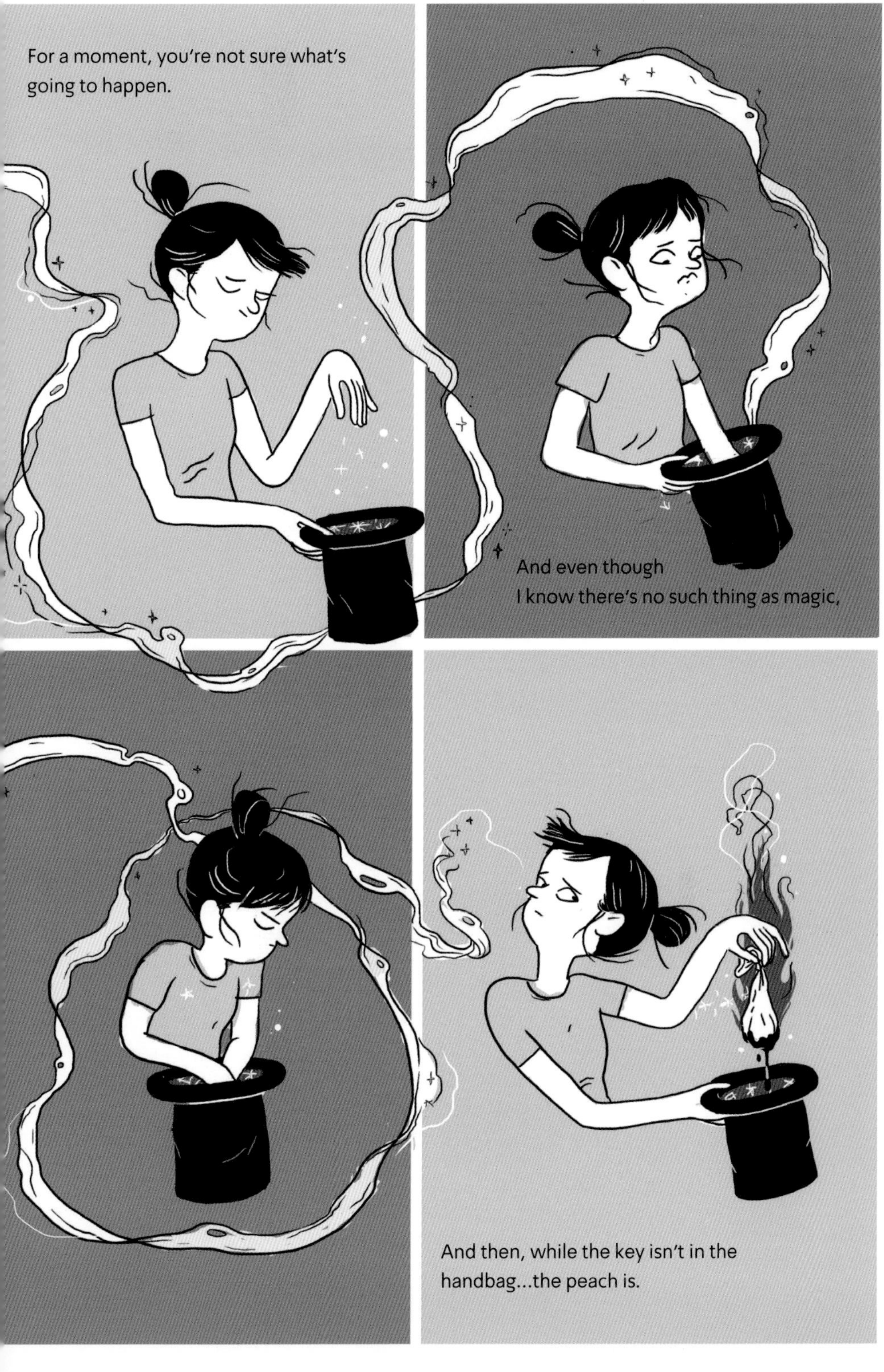
For a moment, you're not sure what's going to happen.
And even though I know there's no such thing as magic,
And then, while the key isn't in the handbag...the peach is.

But sometimes, when I put my hand into my bag to look for the house key--surprisingly, there it is! And when that happens, it feels like magic.

In this guide, I'm not going to try to convince you that messy people can magically become organized. But I will try and prove that we might be able to manage with a handful of tricks and a few miracles.

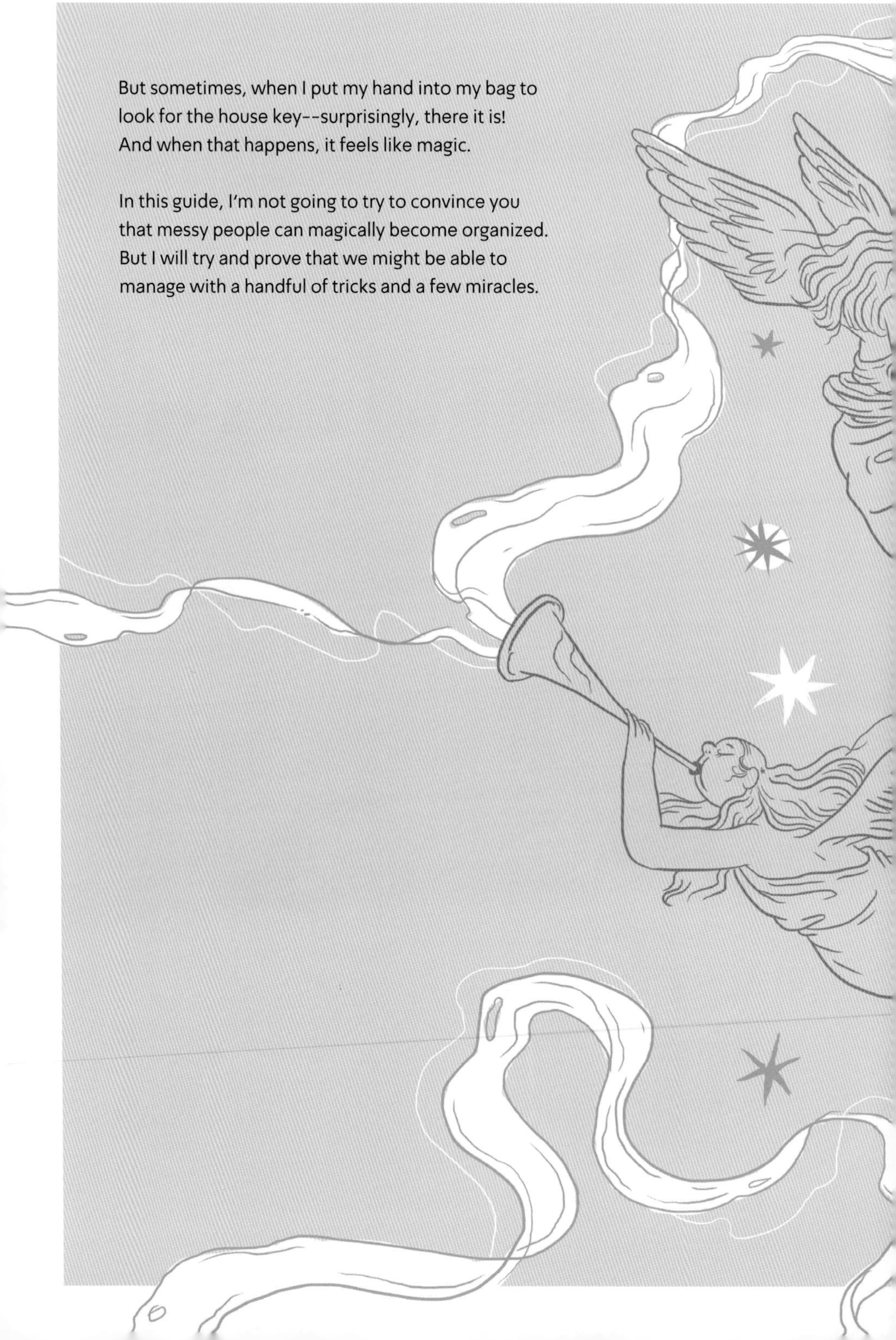

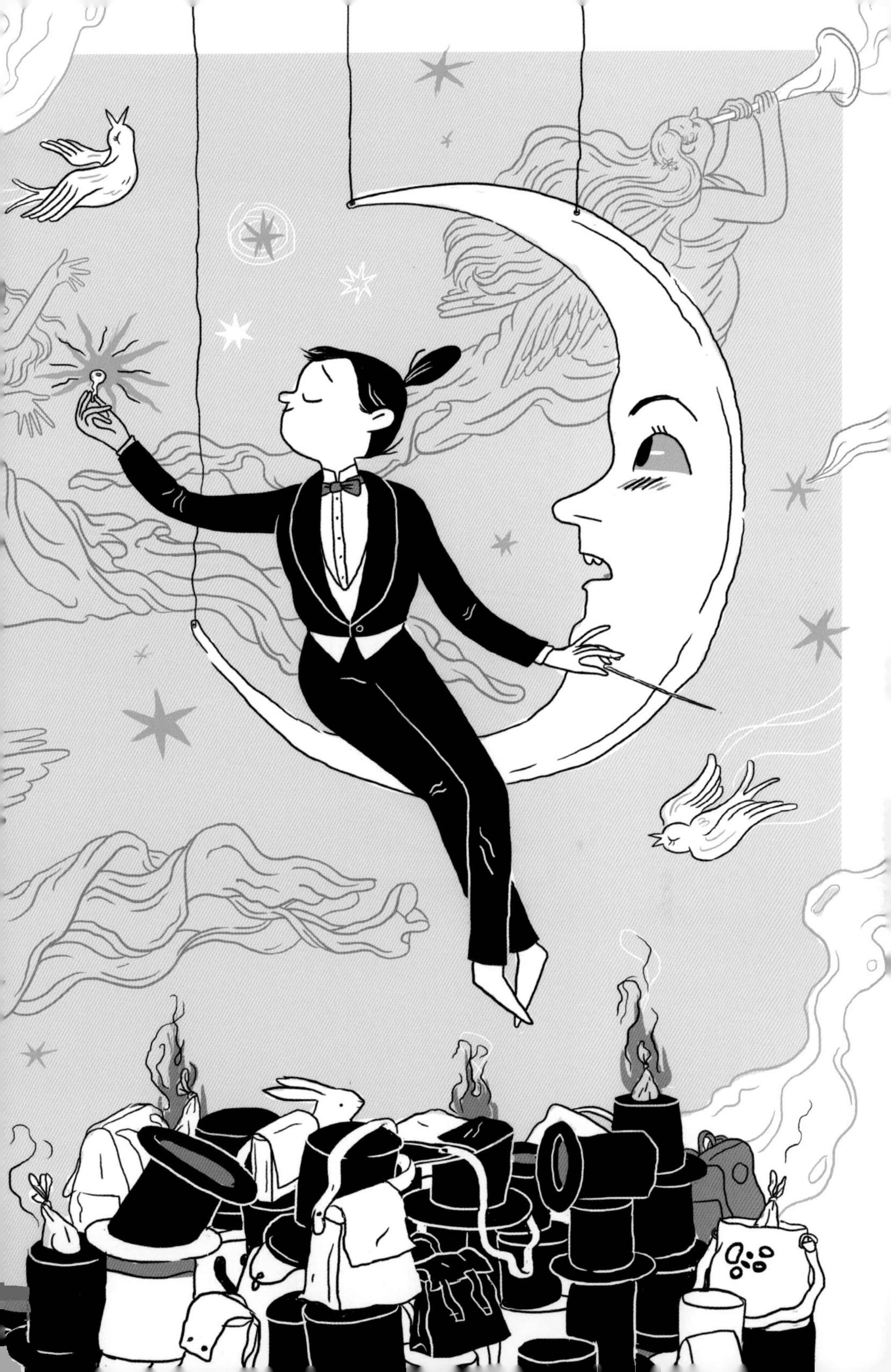

ARE YOU
MESSY?

I suppose that you, wise reader, are starting to ask yourself,
"Am I a messy person, too? And if so, to what extent?"
If you're asking this question while lounging on a nest
of laundry on the couch, you can stop wondering.
But if you're not sure and want to know how much,
then this chapter is for you.

Stage One:
Just how messy are you?

There are five parameters in our daily lives that might
seem trivial at first glance, but they are actually windows to the soul,
and through them, we can assess just how severe your messiness is.

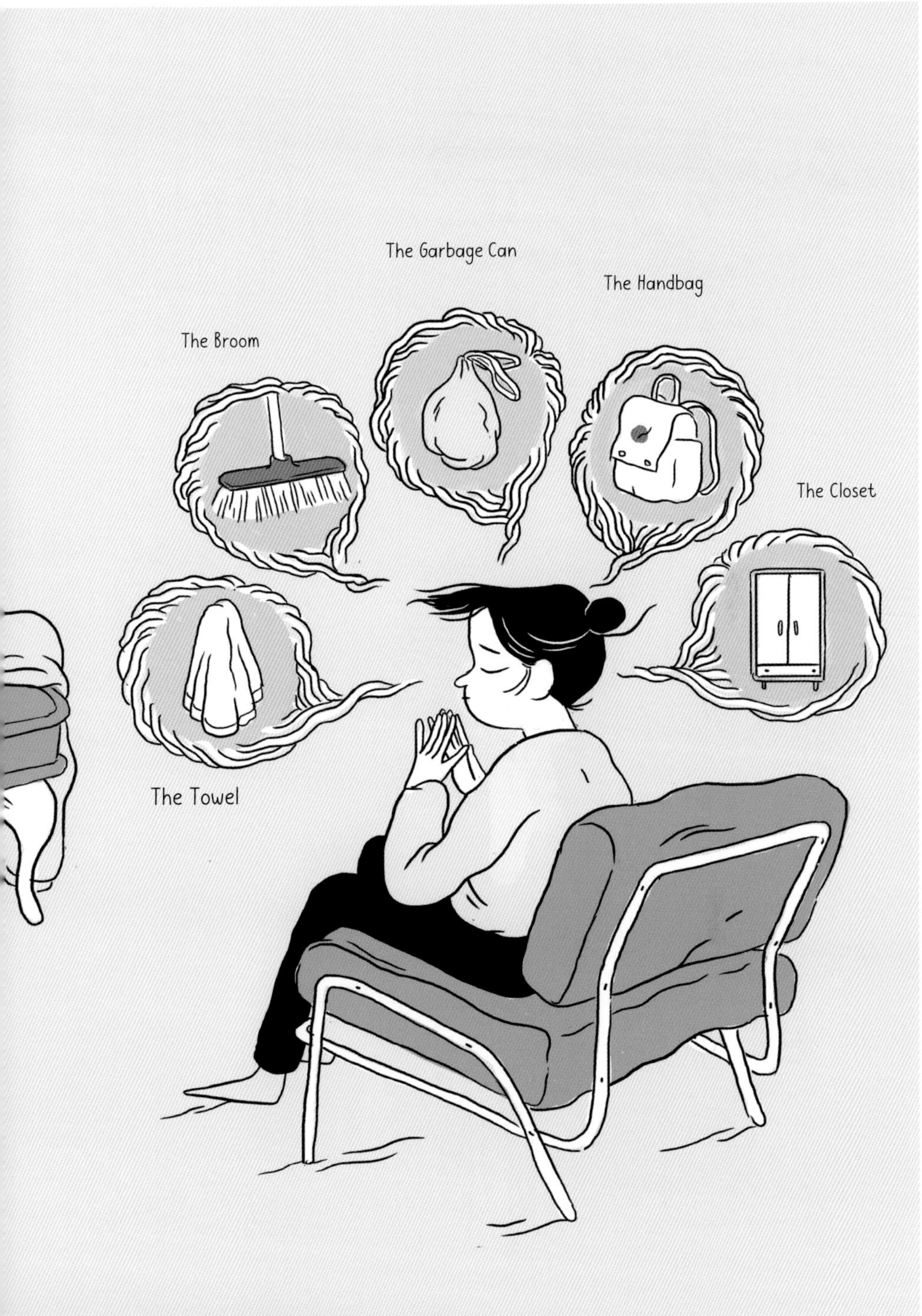
The Garbage Can
The Handbag
The Broom
The Closet
The Towel

1. How many towels do you own?

a. Lots. And they all rest, side by side, in a special woven basket with sachet of potpourri.

b. Towels? Two of each, more or less.

c. One big towel that I took from Mom and Dad and one little towel that my ex-roommate left behind.

2. What sizes?

a. A large wraparound towel. A large bath towel. A long hair-towel. A hand towel for the little ones. A hand towel for the big ones. And a mini-towel for the bidet.

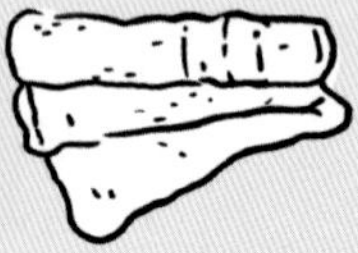

b. Large, medium, and small.

c. A towel.

3. What do you do with the towel after a shower?

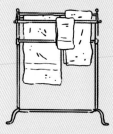

a. Isn't it obvious? I place it on the heated towel rack to dry.

b. I hang it up.

c. I let it fall freely onto the floor on the exact spot that I started getting dressed.

4. One week later, what do you do with the towel?

a. I just pulled it out, warm and fluffy from the dryer, after being washed with a laundry pod and fabric softener.

b. I'll use it a few more times and then put it in the wash.

c. I'll pick it up off the floor where I started getting dressed and will hang it on the door.

5. Do you own a dishtowel?

a. Of course. They're made of organic cotton with my initials embroidered in the corner.

b. Yes, they come in packs of three.

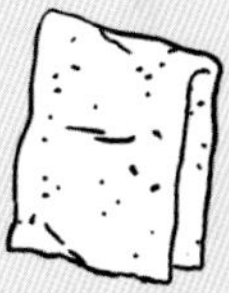

c. Yes, I use the hand towel that my ex-roommate left behind.

6. Bonus question: Do you own a sports towel?

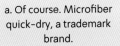

a. Of course. Microfiber quick-dry, a trademark brand.

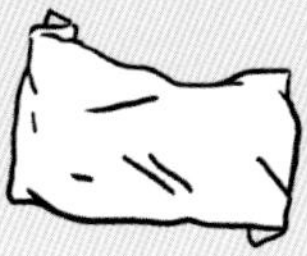

b. Yes. A medium-sized black towel.

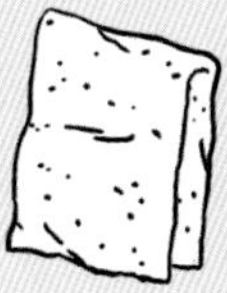

c. I use the kitchen towel my ex-roommate left behind.

1. What type of broom do you have?

a. A state-of-the-art bionic broom with rubber microfibers coated in hair-resistant material.

b. Just a regular broom.

c. An ancient broom inherited from the previous apartment resident and probably once belonged to a chimney sweep.

2. How often do you sweep the apartment?

a. In the morning and in the evening, and whenever else as needed.

b. Once every couple of days or so.

c. After a bag of sugar spills and I can see more ants than floor.

3. Do you have any special sweeping technique for the kitchen?

a. I slowly and calmly sweep up the dirt like raking a Zen garden.

b. I sweep the kitchen from east to west, making my way towards the trash can.

c. I use random sweeping motions that scatter dirt particles in every direction.

4. After sweeping, a line of dirt remains on the edge of the dustpan. What do you do?

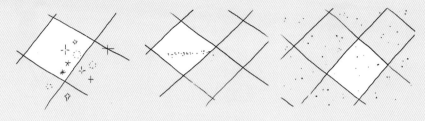

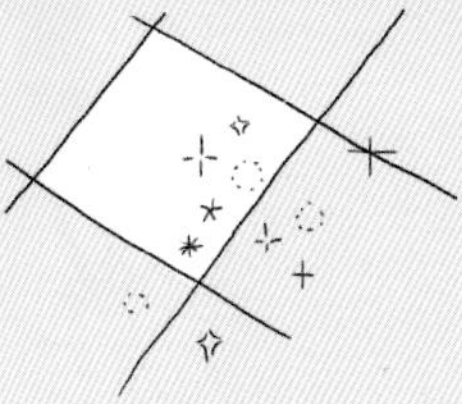

a. A line of dirt?!

b. I'll try again.

c. I gently use the broom to scatter it around. It creates the effect of cleanliness.

5. Describe the contents of your dustpan.

a. A delicate collection of crumbs and dust.

b. Crumbs, dust, and a noodle covered in crumbs and dust.

c. Crumbs, dust, a noodle covered in crumbs and dust, a button, a supermarket receipt, a ring, and a coin from a foreign country.

6. If you can't find the dustpan after you're done sweeping, what do you do?

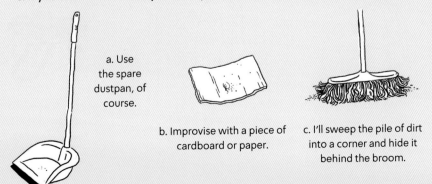

a. Use the spare dustpan, of course.

b. Improvise with a piece of cardboard or paper.

c. I'll sweep the pile of dirt into a corner and hide it behind the broom.

1. When your mobile phone rings in your handbag, what's the first thought that comes to mind?

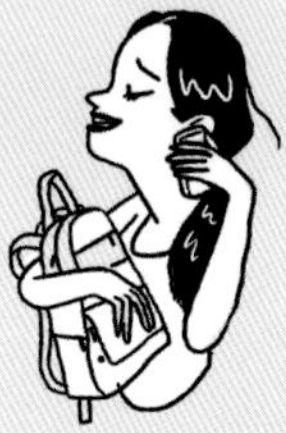

a. Oh, that's my mom's ringtone! I'll take my phone out and answer.

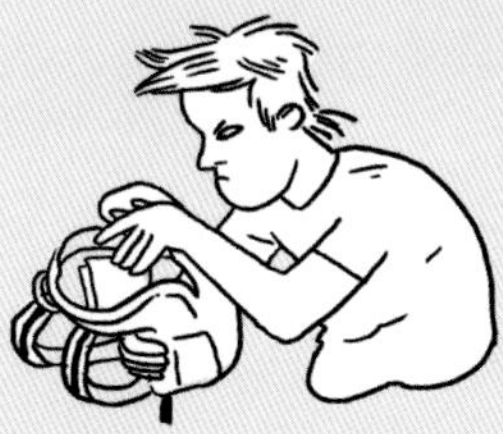

b. Aargh. I thought I put it on mute. I'll dig around in my bag for a little while and I'll put it on mute.

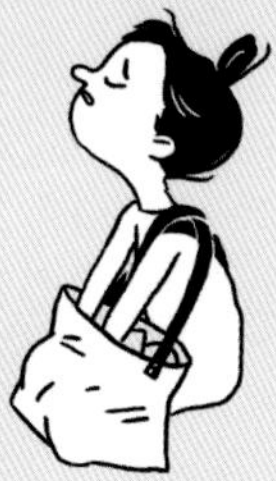

c. Oh no. Finding a ringing phone in a handbag is like birthing a farm animal.

2. A friend asks you for a piece of gum. Do you have any in your handbag?

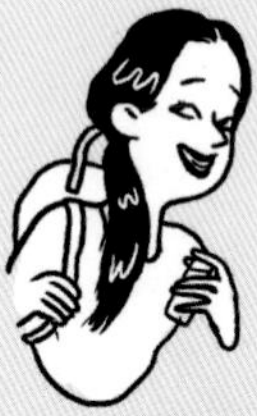

a. Of course. In the small compartment made for storing gum.

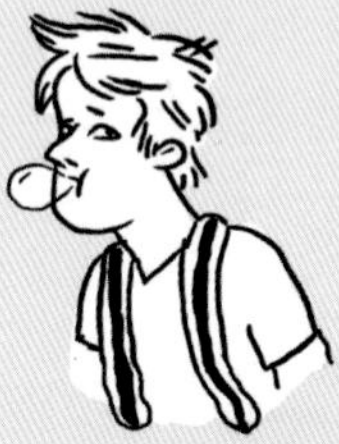

b. I just ate the last piece.

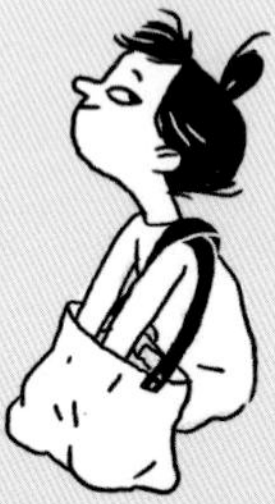

c. I think I have one piece way down at the bottom that fell out of the box. It's a little moist but totally chewable.

3. How many compartments does your handbag have?

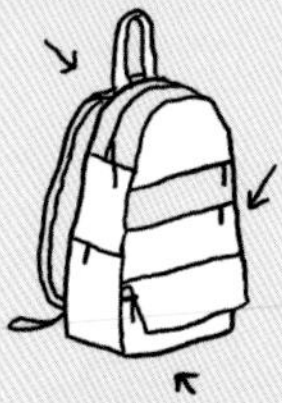

a. Just the basics. A large compartment with two divider, a compartment for my laptop, a front pocket, a side pocket, a hidden front pocket, and a compartment with a zipper on the side.

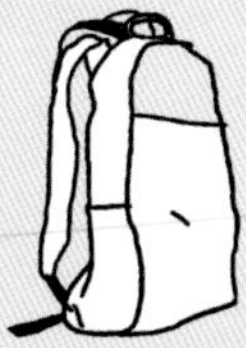

b. One large compartment and one small compartment on the front of the bag.

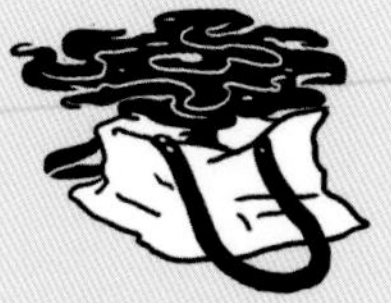

c. My bag is composed of one large space. And a few black holes.

4. Where is your wallet?

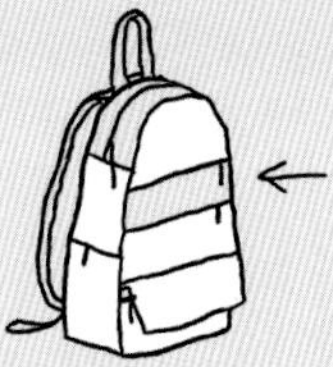

a. In the wallet compartment.

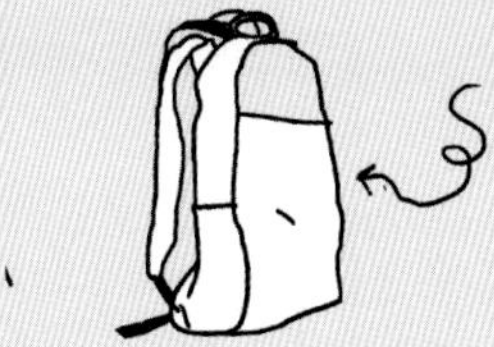

b. In the medium sized compartment or in the front pocket.

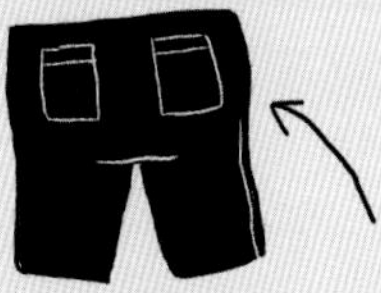

c. In the pocket of the pants that I wore yesterday, and are now in the laundry.

5.What do you do with your handbag when you're not using it?

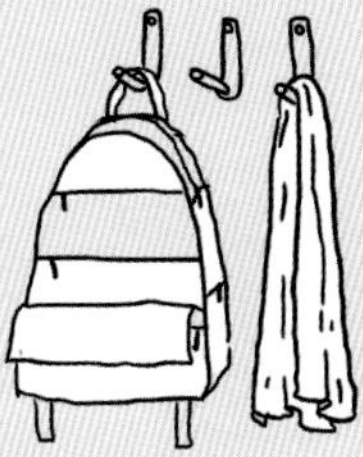

a. I hang it on its hook inside the hall closet.

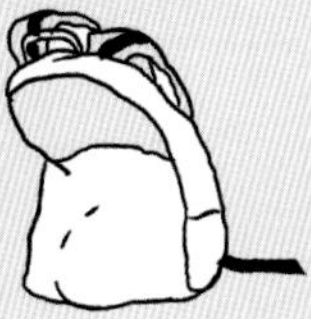

b. I put it in its place at the entrance to the room.

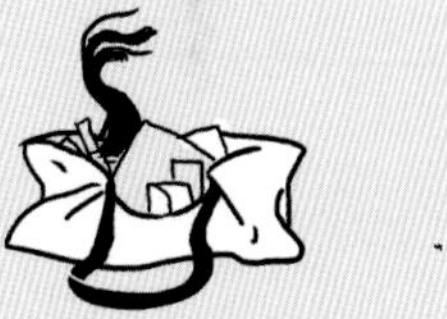

c. I drop it on the floor, a different spot every time.

6.What is in your wallet's coin compartment?

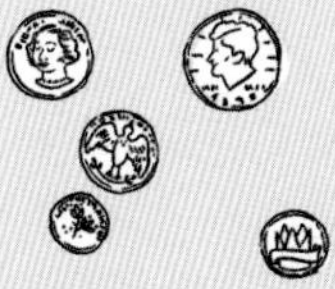

a. Coins, of course.

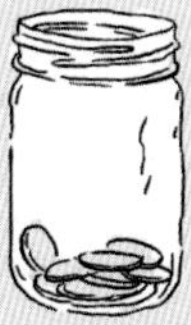

b. I don't have a coin pocket in my wallet. I put them in a tips jar at the local cafe.

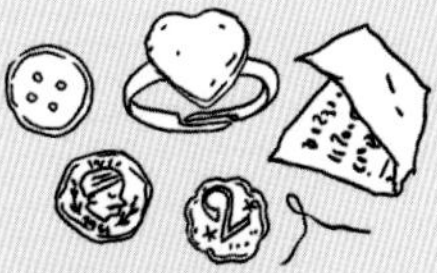

c. A button, a supermarket receipt, a ring and one coin – but there's more coins in my purse, I'm sure.

1. How do you feel about your closet?

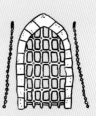

a. My closet is my temple.

b. It's a place to store my clothes.

c. It's the only thing that keeps me from being buried alive under an avalanche of clothes.

2. Do you have a special way of folding clothes?

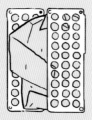

a. I have a manual folding board. It's pretty standard.

b. I fold each piece in half and then into quarters.

c. I roll it into a ball and push as hard as I can.

3. The shirt that you want to wear is at the bottom of the pile. What do you do?

a. I lift the clothes off the top of the pile, remove the shirt, and put the pile back.

b. I try to pull it out quickly so that the pile doesn't notice.

c. My entire closet is the bottom of one big pile.

4. How do you organize your socks?

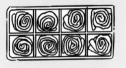

a. In a designated sock organizer.

b. In pairs. Preferably of the same color.

c. I throw them in a drawer and hope each one finds its match.

---

5. What word best describes what you feel when you open your closet?

a. Pleasure.

b. Morning.

c. Mayday!!! Avalanche!!!

1. What do you do when the garbage is full?

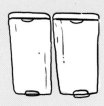 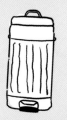 

a. The regular garbage bin or my home recycling bin?

b. Stuff a little more inside and take it out in the morning.

c. Open up a secondary garbage bag.

---

2. What kind of garbage bag do you use?

a. A heavy-duty two-ply garbage bag.

b. Whatever was on sale at the supermarket.

c. I just ran out of garbage bags. I improvise with a shopping bag.

---

3. You took the bag out and it looks like it has a hole. What do you do?

a. That's never happened to me. I buy heavy-duty two-ply garbage bags.

b. I'll put the bag inside a new bag.

c. I'll try and run to the garbage as quickly as possible, even if the handle rips.

4. Who takes out the garbage when the bin is full?

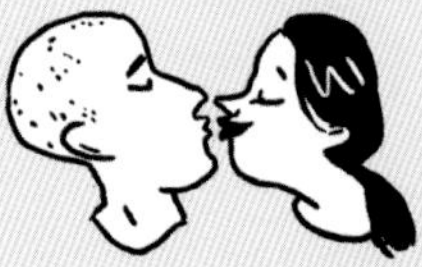

a. That's easy: Whoever notices that the bin is full, of course.

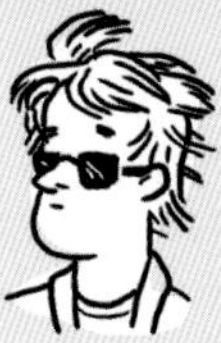

b. Whoever leaves the house first.

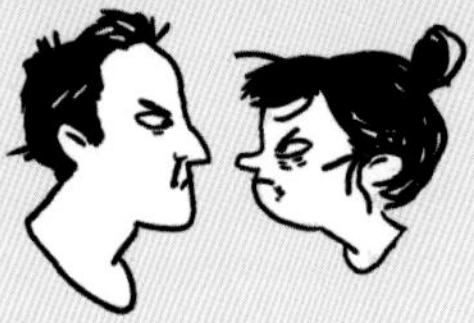

c. The loser.

---

5. What do you feel about the neighborhood dumpster?

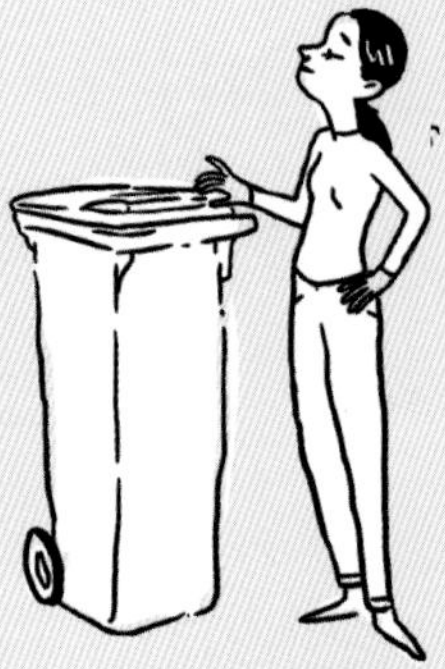

a. Respect and appreciation. It's just a dumpster, nothing to worry about.

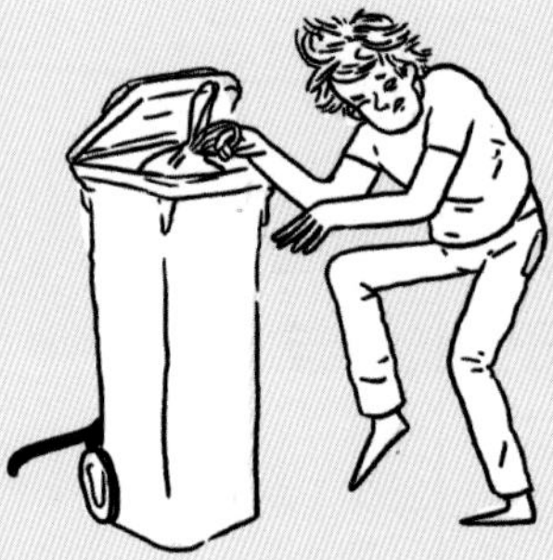

b. I approach it cautiously and then run.

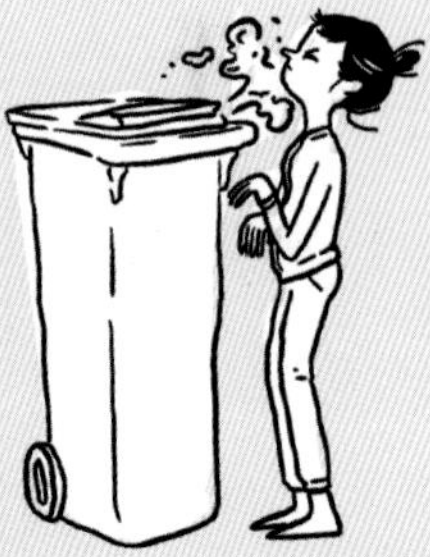

c. I think it detests me.

Bonus question: Do you own a bathroom garbage can?

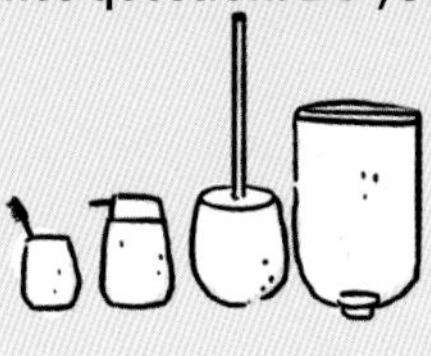

a. Of course. Part of a designer set that matches that rest of the bathroom accessories.

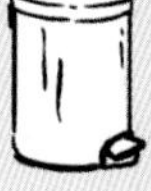

b. Yes. It's hidden in the corner, next to the toilet.

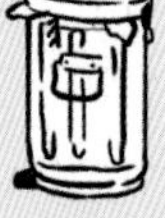

c. I vaguely recall throwing a tampon in one of those, sometime around a year ago.

Imagine the following scenario:

You've boiled water and poured it into a mug with a teaspoon of instant coffee and two teaspoons of sugar. You open the refrigerator but the milk carton feels unusually light in your hand. It turns out that you put the empty carton back after your morning cup of coffee the day before...

What do you do?

I put the carton back into the fridge and drink my coffee black.

I skip the coffee and put the empty carton back into the fridge.

No problem. I have spare cartons of regular, almond, soy, and low-lactose milk.

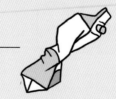

I throw away the carton and go out to buy milk.

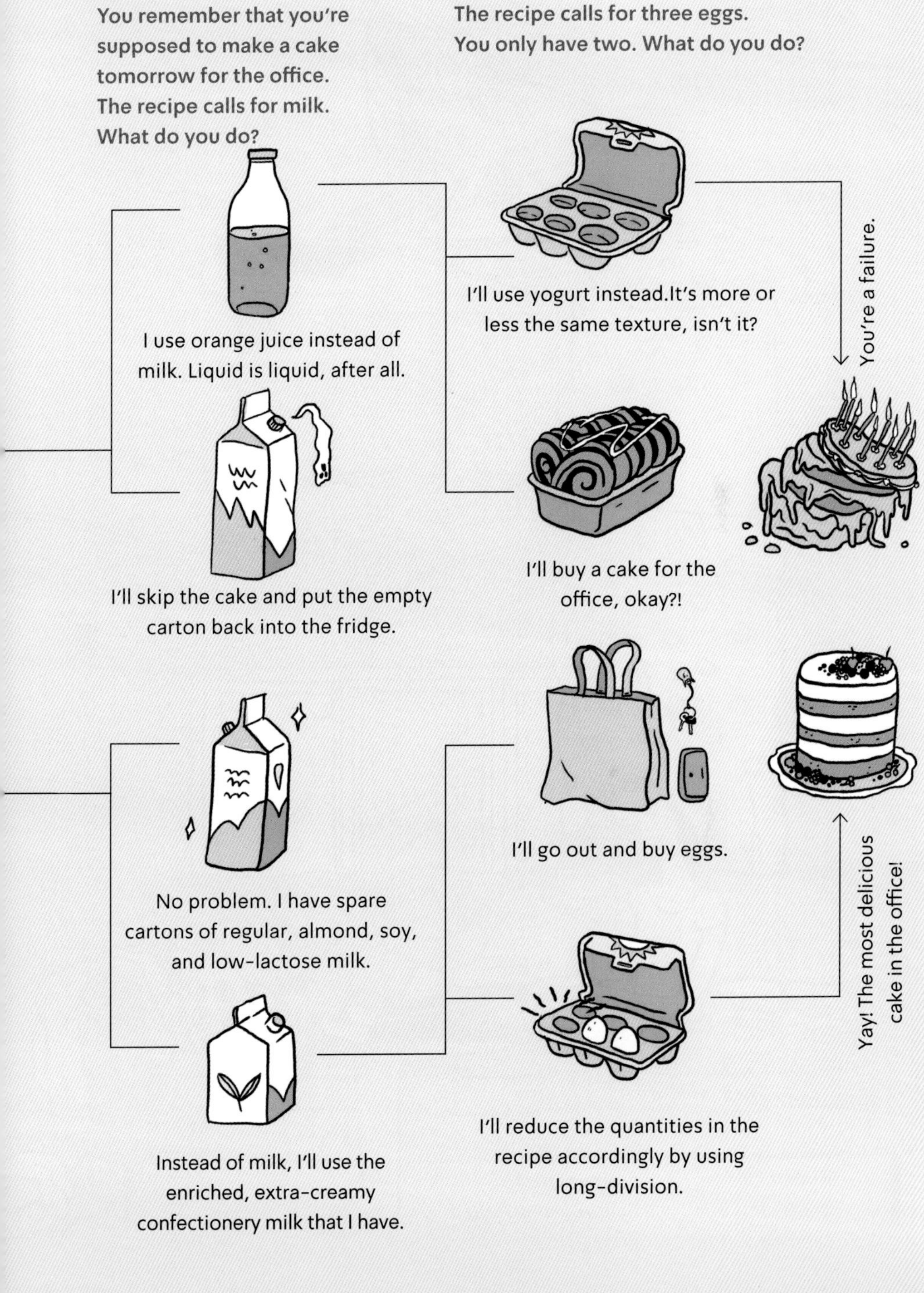
You remember that you're supposed to make a cake tomorrow for the office. The recipe calls for milk. What do you do?
I use orange juice instead of milk. Liquid is liquid, after all.
I'll skip the cake and put the empty carton back into the fridge.
No problem. I have spare cartons of regular, almond, soy, and low-lactose milk.
Instead of milk, I'll use the enriched, extra-creamy confectionery milk that I have.
The recipe calls for three eggs. You only have two. What do you do?
I'll use yogurt instead.It's more or less the same texture, isn't it?
I'll buy a cake for the office, okay?!
I'll go out and buy eggs.
I'll reduce the quantities in the recipe accordingly by using long-division.
You're a failure.
Yay! The most delicious cake in the office!

In Conclusion:
If most of your answers are (a) – just close this book and go iron or reorganize your stamp collection or something.

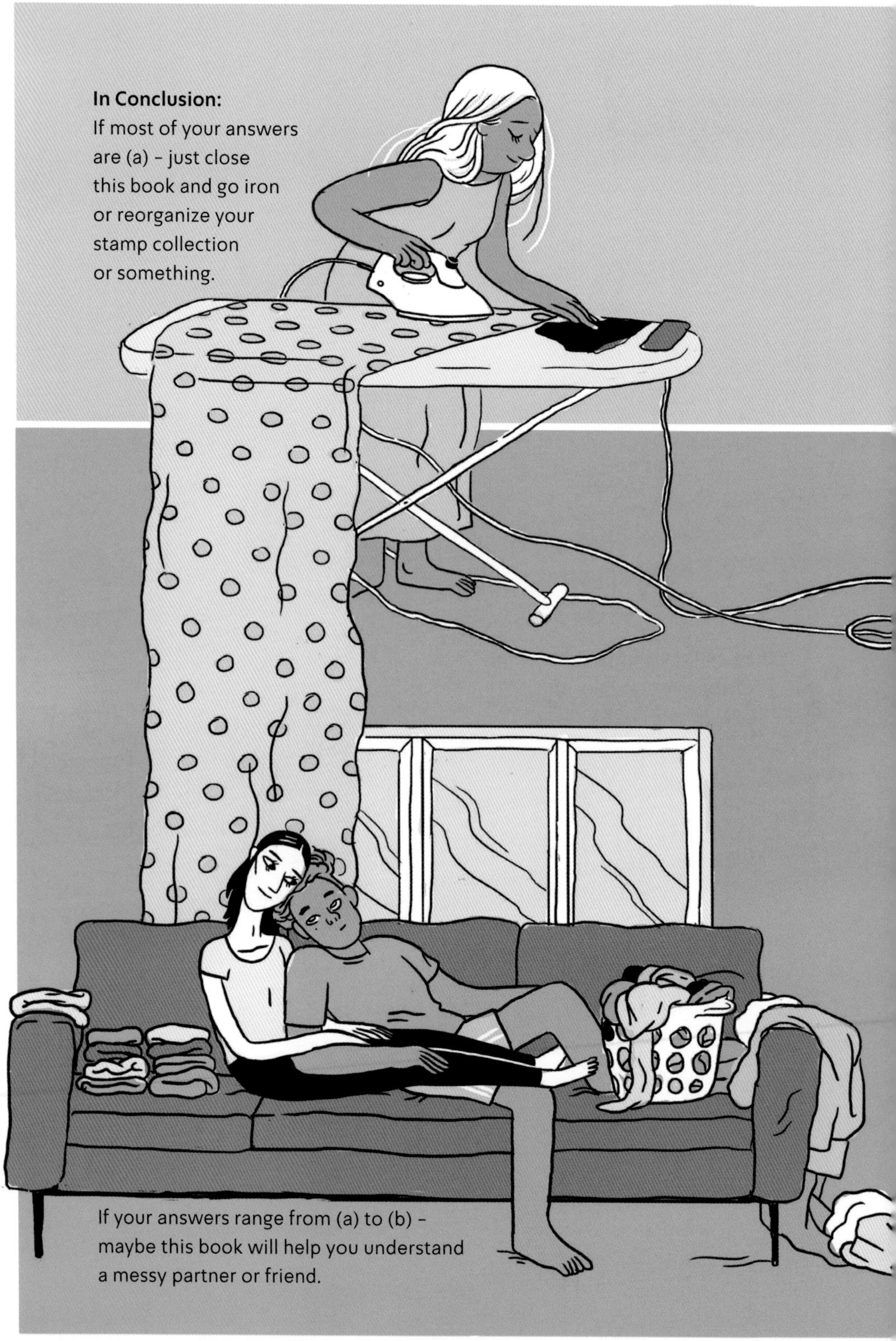

If your answers range from (a) to (b) – maybe this book will help you understand a messy partner or friend.

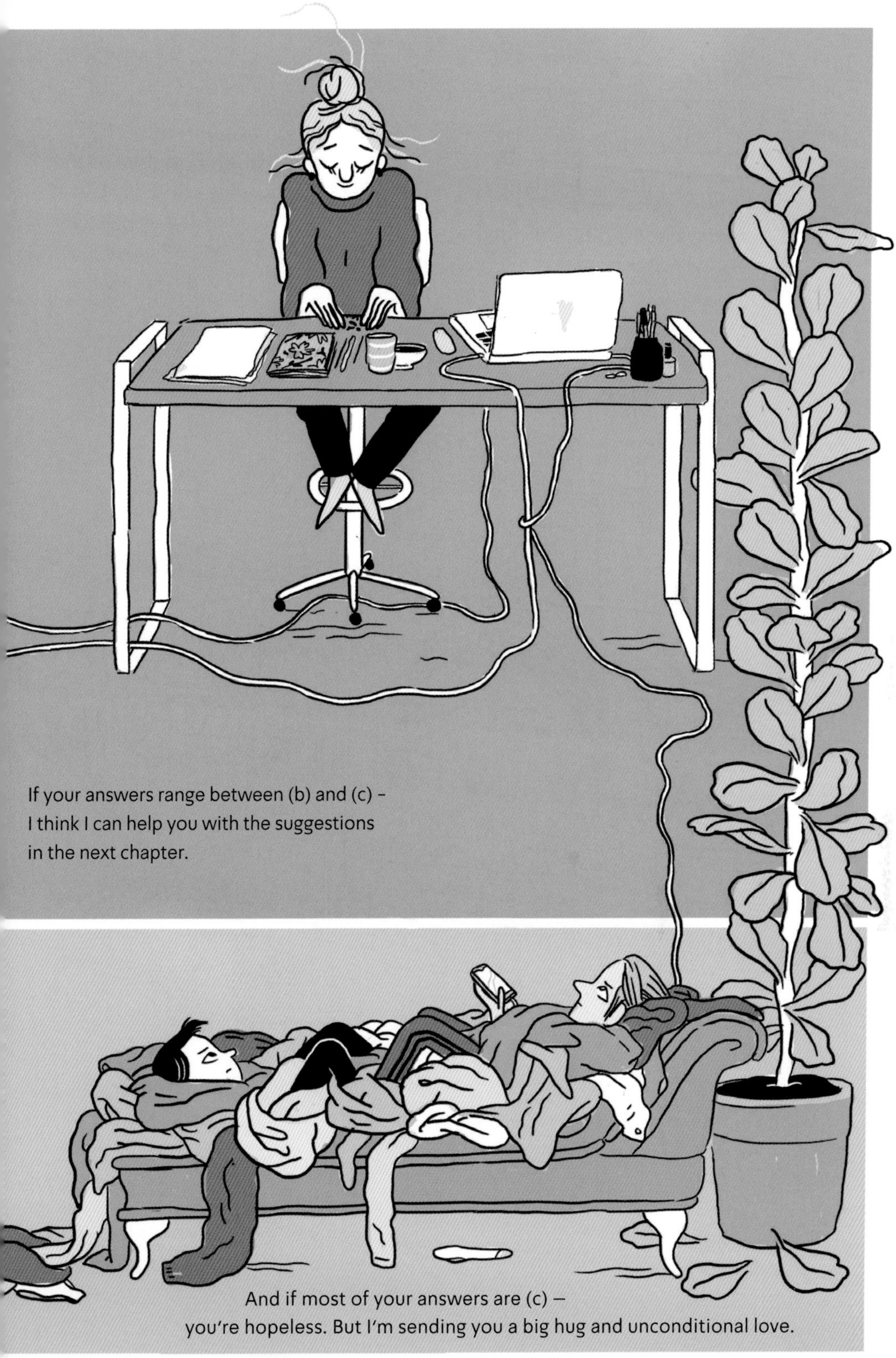
If your answers range between (b) and (c) –
I think I can help you with the suggestions
in the next chapter.
And if most of your answers are (c) –
you're hopeless. But I'm sending you a big hug and unconditional love.

Stage Two: What type of messy person am I?

Messy people can be divided into six main archetypes:

The Bashful
The closet-messes, those who seem to be really organized on the outside, but they actually sweep all their mess underneath the carpet and have tons of junk in their backpacks.

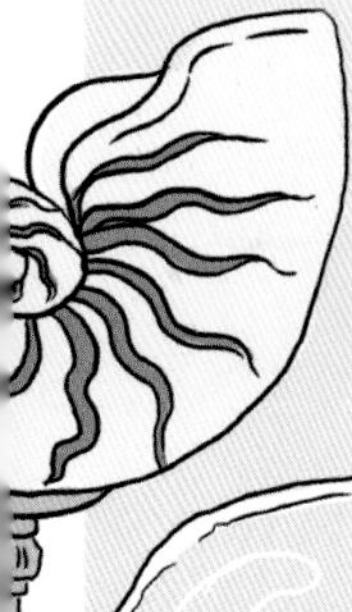

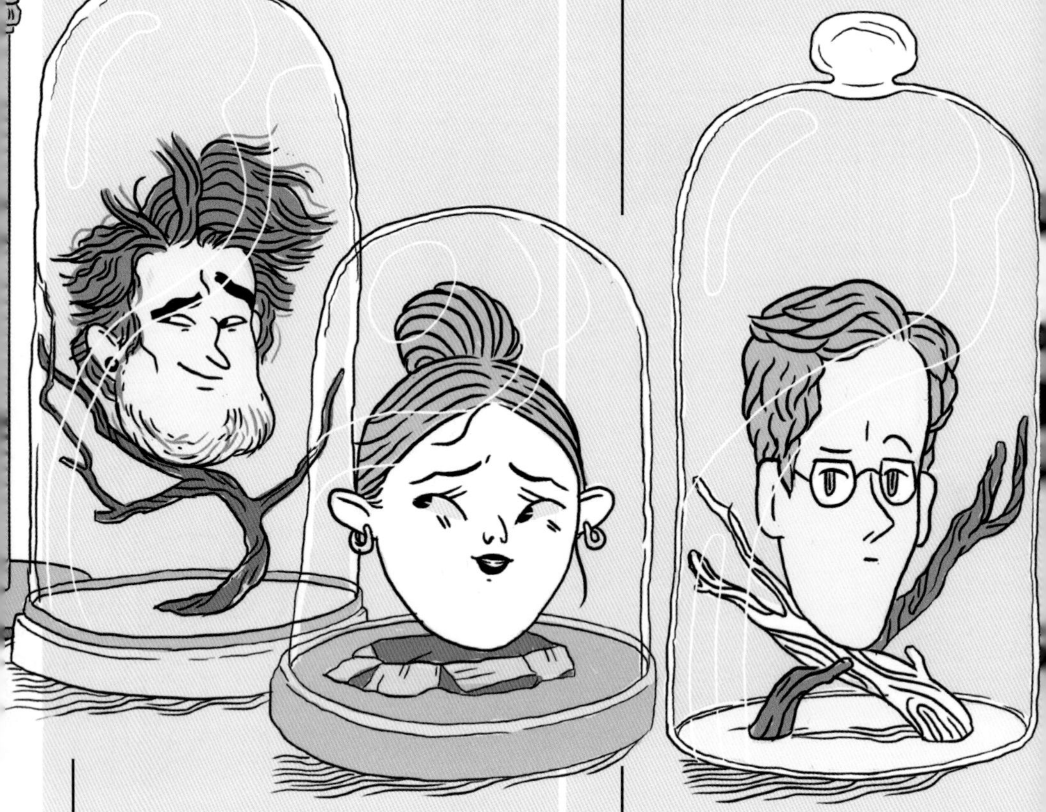

The Sparklers
They turn their mess into part of their style. Their mess is so nonchalant and full of sex appeal, it's perceived more as wild than messy.

The Fabricators
They simply refuse to admit to their messy demeanor and try to push the blame off on others. They'll always say that nobody told them, that they forgot to send a reminder, or someone took the keys after they put them in their place. Anything but admitting who they really are.

The Wee Ones

It's a known fact that kids are the masters of chaos. You could say that aside from a choice few, most people begin their lives in disorder. The mess that kids make is so basic and fundamental that some scientists believe that the combination of kids and Lego will eventually lead to the destruction of planet Earth.

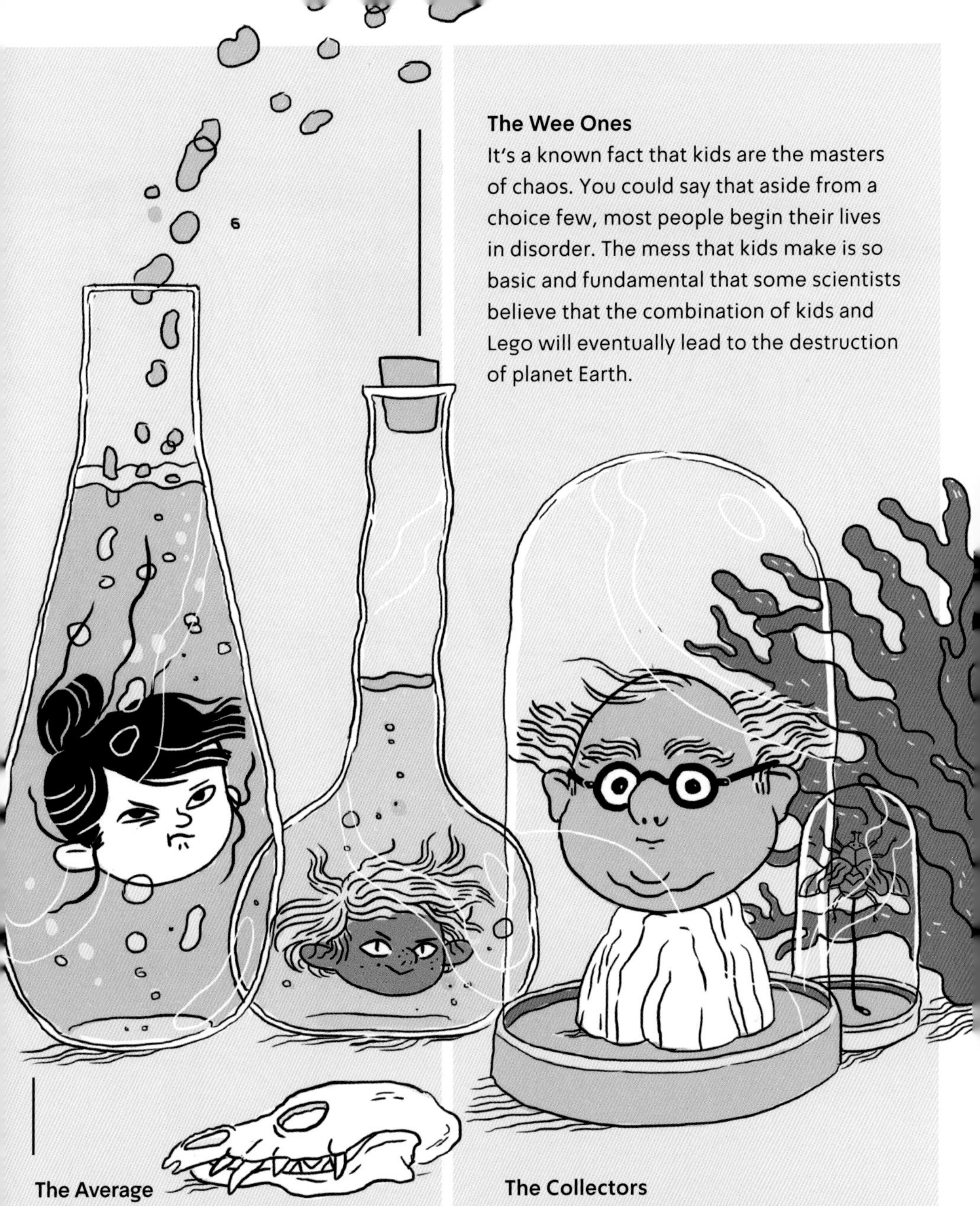

The Average Messy Person, and me and you

The standard, average type who does the best they can. When guests knock at the door, their first instinct is to take everything that's on the living room floor and throw it behind the door of the closest bedroom.

The Collectors

They've turned their mess into a hobby and define it as an eclectic collection to pursue in their spare time.

Of course, it's more complicated than that... There are dozens, if not hundreds of types and varieties of messy people.

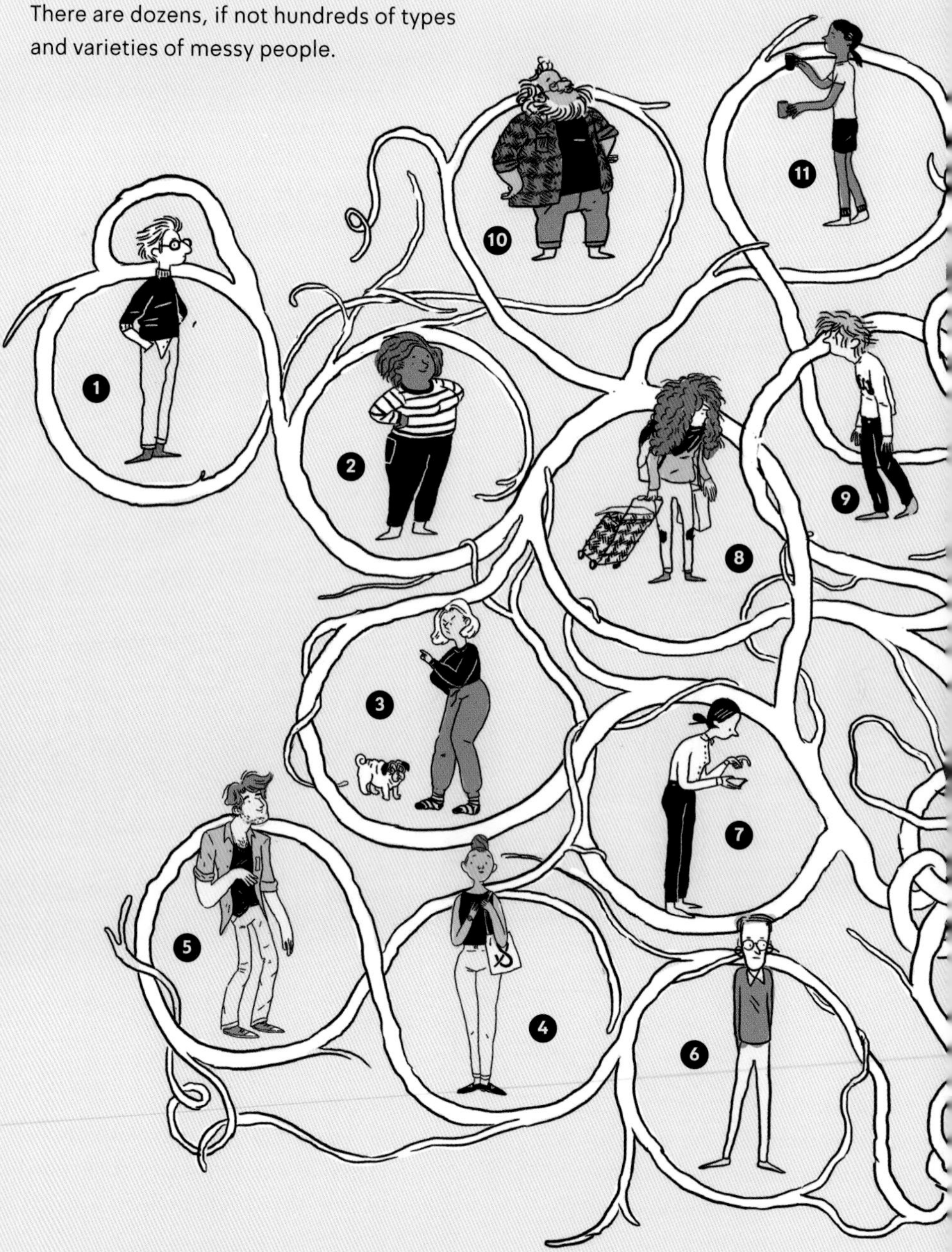

1
2
3
4
5
6
7
8
9
10
11

1. The Procrastinators 2. The Fabricators 3. The Skeptics 4. The Sparklers 5. The Nonchalant 6. The Pretenders 7. The Tenacious 8. The Doubtful 9. The Sloths 10. The Professionals 11. The Slightly Scatterbrained

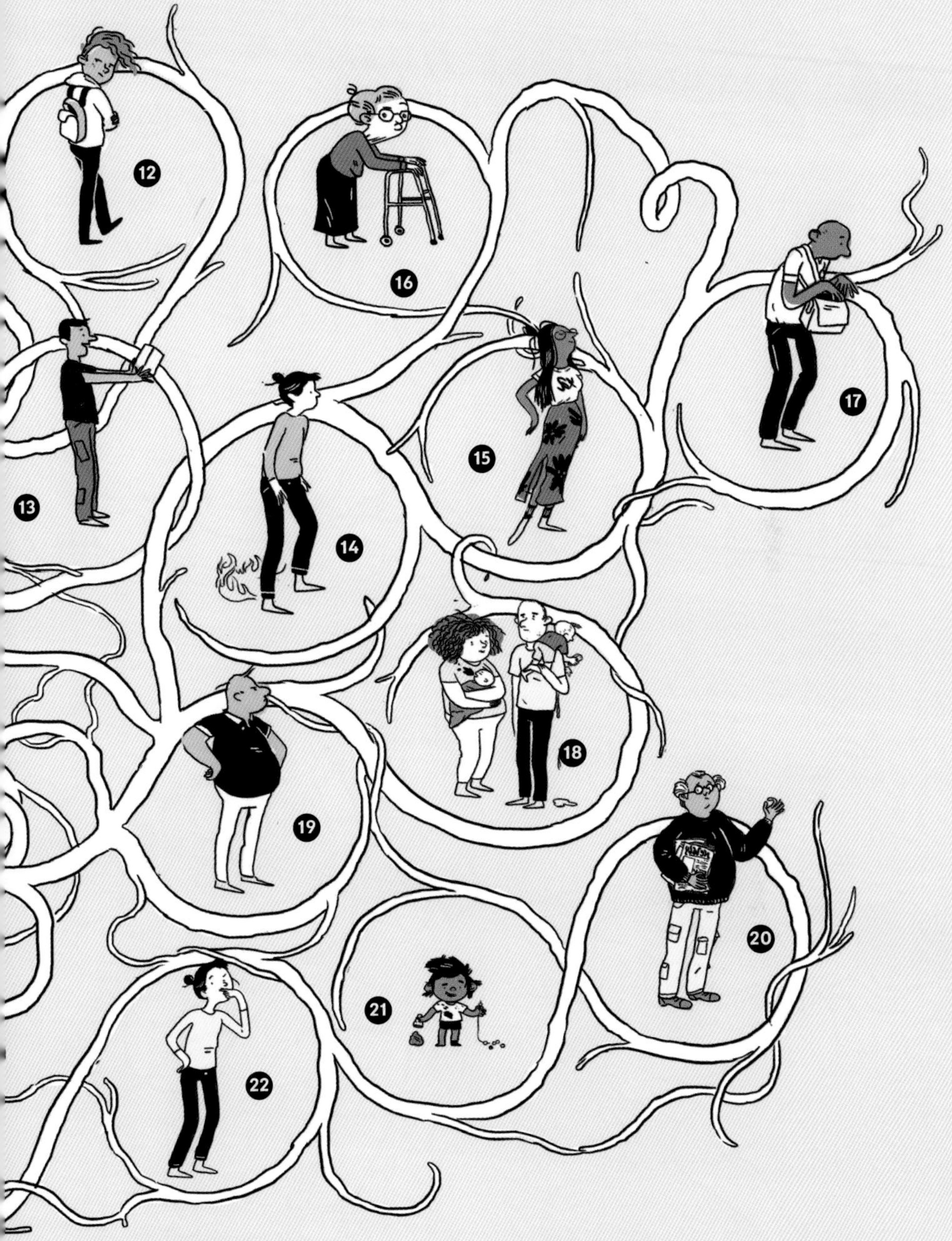
12
16
13
14
15
17
18
19
20
21
22

12. The Rebels 13. The Passionate 14. The Nervous Wrecks 15. The Dramatic
16. The Elders 17. The Forgetful 18. The Parental 19. The Grouches 20. The Collectors
21. The Young Ones 22. The Average

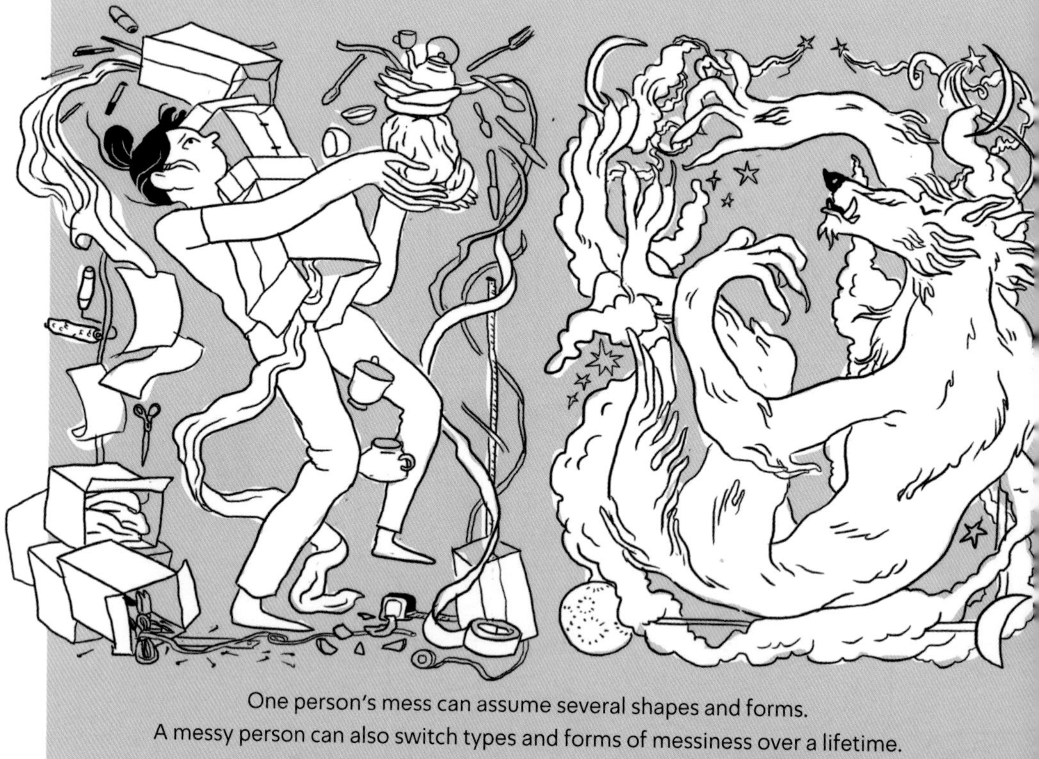

One person's mess can assume several shapes and forms.
A messy person can also switch types and forms of messiness over a lifetime.

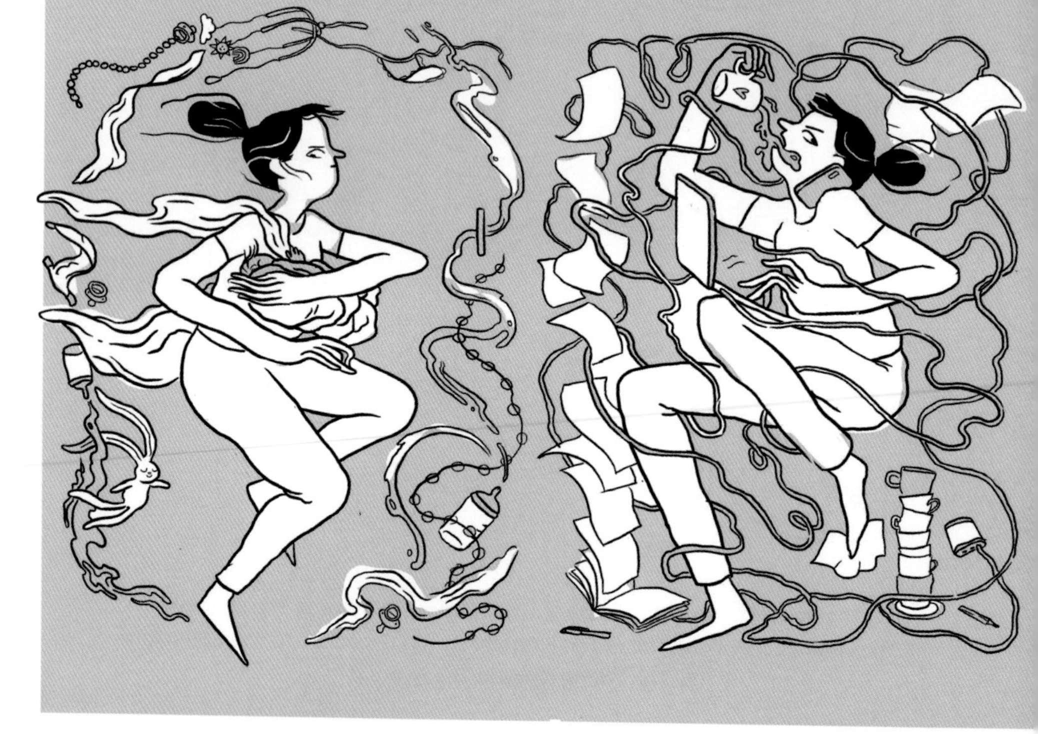

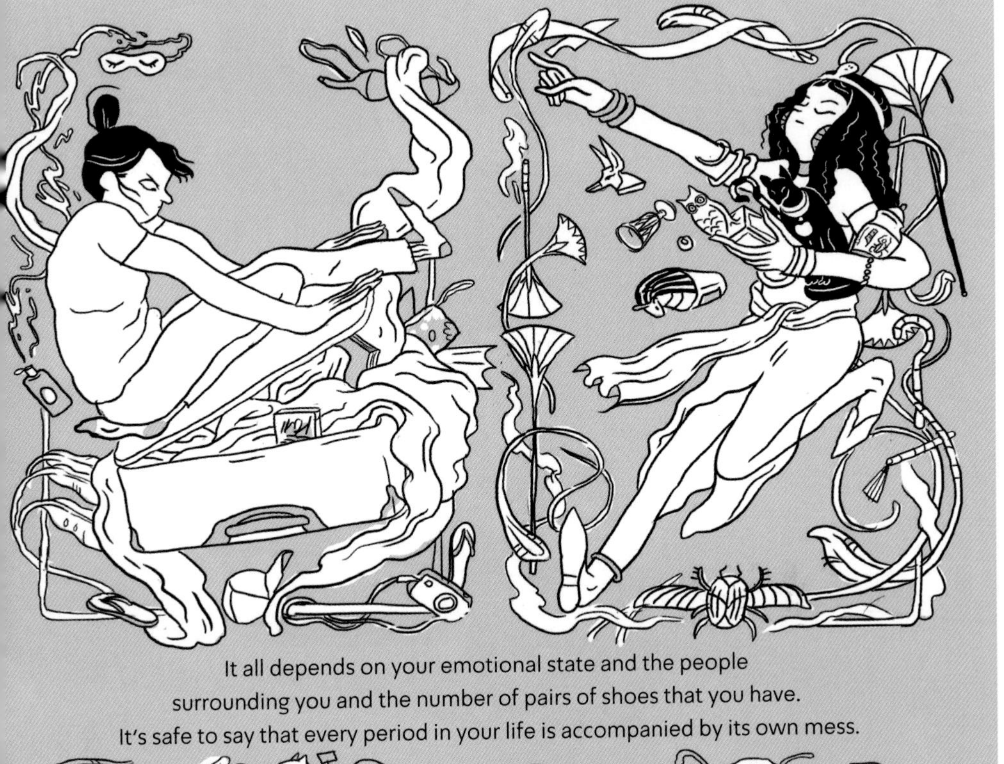

It all depends on your emotional state and the people
surrounding you and the number of pairs of shoes that you have.
It's safe to say that every period in your life is accompanied by its own mess.

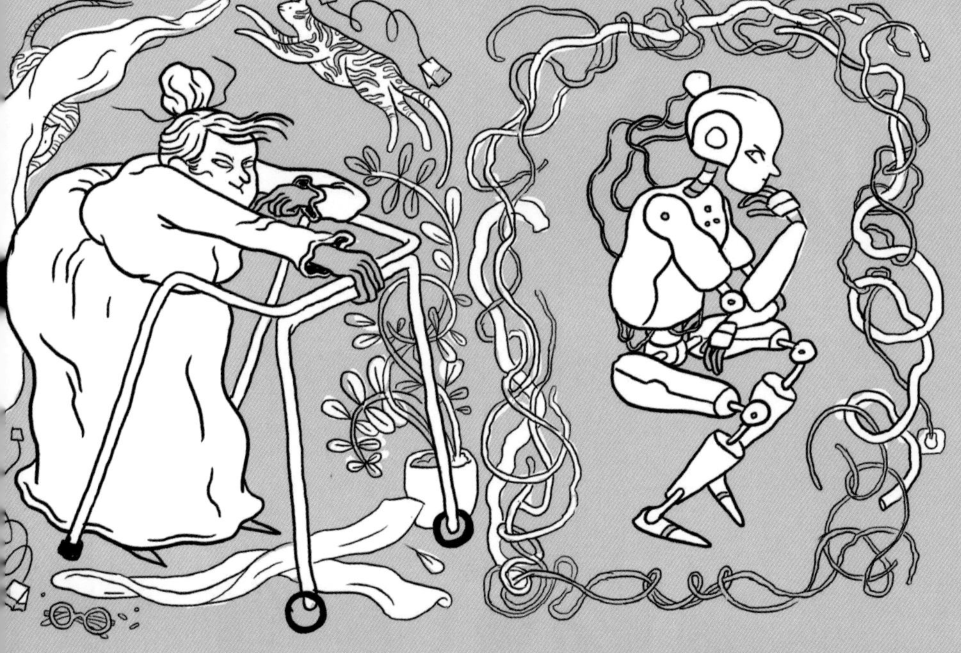

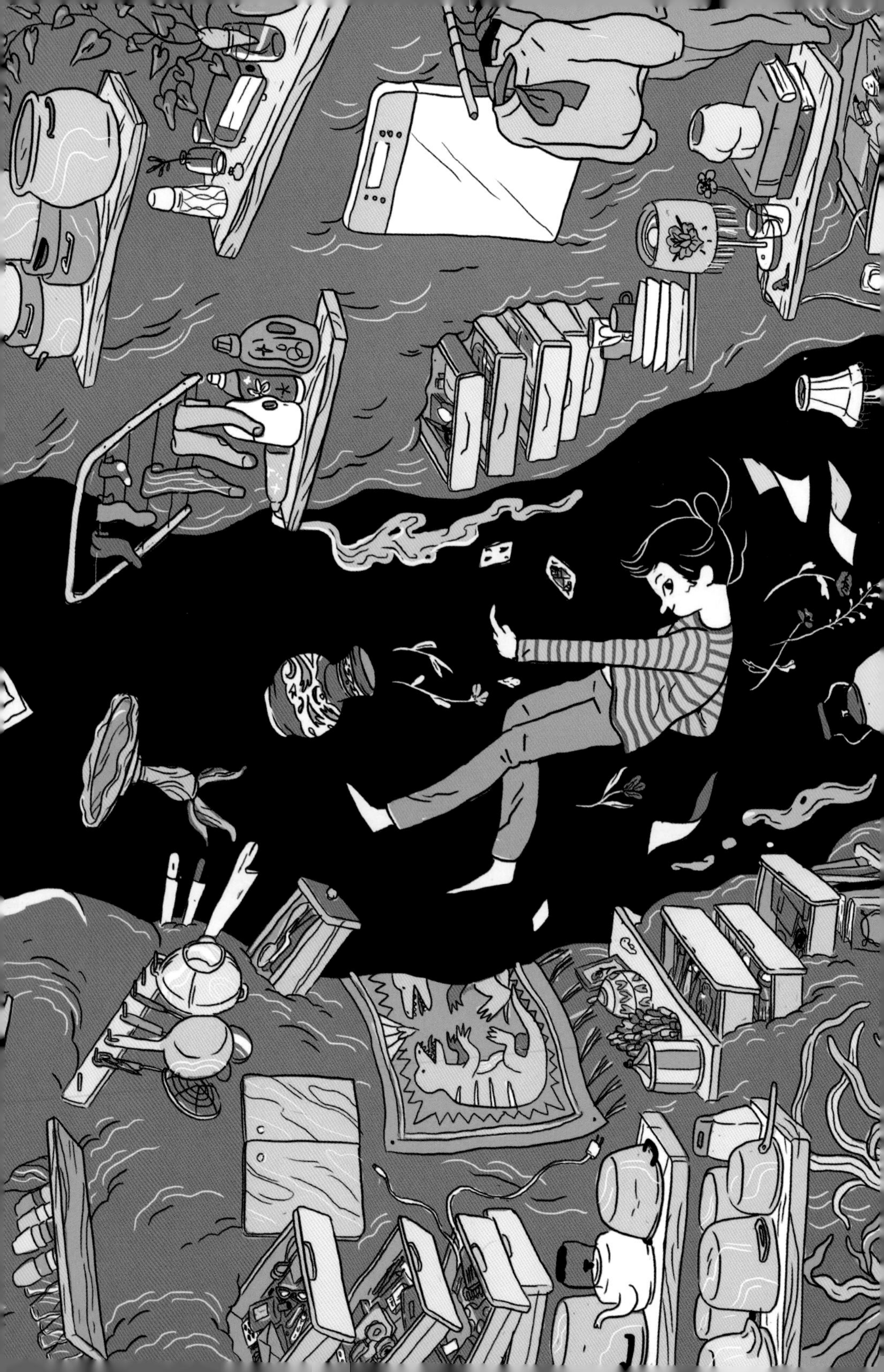

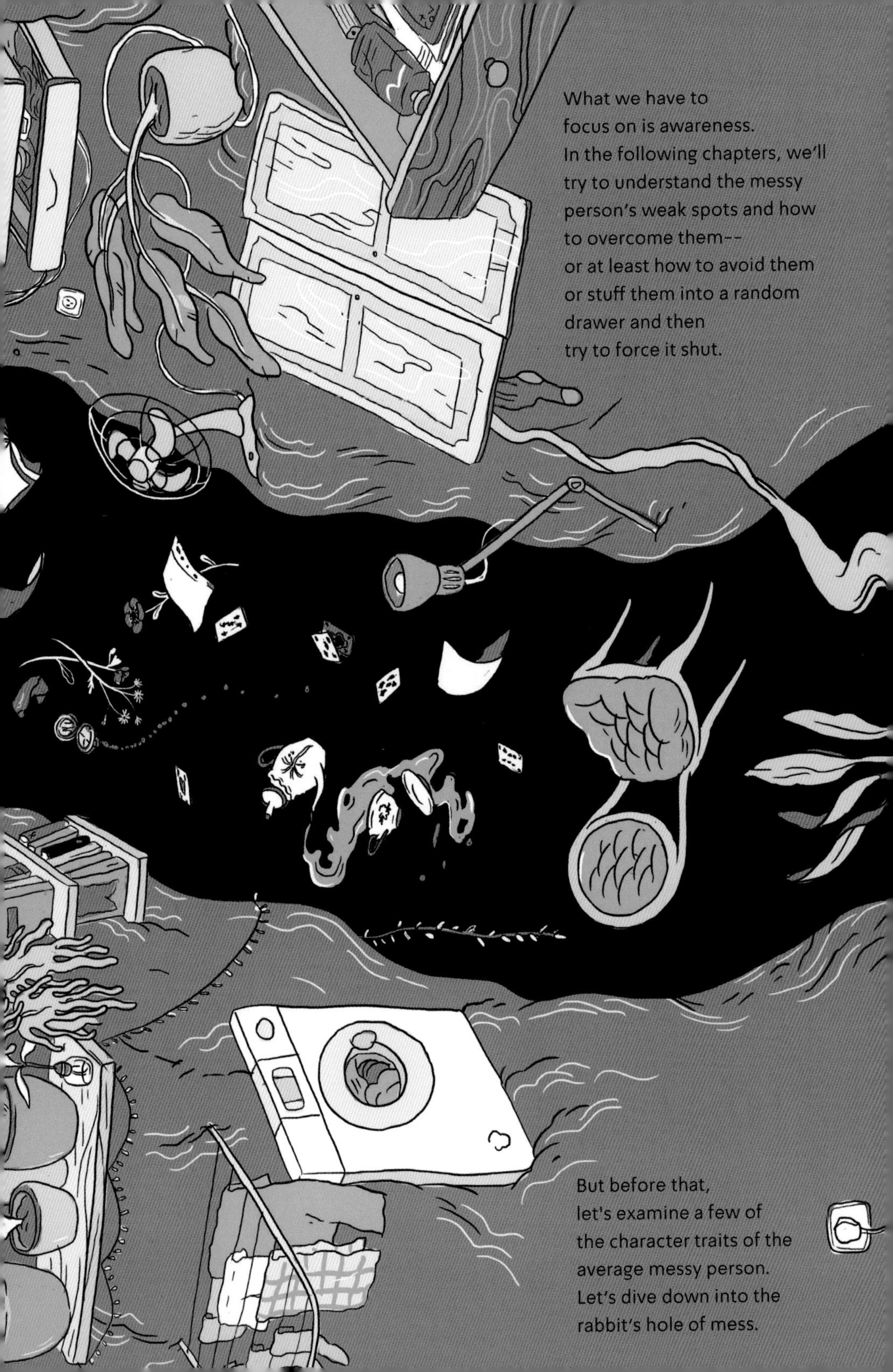
What we have to focus on is awareness. In the following chapters, we'll try to understand the messy person's weak spots and how to overcome them-- or at least how to avoid them or stuff them into a random drawer and then try to force it shut.
But before that, let's examine a few of the character traits of the average messy person. Let's dive down into the rabbit's hole of mess.

WHAT CONSTITUTES A MESS?

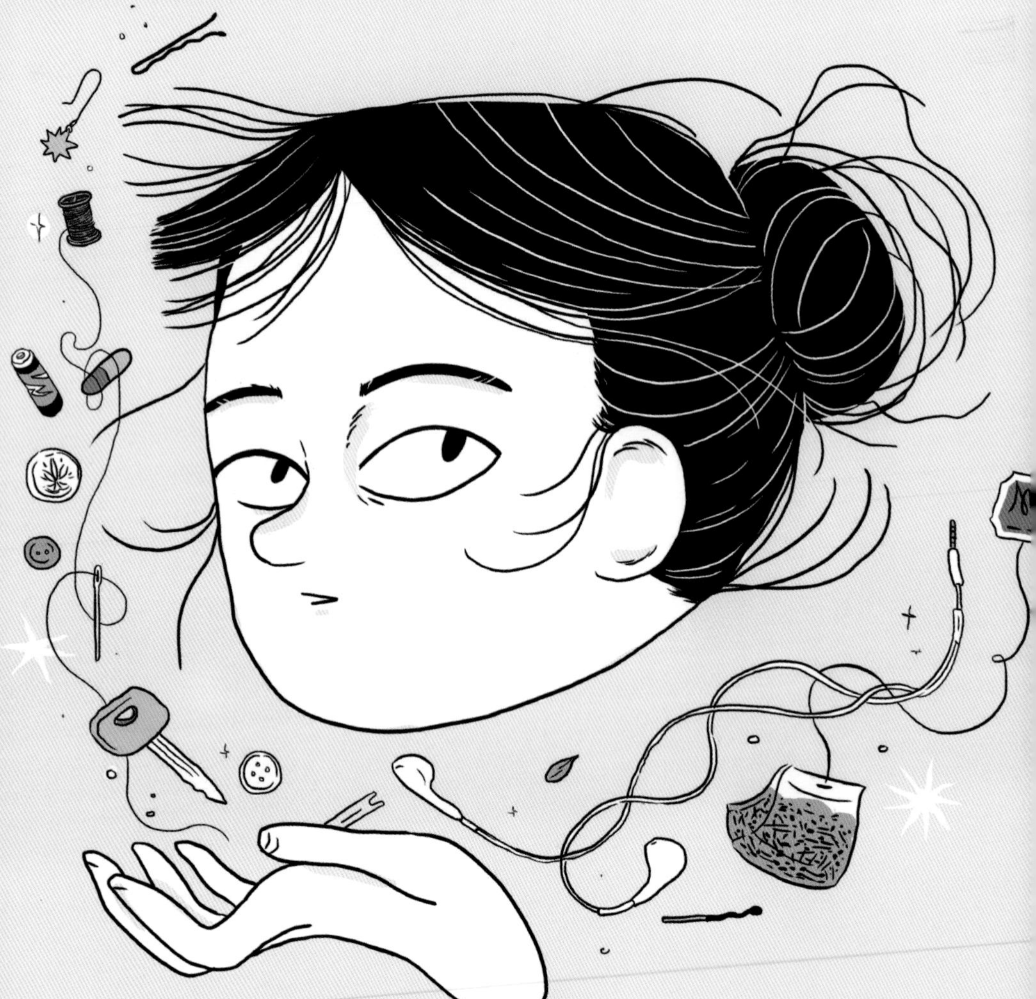

The physical mess is composed of keys, coins, gum at the bottom of a handbag, buttons, batteries, the journal that I bought to be more organized (and then lost) and approximately four umbrellas during an average rainy season.

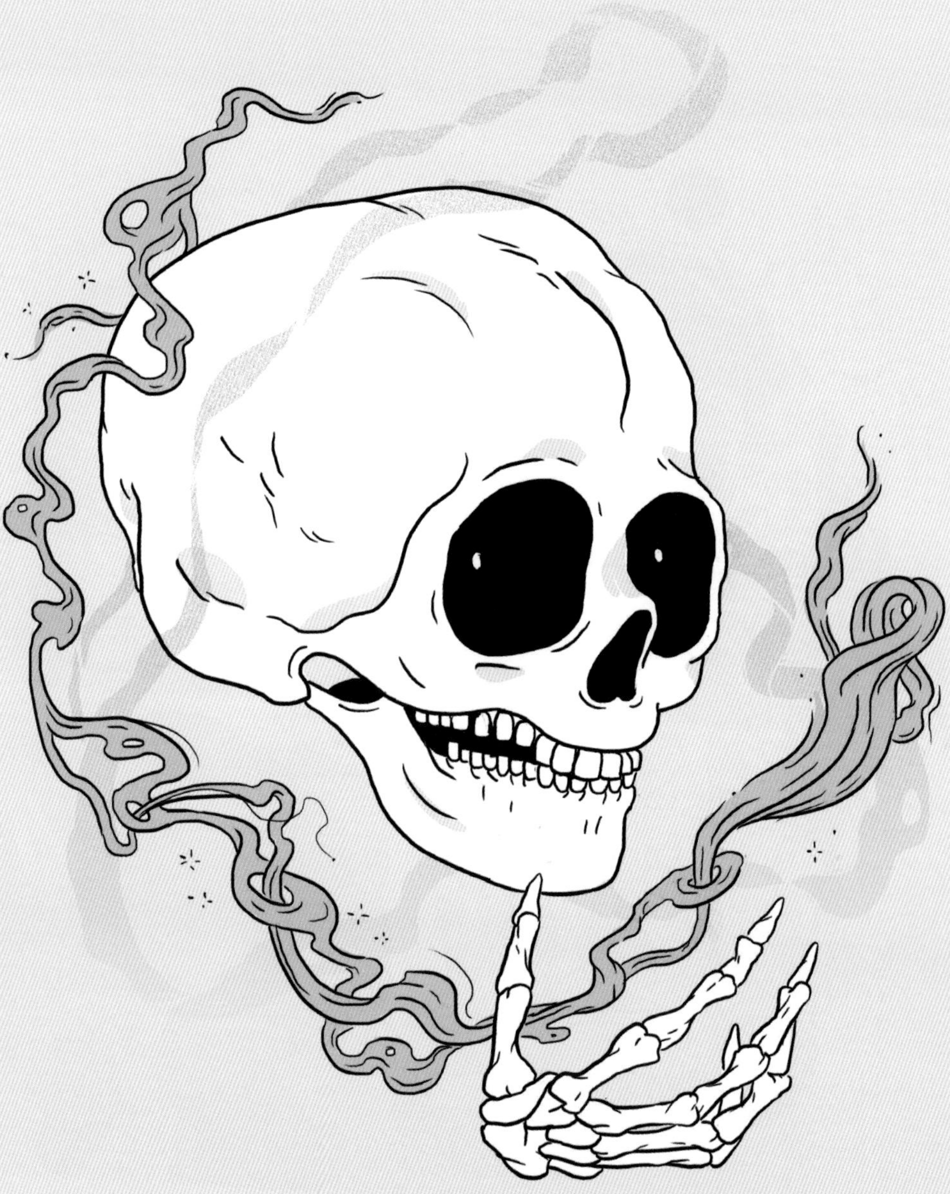

The metaphysical mess isn't about objects--it's about the spirit of things. It is the most basic point of the beginning of the universe, which was also born out of chaos and continues to disperse it on and on.

The most interesting things begin from something disorderly and incohesive,

like the universe

or a birthday cake

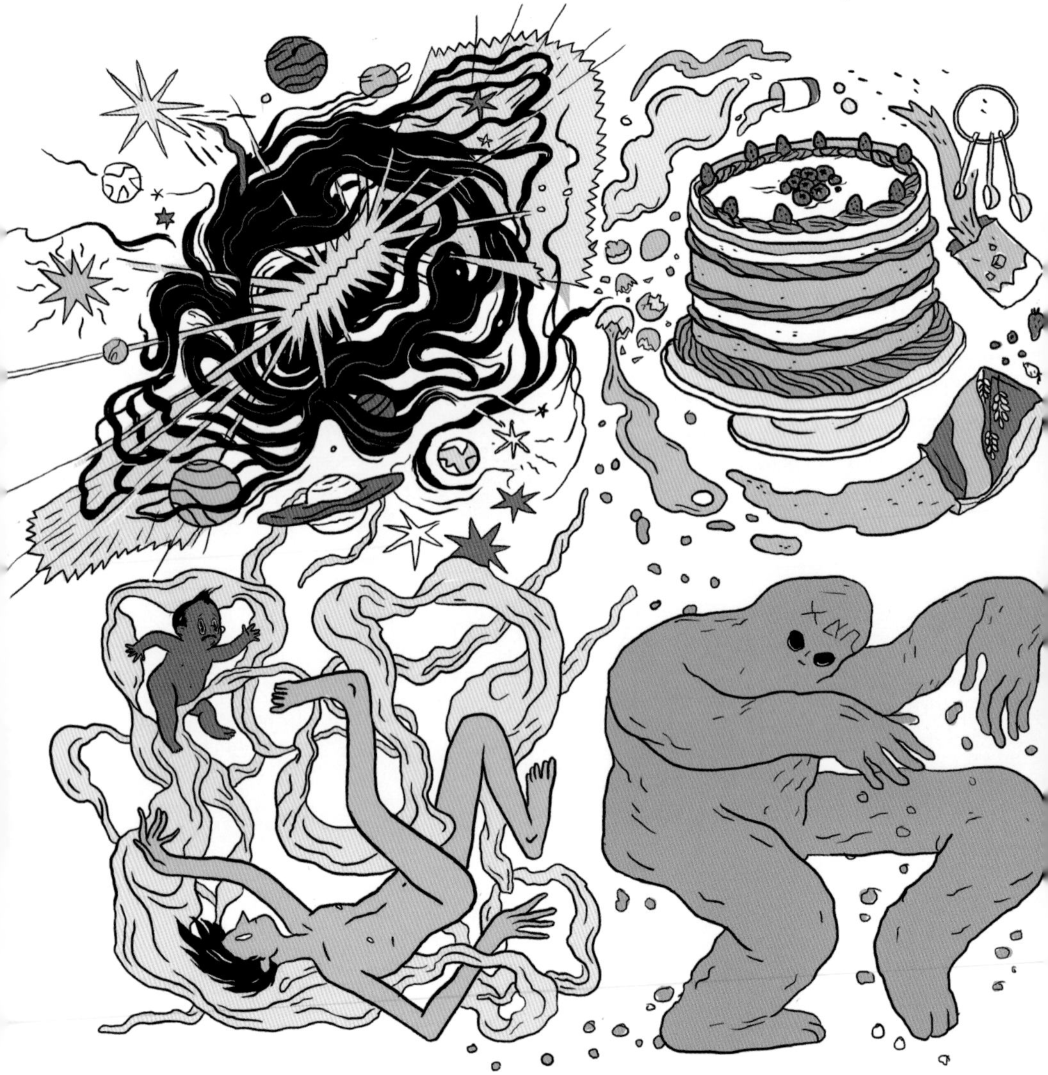

or humans

or golems from Prague.

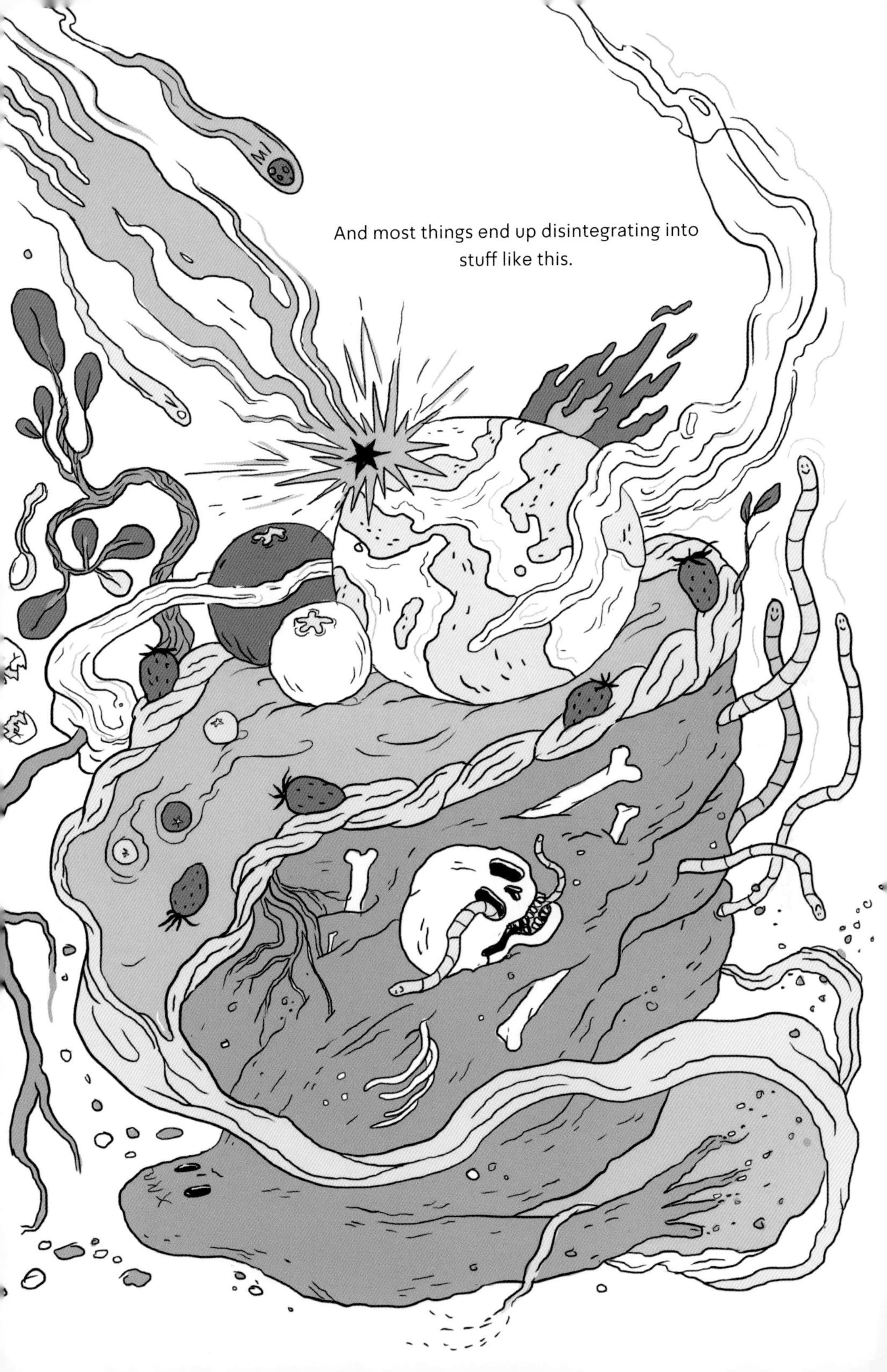
And most things end up disintegrating into stuff like this.

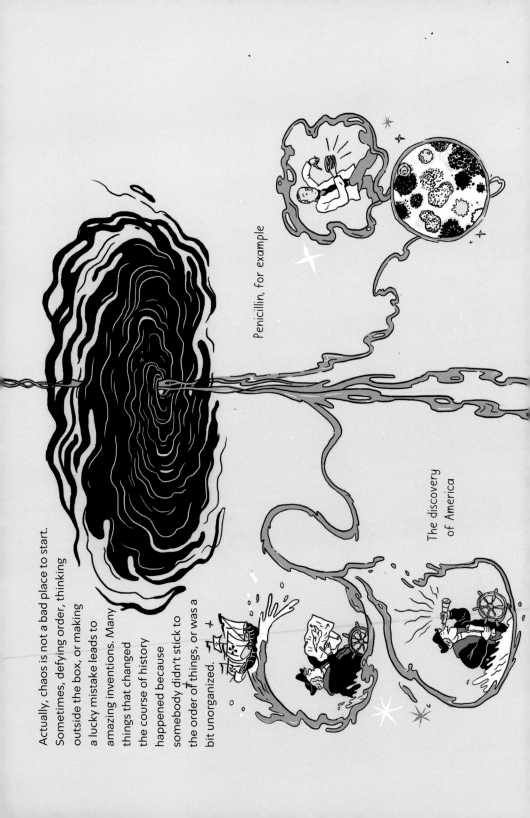

Actually, chaos is not a bad place to start. Sometimes, defying order, thinking outside the box, or making a lucky mistake leads to amazing inventions. Many things that changed the course of history happened because somebody didn't stick to the order of things, or was a bit unorganized.

Penicillin, for example

The discovery of America

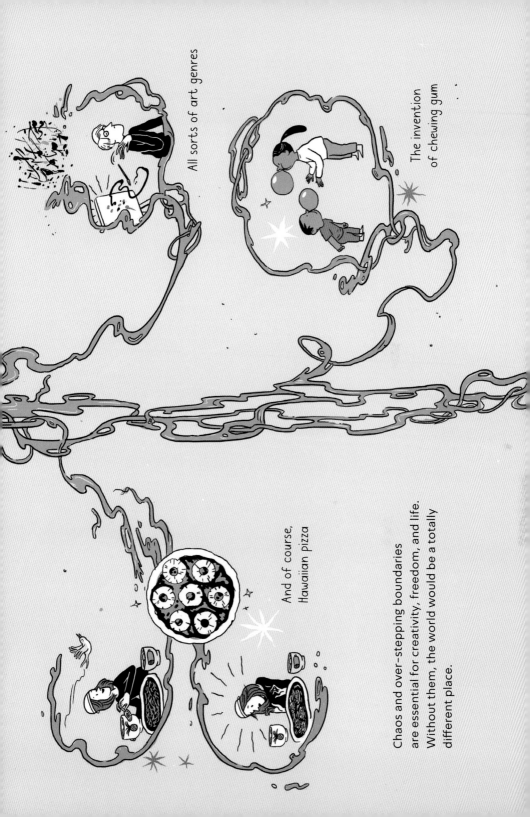

All sorts of art genres

The invention
of chewing gum

And of course,
Hawaiian pizza

Chaos and over-stepping boundaries
are essential for creativity, freedom, and life.
Without them, the world would be a totally
different place.

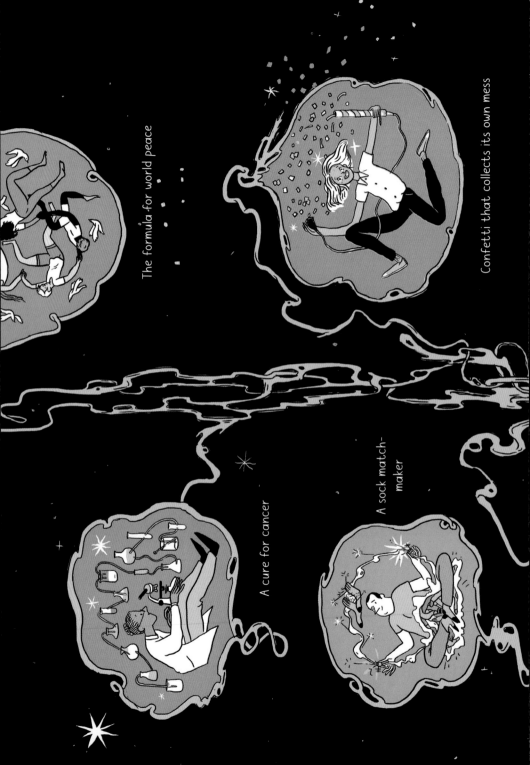

The formula for world peace

Confetti that collects its own mess

A cure for cancer

A sock match-maker

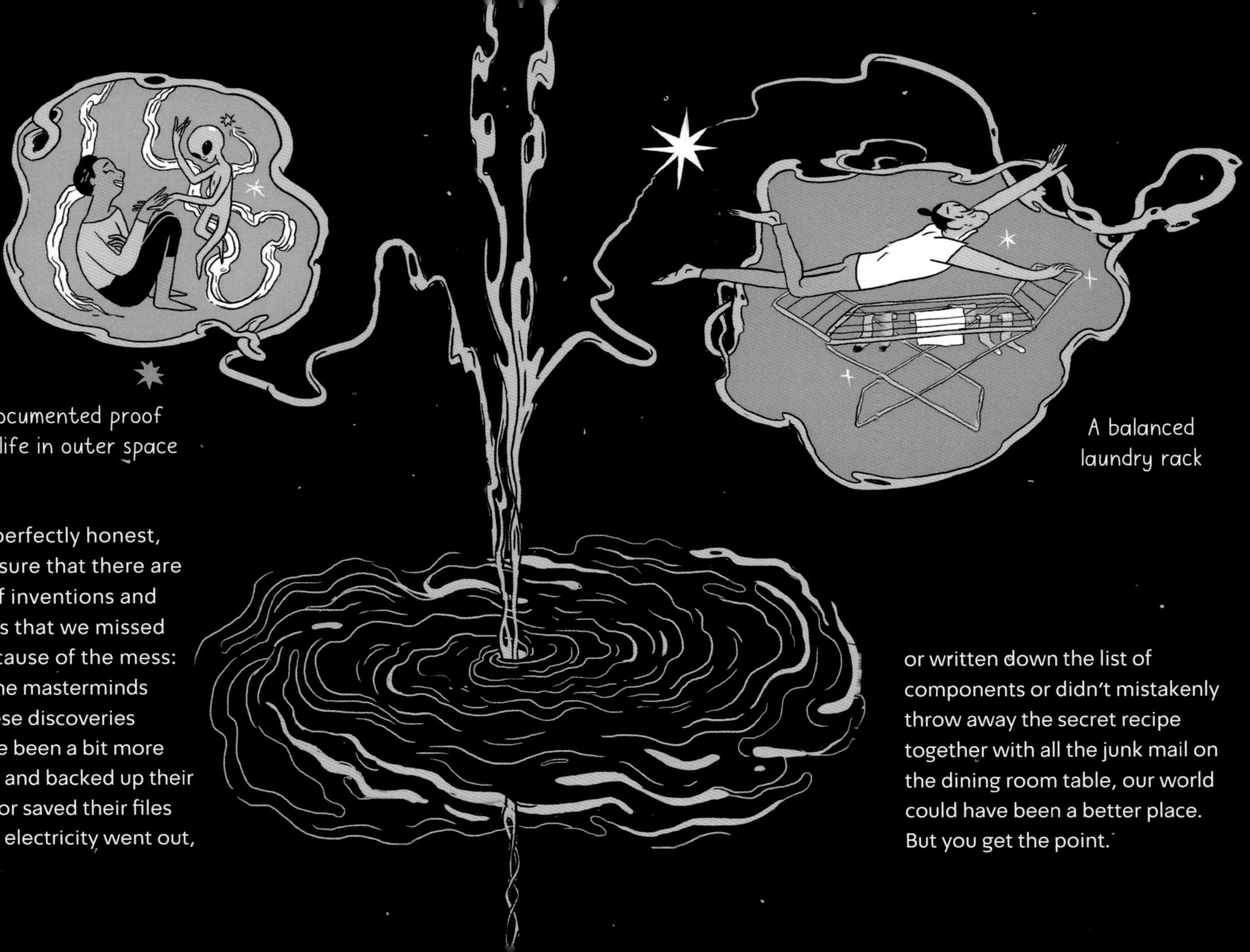

Documented proof of life in outer space
A balanced laundry rack

But to be perfectly honest, I'm pretty sure that there are also lots of inventions and discoveries that we missed out on because of the mess: Maybe if the masterminds behind these discoveries would have been a bit more organized, and backed up their computer or saved their files before the electricity went out, or written down the list of components or didn't mistakenly throw away the secret recipe together with all the junk mail on the dining room table, our world could have been a better place. But you get the point.

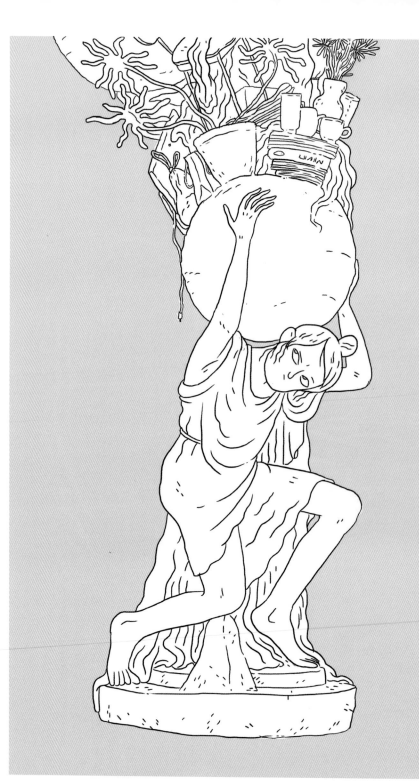

So we saw the metaphysical side of the mess,
but like I said, a mess also has a physical side.
Super physical.

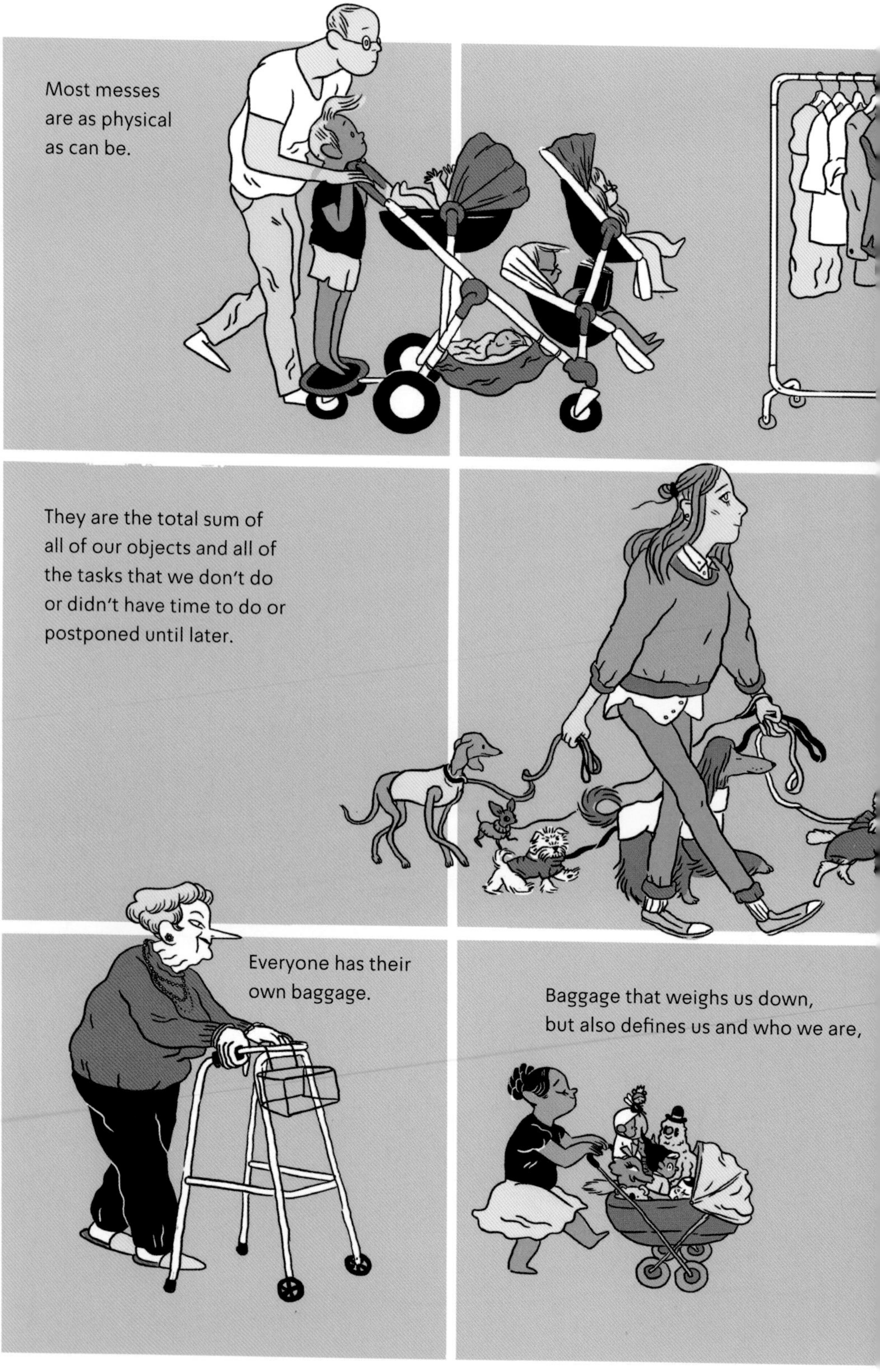
Most messes are as physical as can be.
They are the total sum of all of our objects and all of the tasks that we don't do or didn't have time to do or postponed until later.
Everyone has their own baggage.
Baggage that weighs us down, but also defines us and who we are,

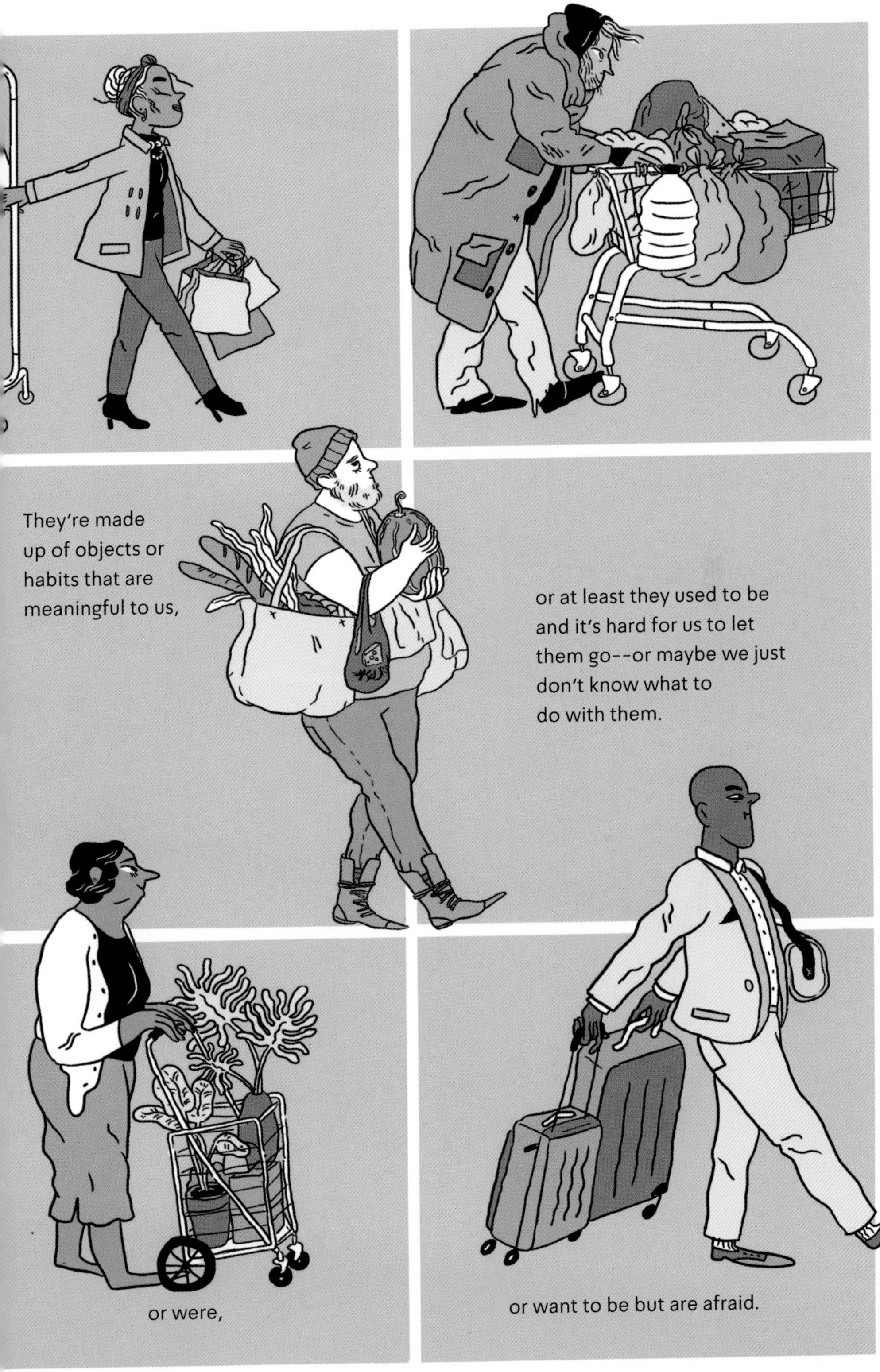
They're made up of objects or habits that are meaningful to us,
or at least they used to be and it's hard for us to let them go--or maybe we just don't know what to do with them.
or were,
or want to be but are afraid.

We waste a lot of time in life on the physical mess, collecting it
and organizing it and putting it all away
so everything looks nice.

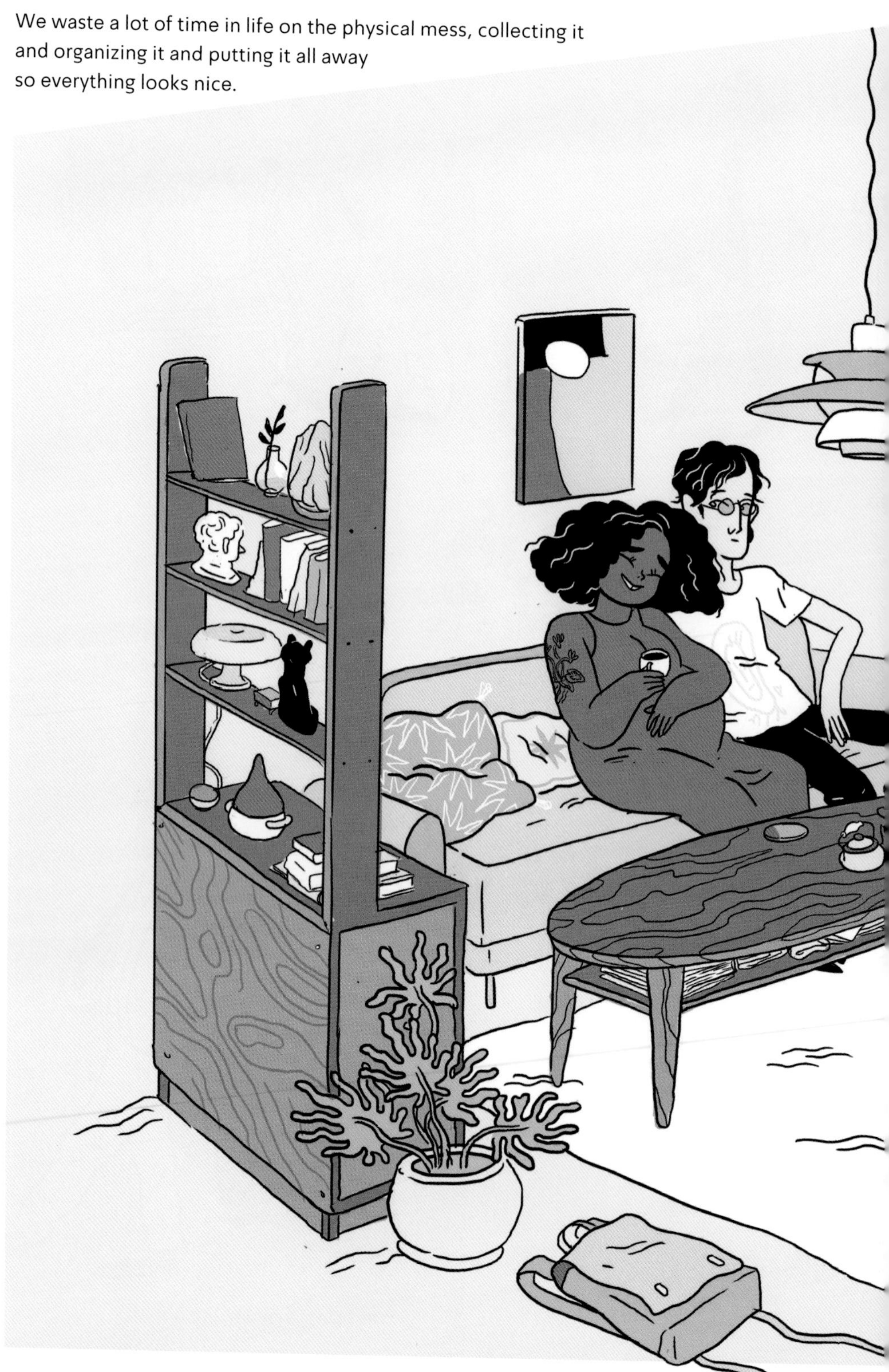

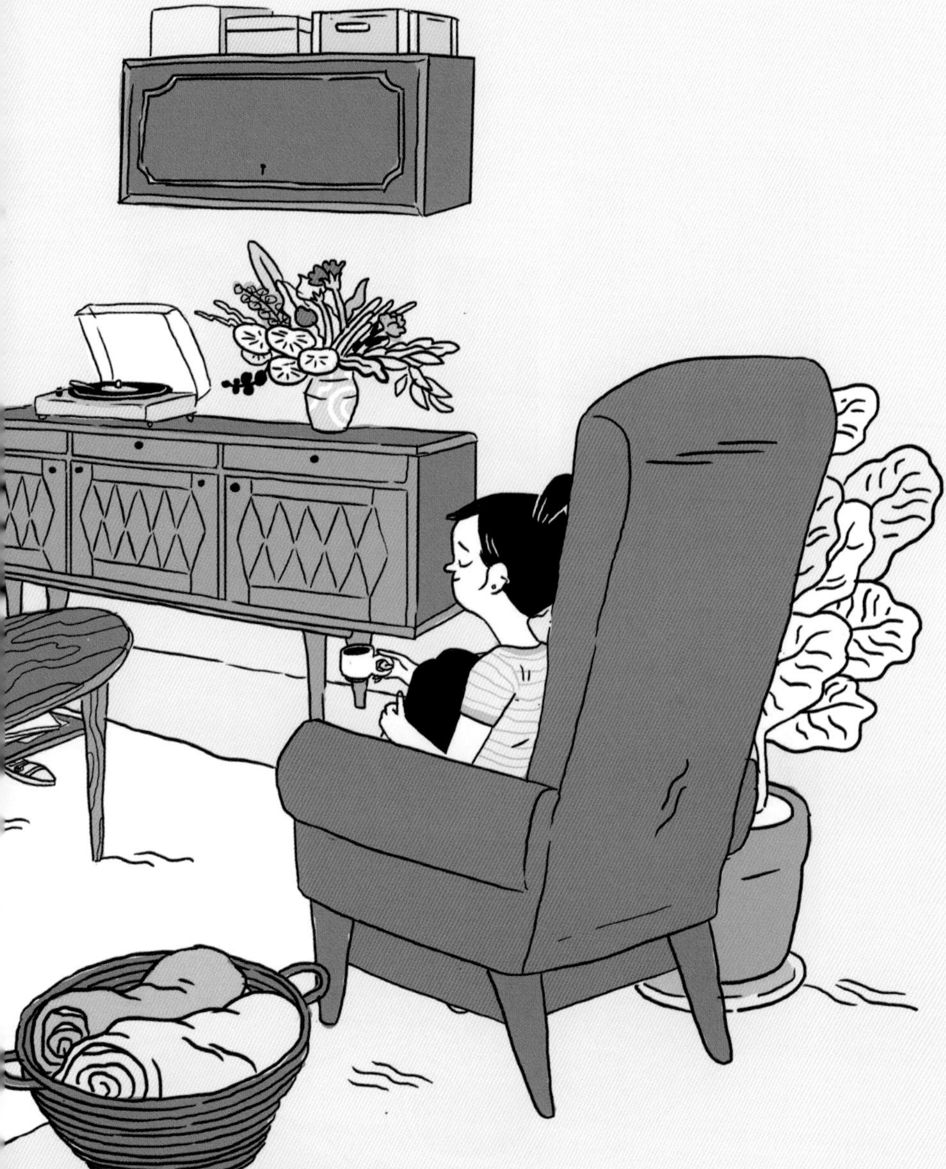

But to me, it sometimes feels like we're all pretending, or concealing a secret deep down inside.

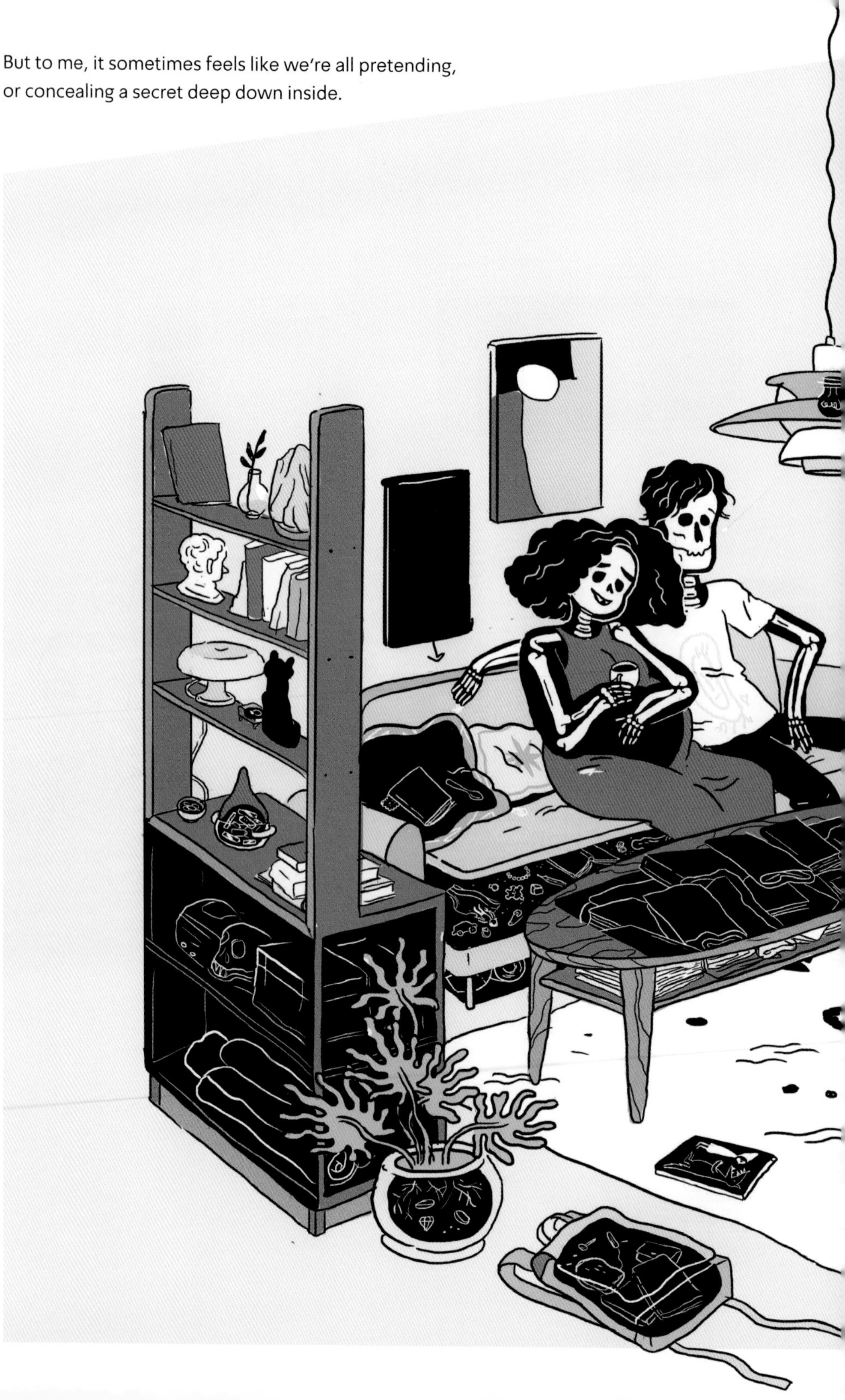

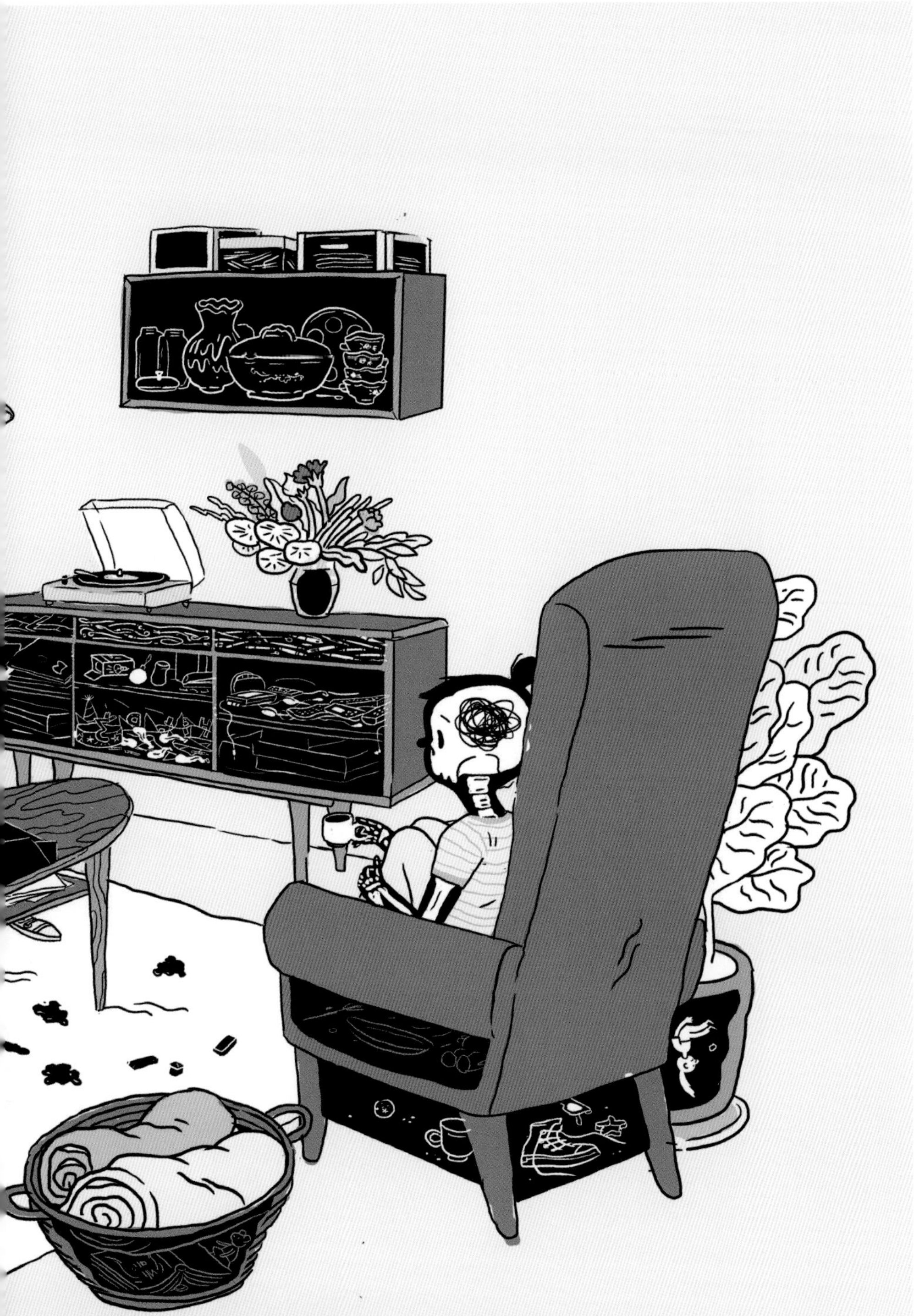

A secret that will eventually come out and erupt...

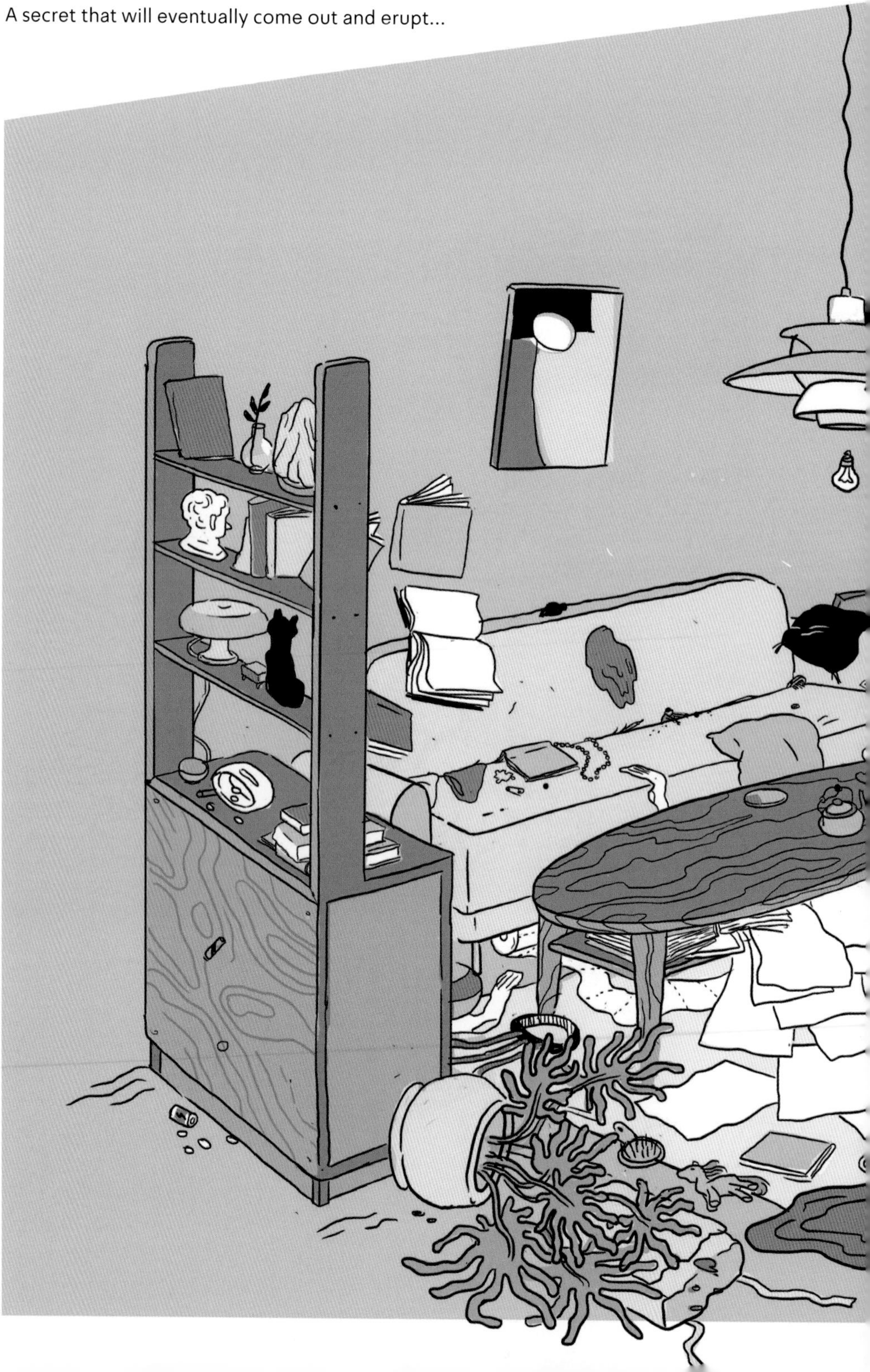

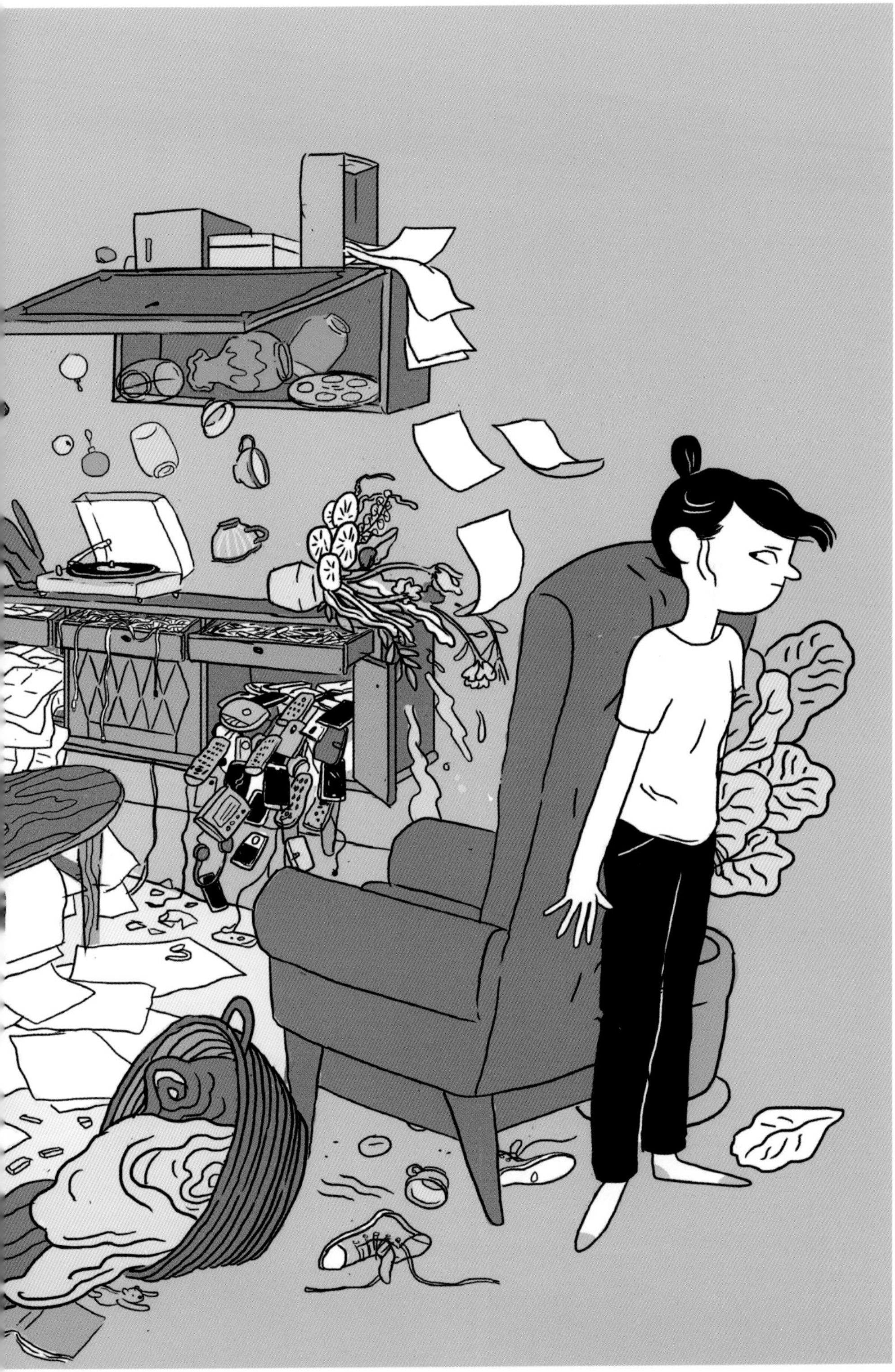

Sweeping everything in its wake

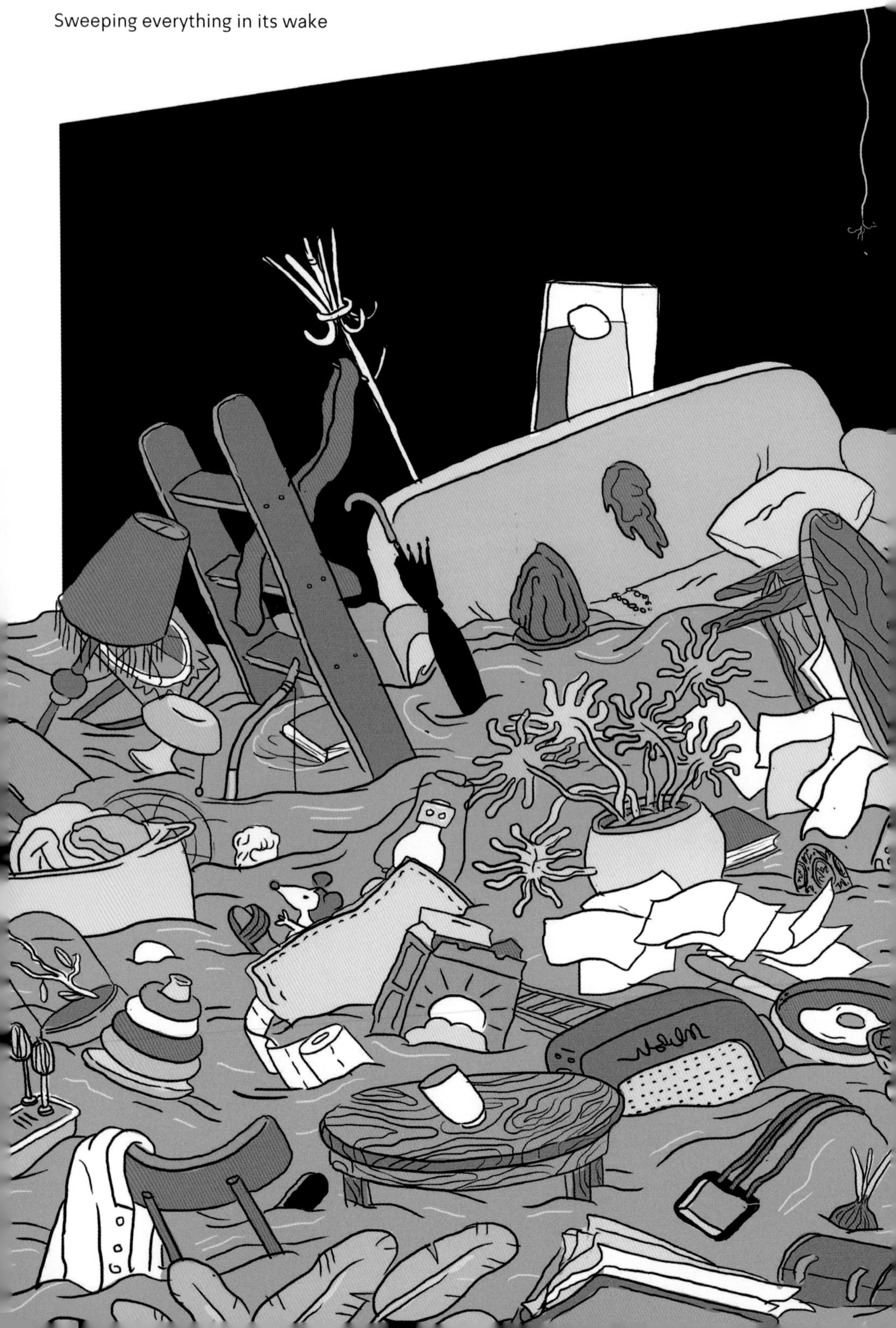

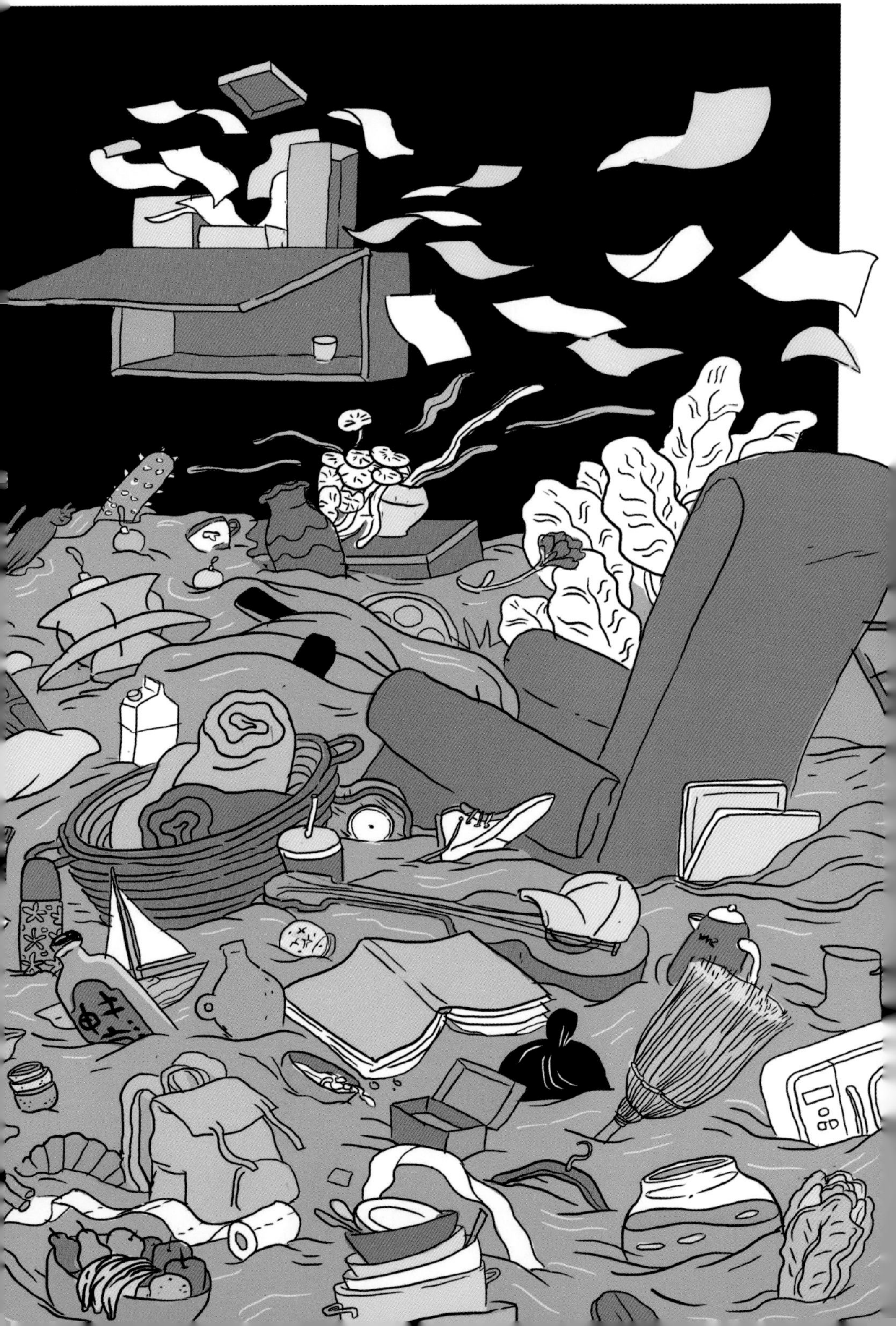

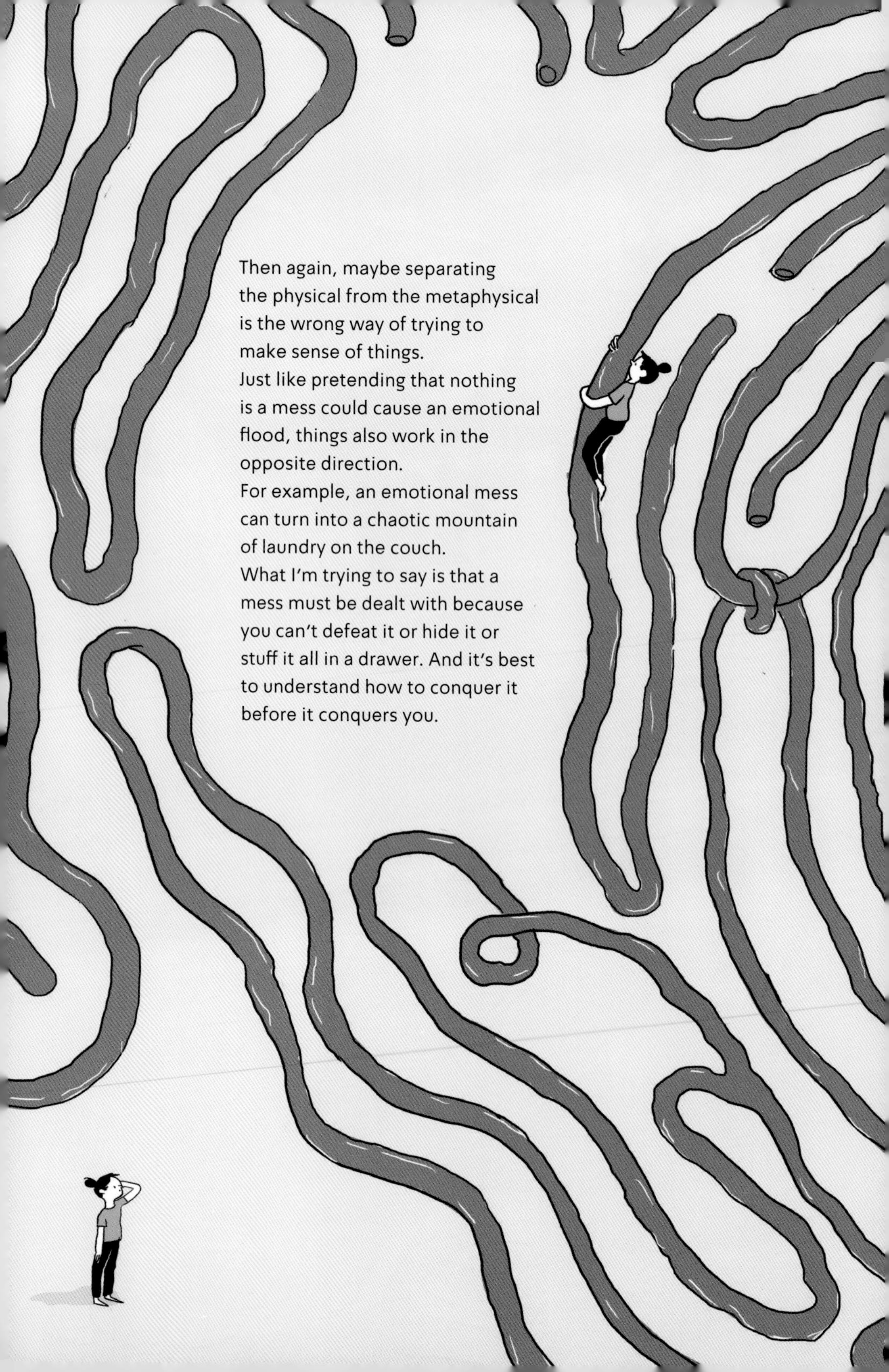

Then again, maybe separating the physical from the metaphysical is the wrong way of trying to make sense of things.
Just like pretending that nothing is a mess could cause an emotional flood, things also work in the opposite direction.
For example, an emotional mess can turn into a chaotic mountain of laundry on the couch.
What I'm trying to say is that a mess must be dealt with because you can't defeat it or hide it or stuff it all in a drawer. And it's best to understand how to conquer it before it conquers you.

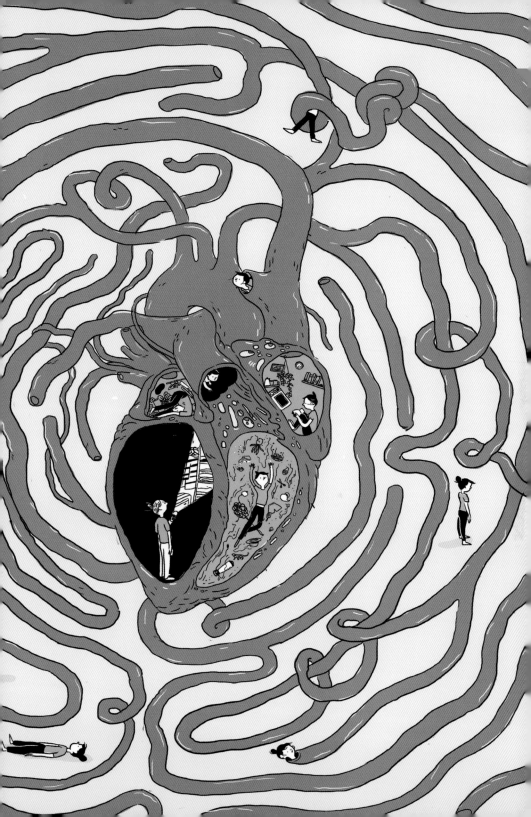

HOW TO DEAL WITH THE MESS

or:

WHAT ARE YOU UP AGAINST?

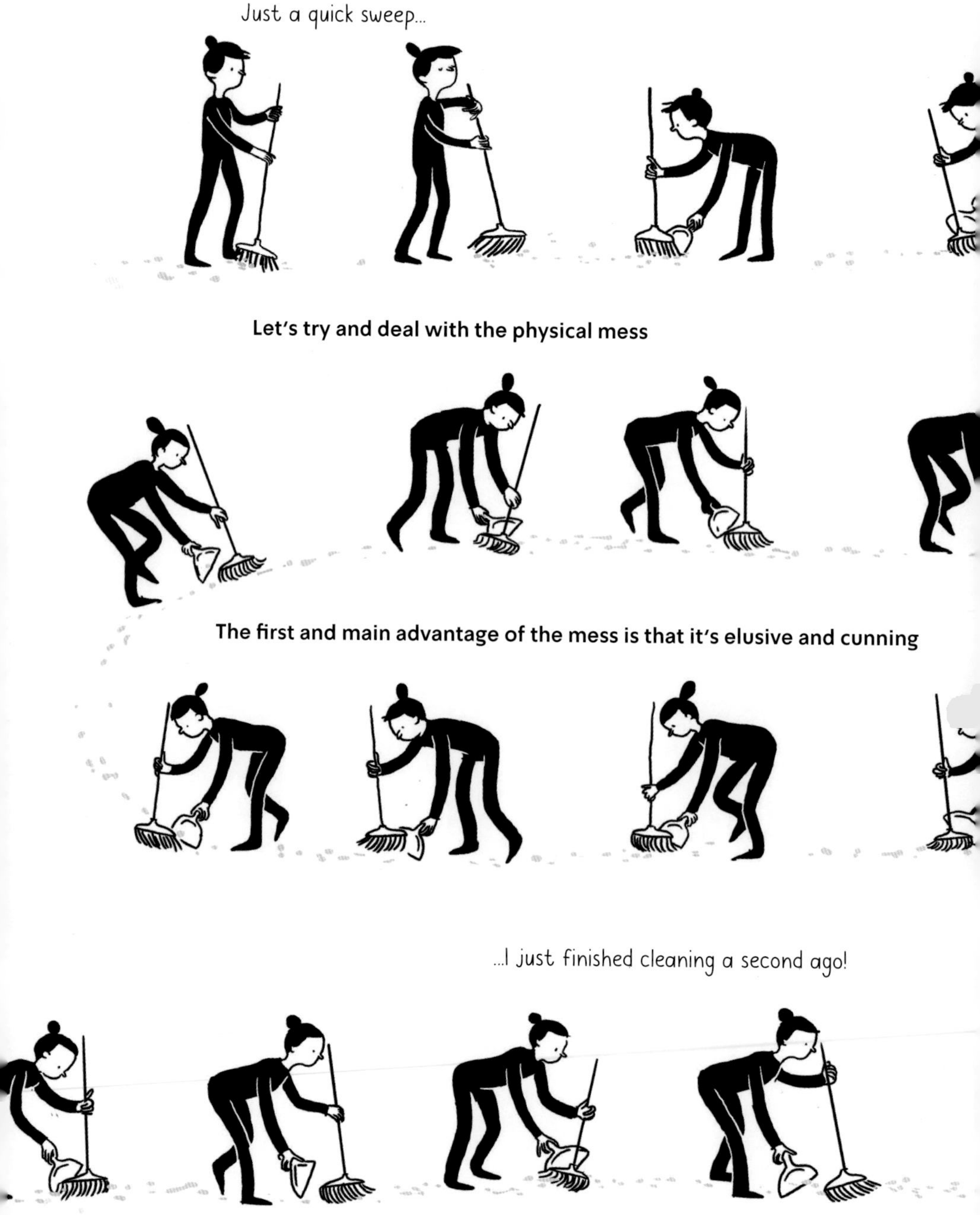
Just a quick sweep...
Let's try and deal with the physical mess
The first and main advantage of the mess is that it's elusive and cunning
...I just finished cleaning a second ago!

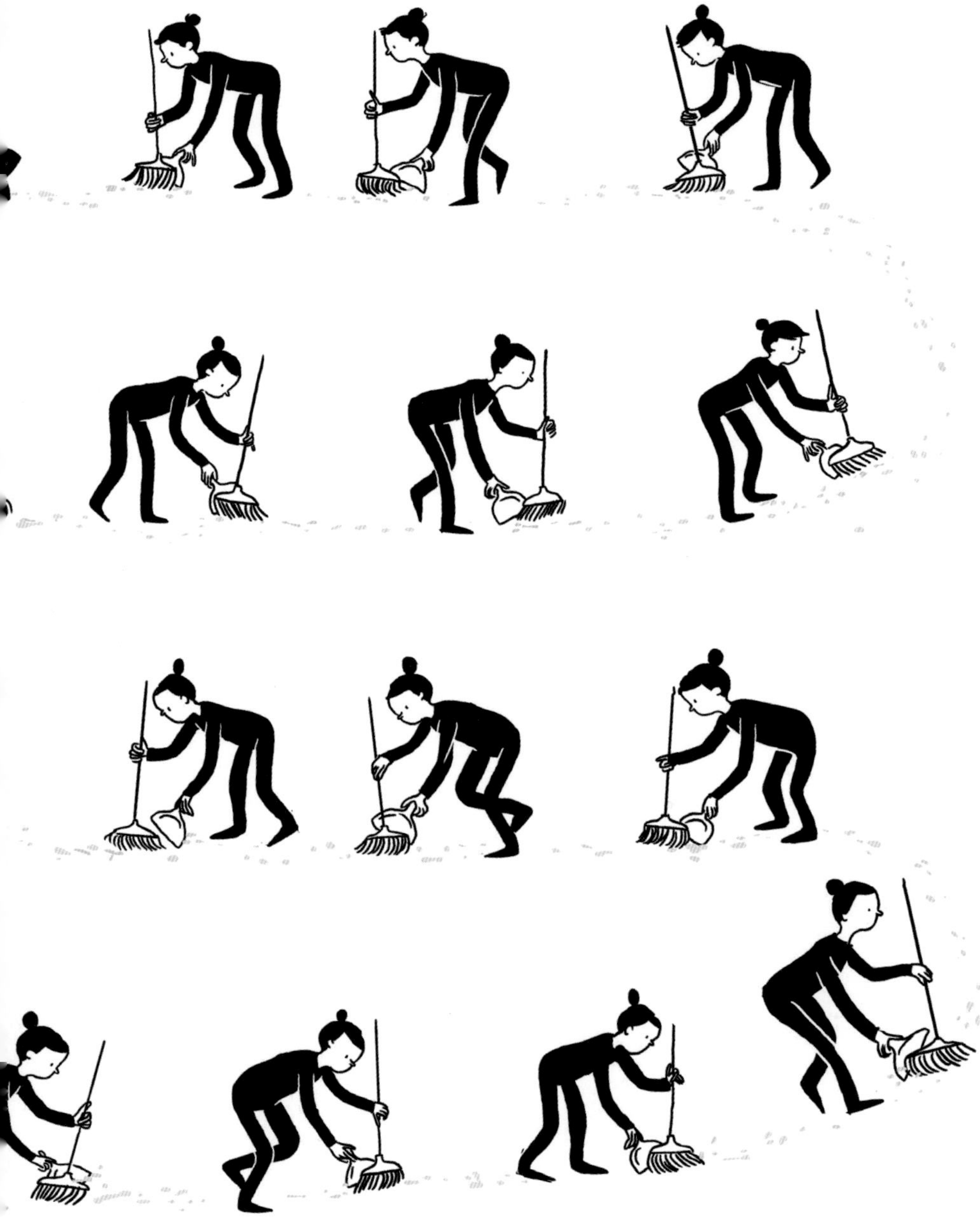

Now there's a towel, three and a half pairs of shoes and two pounds of Legos on the floor.

The second advantage of the mess is that it's a diabolic, endless cycle.

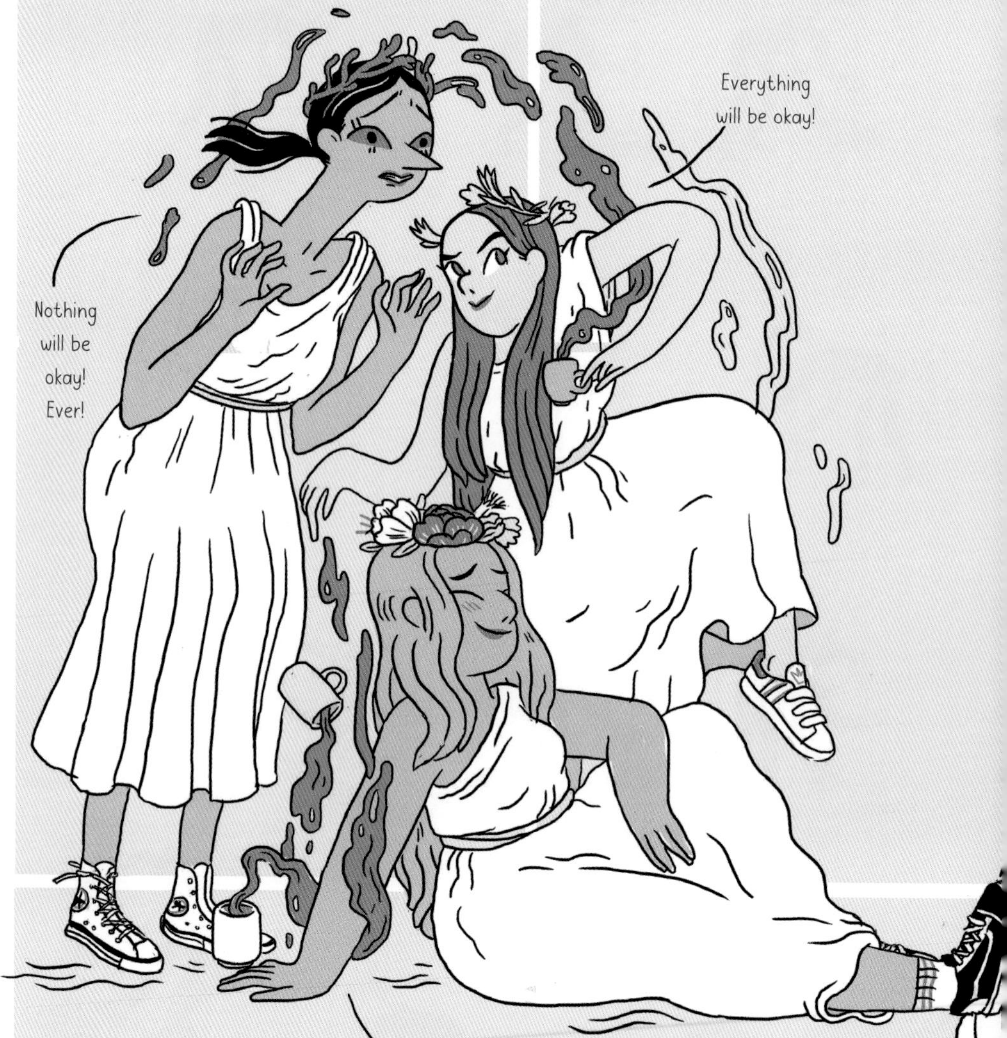
Nothing will be okay! Ever!
Everything will be okay!
Everything's okay...

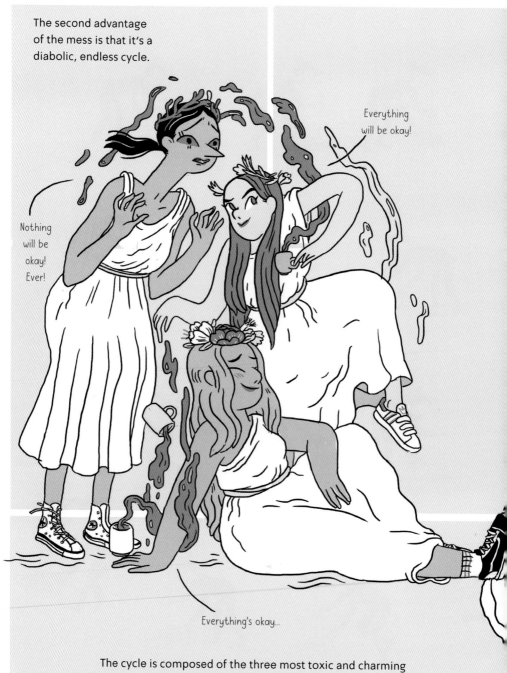

The cycle is composed of the three most toxic and charming weaknesses known to mankind:

Complacency, Procrastination, and Panic

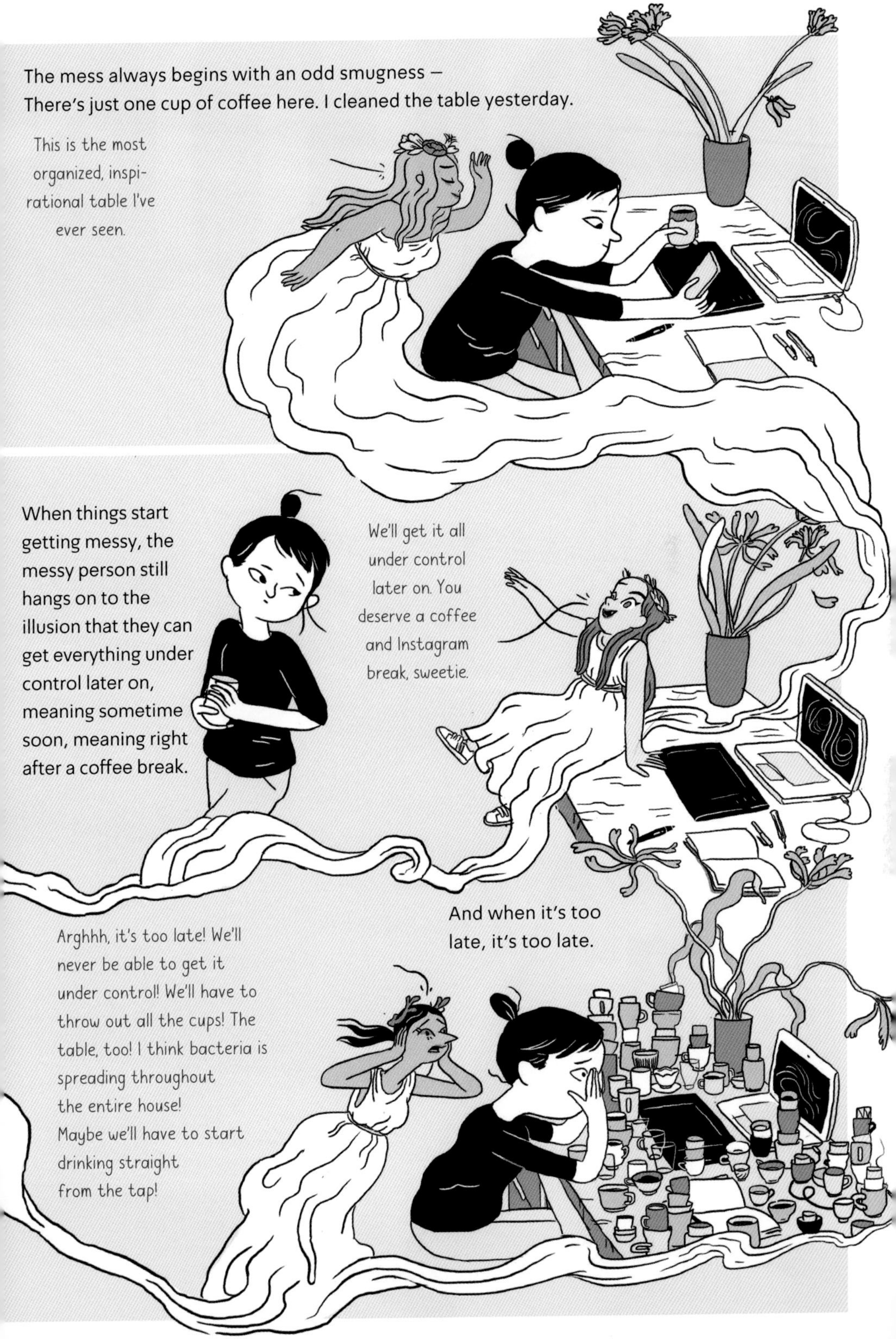
The mess always begins with an odd smugness –
There's just one cup of coffee here. I cleaned the table yesterday.
This is the most organized, inspirational table I've ever seen.
When things start getting messy, the messy person still hangs on to the illusion that they can get everything under control later on, meaning sometime soon, meaning right after a coffee break.
We'll get it all under control later on. You deserve a coffee and Instagram break, sweetie.
And when it's too late, it's too late.
Arghhh, it's too late! We'll never be able to get it under control! We'll have to throw out all the cups! The table, too! I think bacteria is spreading throughout the entire house! Maybe we'll have to start drinking straight from the tap!

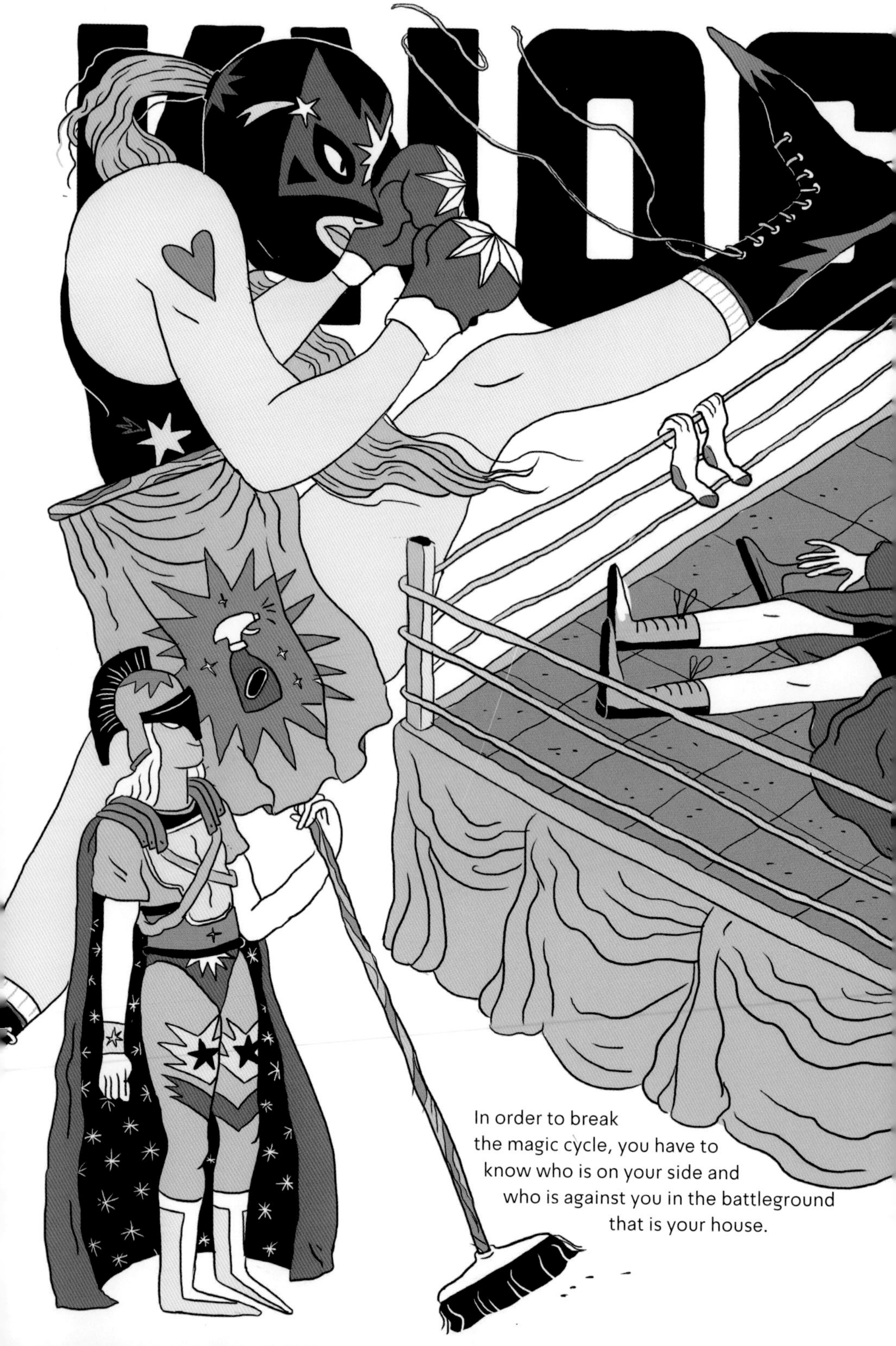
In order to break
the magic cycle, you have to
know who is on your side and
who is against you in the battleground
that is your house.

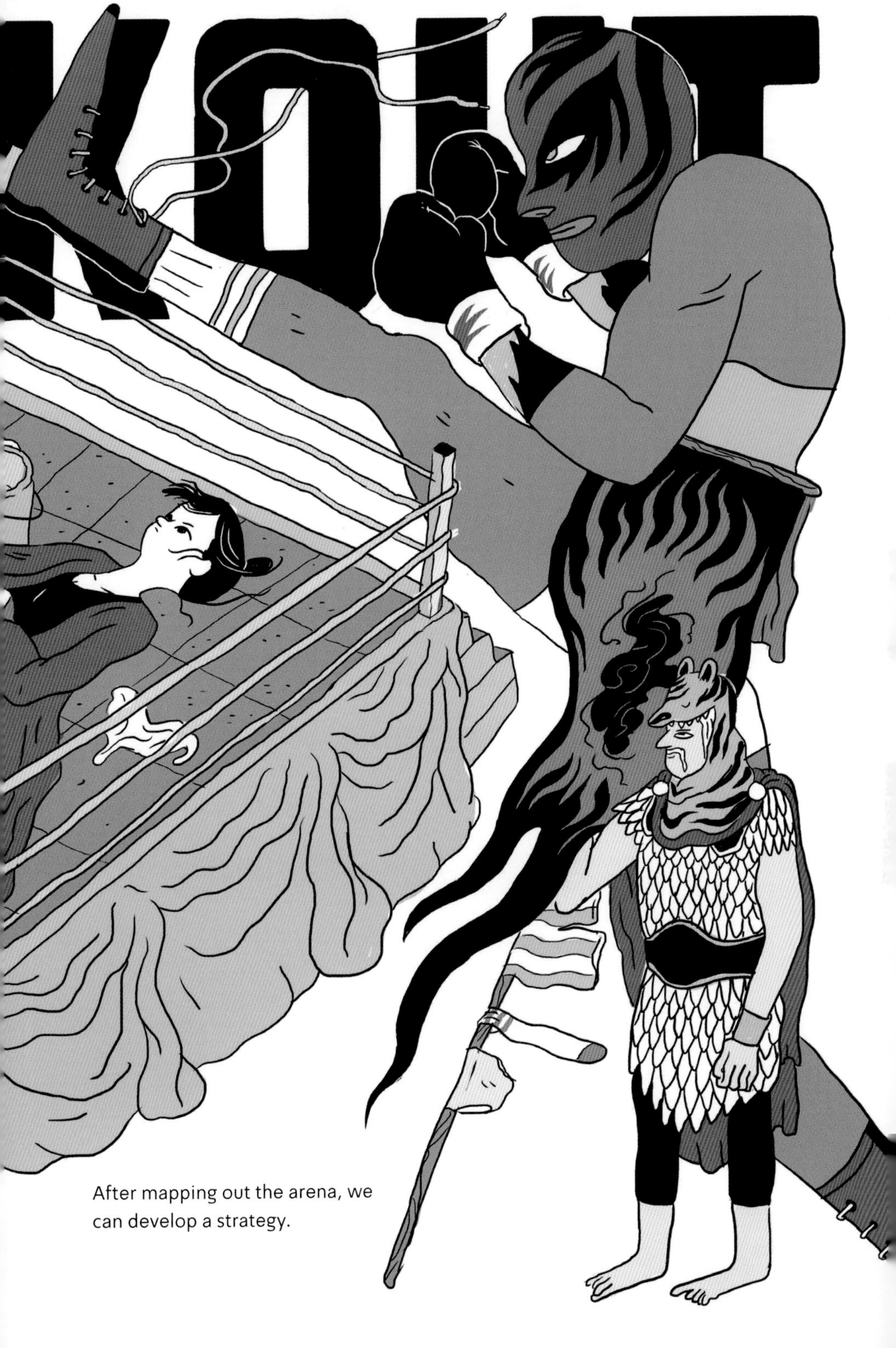
After mapping out the arena, we can develop a strategy.

The Bad Ones

Now, there are objects that clearly side with the bad ones

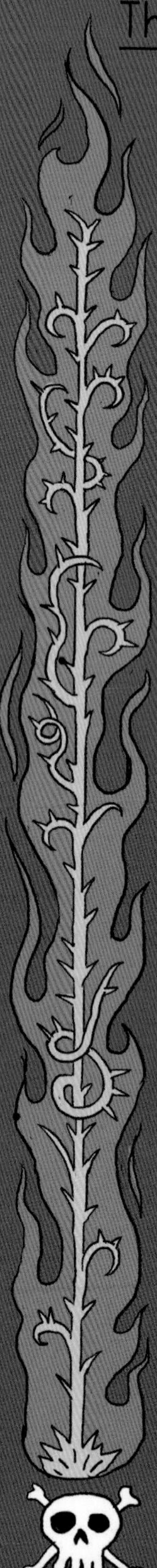

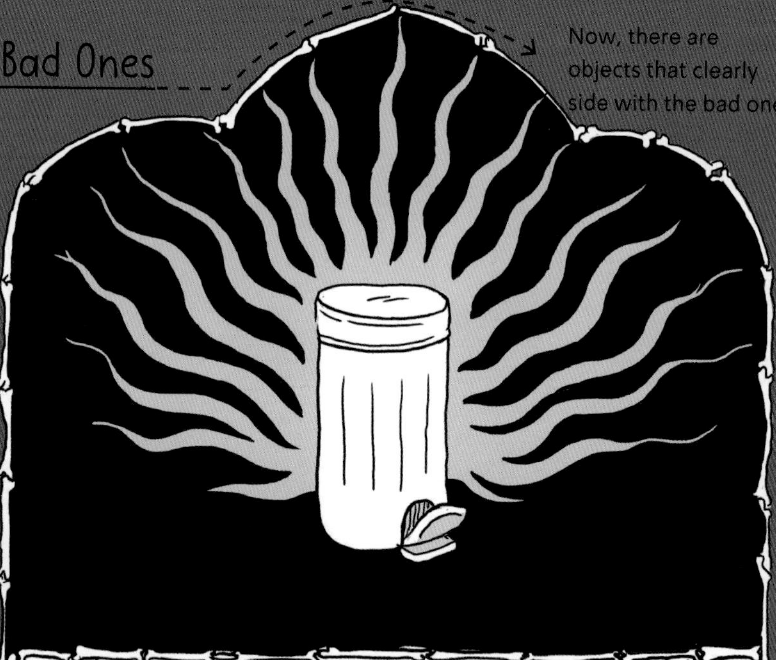

The evil king of objects in the house is, of course, the tiny garbage can near the bathroom. The smaller it is, the more evil. The combination between its miniscule dimensions and the spongy consistency of the things thrown inside create a compressed capsule of mush, reducing your motivation to empty the garbage to once every six months.

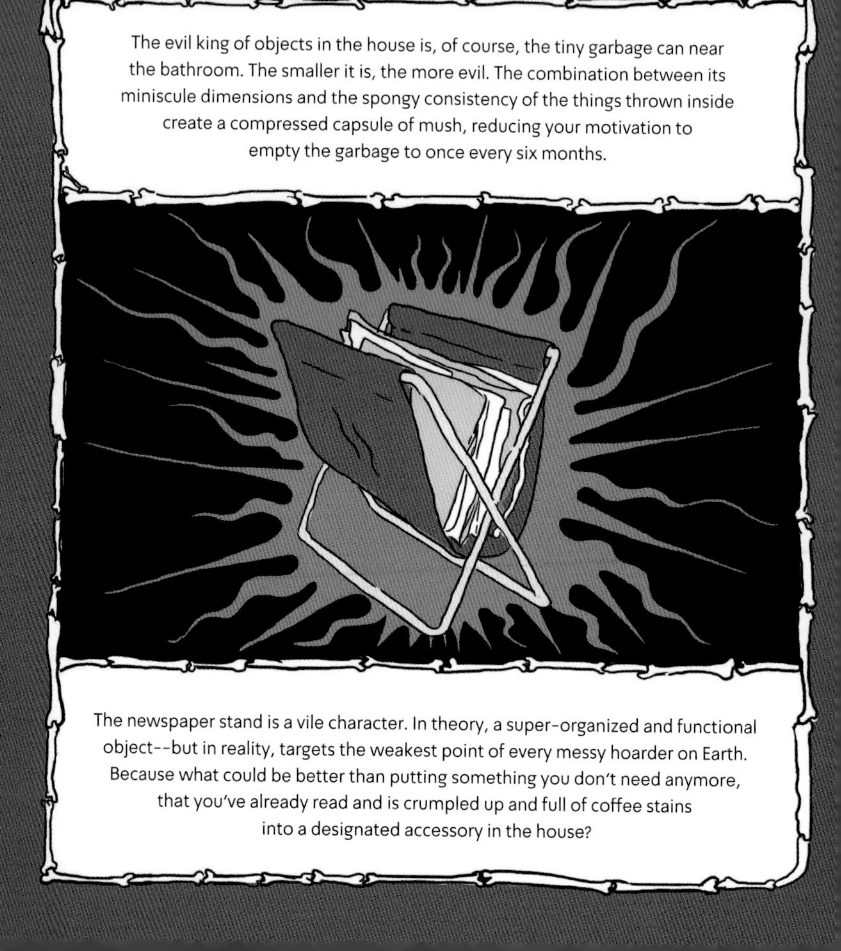

The newspaper stand is a vile character. In theory, a super-organized and functional object--but in reality, targets the weakest point of every messy hoarder on Earth. Because what could be better than putting something you don't need anymore, that you've already read and is crumpled up and full of coffee stains into a designated accessory in the house?

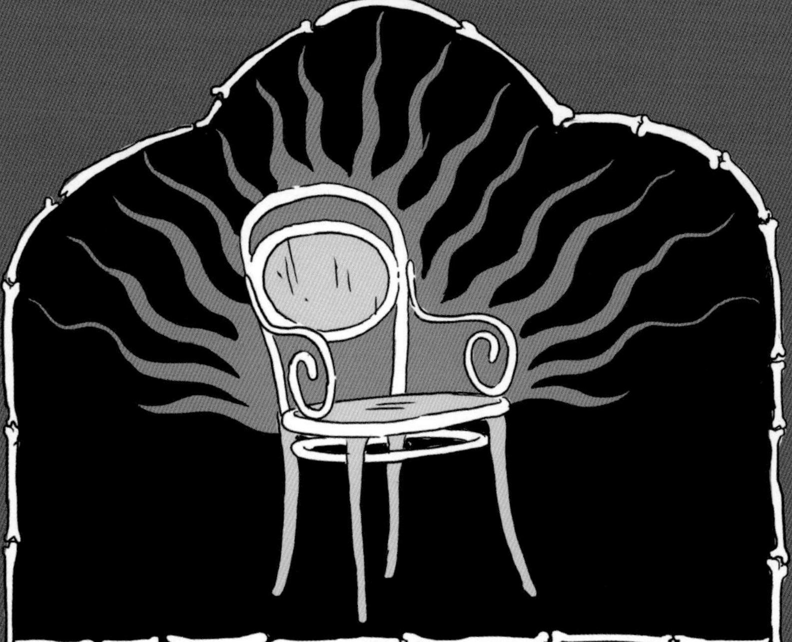

Another arch-enemy is the chair in the corner of the room. The chair is a very sly and sophisticated foe. At first, it seems perfectly harmless, and seems to want to help. But actually, it's a trap. It becomes the resting place of piles of clothing and all sorts of things you didn't know exactly where they belonged when you picked them up off the floor and now, there's no chance of straightening things up again.

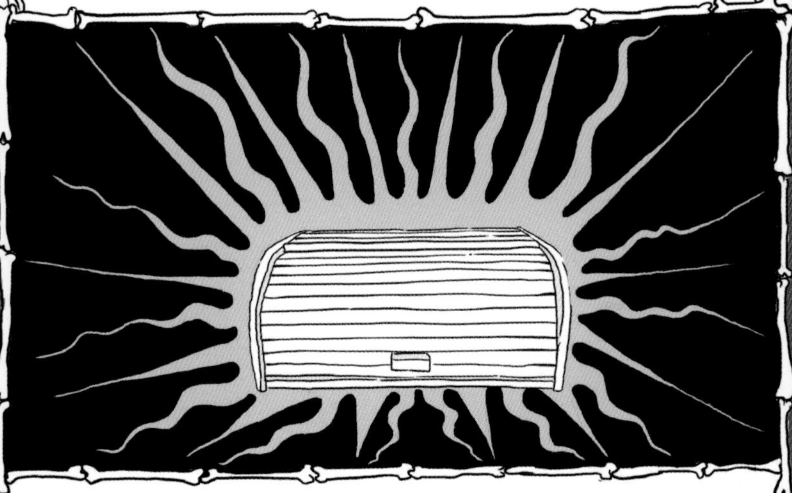

But the most traitorous of all is undoubtedly the bread box. You could even say that it's the double agent of all evil objects. Because under the guise of "the correct and responsible place to store bread," it promises certain failure in the battle between order and mess. There is no chance that any person who isn't Einstein can remember that there is bread inside until the smell begins to spread throughout the kitchen.

The Good Ones

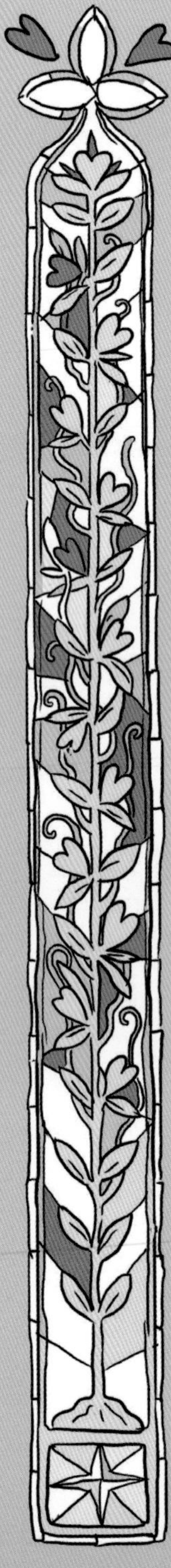

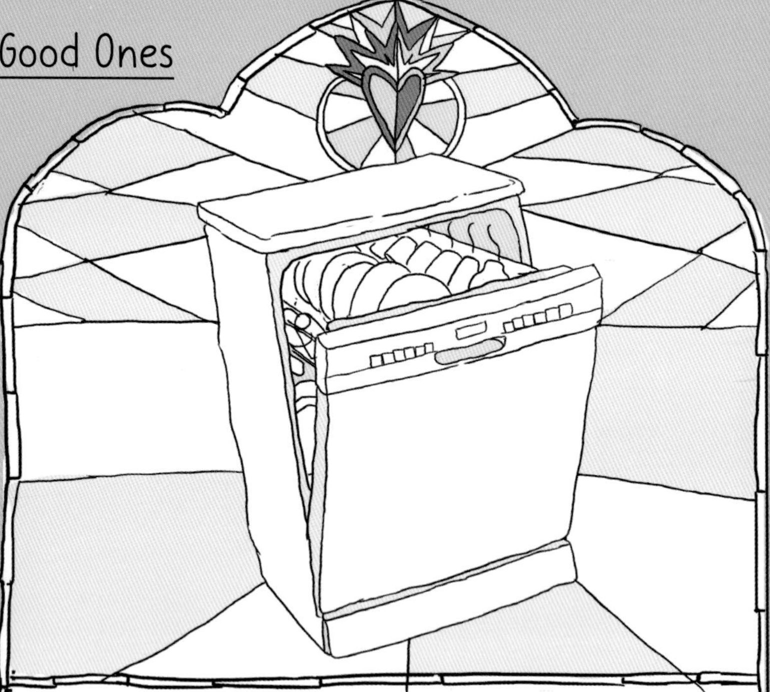

The holiest of all household objects is the dishwasher.
It completes the most annoying task of washing your dishes for you
and also hides them inside until you have time to put them away.

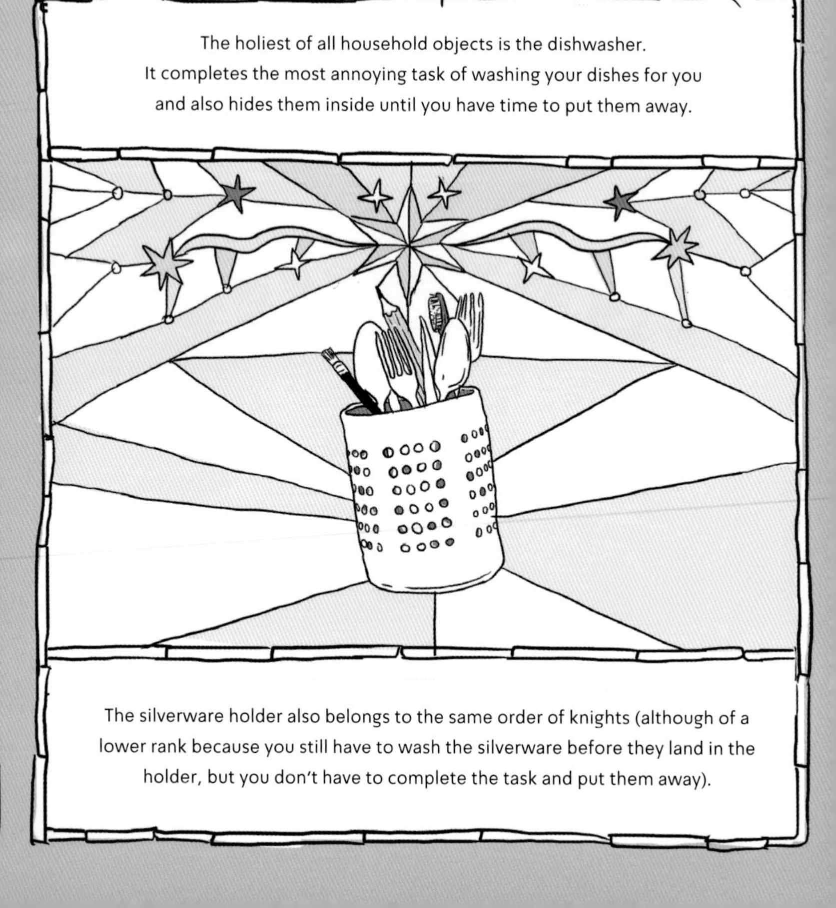

The silverware holder also belongs to the same order of knights (although of a lower rank because you still have to wash the silverware before they land in the holder, but you don't have to complete the task and put them away).

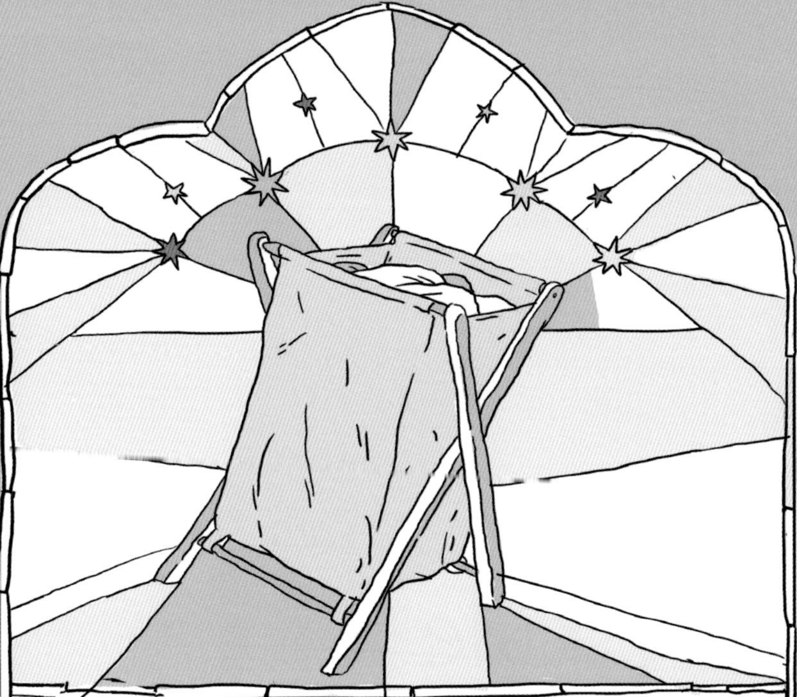

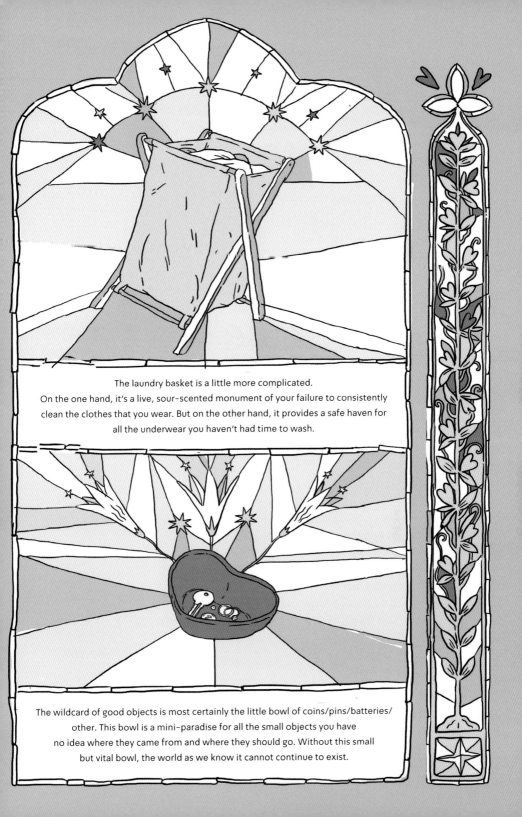

The laundry basket is a little more complicated.
On the one hand, it's a live, sour-scented monument of your failure to consistently clean the clothes that you wear. But on the other hand, it provides a safe haven for all the underwear you haven't had time to wash.

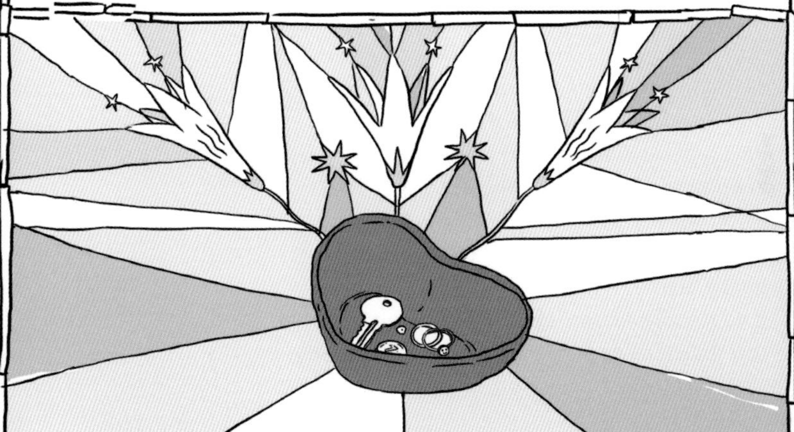

The wildcard of good objects is most certainly the little bowl of coins/pins/batteries/other. This bowl is a mini-paradise for all the small objects you have no idea where they came from and where they should go. Without this small but vital bowl, the world as we know it cannot continue to exist.

After mapping out the main actors, it's time to draw up a few rules for coping with a mess in the most optimal manner. These are five rules (or good suggestions, if you prefer) that will help you fight back, or at least maintain control of the situation. You might even say that these are the five things that separate your house from chaos.

I.
The Rule
of Balance

After accepting the fact that you can't achieve order will not be achieved, you have to learn to live in a controlled mess.
If you haven't washed the dishes for two days and the sink is full, at least try to keep the countertop organized.
If you haven't done laundry for a week, at least collect the clothes and pile them up neatly on the chair in the corner of the room.
If you finally did the laundry and now it's all over the couch, make sure that at least the carpet in the living room is clean, etc. etc.

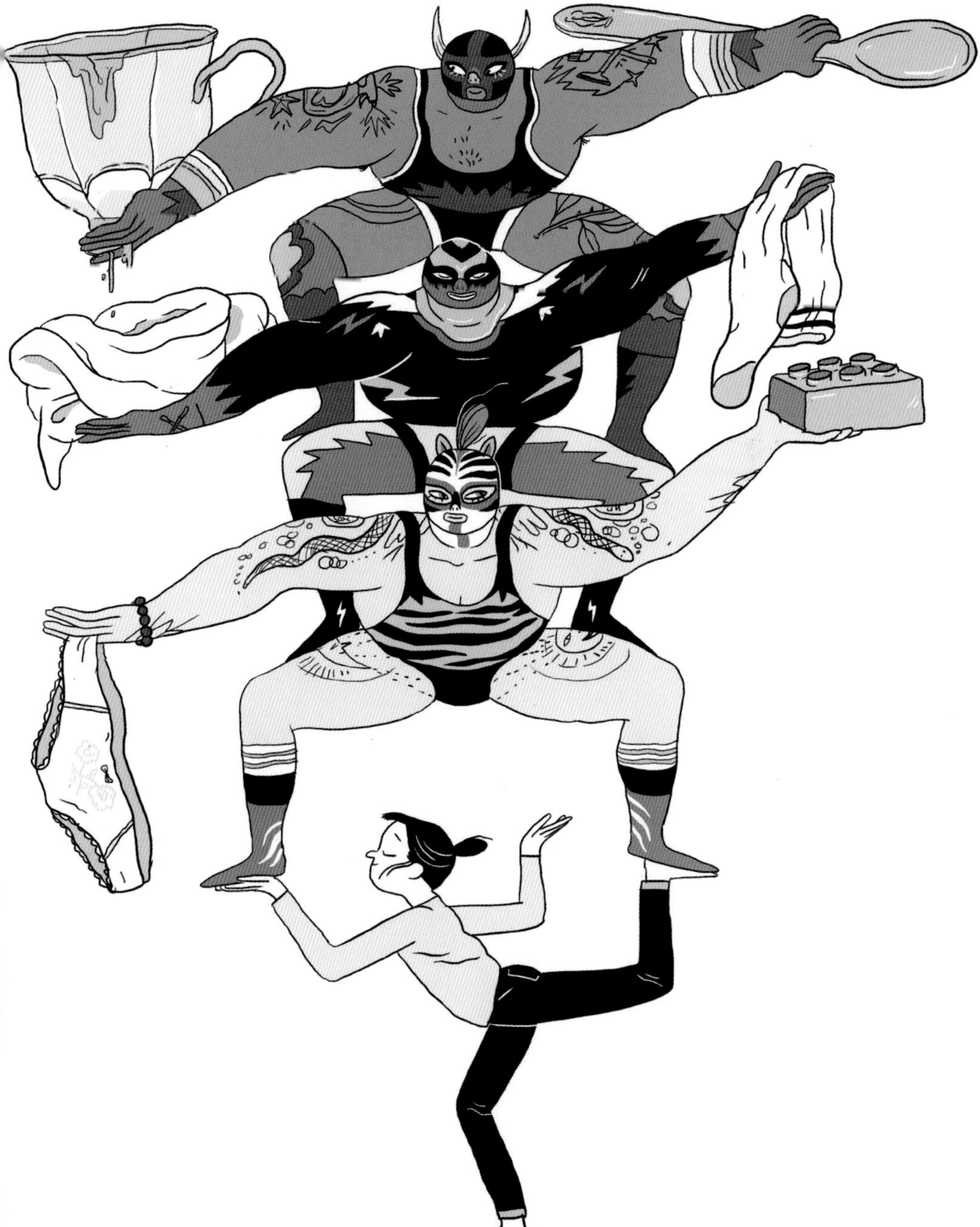

2.
The Rule of the Straight Line

If there are a variety of objects scattered around and you don't know where they came from and where they should go, put them all in a straight line.

This creates a feeling of organization and control. The rule includes the bottles of oil on the countertop (that don't fit in the pantry), the shampoo bottles in the shower (even if half of them are empty), the books on the book shelves, and the mess on the desk.

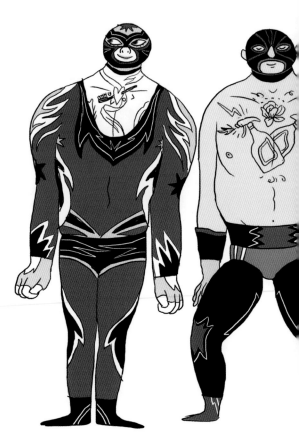

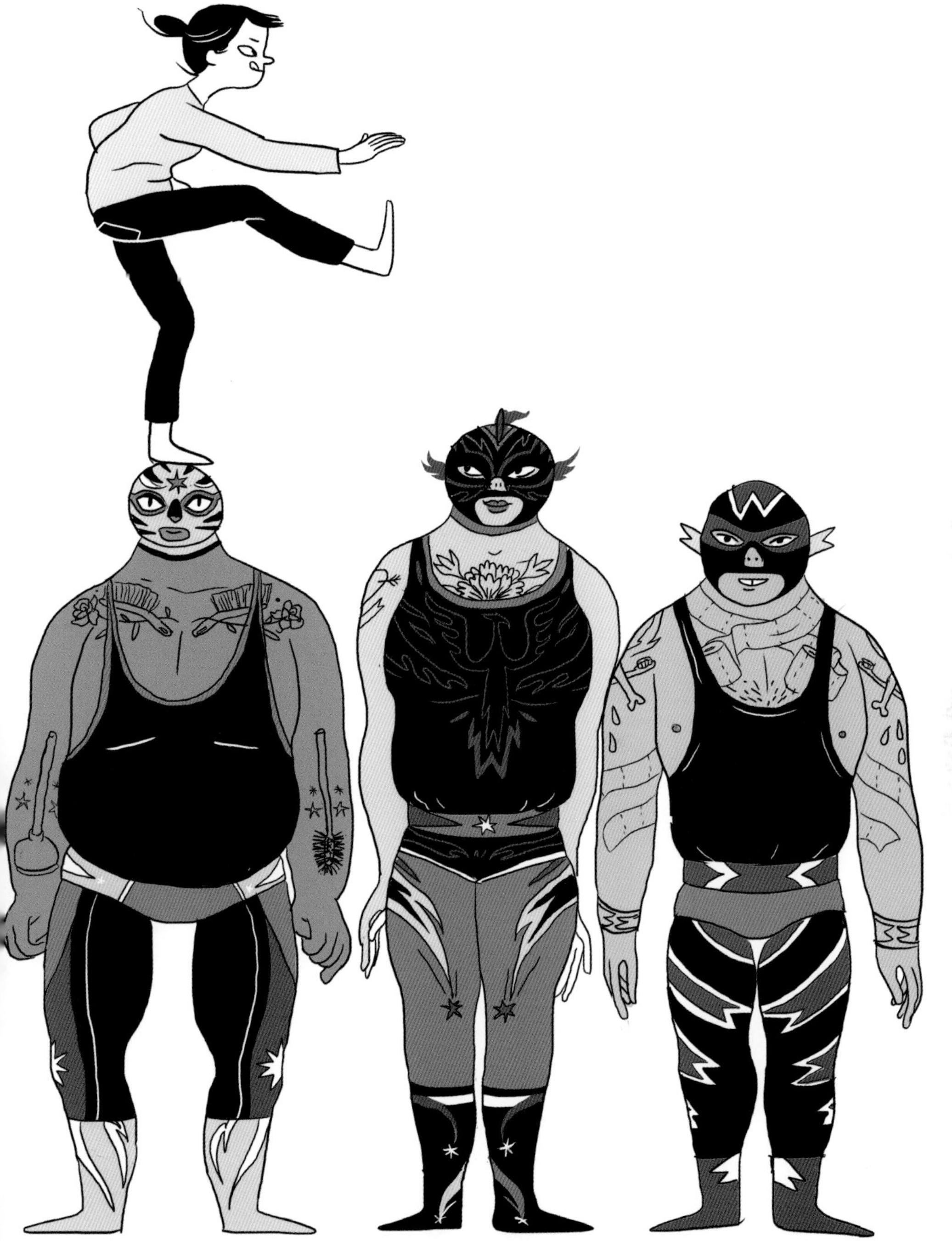

3.
The Rule of the Lowest Common Denominator

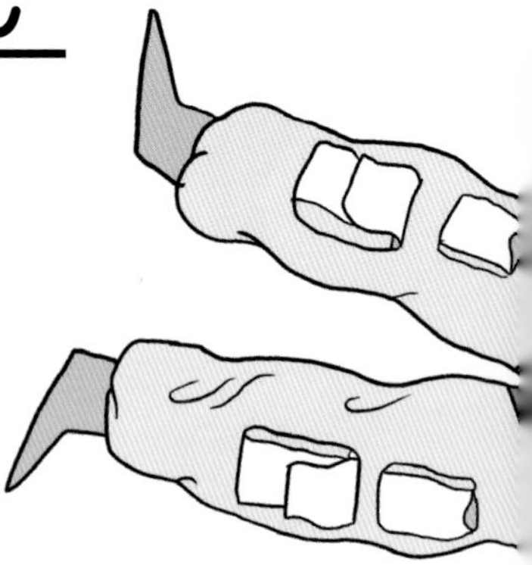

Place similarly shaped objects together. True, the paintbrush doesn't belong in the knives drawer, but since both are the same length and shape, the illusion of order will kick in. Sometimes this is even useful because the unexpected location helps remind you where you last saw the object.

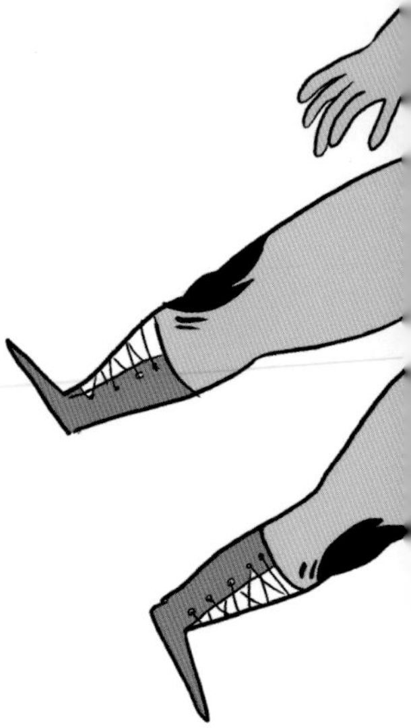

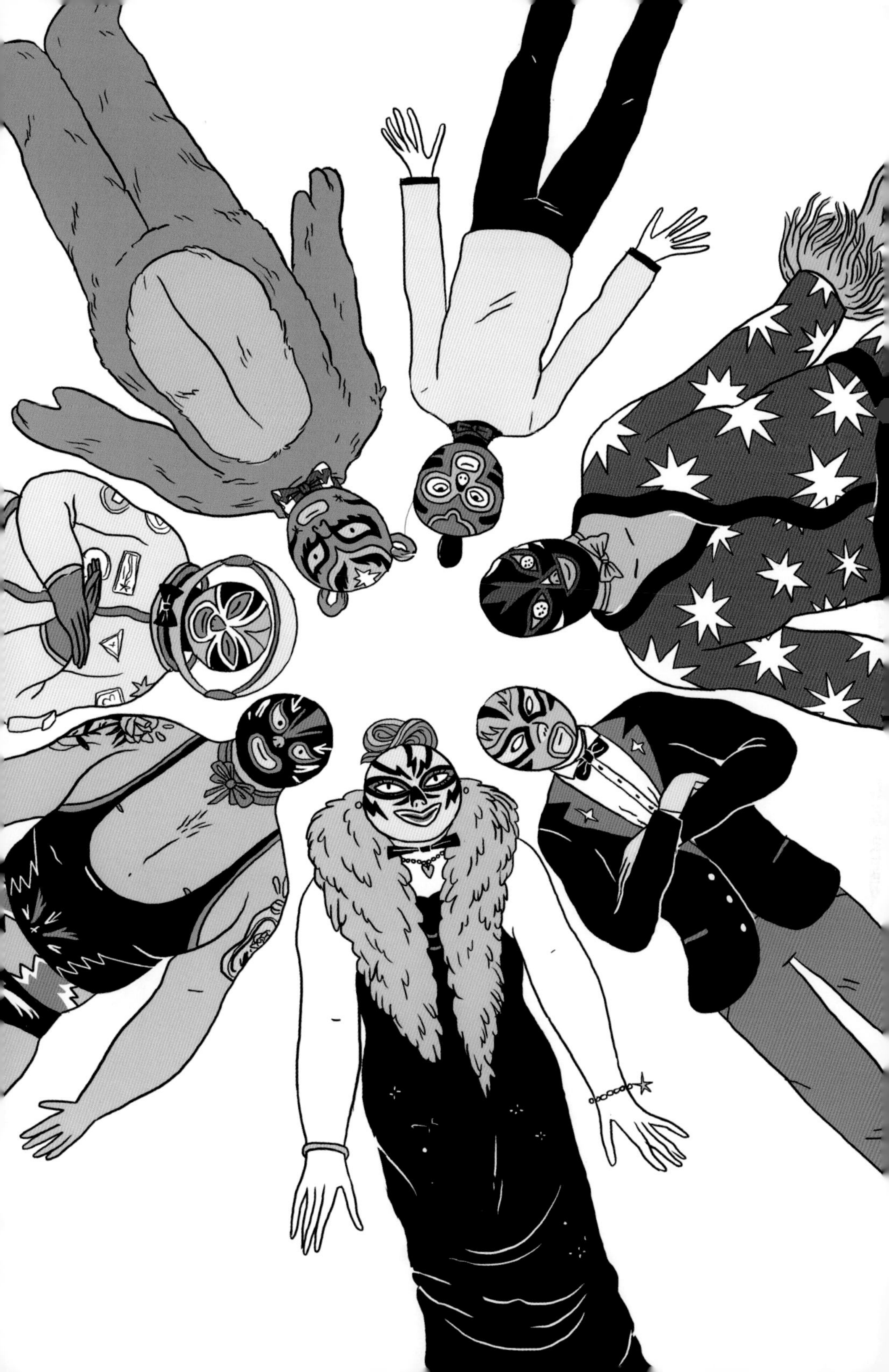

4. The "Rose Among Thorns" Rule

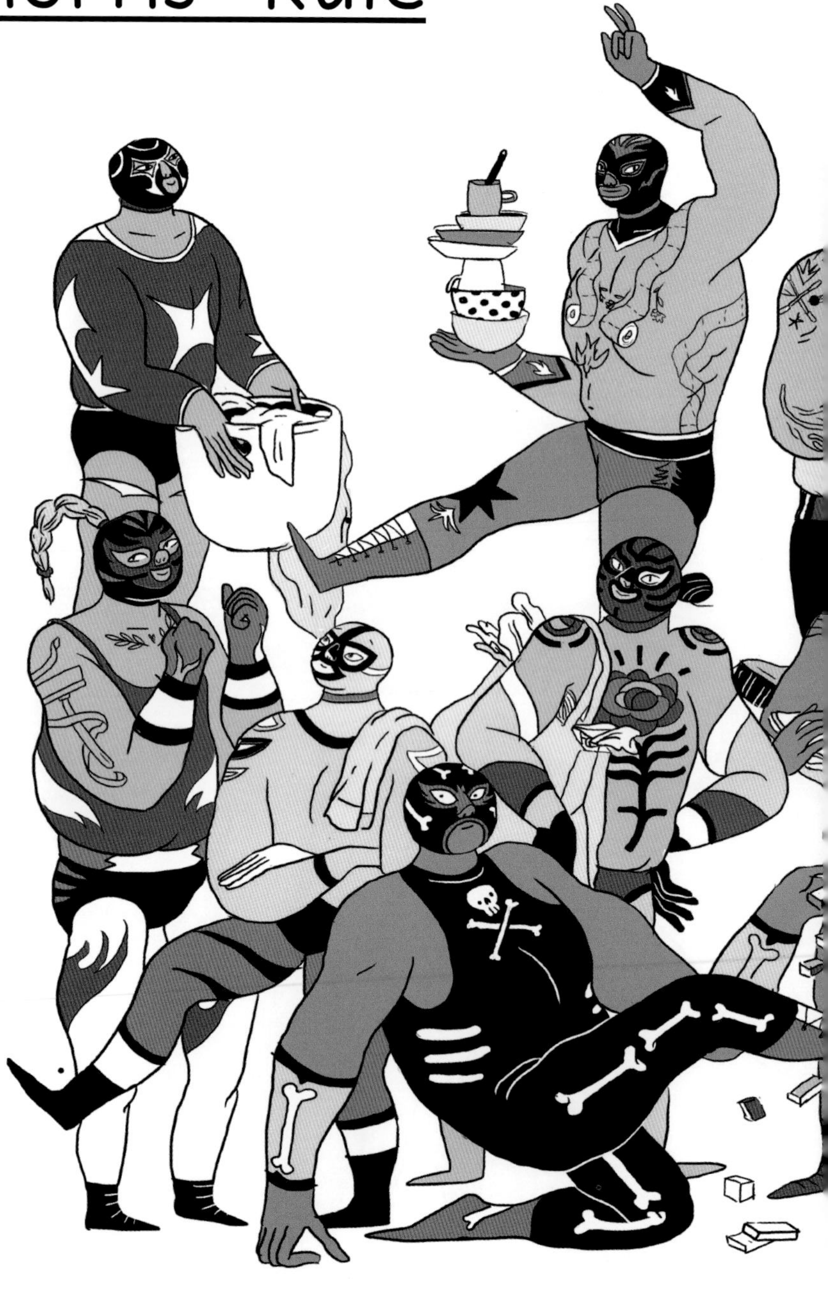

Showcase a beautiful object in a central location in the room.
This won't create a feeling of order,
but it will add character and
good taste to the area.

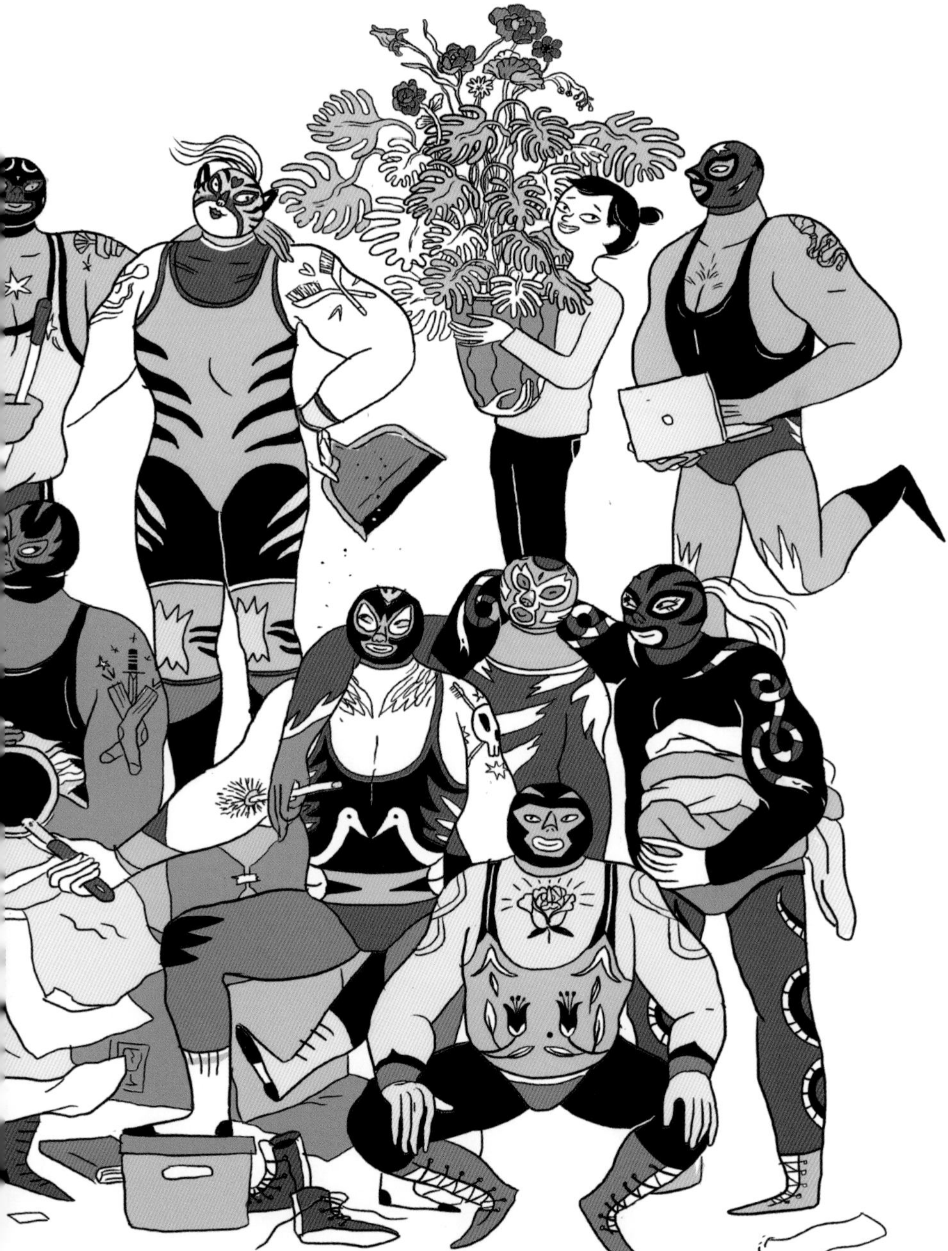

5. The Rug Rule – If it's not there, it doesn't exist

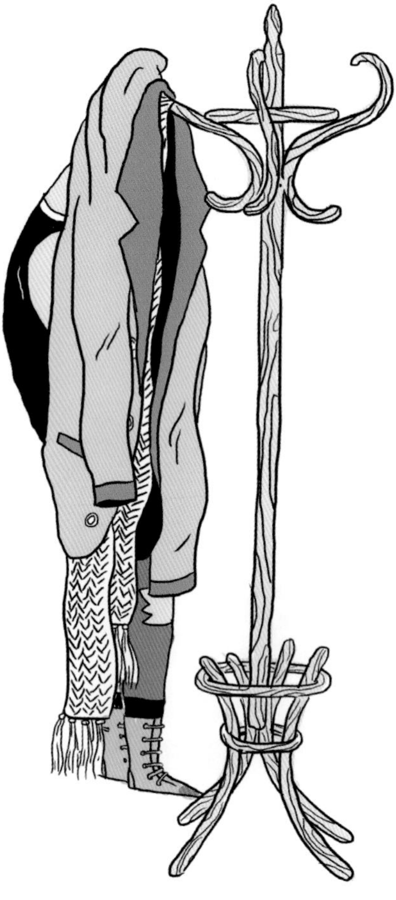

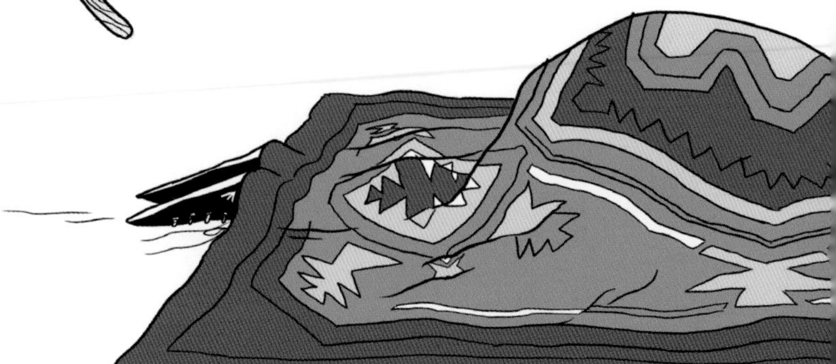

If, despite your best efforts, you don't know where to put something, ust sweep it under the rug or stick it in a closet, or shove it into a drawer. If it's something small, you can always put it in the little bowl.

5.5. Bonus! The Field Trip Rule

If you get lost, stay right where you are, and if you don't feel like cleaning up, simply leave everything just where it is. This will increase the chance of finding things later (more about that in Chapter 7).

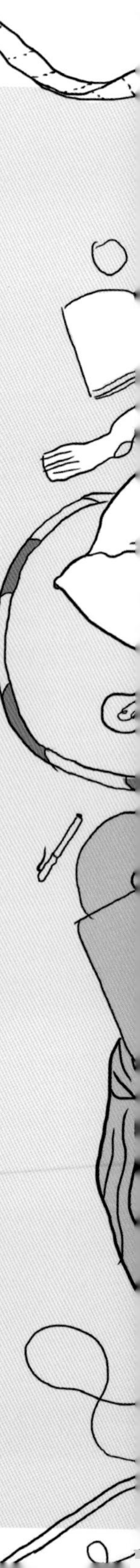

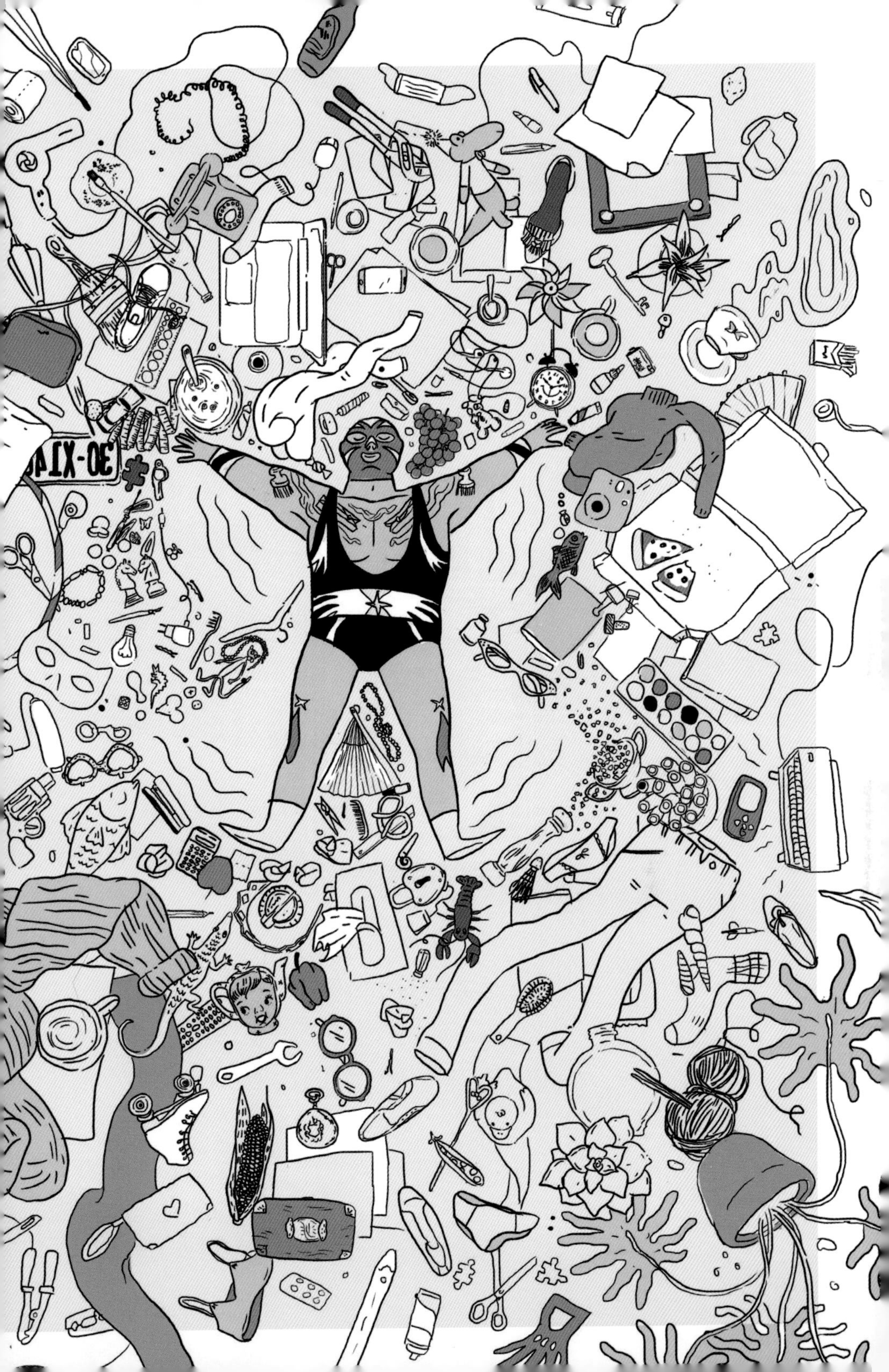

HOW TO ORGANIZE WITHOUT GETTING ORGANIZED

Every battle plan that respects itself needs a map. Now, there may be changes in the master plan but the

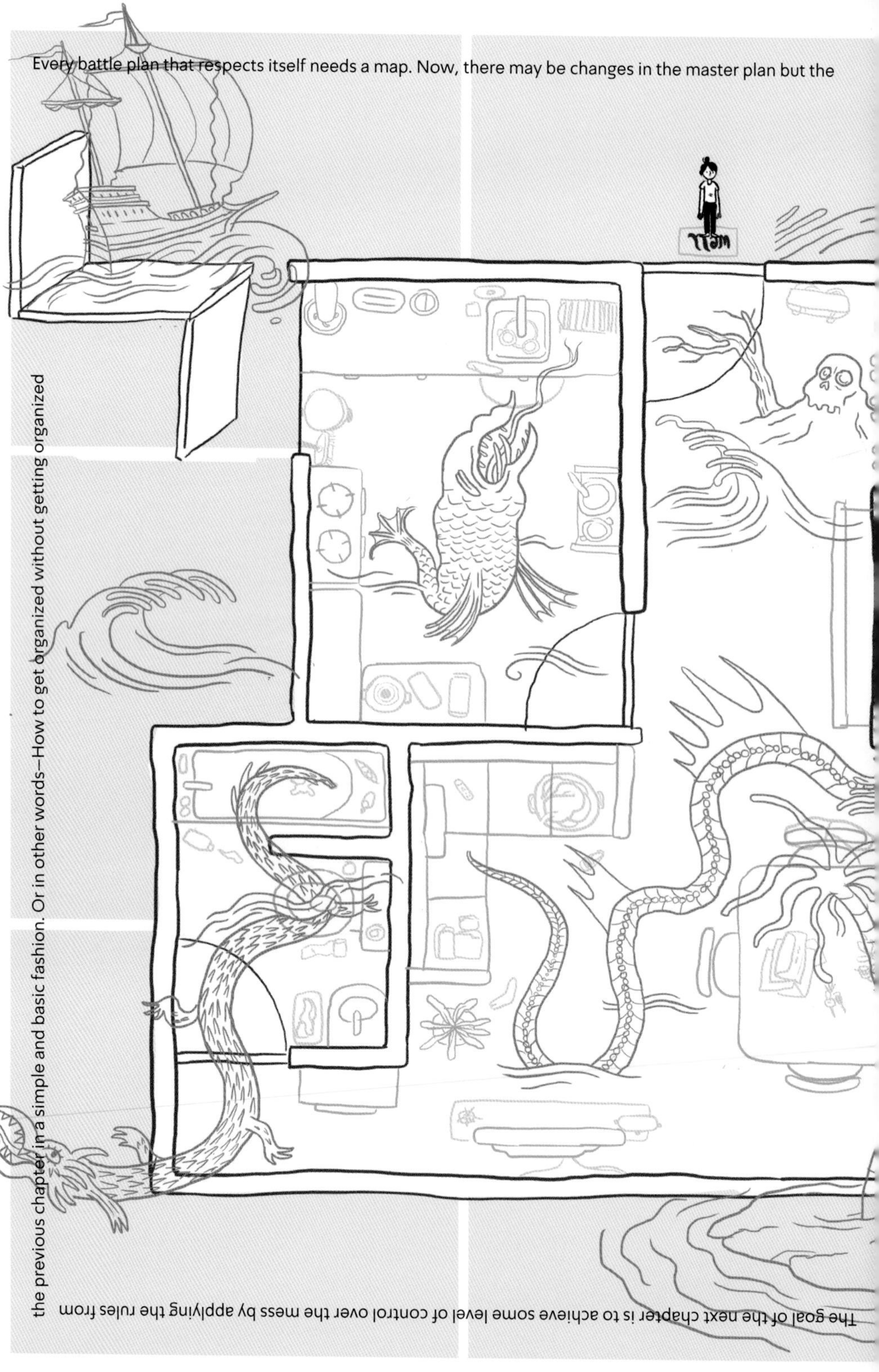

The goal of the next chapter is to achieve some level of control over the mess by applying the rules from the previous chapter in a simple and basic fashion. Or in other words—How to get organized without getting organized

idea remains the same because all messy families are quite similar. The mess usually congregates in areas in which people live. If one part of the house stays organized, you're probably not making use of it or else you are a soulless zombies, or else a crazy load of stuff has piled up in that area, creating a sort of storage room. (And that is how storage rooms are born.)

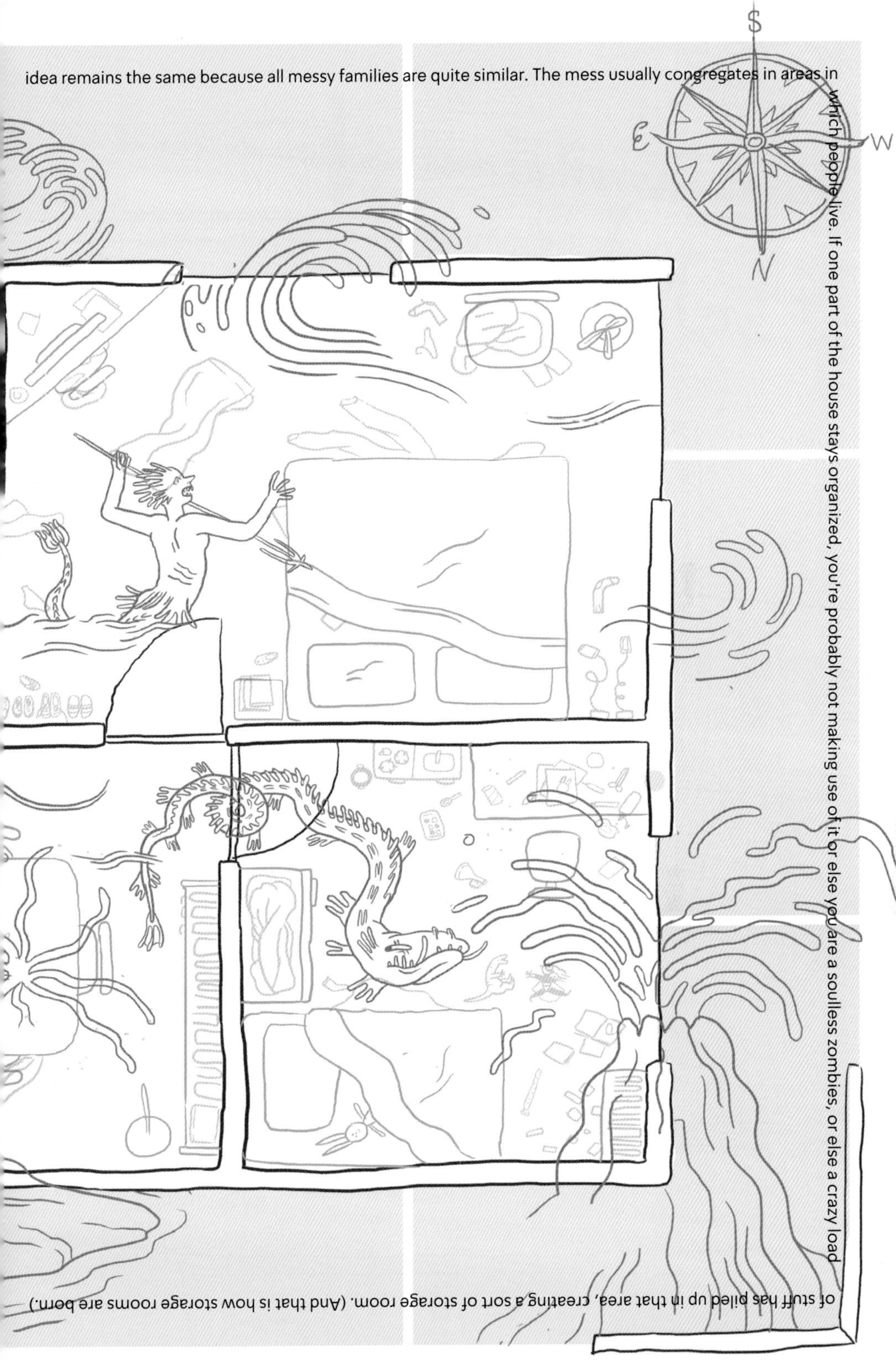
S
E
W
N

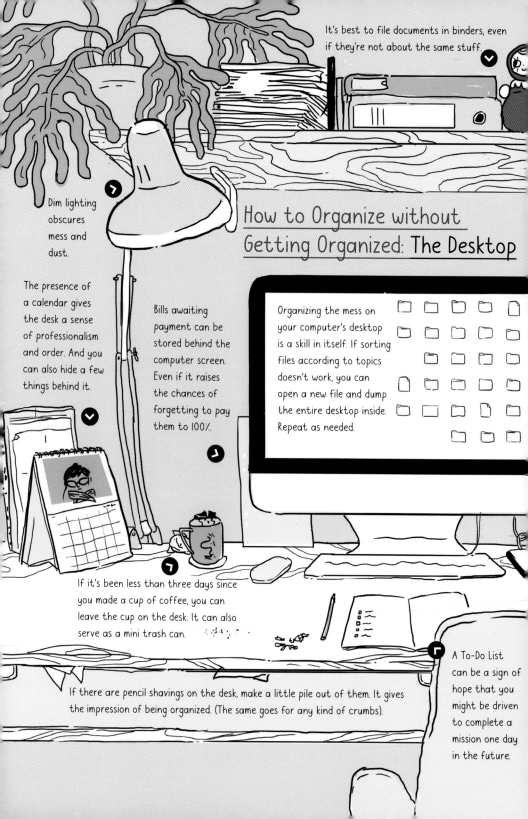

It's best to file documents in binders, even if they're not about the same stuff.

Dim lighting obscures mess and dust.

How to Organize without Getting Organized: The Desktop

The presence of a calendar gives the desk a sense of professionalism and order. And you can also hide a few things behind it.

Bills awaiting payment can be stored behind the computer screen. Even if it raises the chances of forgetting to pay them to 100%.

Organizing the mess on your computer's desktop is a skill in itself. If sorting files according to topics doesn't work, you can open a new file and dump the entire desktop inside. Repeat as needed.

If it's been less than three days since you made a cup of coffee, you can leave the cup on the desk. It can also serve as a mini trash can.

A To-Do List can be a sign of hope that you might be driven to complete a mission one day in the future.

If there are pencil shavings on the desk, make a little pile out of them. It gives the impression of being organized. (The same goes for any kind of crumbs).

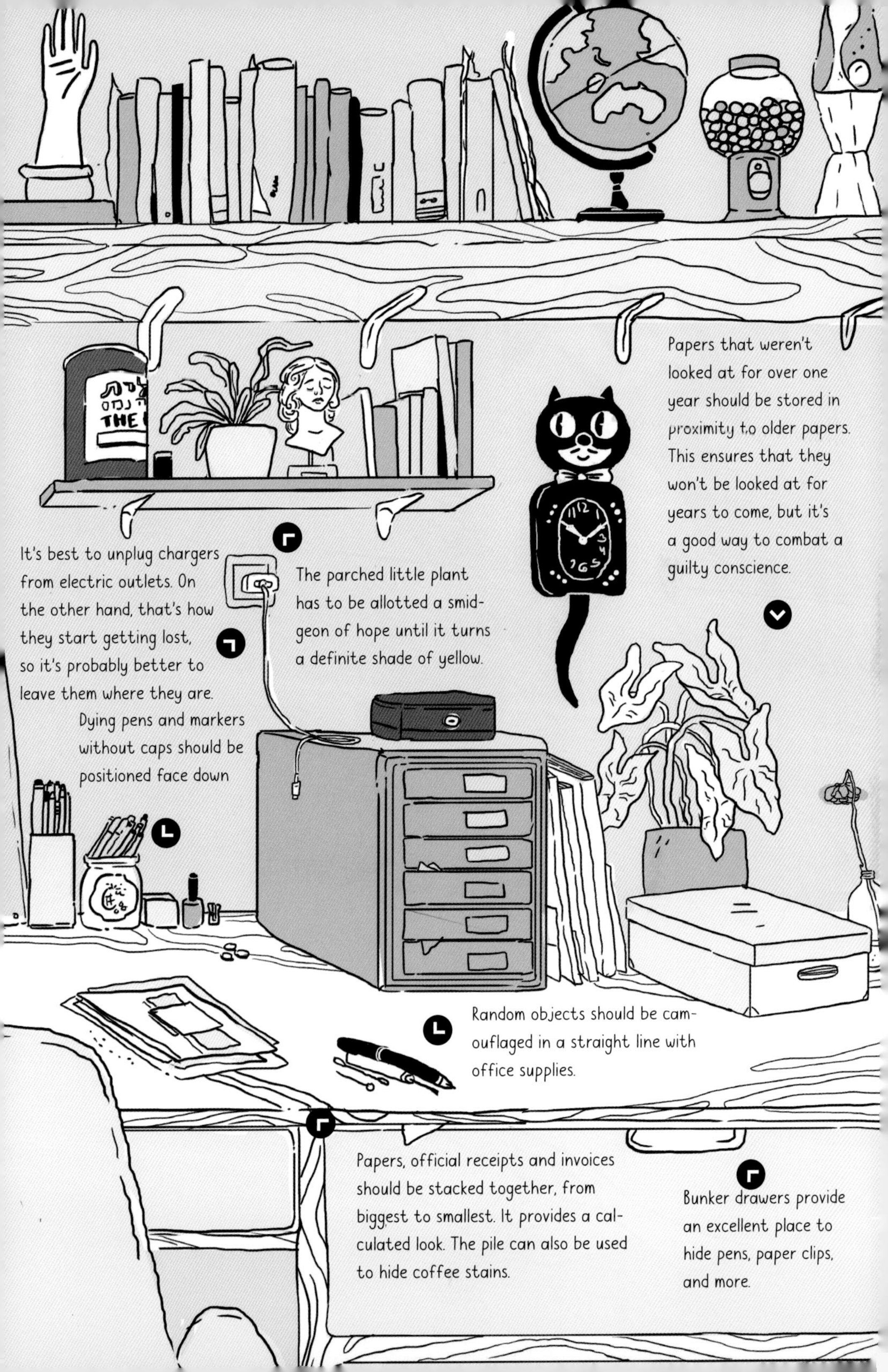

It's best to unplug chargers from electric outlets. On the other hand, that's how they start getting lost, so it's probably better to leave them where they are.
The parched little plant has to be allotted a smidgeon of hope until it turns a definite shade of yellow.
Papers that weren't looked at for over one year should be stored in proximity to older papers. This ensures that they won't be looked at for years to come, but it's a good way to combat a guilty conscience.
Dying pens and markers without caps should be positioned face down
Random objects should be camouflaged in a straight line with office supplies.
Papers, official receipts and invoices should be stacked together, from biggest to smallest. It provides a calculated look. The pile can also be used to hide coffee stains.
Bunker drawers provide an excellent place to hide pens, paper clips, and more.

The Desk Piles Conundrum

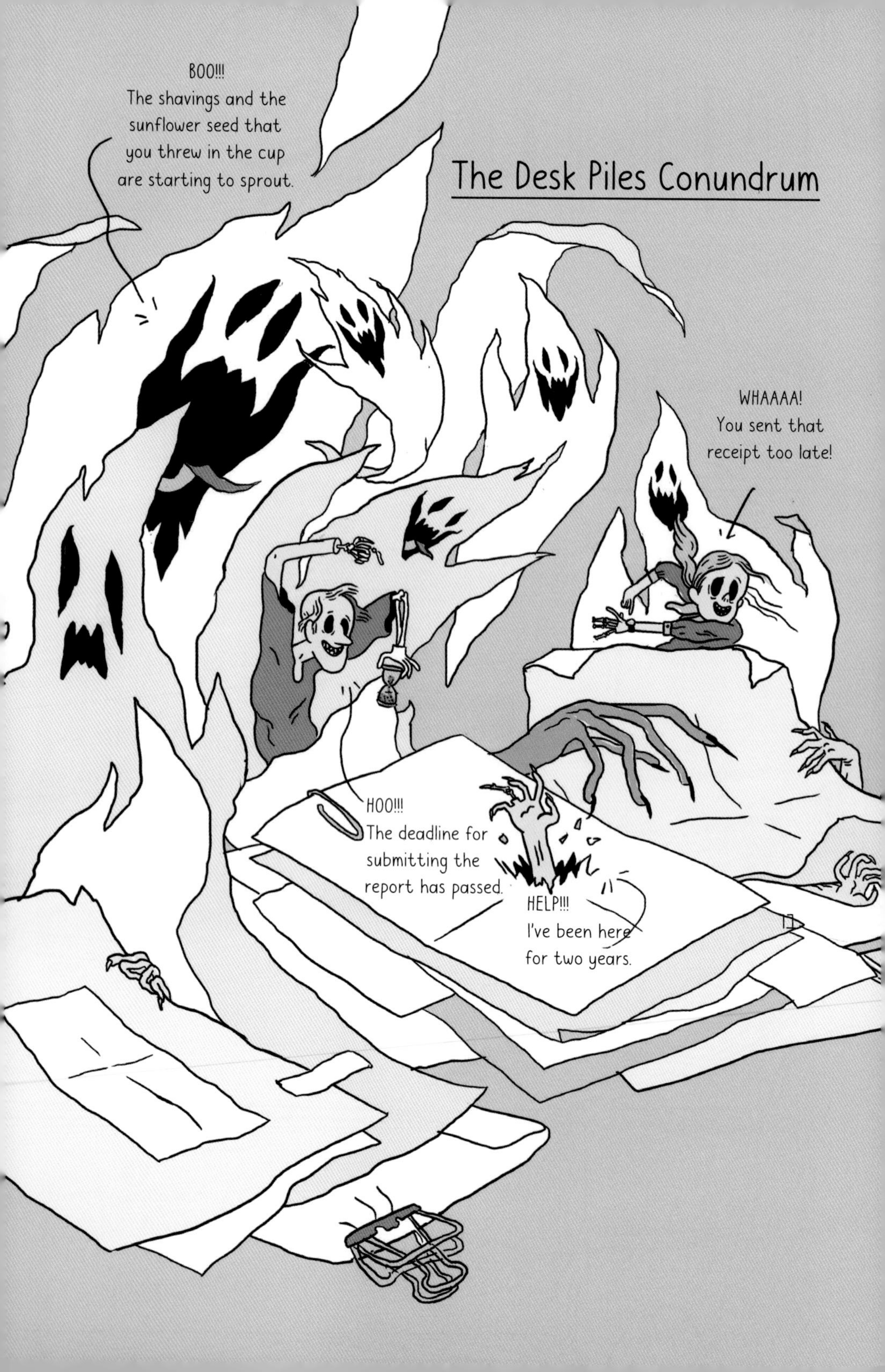
BOO!!!
The shavings and the sunflower seed that you threw in the cup are starting to sprout.
WHAAAA!
You sent that receipt too late!
HOO!!!
The deadline for submitting the report has passed.
HELP!!!
I've been here for two years.

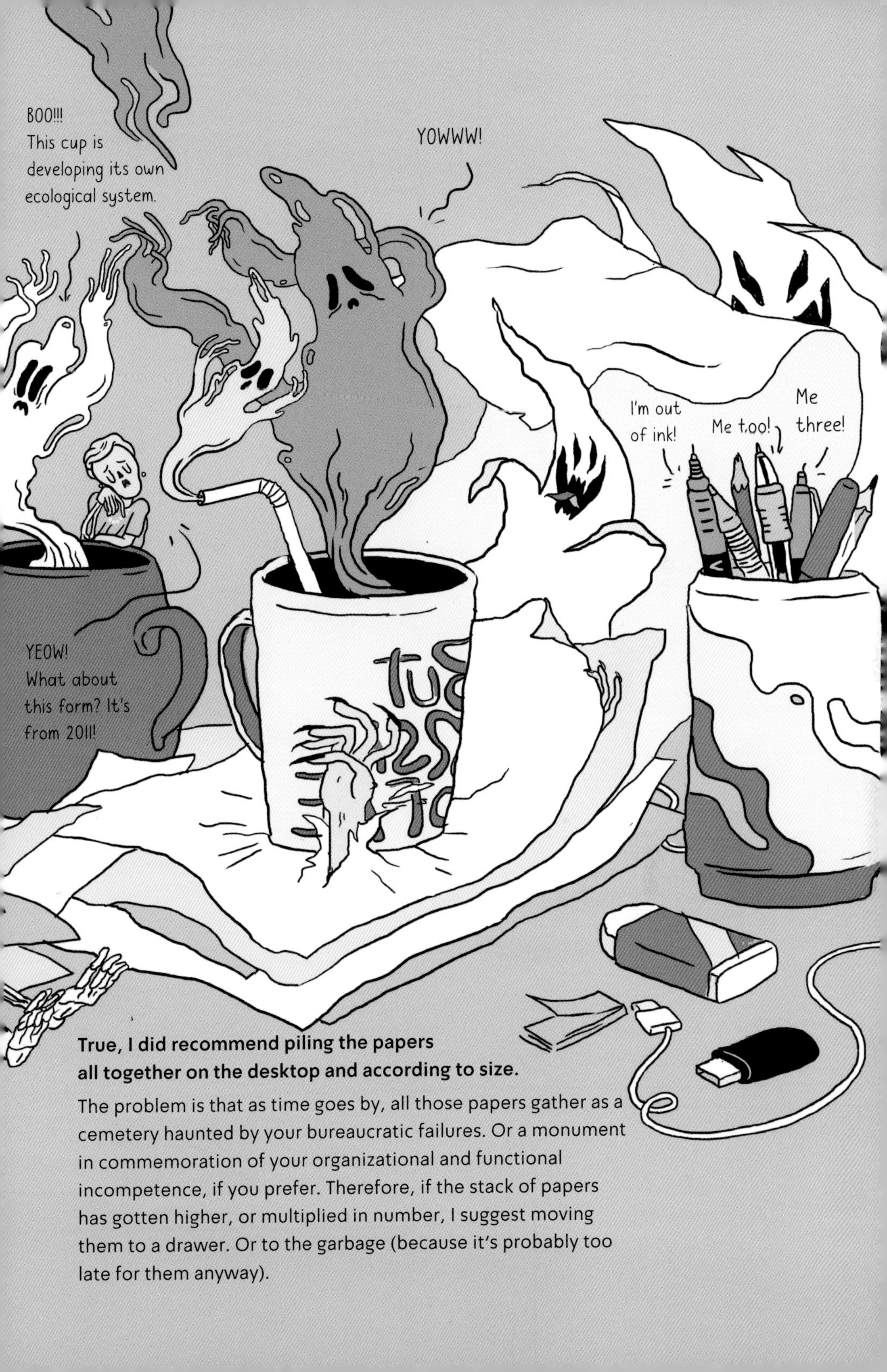
BOO!!!
This cup is developing its own ecological system.
YOWWW!
YEOW!
What about this form? It's from 2011!
I'm out of ink!
Me too!
Me three!

True, I did recommend piling the papers all together on the desktop and according to size.

The problem is that as time goes by, all those papers gather as a cemetery haunted by your bureaucratic failures. Or a monument in commemoration of your organizational and functional incompetence, if you prefer. Therefore, if the stack of papers has gotten higher, or multiplied in number, I suggest moving them to a drawer. Or to the garbage (because it's probably too late for them anyway).

How to Organize without Getting Organized: The Kitchen

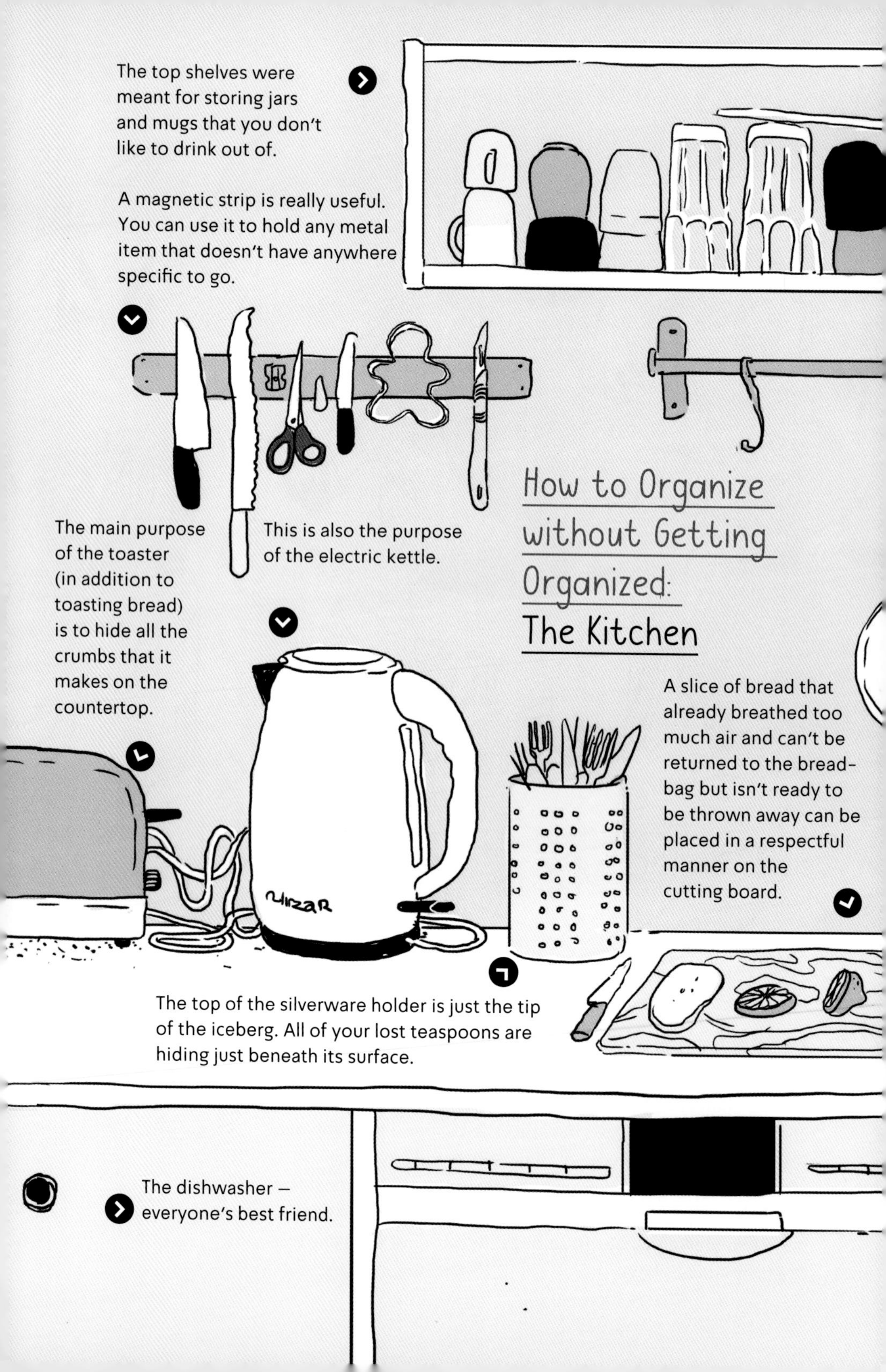
The top shelves were meant for storing jars and mugs that you don't like to drink out of.
A magnetic strip is really useful. You can use it to hold any metal item that doesn't have anywhere specific to go.
The main purpose of the toaster (in addition to toasting bread) is to hide all the crumbs that it makes on the countertop.
This is also the purpose of the electric kettle.
A slice of bread that already breathed too much air and can't be returned to the bread-bag but isn't ready to be thrown away can be placed in a respectful manner on the cutting board.
The top of the silverware holder is just the tip of the iceberg. All of your lost teaspoons are hiding just beneath its surface.
The dishwasher – everyone's best friend.

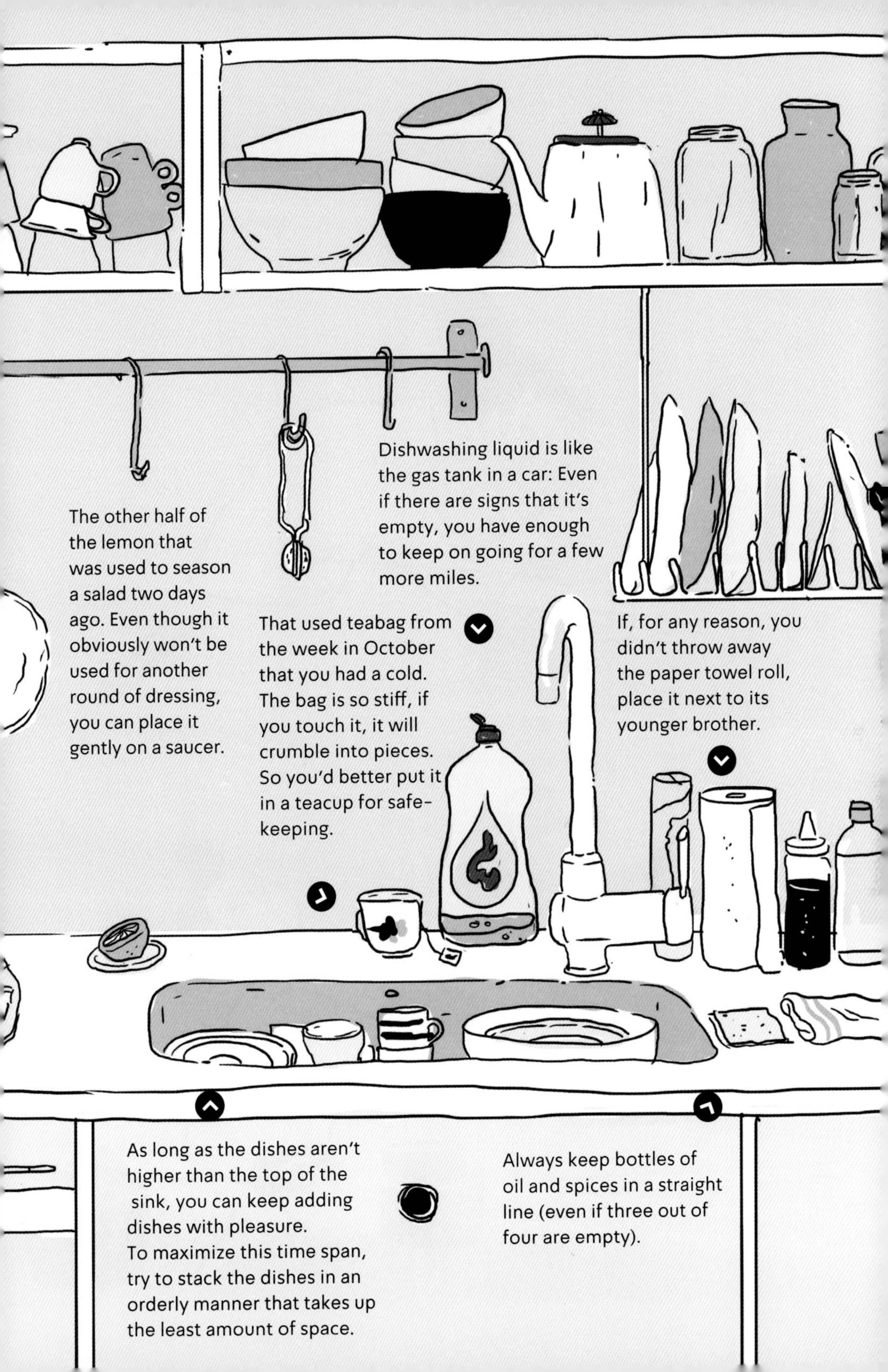

Dishwashing liquid is like the gas tank in a car: Even if there are signs that it's empty, you have enough to keep on going for a few more miles.
The other half of the lemon that was used to season a salad two days ago. Even though it obviously won't be used for another round of dressing, you can place it gently on a saucer.
That used teabag from the week in October that you had a cold. The bag is so stiff, if you touch it, it will crumble into pieces. So you'd better put it in a teacup for safe-keeping.
If, for any reason, you didn't throw away the paper towel roll, place it next to its younger brother.
As long as the dishes aren't higher than the top of the sink, you can keep adding dishes with pleasure. To maximize this time span, try to stack the dishes in an orderly manner that takes up the least amount of space.
Always keep bottles of oil and spices in a straight line (even if three out of four are empty).

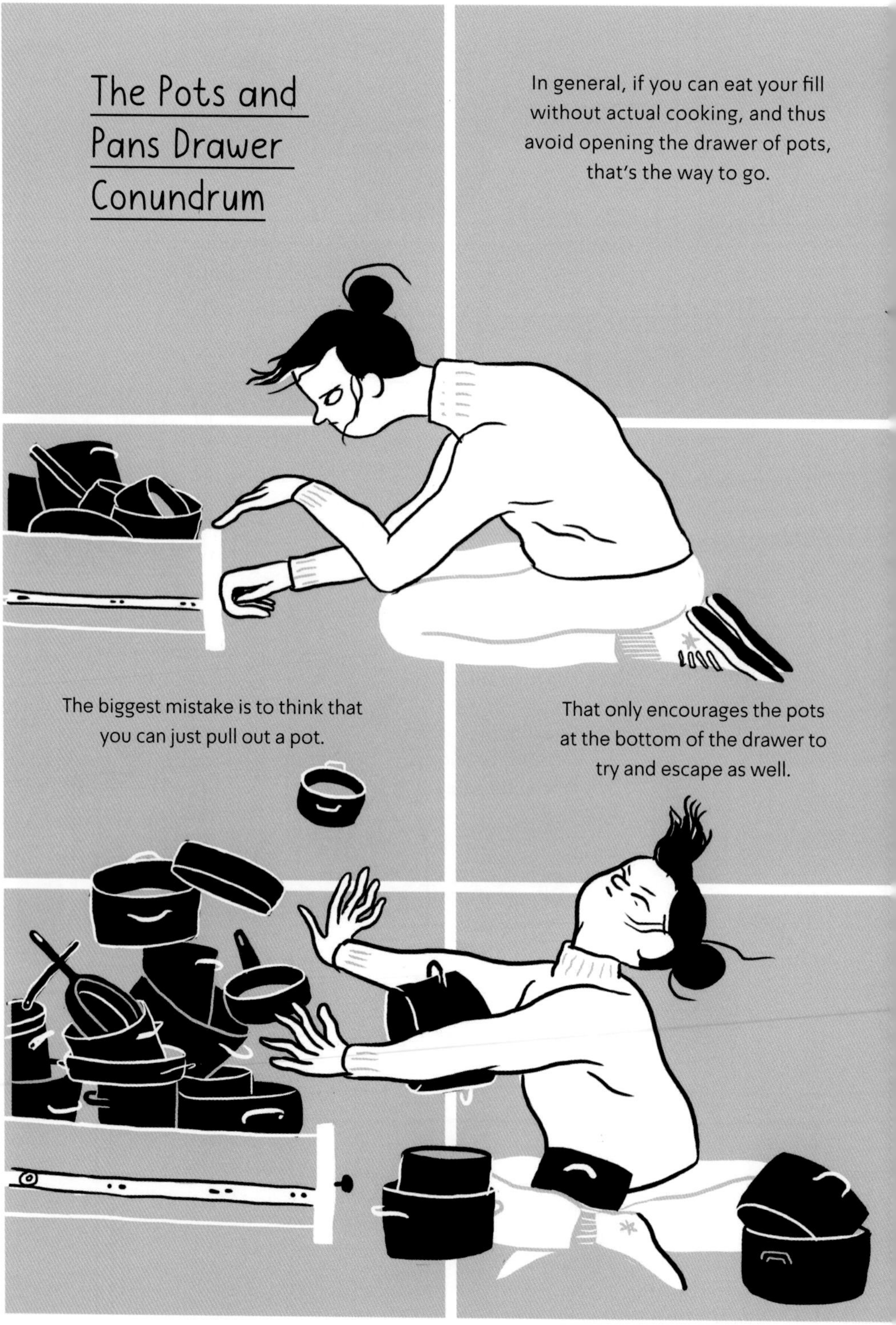
The Pots and Pans Drawer Conundrum
In general, if you can eat your fill without actual cooking, and thus avoid opening the drawer of pots, that's the way to go.
The biggest mistake is to think that you can just pull out a pot.
That only encourages the pots at the bottom of the drawer to try and escape as well.

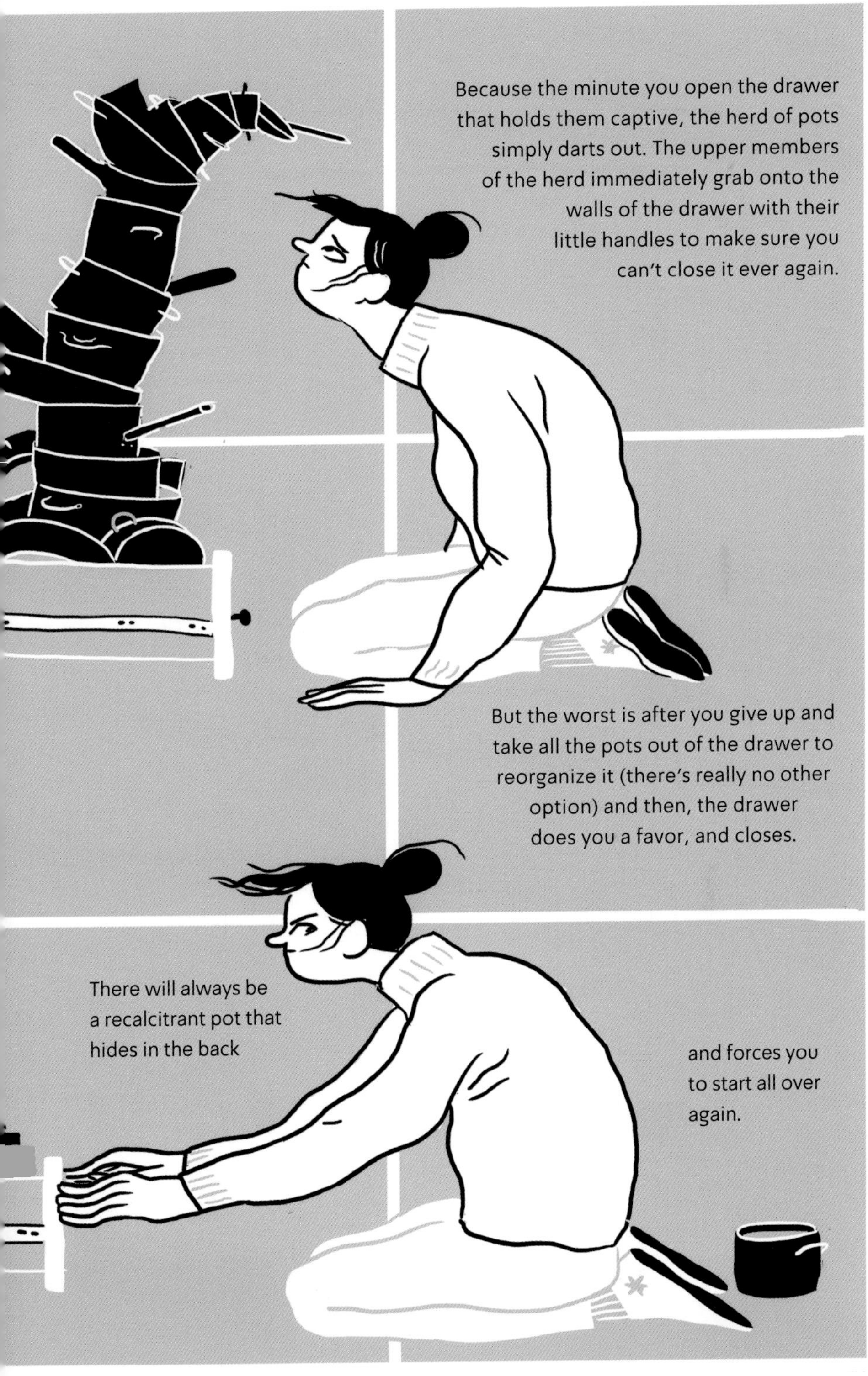
Because the minute you open the drawer that holds them captive, the herd of pots simply darts out. The upper members of the herd immediately grab onto the walls of the drawer with their little handles to make sure you can't close it ever again.
But the worst is after you give up and take all the pots out of the drawer to reorganize it (there's really no other option) and then, the drawer does you a favor, and closes.
There will always be a recalcitrant pot that hides in the back
and forces you to start all over again.

How to Organize without Organizing:
The Refrigerator (on the outside)

To balance out the composition, magnets advertising local services and deliveries can be arranged in the upper corner. These magnets tend to have odd shapes and therefore will not fit in the square grid of the photos and tickets. Children's drawings should be treated like rotating exhibitions, displaying only one piece at a time.

Otherwise, it's just a mess.

For a messy person, the front of the refrigerator is a combination of an office and a family history project. Since you'll never throw anything away (even though you'll never pay the parking tickets and half of the photo magnets are from weddings that ended in divorce), you can still create a feeling of order on your refrigerator.

Start by sorting items according to type and common denominator. All parking tickets in one row, and all photos in the next. You can also arrange them in chronological order, to document the recent trends in traffic tickets.

The bottom section of the refrigerator has the vibe of serving suggestions and footnotes; that's the place for outdated invitations and drawings.

How to Organize without Organizing: The Refrigerator (on the inside)

The shelves on the refrigerator door are a combination of an incarceration facility for dangerous prisoners and an incubator. Therefore, it's best not to move most of the things in there, just reorganize them according to size and common denominator.

The top shelf is higher than the height of an average person's eyes and so it's best to use the shelf for things you don't need often, want to avoid, or are dear to you and you don't want to make others jealous.

Inside the refrigerator, use the Straight Line Rule — vertically.

The cheese suite.

The rule of the common denominator will be useful for an entire congregation of the end slices of bread that can always be found in the refrigerator.

This is a good time to note that the refrigerator is one of the most personal and private places a person can own. Opening someone else's refrigerator is the equivalent of peeking into the depths of their soul or opening their underwear drawer.

The bottom drawers are to be used like any other drawer: a place to hide things you want to put off dealing with until later.

The pharmacy shelf

The exotic shelf — with sauces from the era in which you thought food should be interesting.

The sticky shelf. Something spilled on it and fermented. Now, it's part of the shelf.

The (relatively) useful shelf. With an almost empty carton of milk, and half-full bottle of champagne from New Year's 2006.

The best advice I can give you about organizing the freezer is to try to keep it as empty as possible. The freezer is a real mess-trap, and the last place on earth where icebergs don't melt. In the freezer, try to store only an ice cube tray (which you'll always forget to fill, of course).

The Refrigerator Conundrum

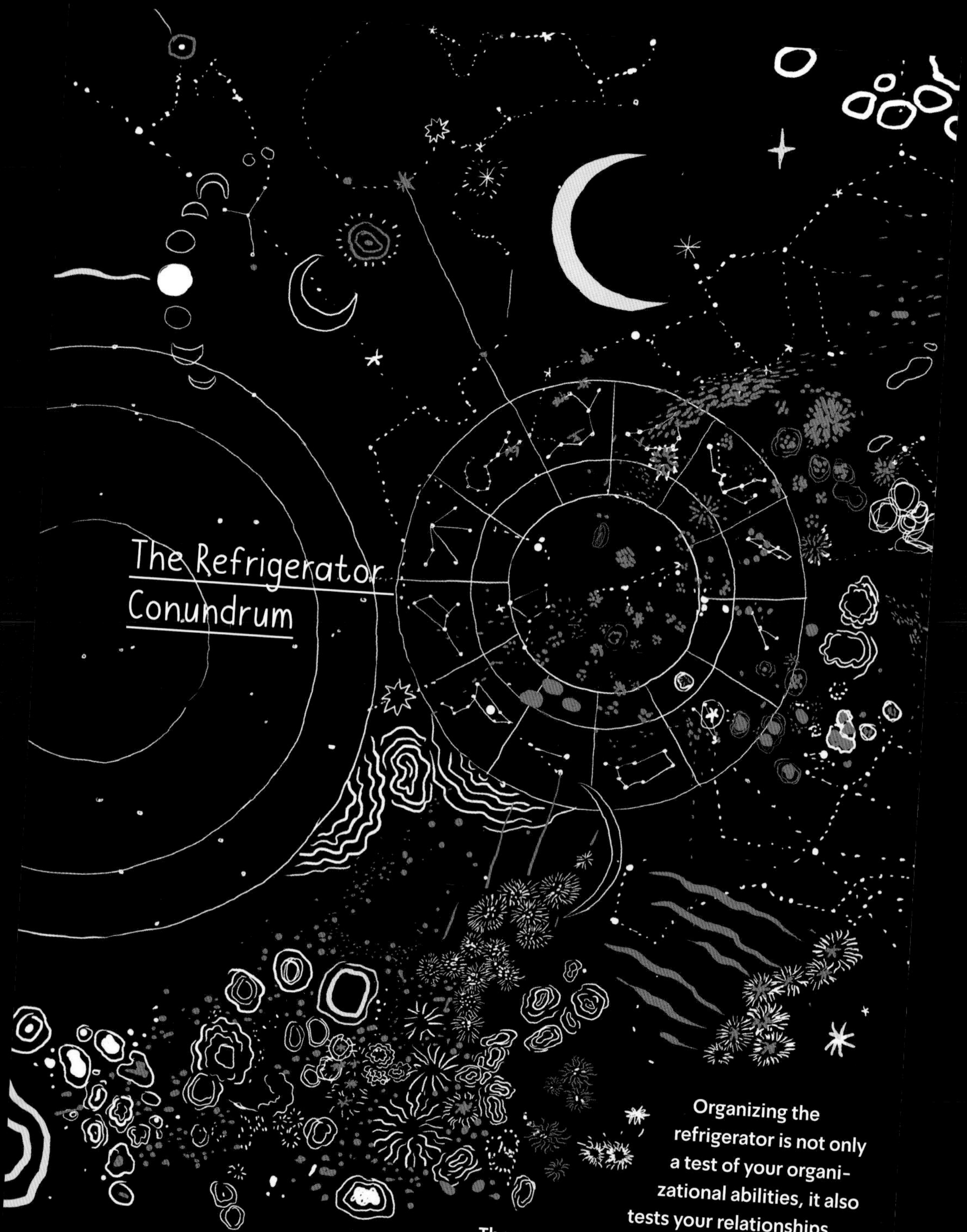

Organizing the refrigerator is not only a test of your organizational abilities, it also tests your relationships. The way you divide up the task of removing the hairy horrors that grow in the refrigerator can teach a lot about your strengths and weaknesses as a couple. Some also claim that you can create an exact astrological map of your relationships using the moldy constellations that accumulate in the refrigerator, but don't try it at home.

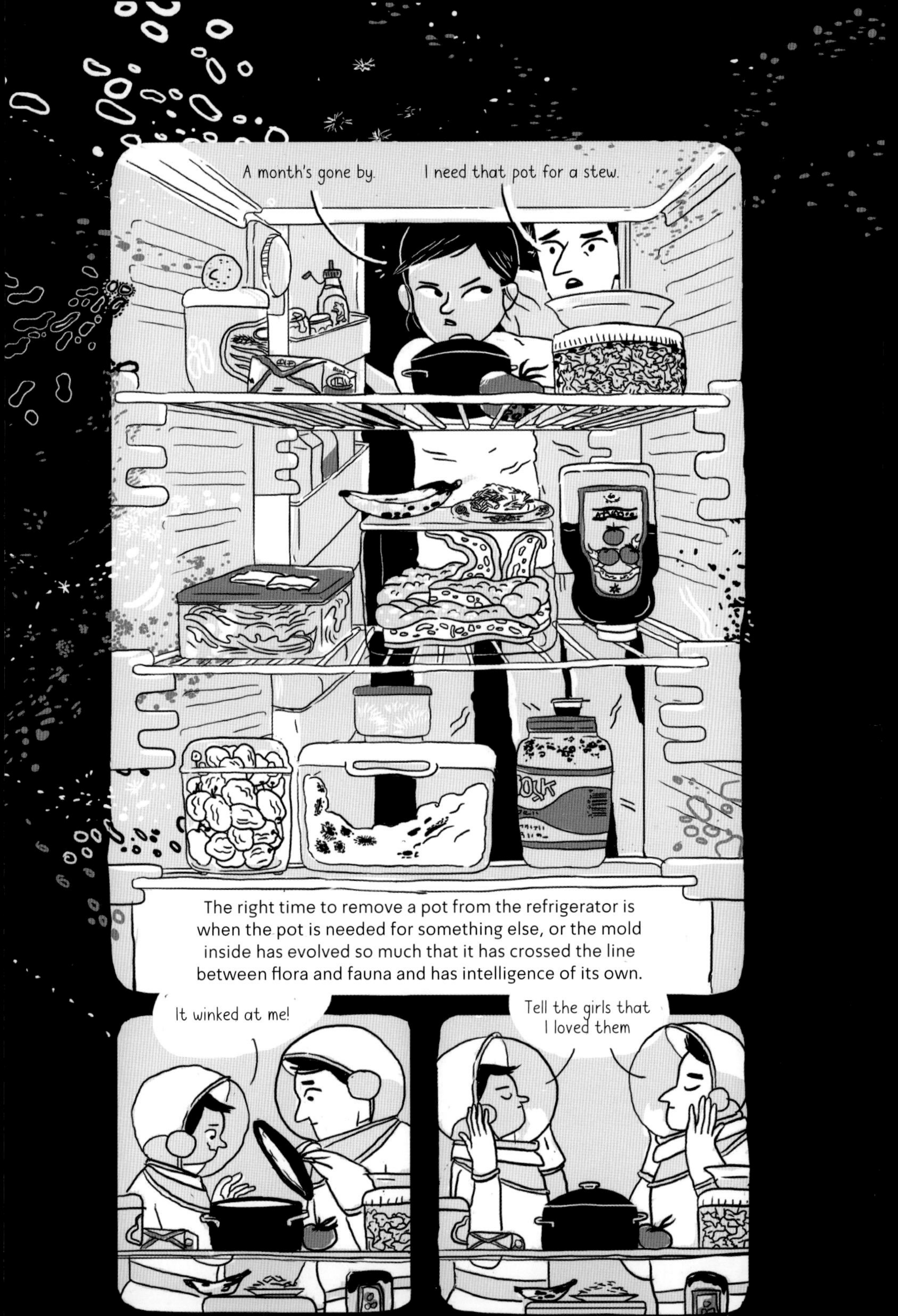
A month's gone by.
I need that pot for a stew.
The right time to remove a pot from the refrigerator is when the pot is needed for something else, or the mold inside has evolved so much that it has crossed the line between flora and fauna and has intelligence of its own.
It winked at me!
Tell the girls that I loved them

How to Organize without Organizing: The Living Room

The living room is the skeleton closet of the house. Mainly because of the couch. On one hand, the couch is the social and aesthetic center of the house. On the other hand, it is a black hole that swallows and hordes an unfathomable number of coins, crumbs, and unlucky toys.

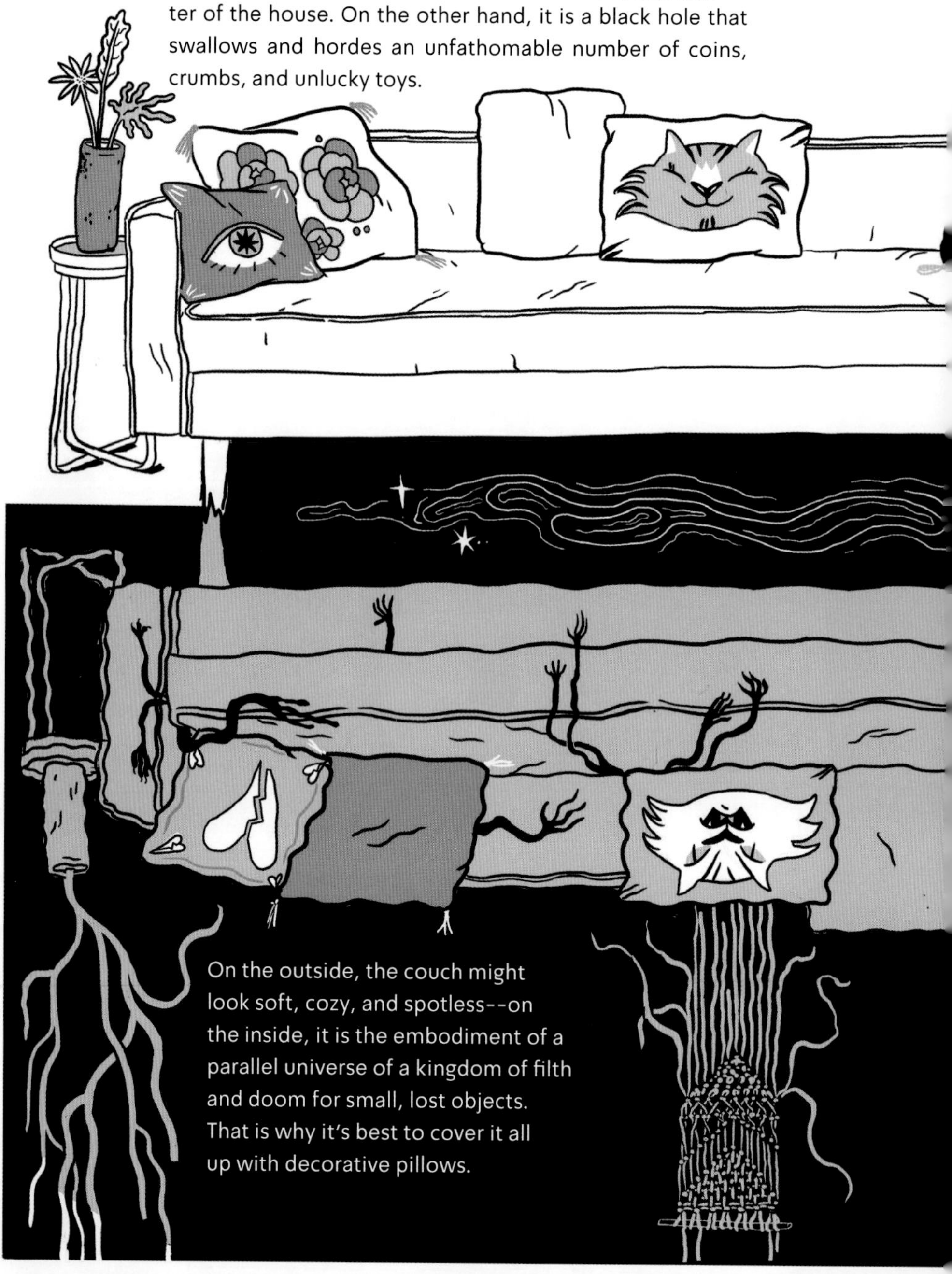

On the outside, the couch might look soft, cozy, and spotless--on the inside, it is the embodiment of a parallel universe of a kingdom of filth and doom for small, lost objects. That is why it's best to cover it all up with decorative pillows.

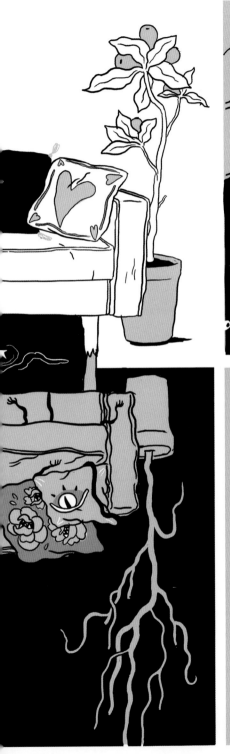

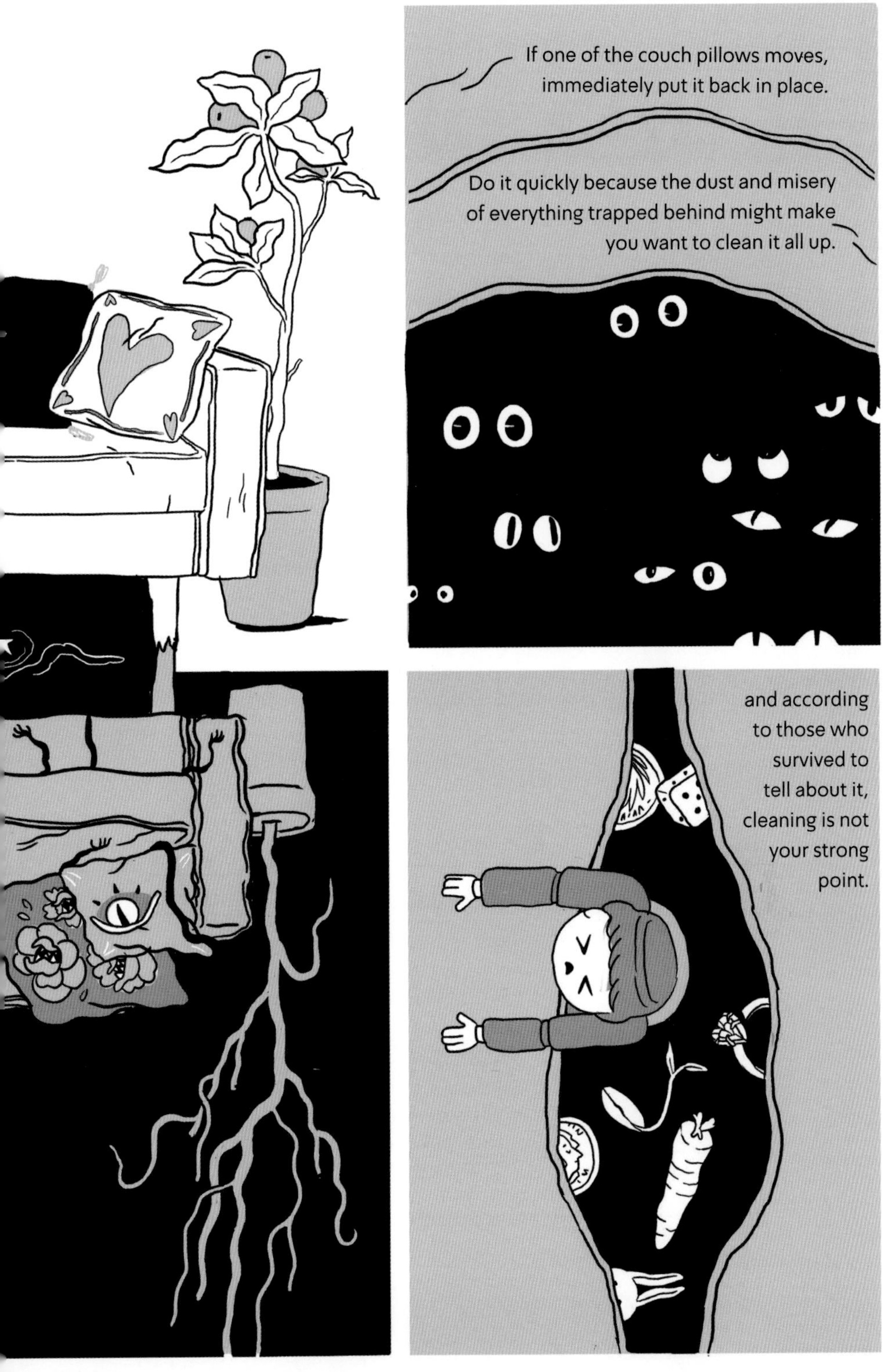

If one of the couch pillows moves, immediately put it back in place.

Do it quickly because the dust and misery of everything trapped behind might make you want to clean it all up.

and according to those who survived to tell about it, cleaning is not your strong point.

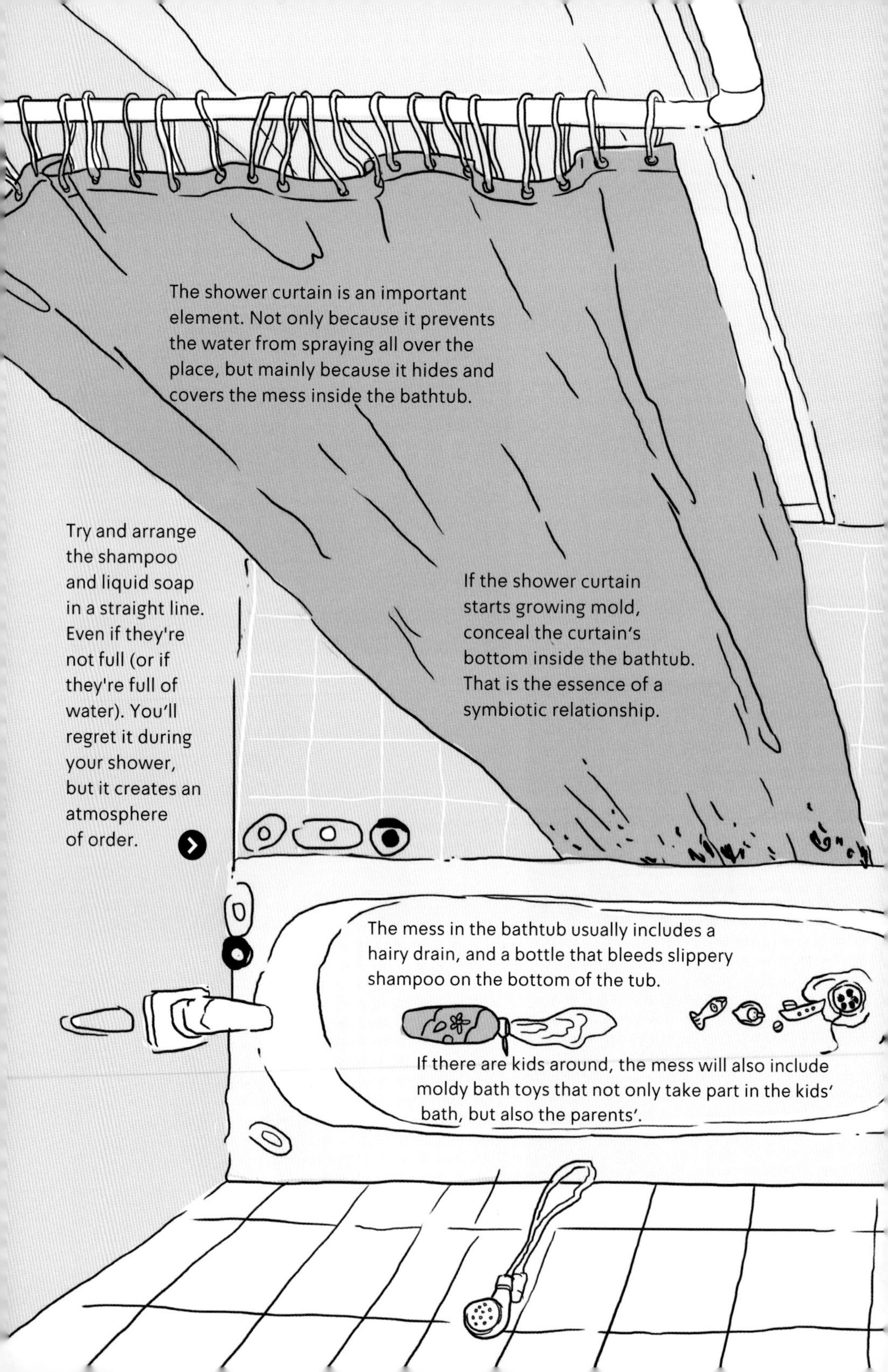
The shower curtain is an important element. Not only because it prevents the water from spraying all over the place, but mainly because it hides and covers the mess inside the bathtub.
Try and arrange the shampoo and liquid soap in a straight line. Even if they're not full (or if they're full of water). You'll regret it during your shower, but it creates an atmosphere of order.
If the shower curtain starts growing mold, conceal the curtain's bottom inside the bathtub. That is the essence of a symbiotic relationship.
The mess in the bathtub usually includes a hairy drain, and a bottle that bleeds slippery shampoo on the bottom of the tub.
If there are kids around, the mess will also include moldy bath toys that not only take part in the kids' bath, but also the parents'.

How to Organize without Organizing: The Bathroom

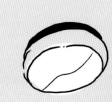

The little bathroom cabinet (more about that later) functions in the bathroom like a drawer. Hide as many things as you can inside. ⌄

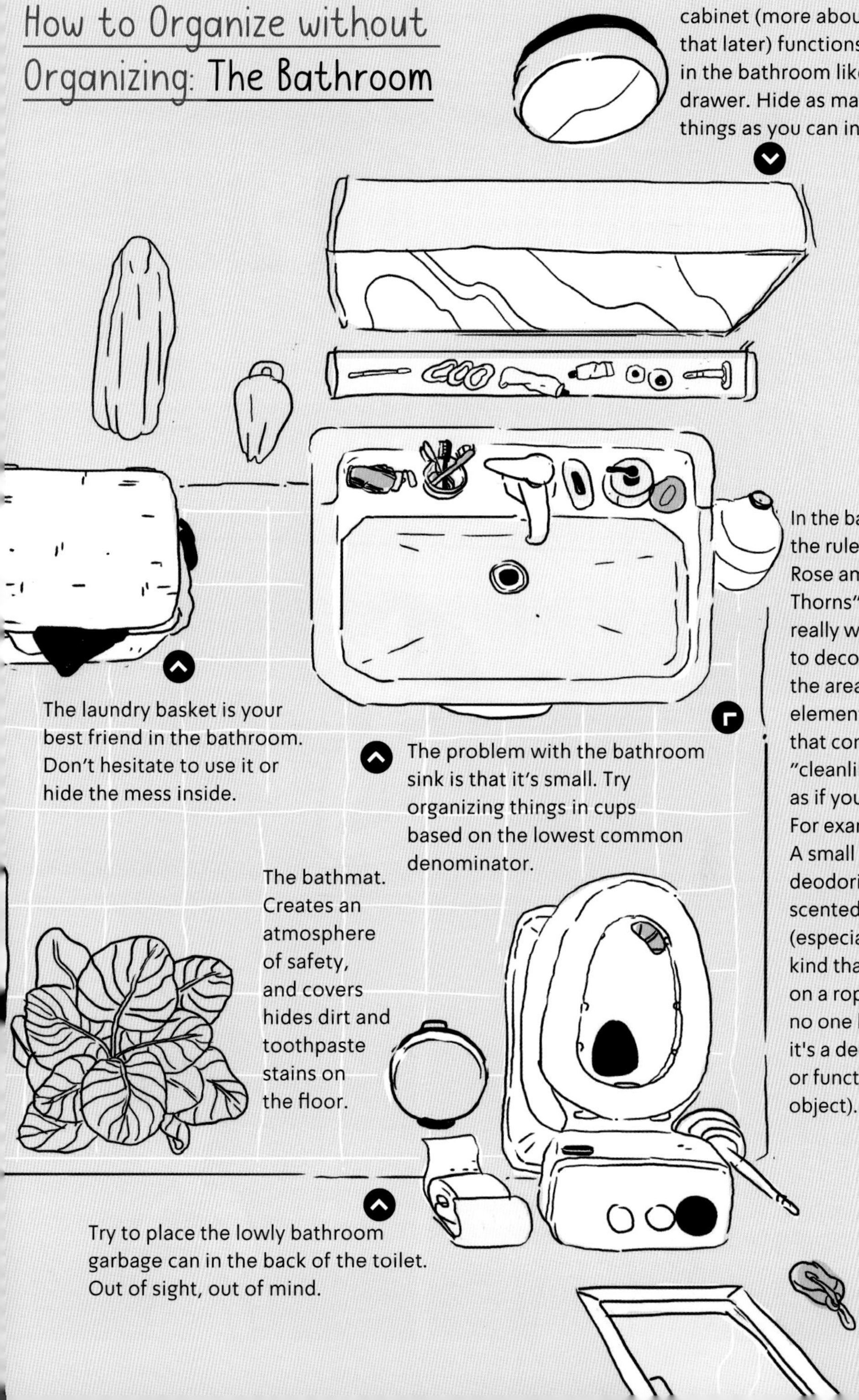

In the bathroom, the rule of "The Rose among Thorns" works really well. Try to decorate the area with elements that convey "cleanliness" as if you care. For example: A small toilet deodorizer or scented soap (especially the kind that hangs on a rope and no one knows if it's a decorative or functional object).

The laundry basket is your best friend in the bathroom. Don't hesitate to use it or hide the mess inside. ⌃

The problem with the bathroom sink is that it's small. Try organizing things in cups based on the lowest common denominator. ⌃

The bathmat. Creates an atmosphere of safety, and covers hides dirt and toothpaste stains on the floor.

Try to place the lowly bathroom garbage can in the back of the toilet. Out of sight, out of mind. ⌃

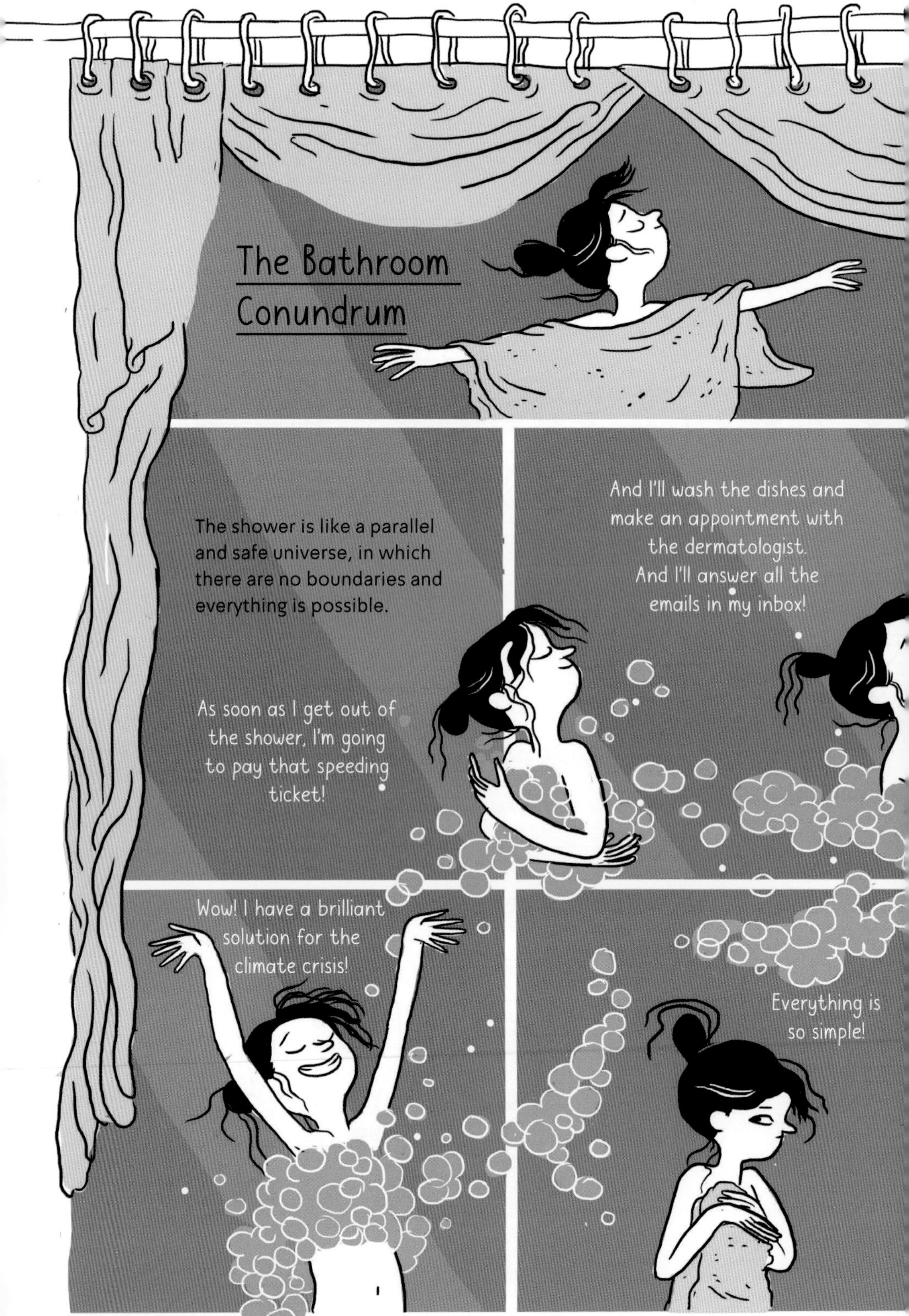

The Bathroom Conundrum
The shower is like a parallel and safe universe, in which there are no boundaries and everything is possible.
As soon as I get out of the shower, I'm going to pay that speeding ticket!
And I'll wash the dishes and make an appointment with the dermatologist.
And I'll answer all the emails in my inbox!
Wow! I have a brilliant solution for the climate crisis!
Everything is so simple!

It fills you with a false sense of vitality and decisiveness.
Suddenly, every problem is small and can be solved. And every idea seems ingenious and groundbreaking.
I'll calmly explain to my boss that I demand a raise or I'll quit!
The problem with the shower is that every shower comes to an end.
Ah, I'm tired. I'm going to sleep.

One of the organized figures in Greek mythology was the girl Pandora. Instead of understanding the importance of leaving things in the box, she thought she could organize everything in an IKEA sock organizer, and brought upon us all a world full of doom, disease, and disorder.

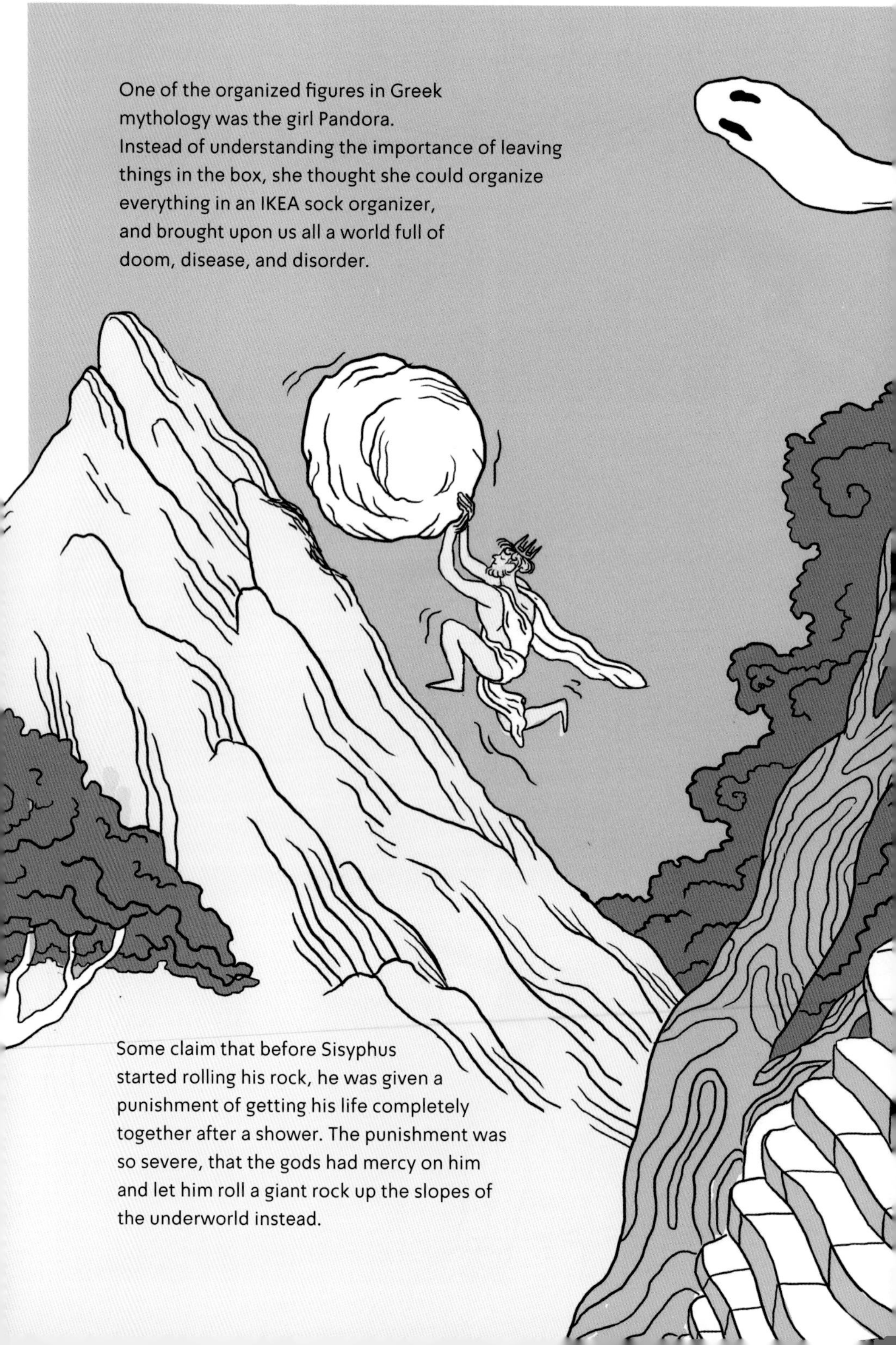

Some claim that before Sisyphus started rolling his rock, he was given a punishment of getting his life completely together after a shower. The punishment was so severe, that the gods had mercy on him and let him roll a giant rock up the slopes of the underworld instead.

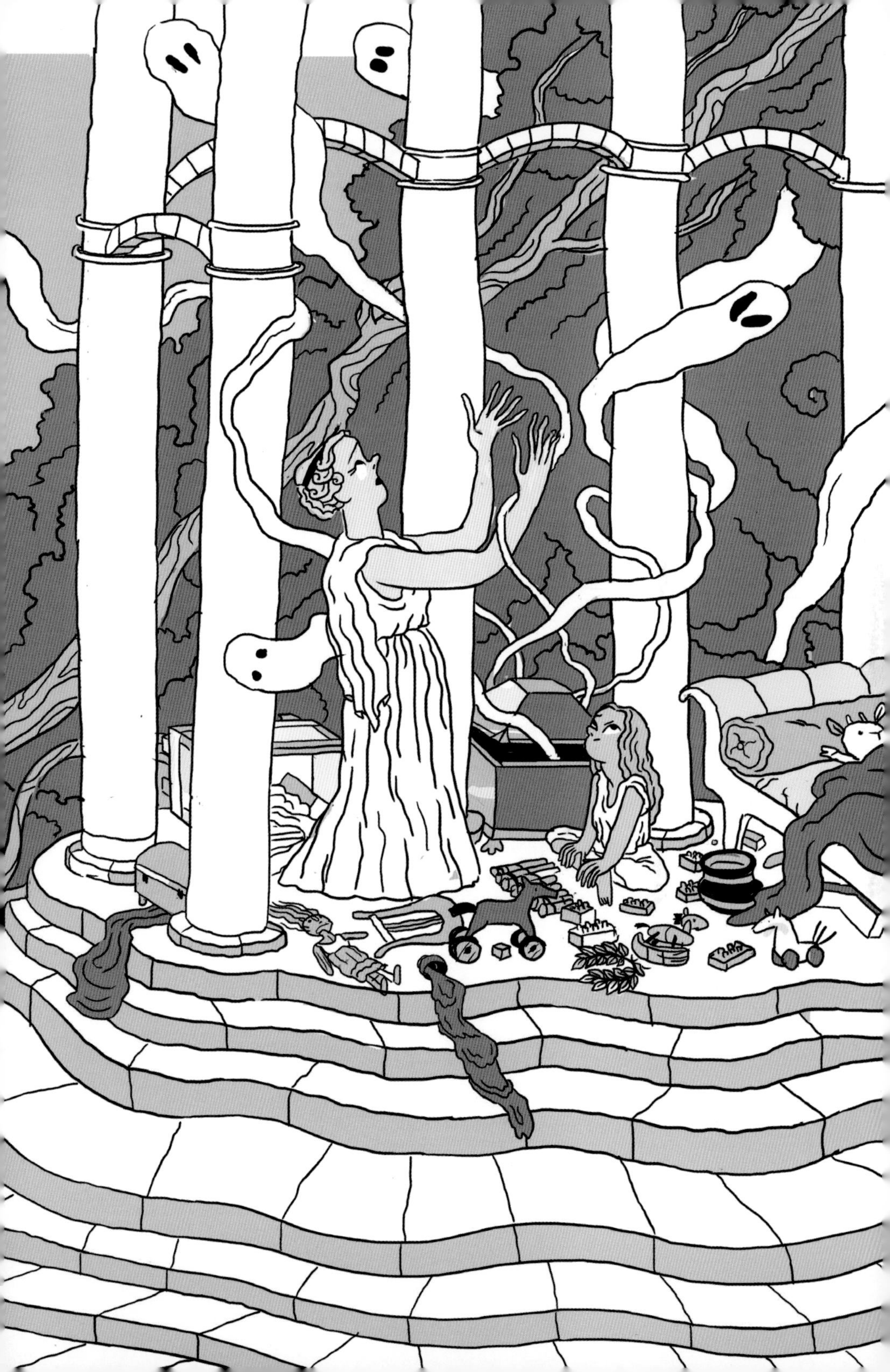

THE ORGANIZED ONES

This chapter will discuss that golden group of gods: The Organized Ones. I don't hate organized people. Some of my closest friends are organized. I'm just jealous of them. Because from where I see it, they represent a model of life that is organized, functional, and almost make believe. Maybe that's how it looks from the side, or rather – from the couch piled with laundry, but by organized people, everything looks clean and sparkling, efficient, and neat. And they always seem to have insights and tips on the matter.

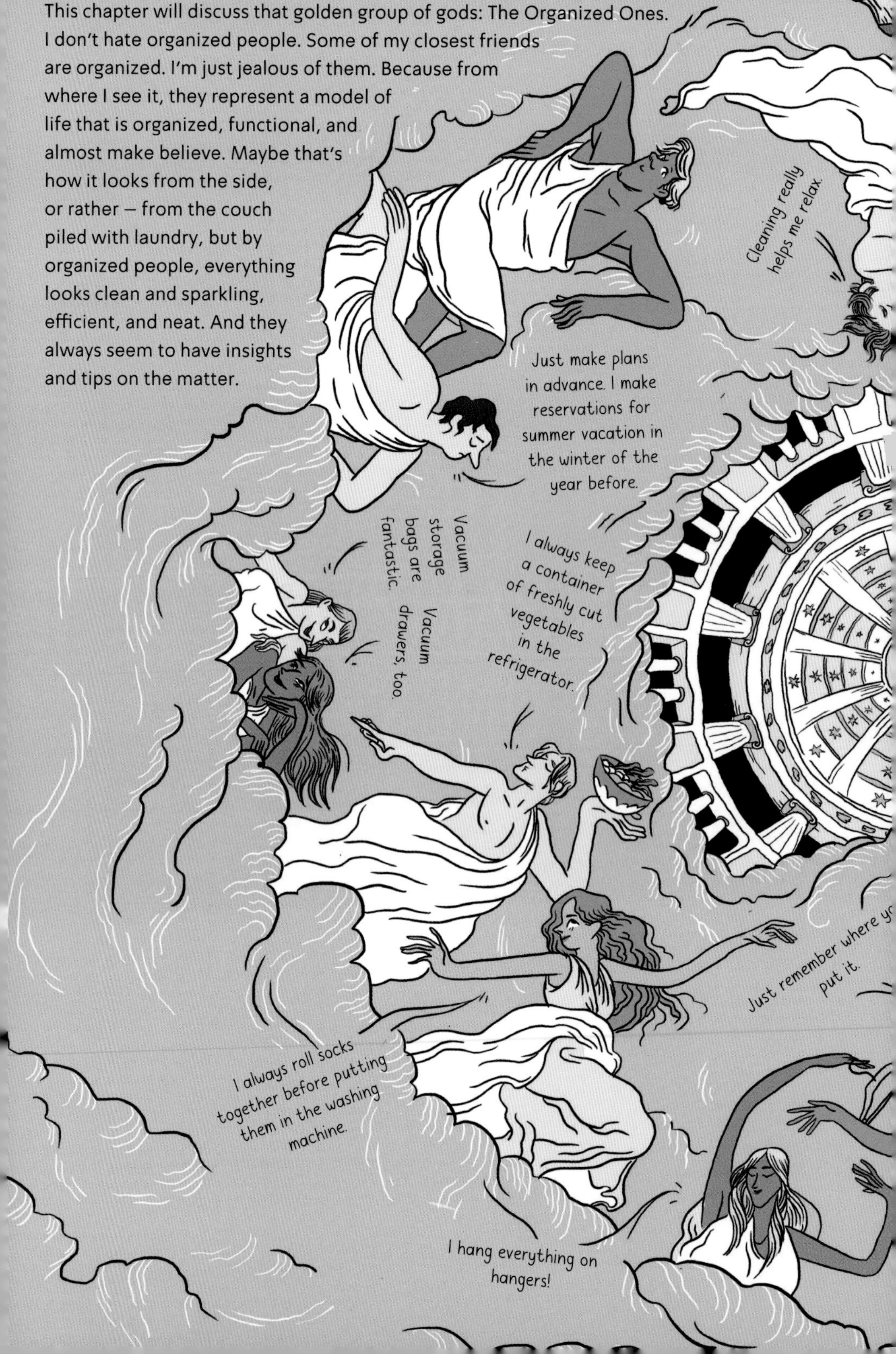
Cleaning really helps me relax.
Just make plans in advance. I make reservations for summer vacation in the winter of the year before.
Vacuum storage bags are fantastic.
Vacuum drawers, too.
I always keep a container of freshly cut vegetables in the refrigerator.
Just remember where you put it.
I always roll socks together before putting them in the washing machine.
I hang everything on hangers!

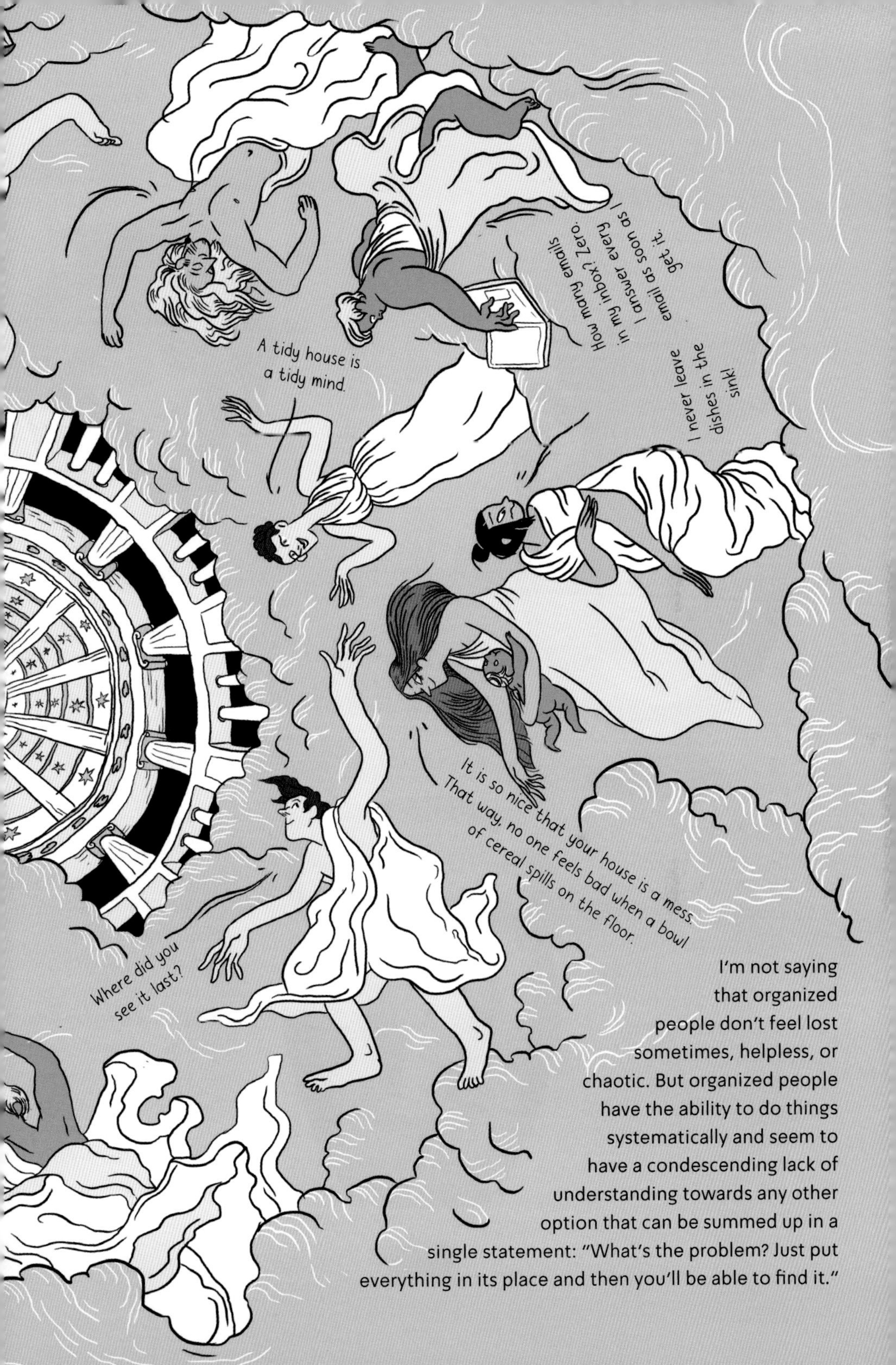
How many emails in my inbox? Zero. I answer every email as soon as I get it.
A tidy house is a tidy mind.
I never leave dishes in the sink!
It is so nice that your house is a mess. That way, no one feels bad when a bowl of cereal spills on the floor.
Where did you see it last?

I'm not saying that organized people don't feel lost sometimes, helpless, or chaotic. But organized people have the ability to do things systematically and seem to have a condescending lack of understanding towards any other option that can be summed up in a single statement: "What's the problem? Just put everything in its place and then you'll be able to find it."

Of course, just like with messy people, organized people are not all alike. And even the members of this restricted club come in different ranks and classes.

The Un-Naturals
Tidiness doesn't come naturally to this type, but it's really important to them (probably something from their childhood) and they invest so much energy in getting organized that they don't have much energy or patience for other things.

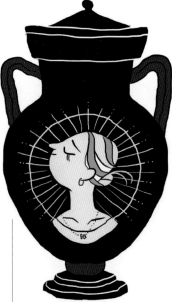

The Shampoo Halos
The tidiness of these types is infused with style — it's not just functional, it's a form of art. They have small, quaint baskets for towels and potpourri and all sorts of other things that go in small, quaint baskets. And they always leave a fresh whiff of herbal shampoo in their wake. Even at three in the afternoon.

The Naturals
Organization and planning come naturally for people of this status. They have different colors on the calendar for business meetings, family events, and school events. Since being organized doesn't demand much energy, they are vibrant and full of energy on a daily basis.

The Reformed

Messy people who turn over a new (and tidy) leaf will always try to convince you to see the light, to buy sock-divider drawers from IKEA, and to remember where you last saw your house key.

The Revelations

You can't tell these people are organized just by looking at them. They look like regular people. But their organizational skills are revealed when you're assigned to their team at work/school/social event/kindergarten party, or when they cut their food into very, very precise pieces.

The Rankled

Their tidiness is on edge; they're fed up with the order and organization that the modern world demands of them and they're one step away from crossing over to the messy side. They'll always suggest a guidebook to tidiness that changed their lives. (And I don't mean this guidebook...)

But while messy people change their old ways and try out new ones, the organized ones usually keep everything organized and stay that way.

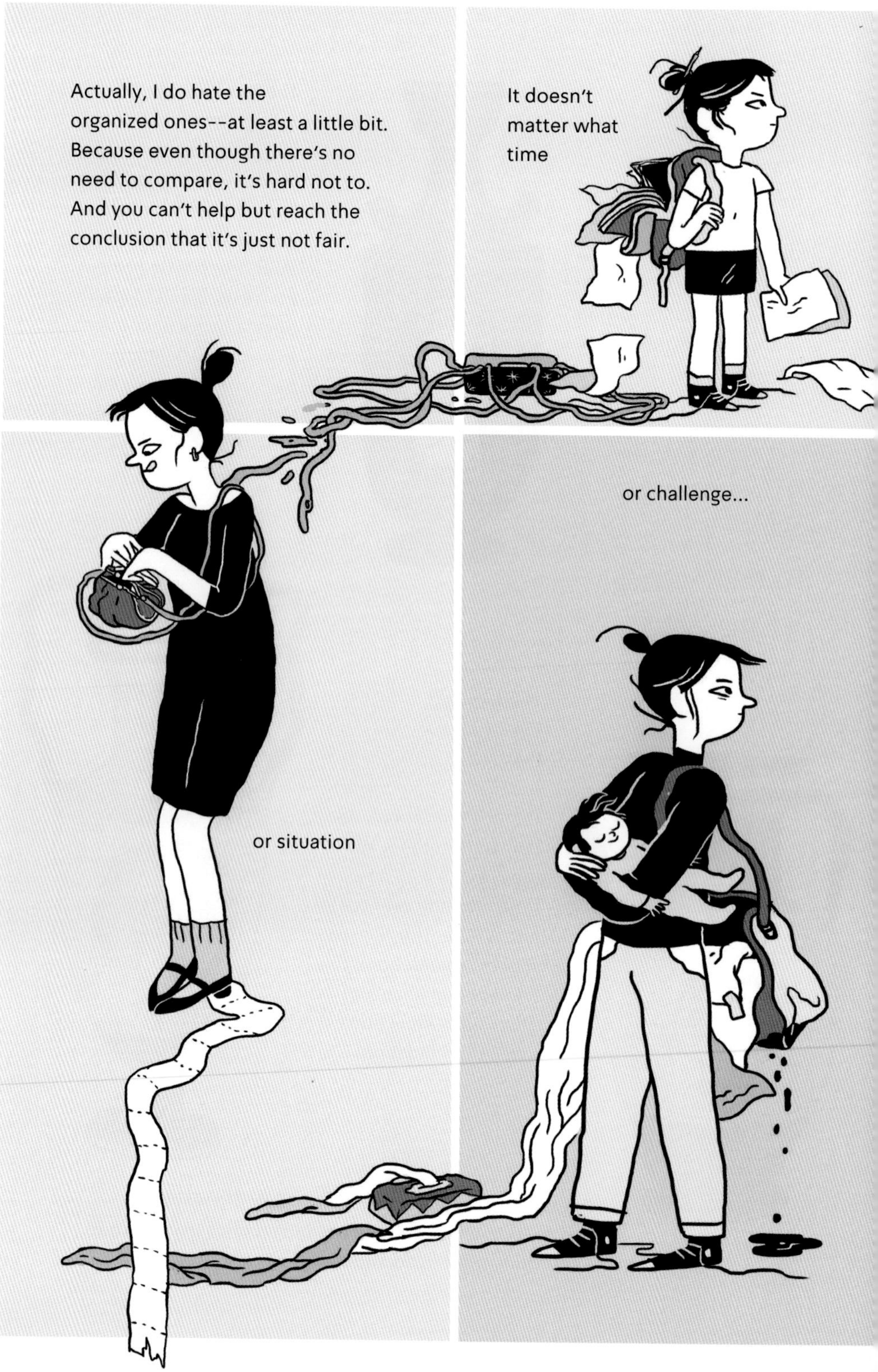
Actually, I do hate the organized ones--at least a little bit. Because even though there's no need to compare, it's hard not to. And you can't help but reach the conclusion that it's just not fair.
It doesn't matter what time
or situation
or challenge...

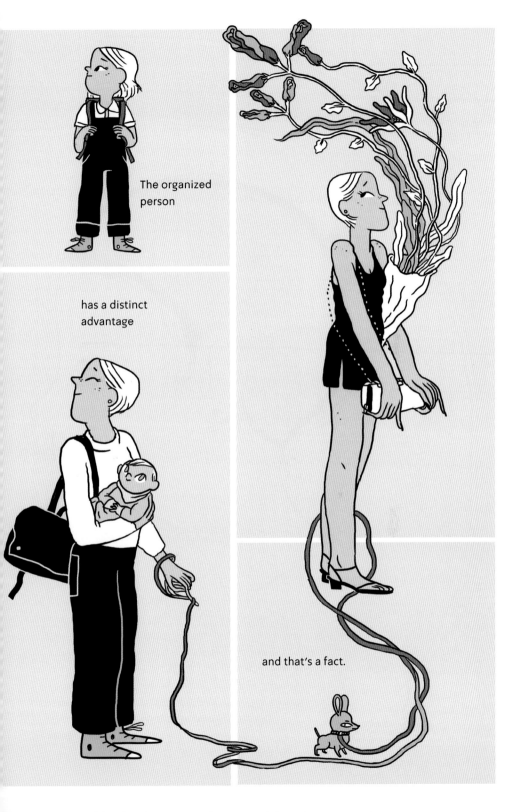

The organized person

has a distinct advantage

and that's a fact.

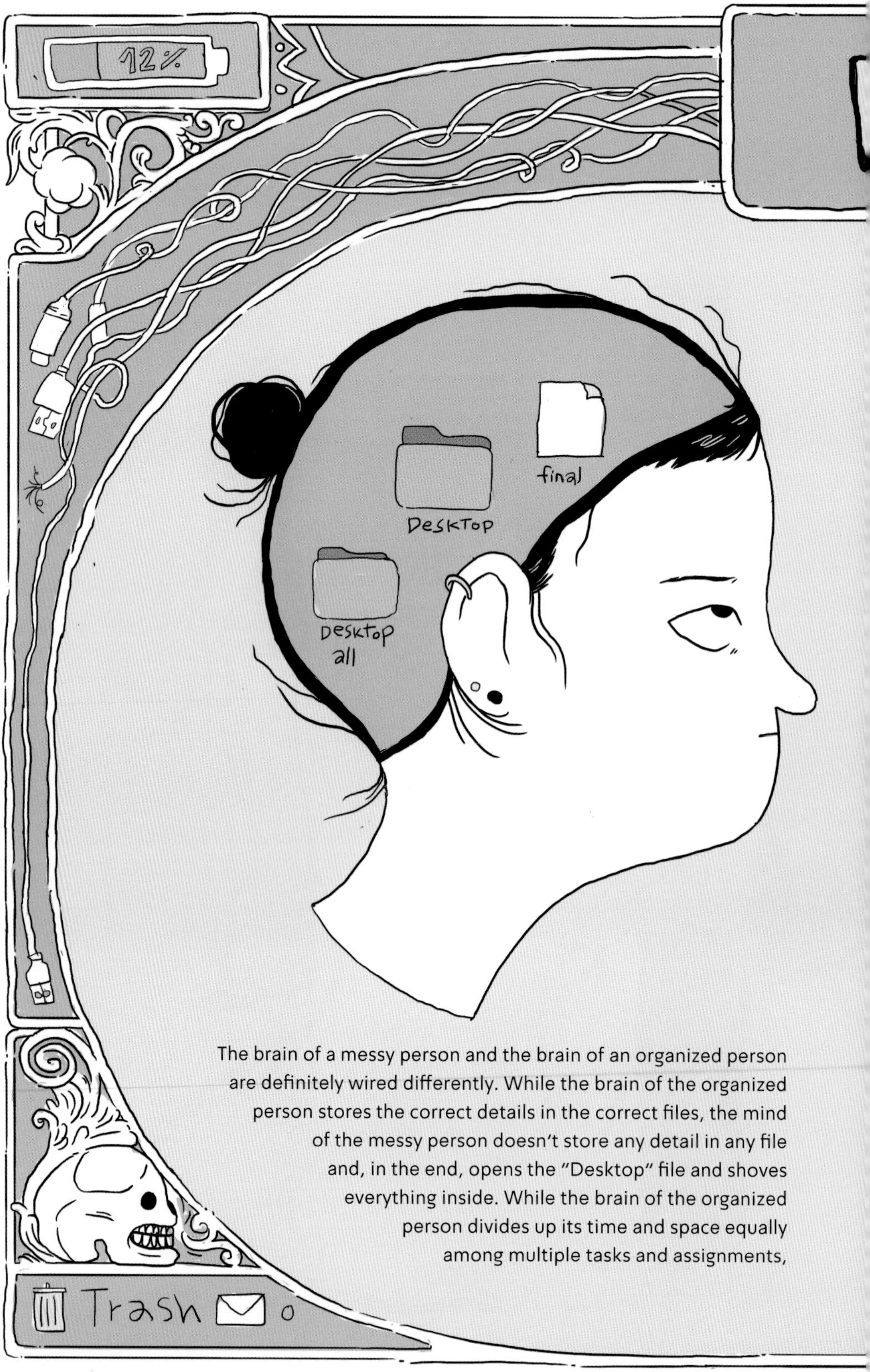
12%
DESKTOP
final
DESKTOP
all
Trash
0

The brain of a messy person and the brain of an organized person are definitely wired differently. While the brain of the organized person stores the correct details in the correct files, the mind of the messy person doesn't store any detail in any file and, in the end, opens the "Desktop" file and shoves everything inside. While the brain of the organized person divides up its time and space equally among multiple tasks and assignments,

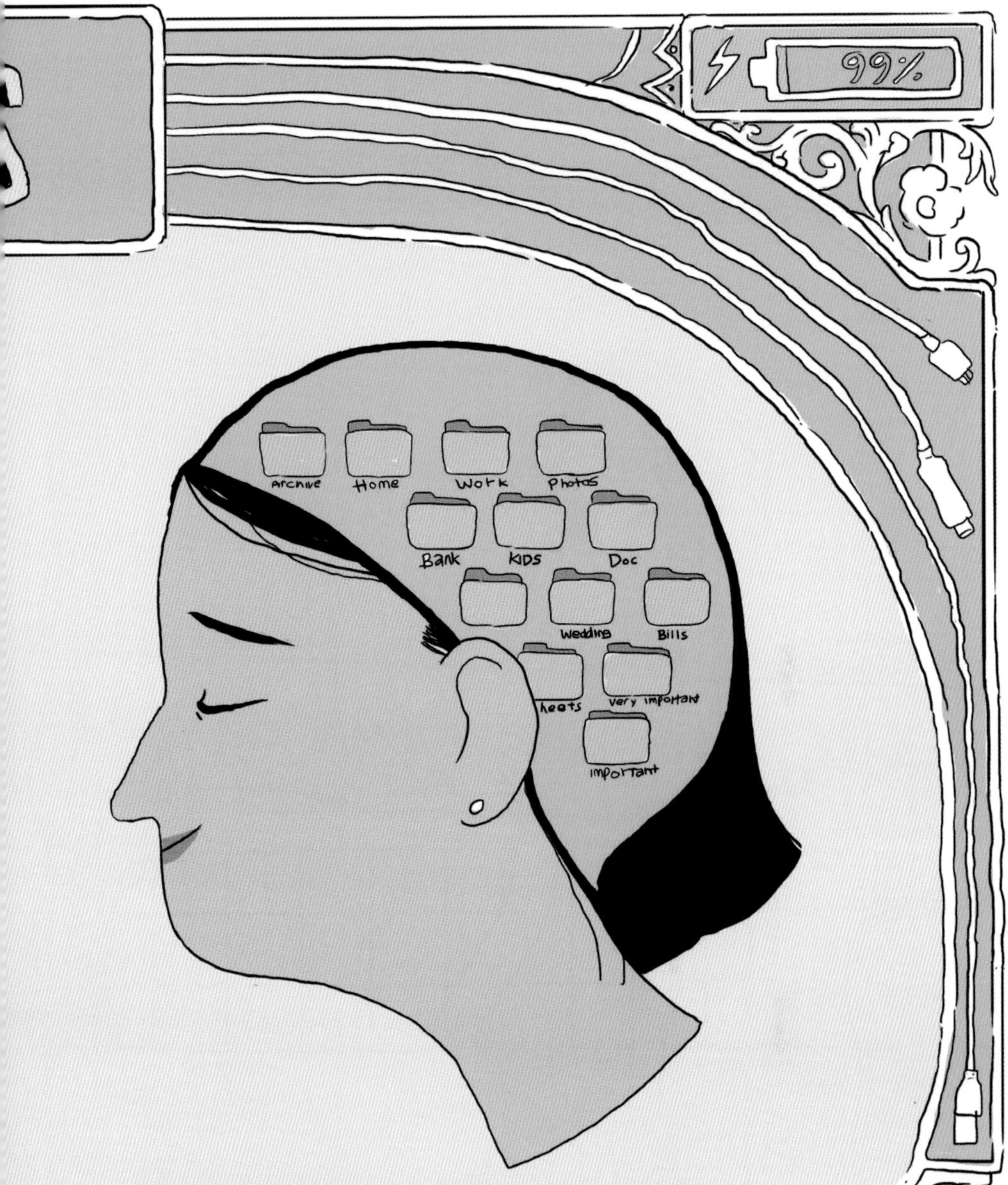
99%
Archive
Home
Work
Photos
Bank
KIDS
Doc
Wedding
Bills
heets
very important
important

the brain of the messy person takes an Xbox break or stops for a second to read an entire article about fire ants on Wikipedia. The brain of the organized person plans ahead of time, and always remembers to bring a towel before going into the shower. It would be a big surprise if the brain of a messy person would remember to bring a towel (and in any case, chances are that it would end up being a medium-sized hand towel).

Let's make a brief comparison in a few sectors.

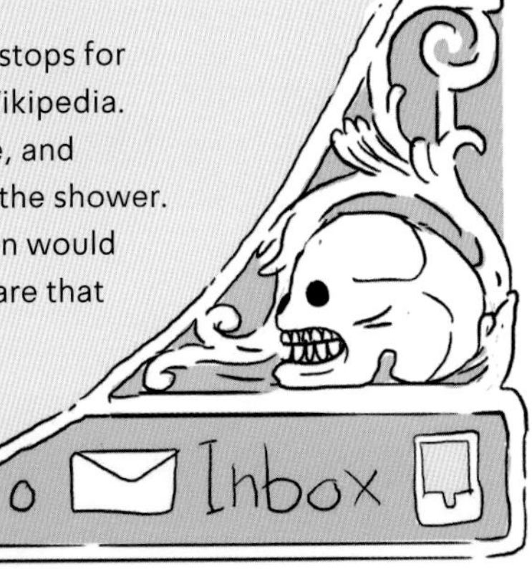
0
Inbox

The Shower

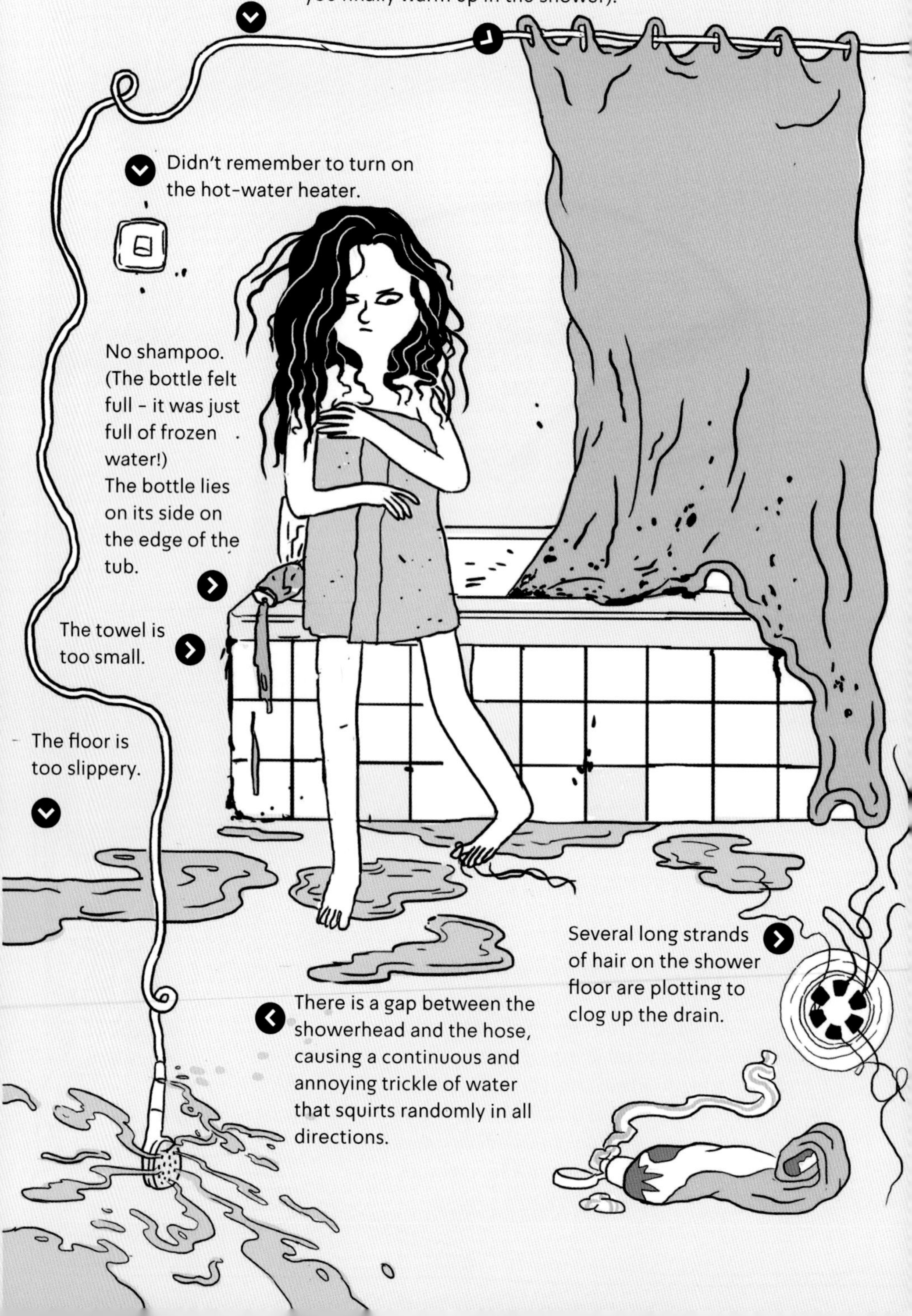
A shower curtain that always blows towards you and sticks to your body when you're least expecting it (usually after you finally warm up in the shower).
Didn't remember to turn on the hot-water heater.
No shampoo. (The bottle felt full - it was just full of frozen water!) The bottle lies on its side on the edge of the tub.
The towel is too small.
The floor is too slippery.
There is a gap between the showerhead and the hose, causing a continuous and annoying trickle of water that squirts randomly in all directions.
Several long strands of hair on the shower floor are plotting to clog up the drain.

A timer for the hot-water heater that is set for 30 minutes before waking up for a refreshing morning shower and then for 30 minutes before getting home from work in the evening.

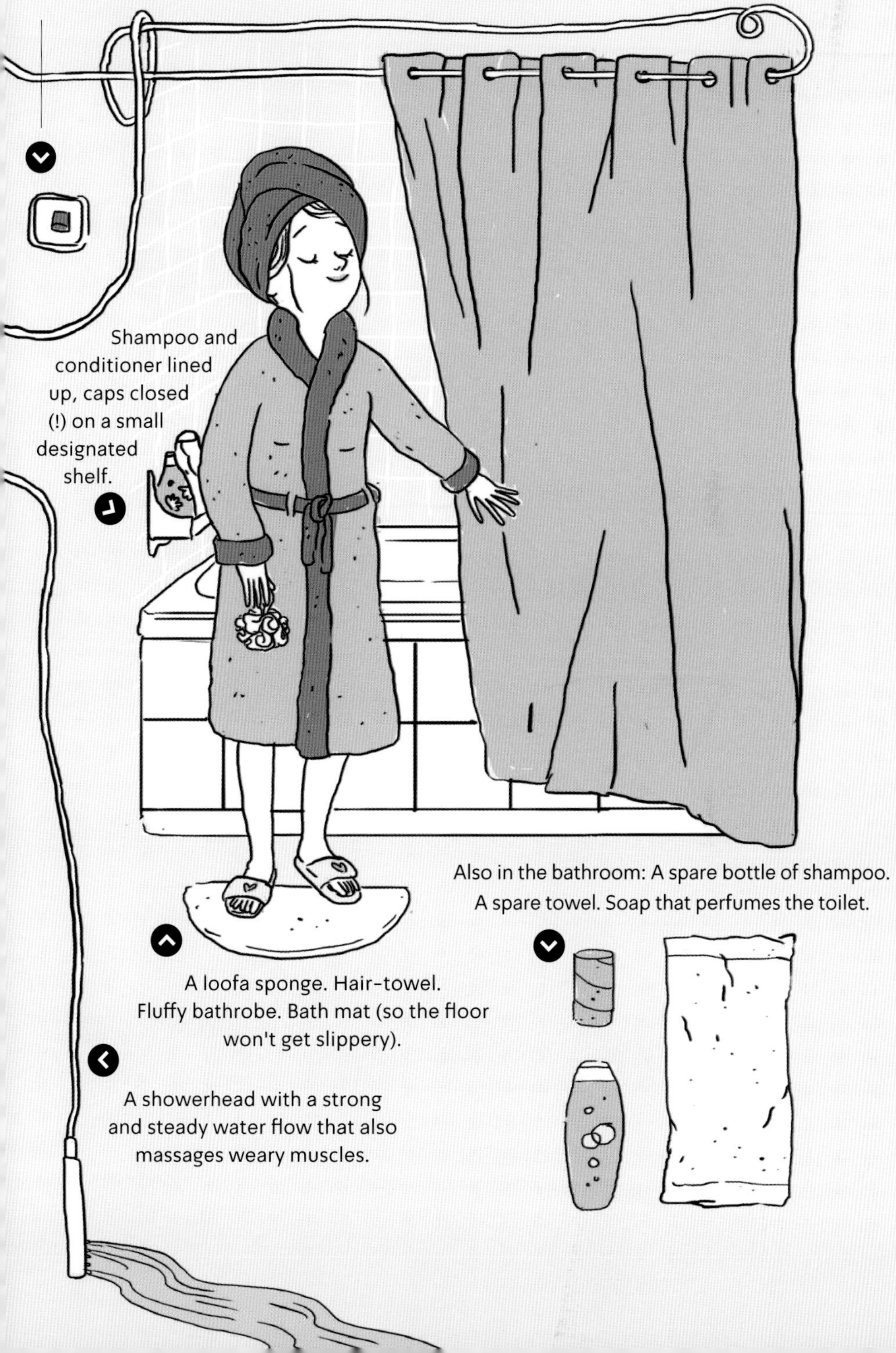
Shampoo and conditioner lined up, caps closed (!) on a small designated shelf.
Also in the bathroom: A spare bottle of shampoo. A spare towel. Soap that perfumes the toilet.
A loofa sponge. Hair-towel. Fluffy bathrobe. Bath mat (so the floor won't get slippery).
A showerhead with a strong and steady water flow that also massages weary muscles.

Family Dinner

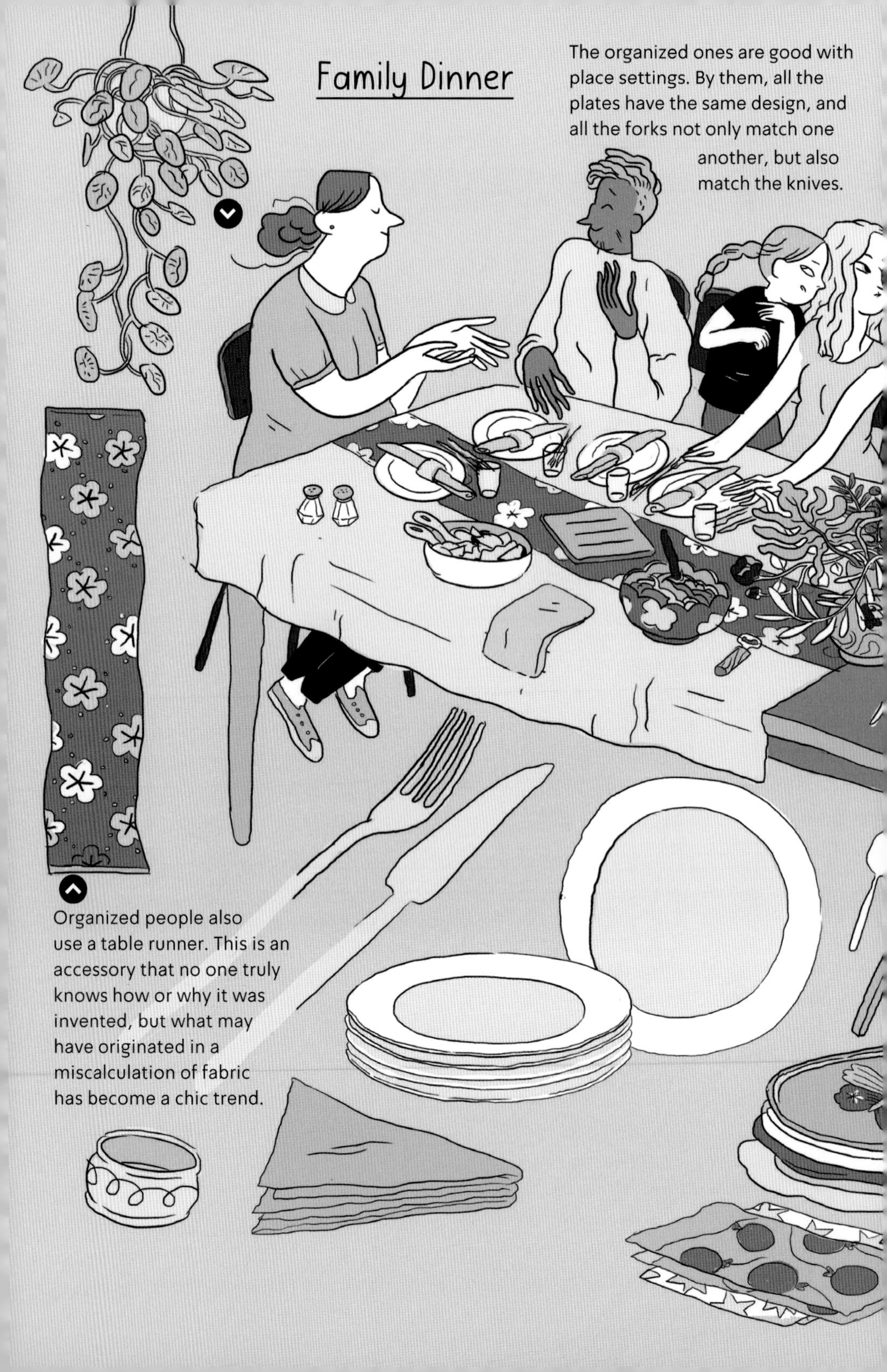

The organized ones are good with place settings. By them, all the plates have the same design, and all the forks not only match one another, but also match the knives.

Organized people also use a table runner. This is an accessory that no one truly knows how or why it was invented, but what may have originated in a miscalculation of fabric has become a chic trend.

The organized ones have all sorts of kitchen accessories that the messy ones don't, for example: a beer bottle opener every time one is needed, napkin rings, cheese forks, and that little scoop thingy that looks like an embalming tool and turns a melon into little balls.

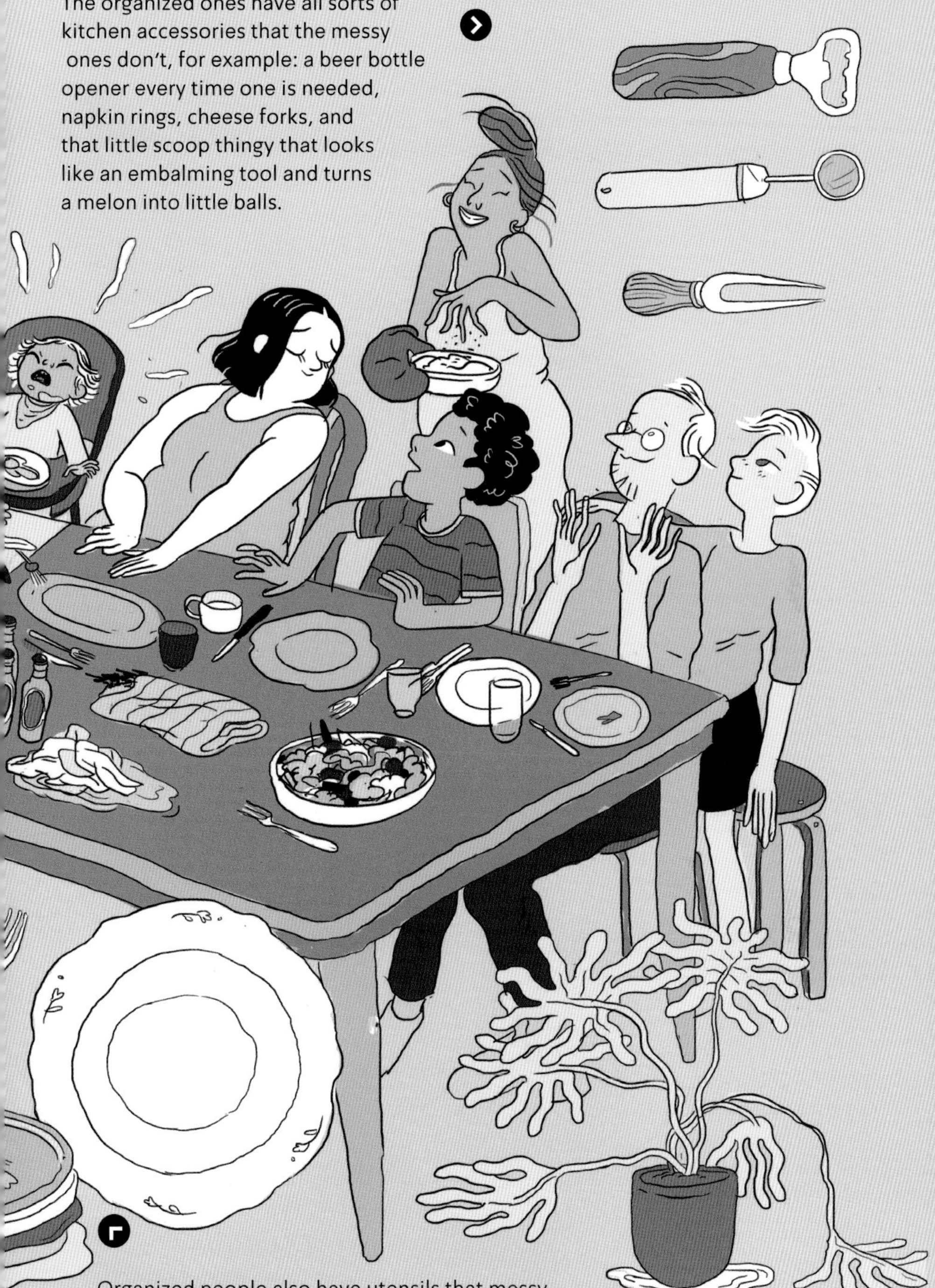

Organized people also have utensils that messy people have, but they actually remember where they put them and can find them when they're needed. These include salad tongs, oven mitts, and placemats for hot pots (a towel with a burnt corner doesn't count).

Lists

Lists are one of the pillars of the organized life. There's something ceremonial and even mystical about lists. You write things down and they happen! Well, you do them, I mean. If you're an organized person. So when organized people write a list, they will use:

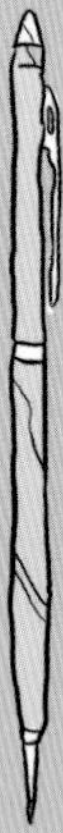

A specific pen that's always in its place (in the pen pouch of their handbag).

And a designated notebook.

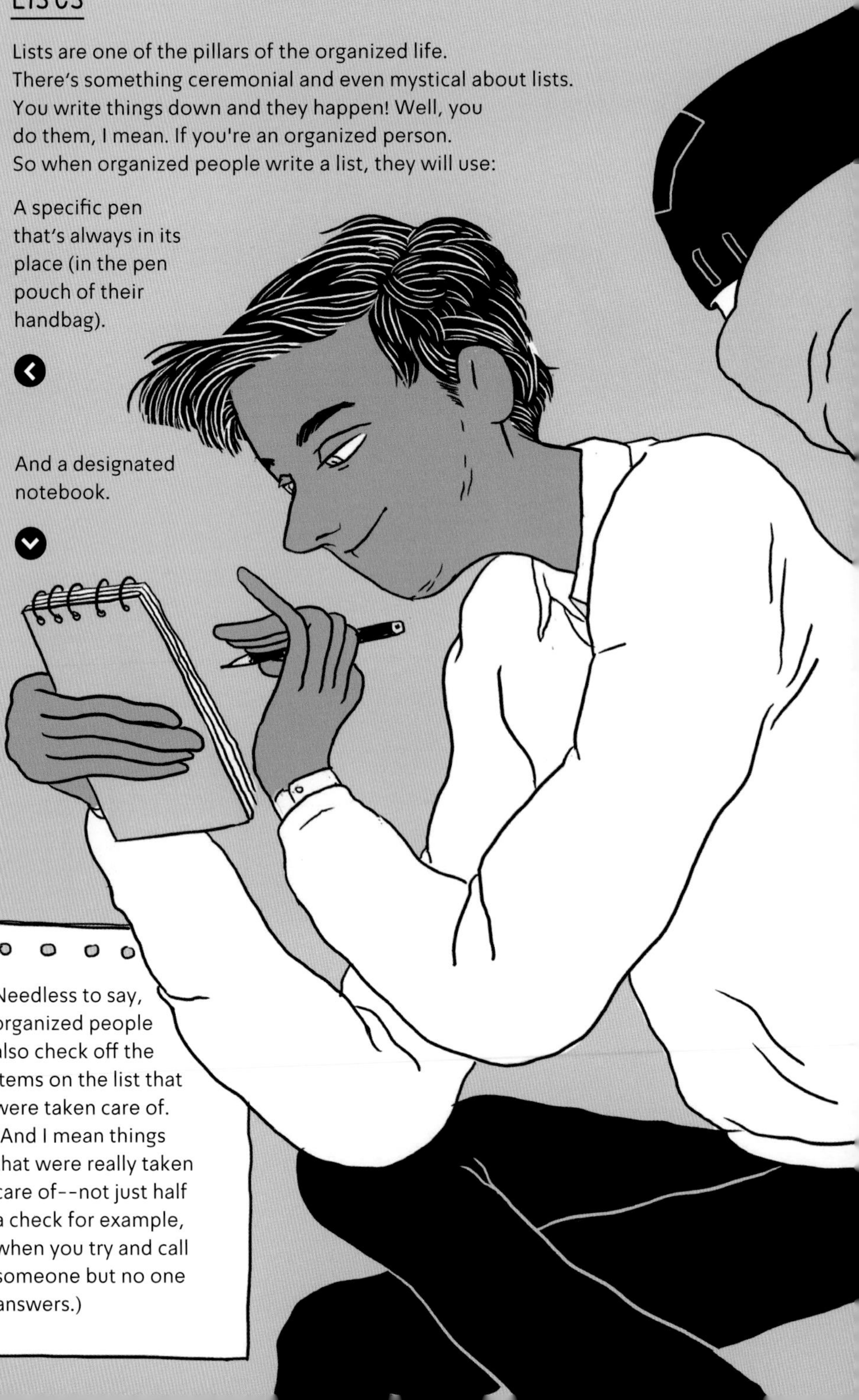

Needless to say, organized people also check off the items on the list that were taken care of. (And I mean things that were really taken care of--not just half a check for example, when you try and call someone but no one answers.)

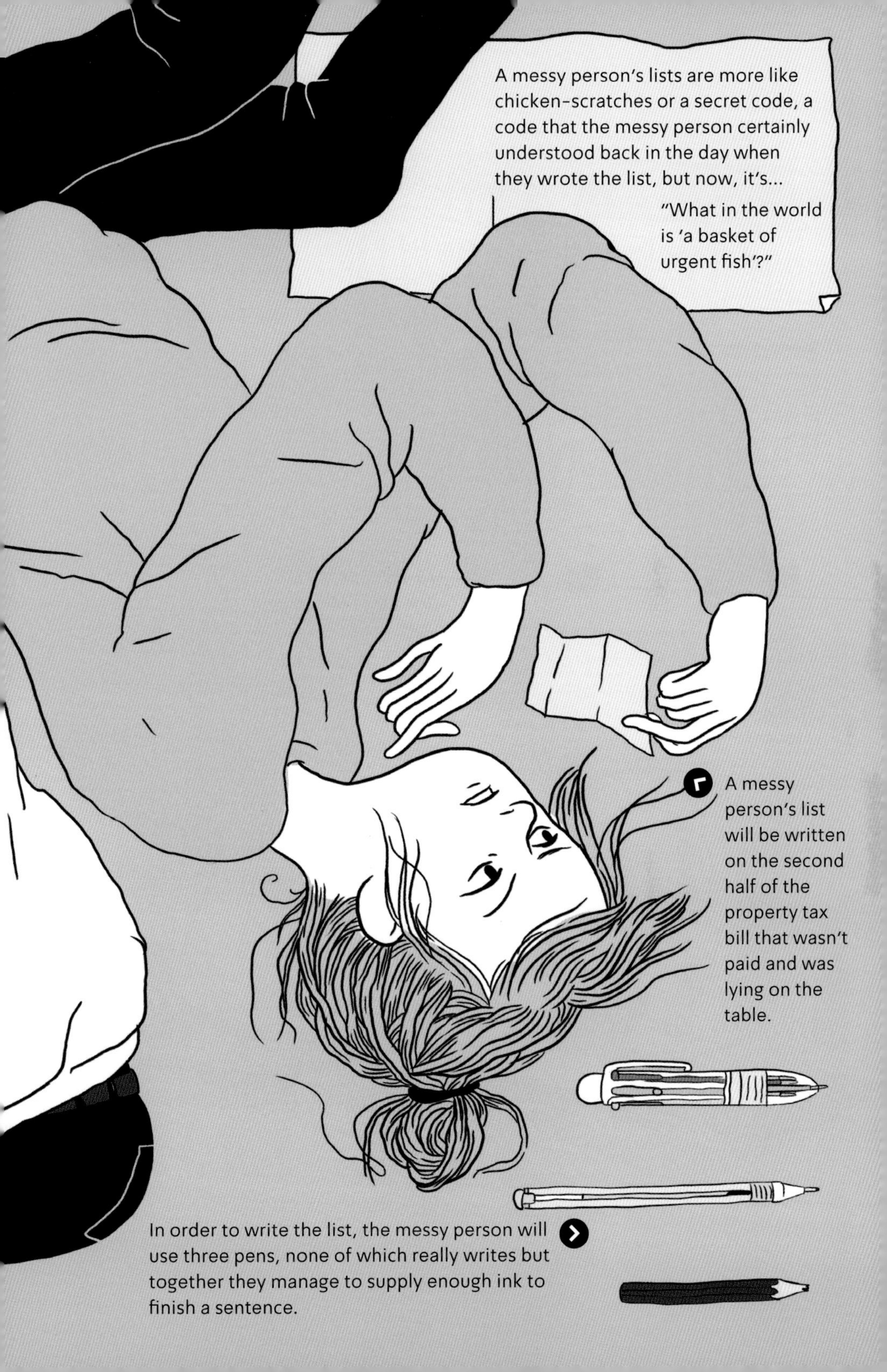
A messy person's lists are more like chicken-scratches or a secret code, a code that the messy person certainly understood back in the day when they wrote the list, but now, it's...
"What in the world is 'a basket of urgent fish'?"
A messy person's list will be written on the second half of the property tax bill that wasn't paid and was lying on the table.
In order to write the list, the messy person will use three pens, none of which really writes but together they manage to supply enough ink to finish a sentence.

Packing

The organized person's suitcase corresponds to the travel destination, the climate, the length of the trip, and the importance of brushing one's teeth.

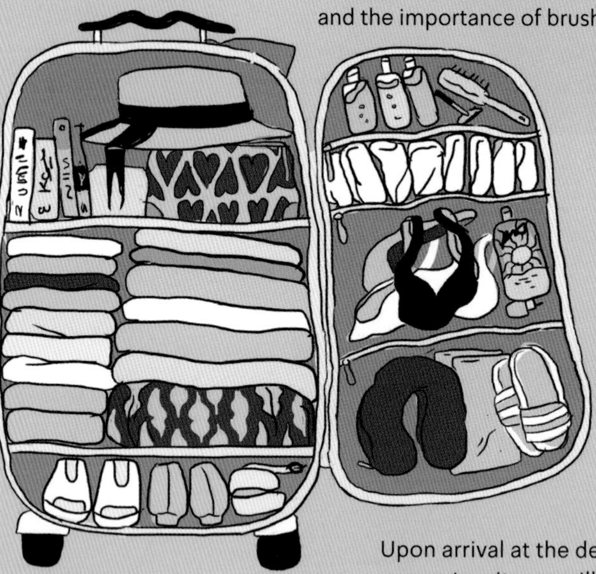

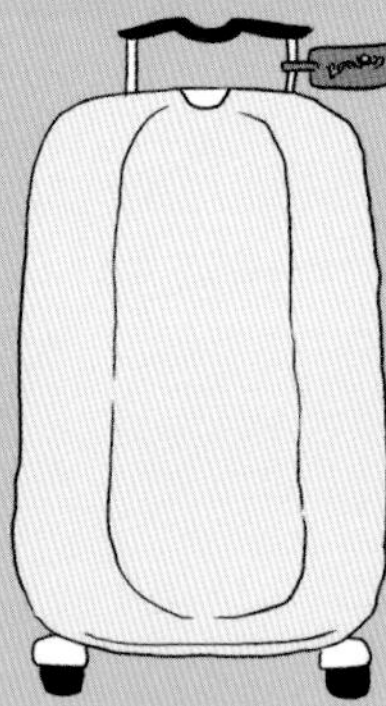

This includes maximizing the hierarchy of the suitcase and its various compartments and using waterproof plastic bags for creams or lotions.

Upon arrival at the destination, the organized person's suitcase will be immediately unpacked onto designated shelves, and will be repacked at the end of the trip. Upon returning home, we can expect all the clothes to be back in their closet within two hours.

Although it goes without saying, I will note that the number of underpants that arrive at the destination match the number of vacation days along with whatever else is needed on the vacation.

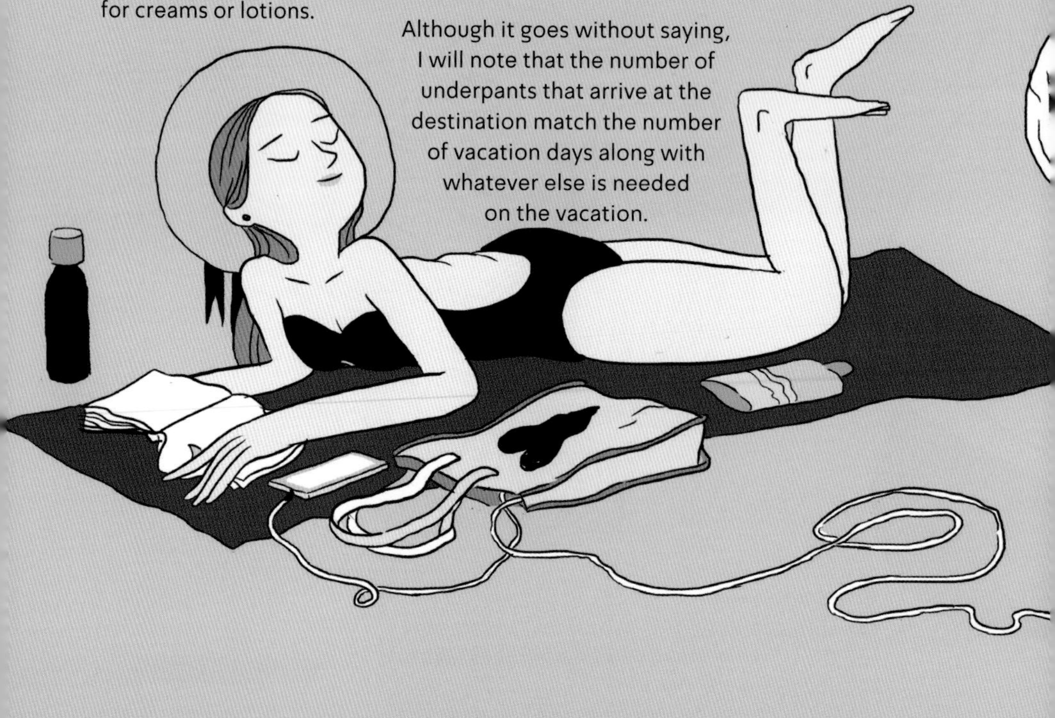

The messy person's suitcase is more like a stream of consciousness devoid of any long-term contemplation. It holds all sorts of items--some from the clean laundry pile, a book, and a cosmetic bag with a tube of toothpaste that doesn't close so well.

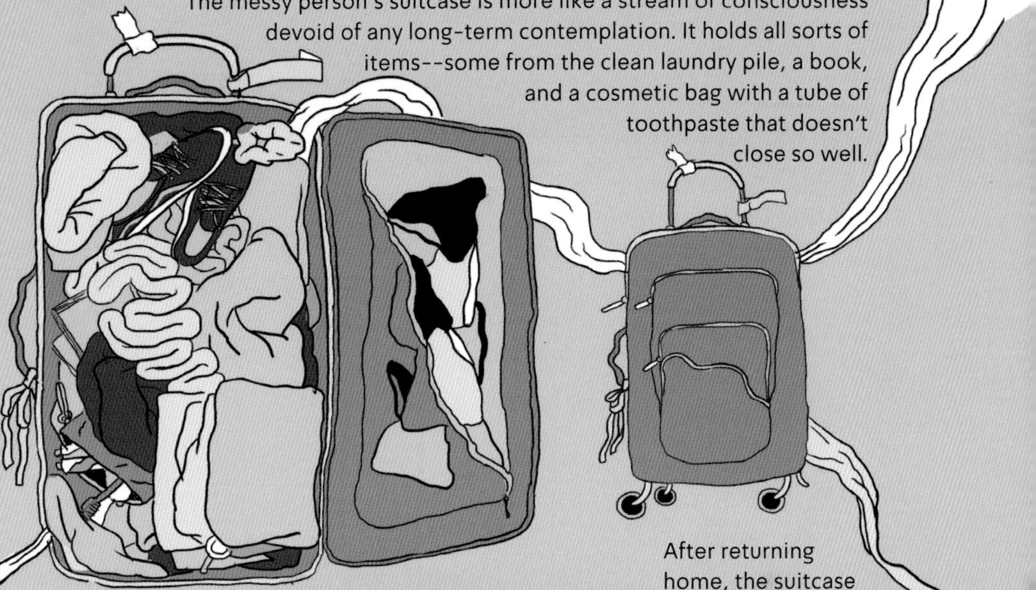

The messy person's suitcase will stay just like it is when it arrives at the destination, and will be used like a portable closet. With the exception of the cosmetic bag that must be cleaned because the toothpaste tube was not closed well and exploded on the contents of the cosmetic bag.

After returning home, the suitcase will remain as is for one to two weeks at best (with the exception of the cosmetic bag that still hasn't dried out).

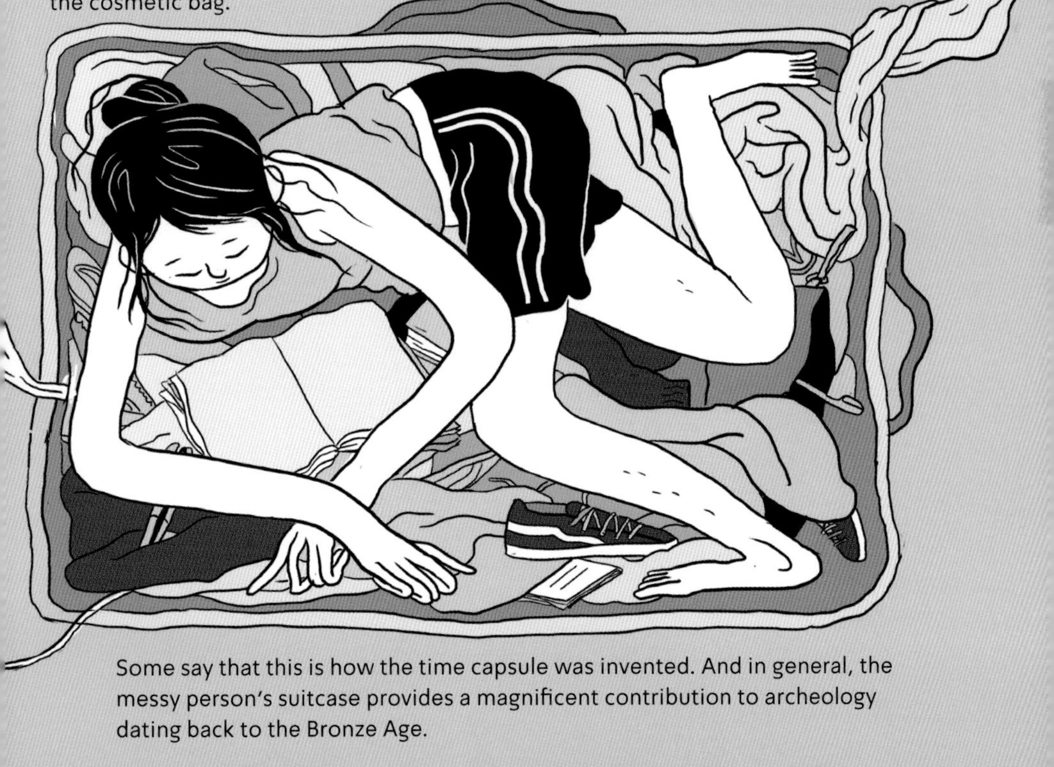

Some say that this is how the time capsule was invented. And in general, the messy person's suitcase provides a magnificent contribution to archeology dating back to the Bronze Age.

The Seasons

Unexpected changes in schedule don't work well for the messy person (and most changes will be unexpected, because messy people don't always check their messages or remember the updates). Therefore, the change of seasons always catches them by surprise. The tidy, organized person has no such problem. Their superiority over the messy person is clear.

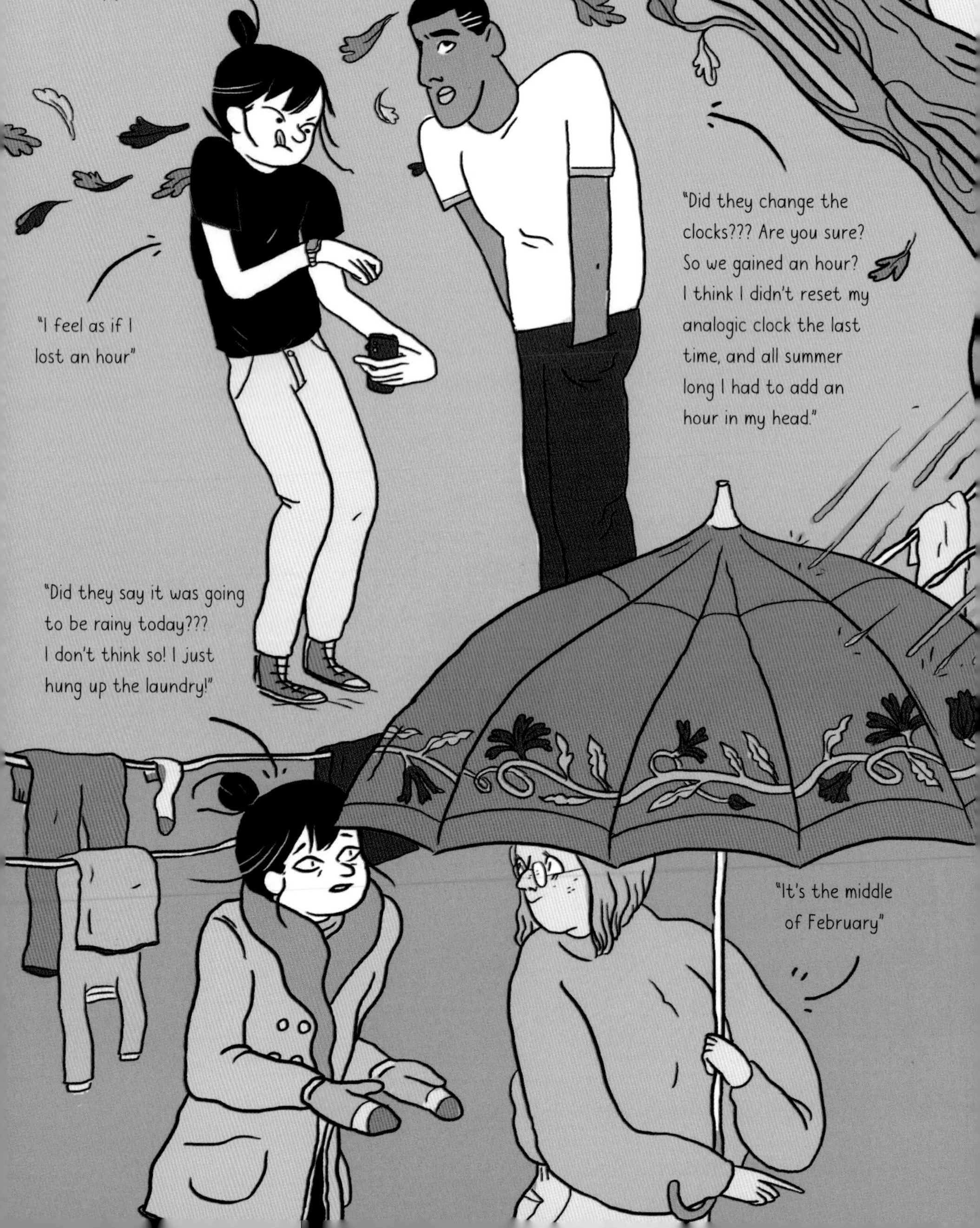
"I feel as if I lost an hour"
"Did they change the clocks??? Are you sure? So we gained an hour? I think I didn't reset my analogic clock the last time, and all summer long I had to add an hour in my head."
"Did they say it was going to be rainy today??? I don't think so! I just hung up the laundry!"
"It's the middle of February"

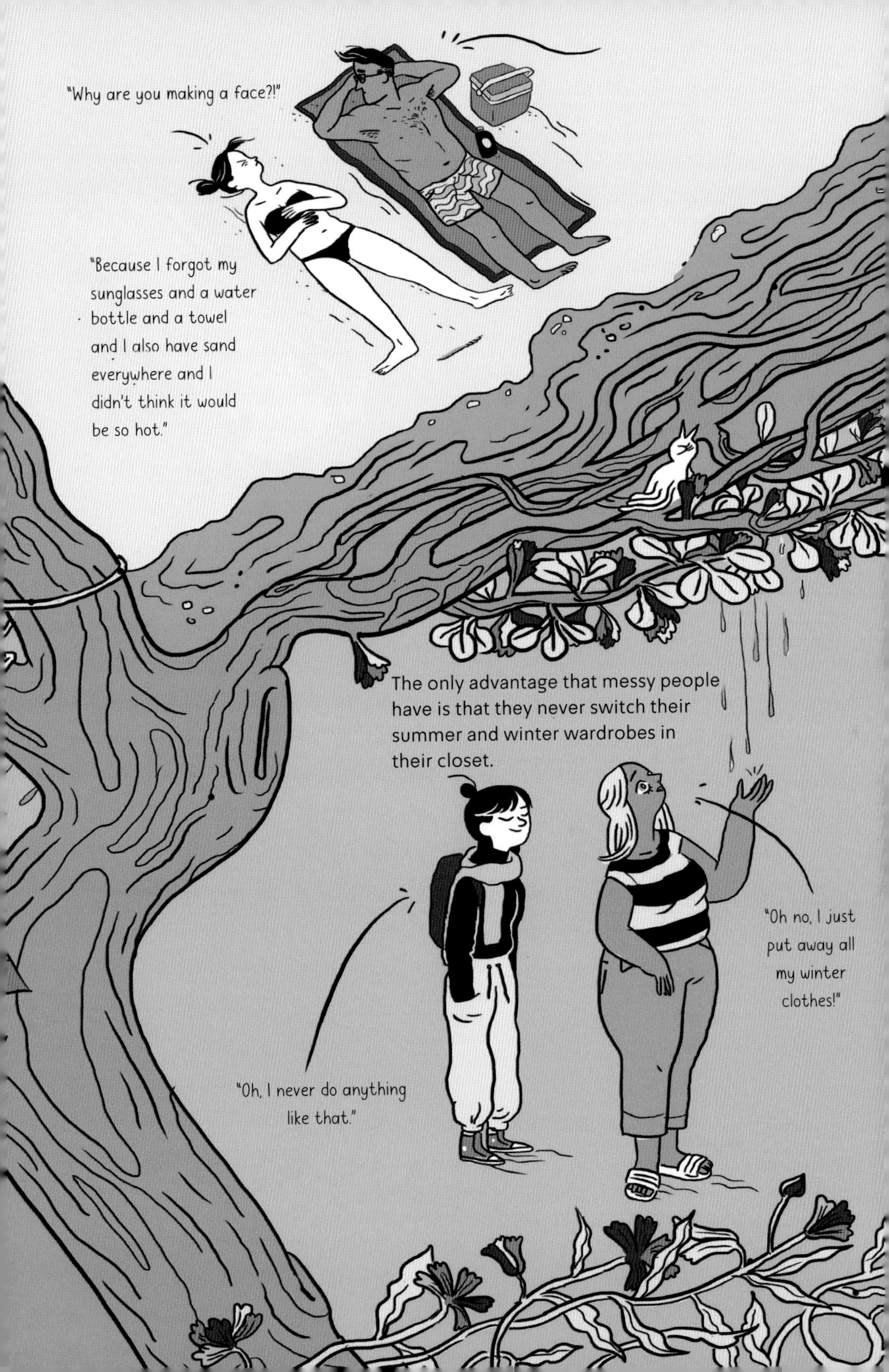
"Why are you making a face?!"
"Because I forgot my sunglasses and a water bottle and a towel and I also have sand everywhere and I didn't think it would be so hot."
The only advantage that messy people have is that they never switch their summer and winter wardrobes in their closet.
"Oh no, I just put away all my winter clothes!"
"Oh, I never do anything like that."

The Little Bathroom Cabinet

For an organized person, the little bathroom cabinet is a compact, useful cabinet. It holds everything one needs for the maintenance of daily hygiene and grooming. And of course, there is also a section that's categorized as first aid.

A very thorough tidy, organized person also has a few types of every item.

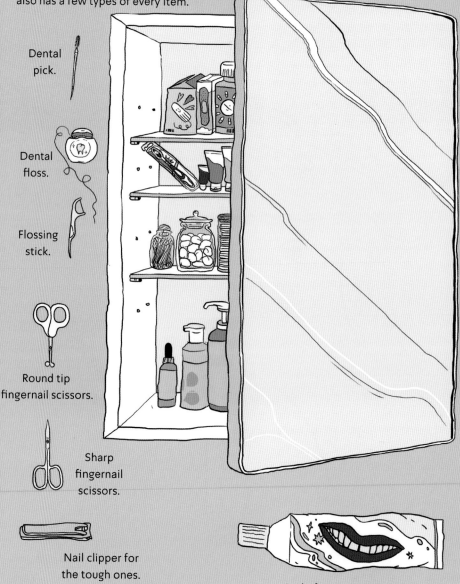

Dental pick.

Dental floss.

Flossing stick.

Round tip fingernail scissors.

Sharp fingernail scissors.

Nail clipper for the tough ones.

And of course, a spare tube of toothpaste.

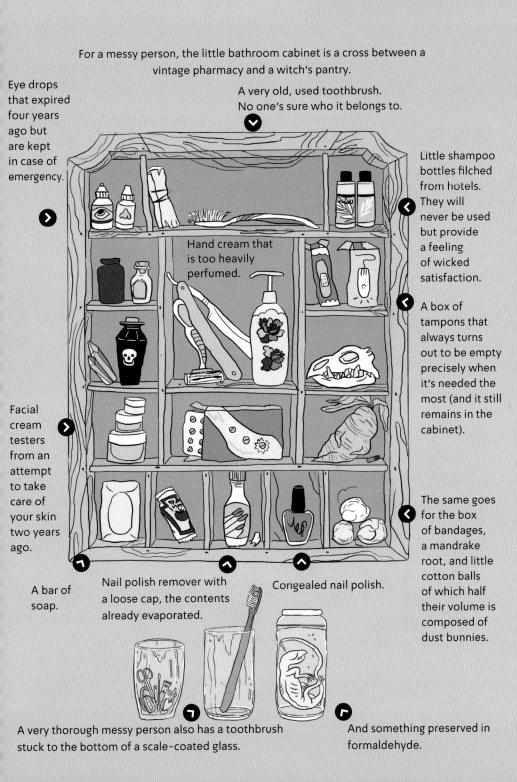

For a messy person, the little bathroom cabinet is a cross between a vintage pharmacy and a witch's pantry.

A very old, used toothbrush. No one's sure who it belongs to.

Eye drops that expired four years ago but are kept in case of emergency.

Little shampoo bottles filched from hotels. They will never be used but provide a feeling of wicked satisfaction.

Hand cream that is too heavily perfumed.

A box of tampons that always turns out to be empty precisely when it's needed the most (and it still remains in the cabinet).

Facial cream testers from an attempt to take care of your skin two years ago.

The same goes for the box of bandages, a mandrake root, and little cotton balls of which half their volume is composed of dust bunnies.

A bar of soap.

Nail polish remover with a loose cap, the contents already evaporated.

Congealed nail polish.

A very thorough messy person also has a toothbrush stuck to the bottom of a scale-coated glass.

And something preserved in formaldehyde.

The Bedroom

Sleep is the most important meal of the day, and the bedroom is the temple of the dreamer. Therefore, the organized person uses their bedroom mainly as a bedroom, while the messy person less so. For the messy person, the bedroom is more like a floor closet. In a messy person's bedroom there are lots of clothes on the floor, objects on the bed (and under it!), and one lone slipper.

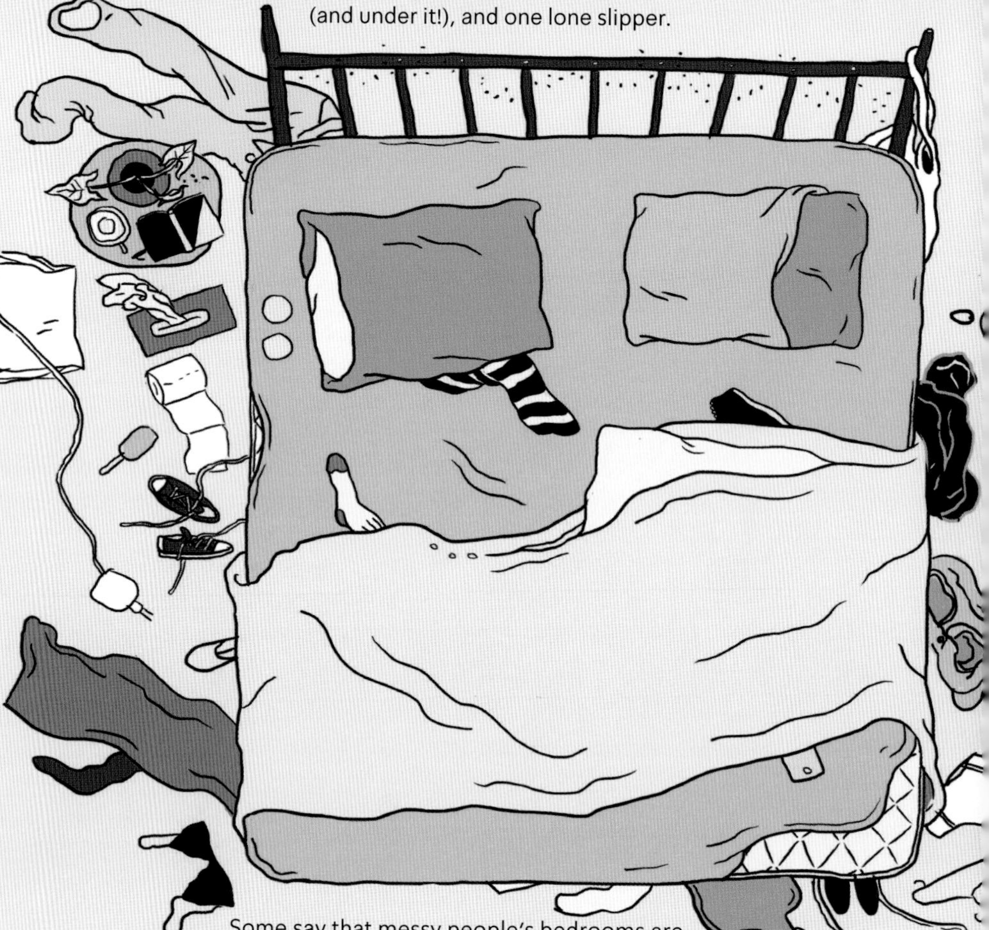

Some say that messy people's bedrooms are where the legends about monsters under the bed were born.

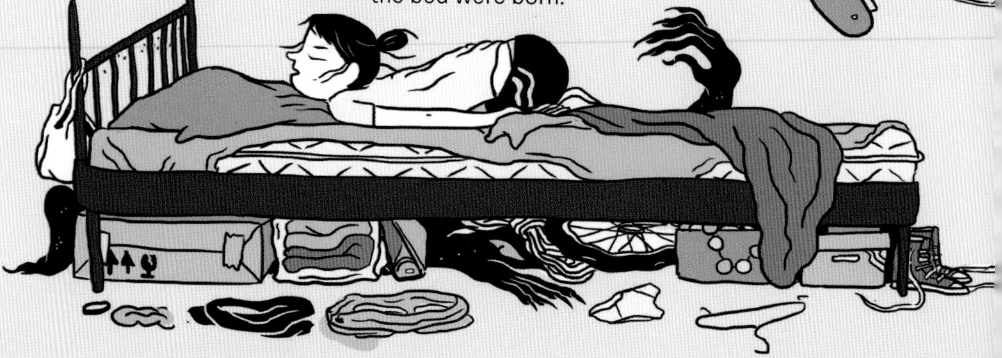

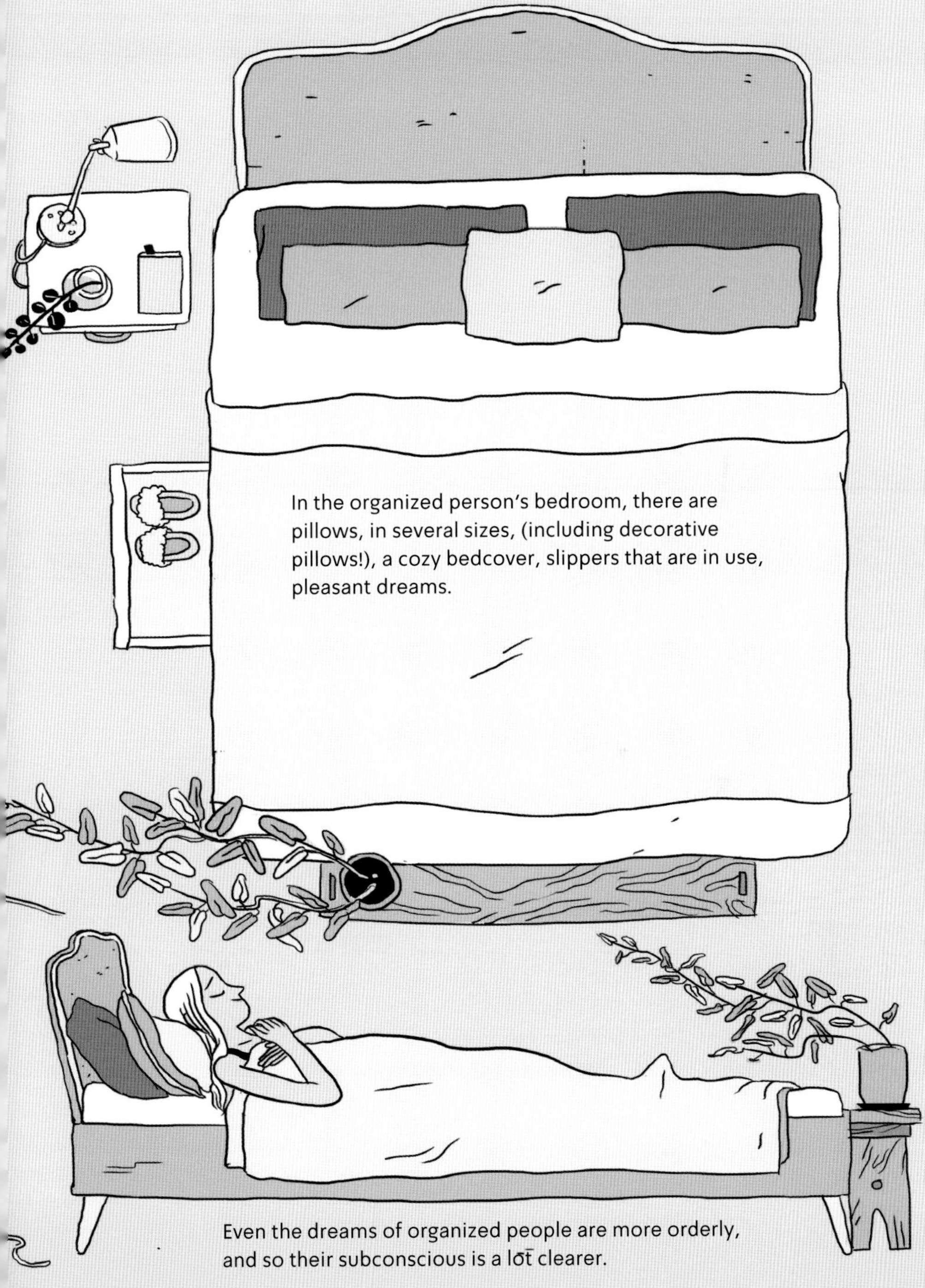
In the organized person's bedroom, there are pillows, in several sizes, (including decorative pillows!), a cozy bedcover, slippers that are in use, pleasant dreams.
Even the dreams of organized people are more orderly, and so their subconscious is a lot clearer.

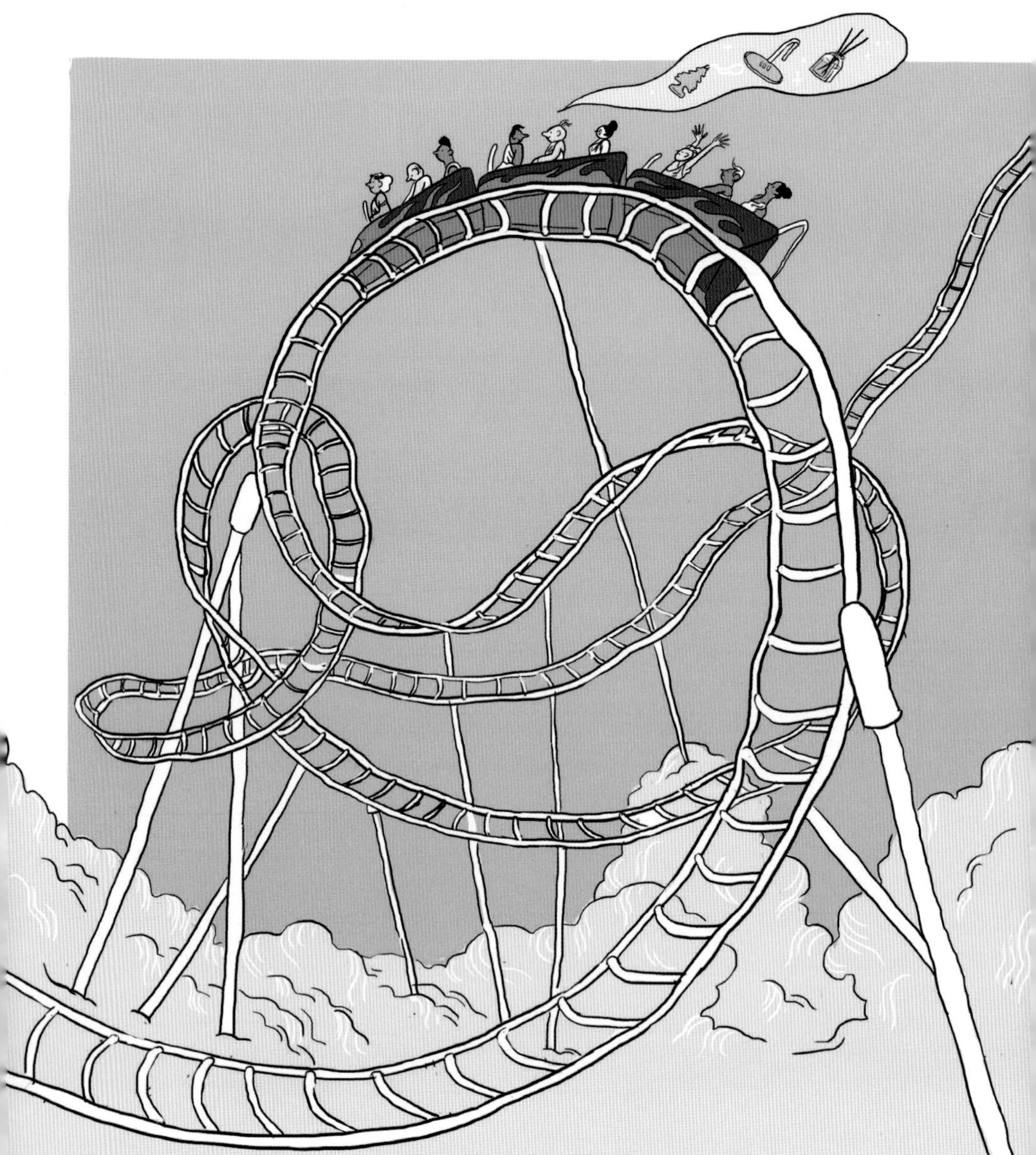

To sum up this chapter, all of our lives are filled with ups and downs. But in the segments relevant to this guide, the organized person will have new highs and lows of order and efficiency that will give them an opportunity to rise up again.

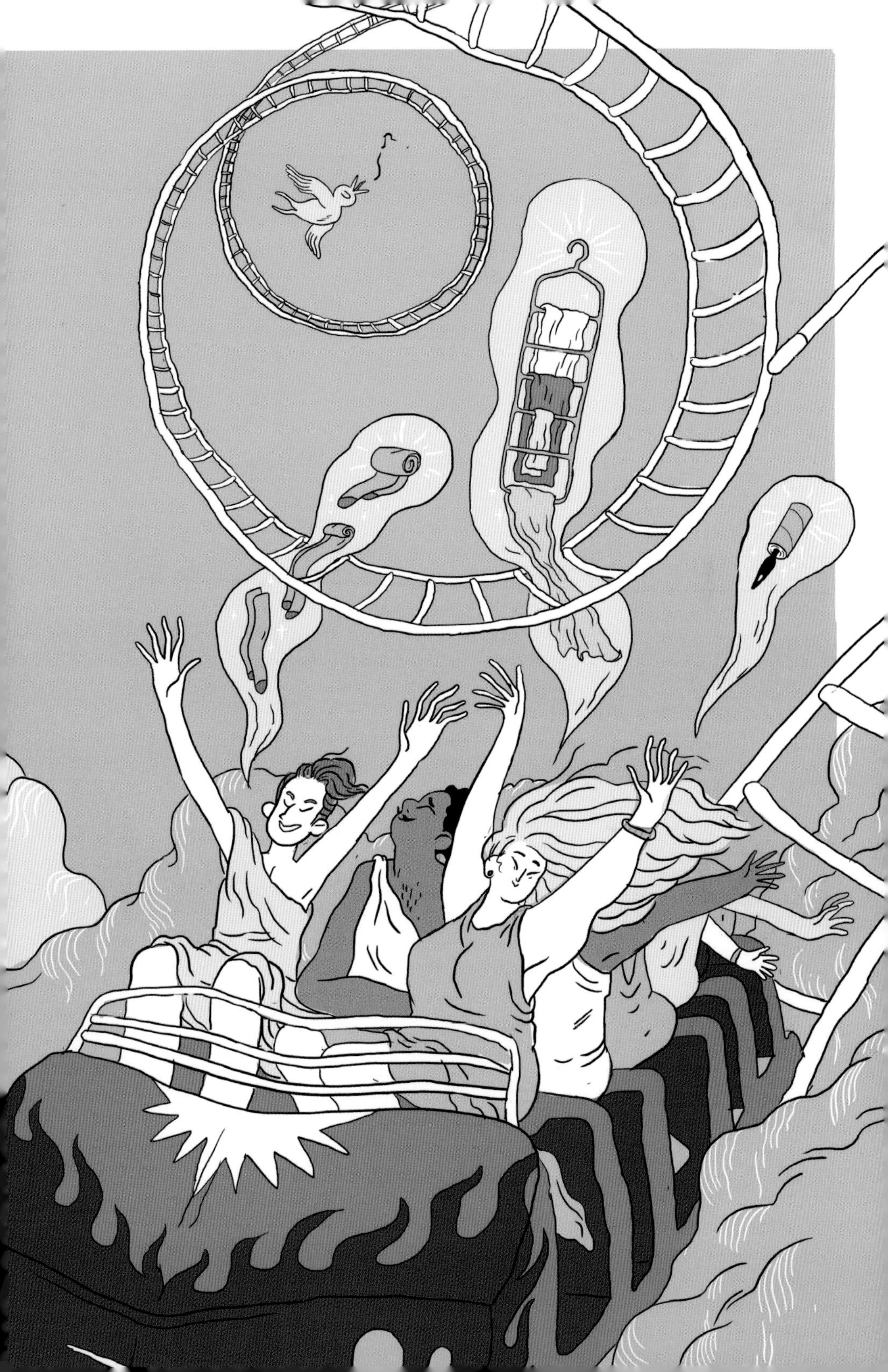

As for the messy person, they stumble along on a journey in search of a little tidiness and organization, with a short-lived dedication to reminders on Google Calendar and a desperate attempt to decipher why the word "wings" is written on Sunday, March 3rd. To make a long story short, I don't think that organized people are better. But there's no doubt that they make me feel worse about myself.

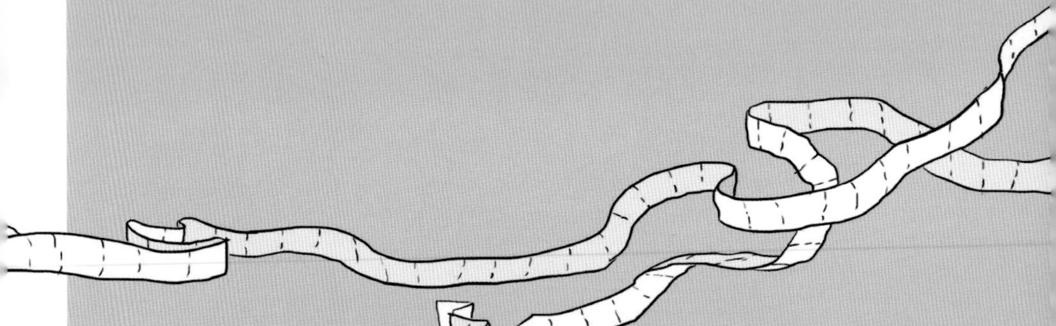

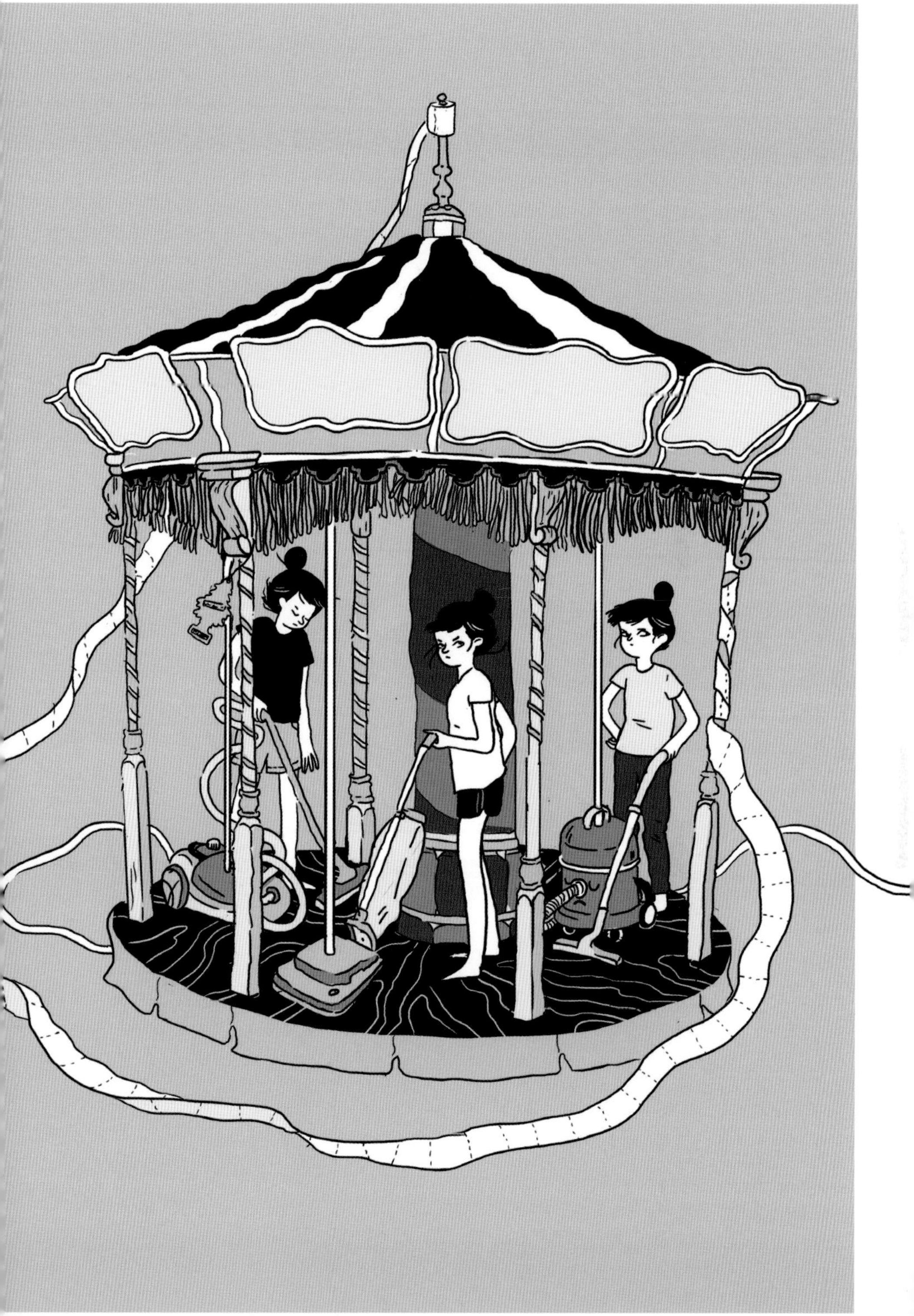

THE EVOLUTIONARY ADVANTAGES OF BEING MESSY

To summarize what we learned in the previous chapter, organized people are heroes who know deep down in their hearts exactly what to do, and messy people are the antithesis who might succeed against all odds (or not). It's pretty simple. Being messy is not a glamorous trait. It's not something that is beautifully woven into a story or goes well with legendary, larger-than-life figures. Strong fairy tale princesses are never grungy, and epic heroes always put their swords back where they belong. And even a proper villain needs structure and order - without that, they'd never be able to take over the world.

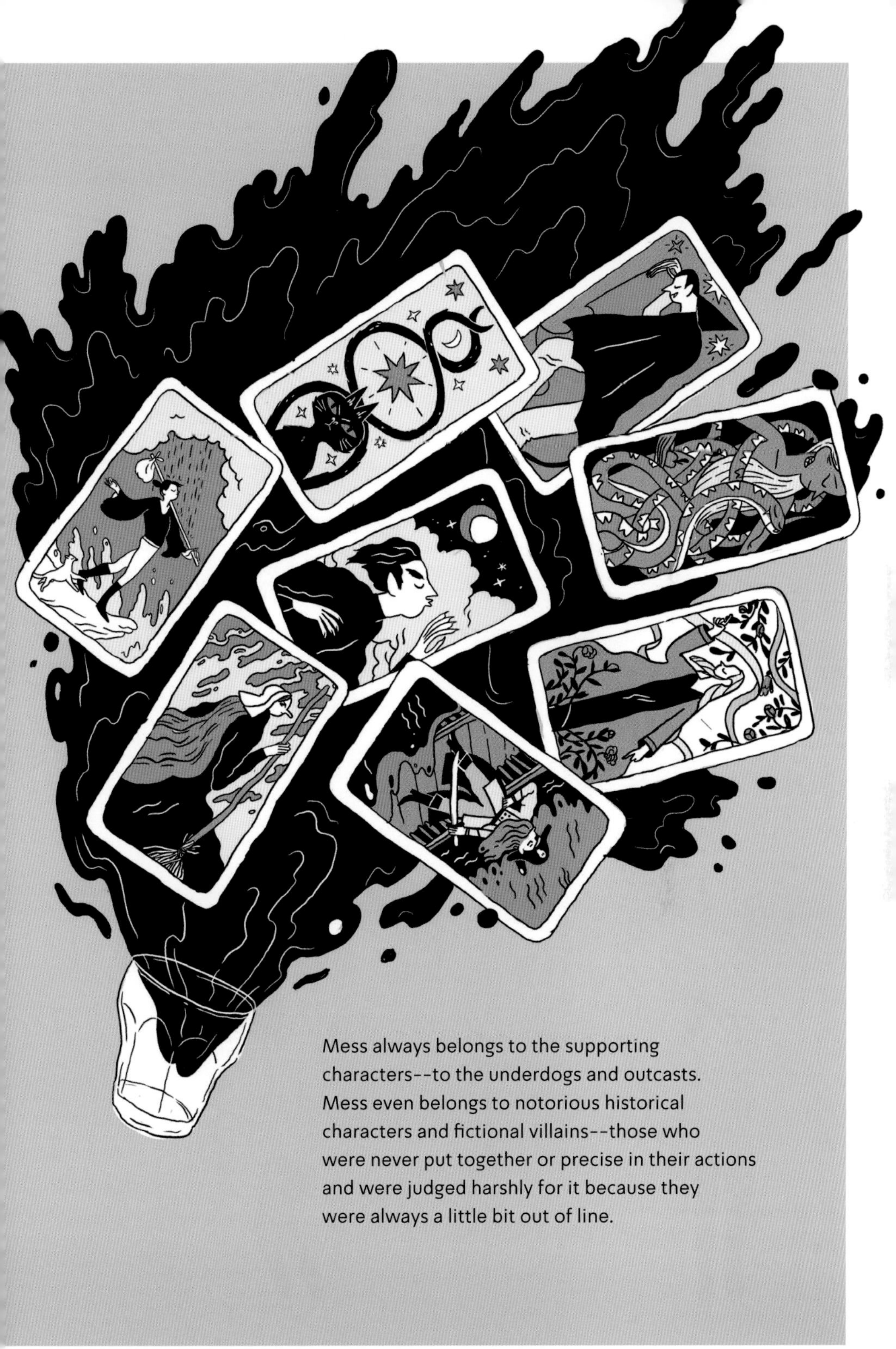

Mess always belongs to the supporting characters--to the underdogs and outcasts. Mess even belongs to notorious historical characters and fictional villains--those who were never put together or precise in their actions and were judged harshly for it because they were always a little bit out of line.

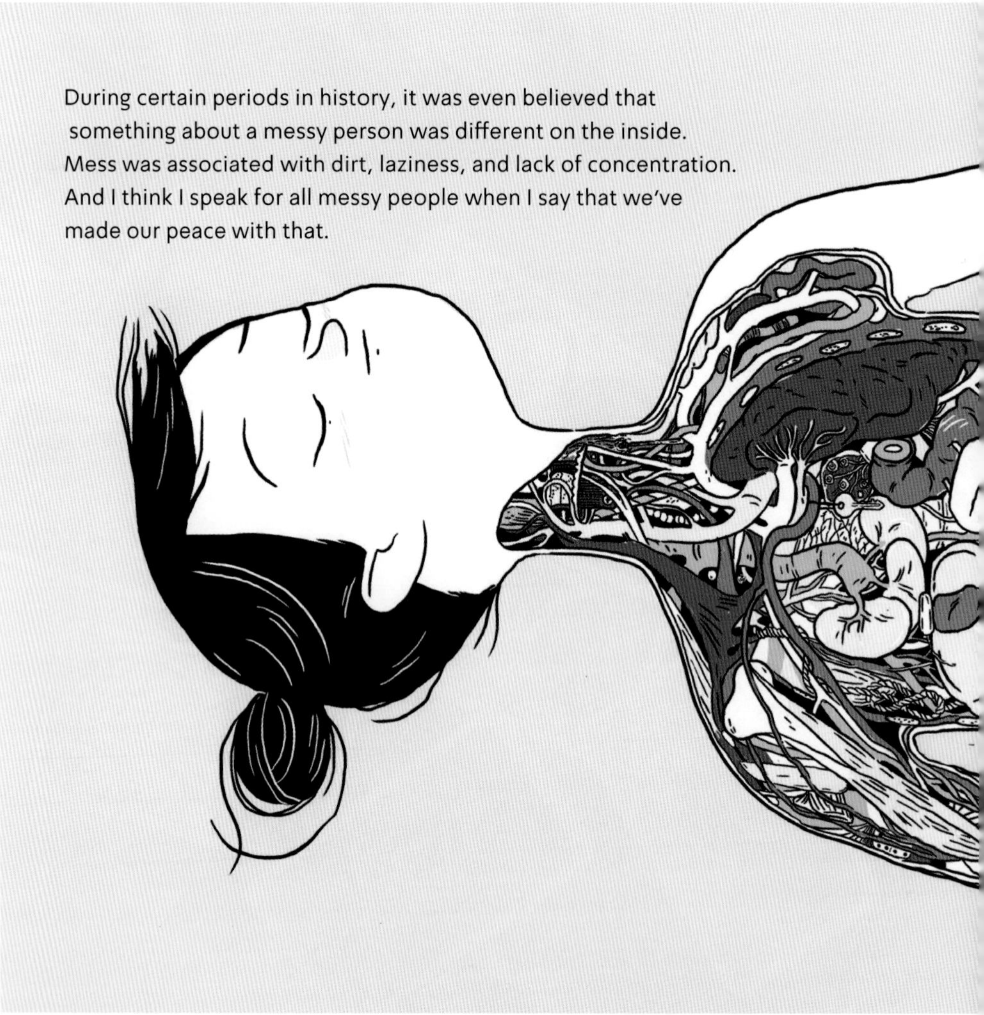
During certain periods in history, it was even believed that something about a messy person was different on the inside. Mess was associated with dirt, laziness, and lack of concentration. And I think I speak for all messy people when I say that we've made our peace with that.

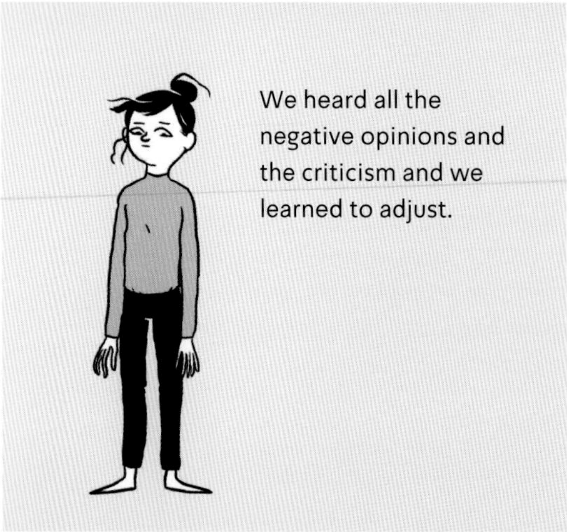
We heard all the negative opinions and the criticism and we learned to adjust.

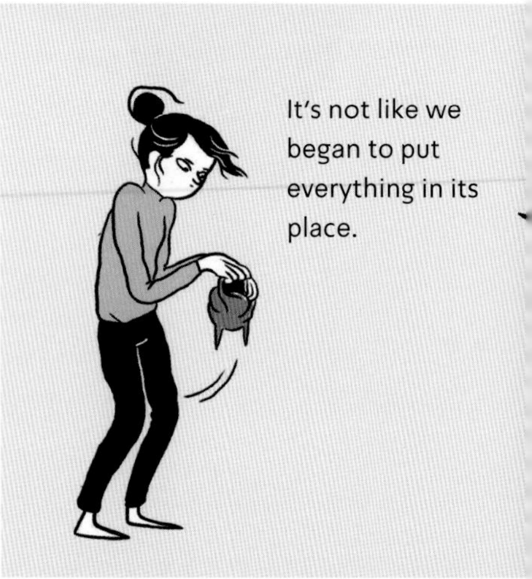
It's not like we began to put everything in its place.

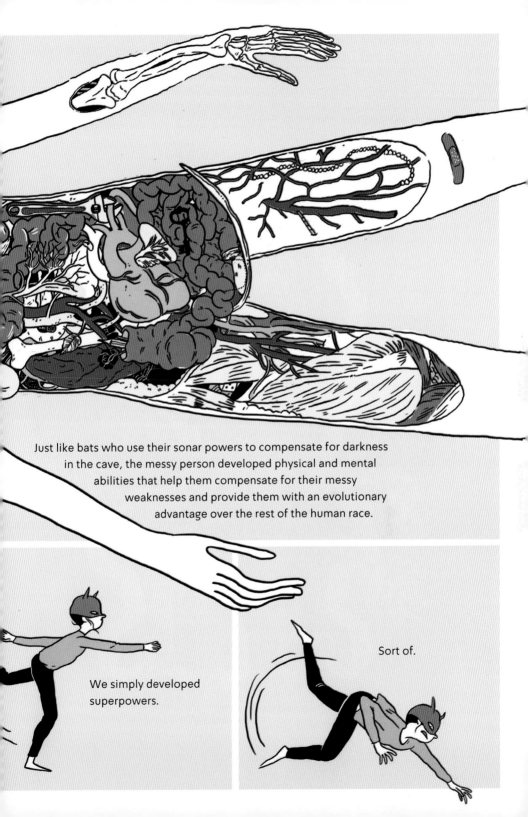

Just like bats who use their sonar powers to compensate for darkness in the cave, the messy person developed physical and mental abilities that help them compensate for their messy weaknesses and provide them with an evolutionary advantage over the rest of the human race.

We simply developed superpowers.

Sort of.

I. The Power of Improvisation

Since a messy person doesn't have what they need more than fifty percent of the time because they didn't think about it beforehand--or lost whatever they needed--the improvisational and creative skills of messy people are twice as great as that of the average person. The power of improvisation helps messy people extricate themselves from the unfortunate situations that they tend to fall into.

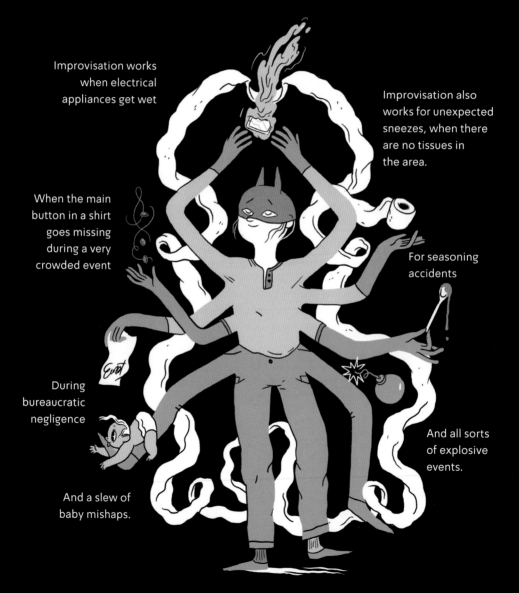

Improvisation works when electrical appliances get wet

Improvisation also works for unexpected sneezes, when there are no tissues in the area.

When the main button in a shirt goes missing during a very crowded event

For seasoning accidents

During bureaucratic negligence

And all sorts of explosive events.

And a slew of baby mishaps.

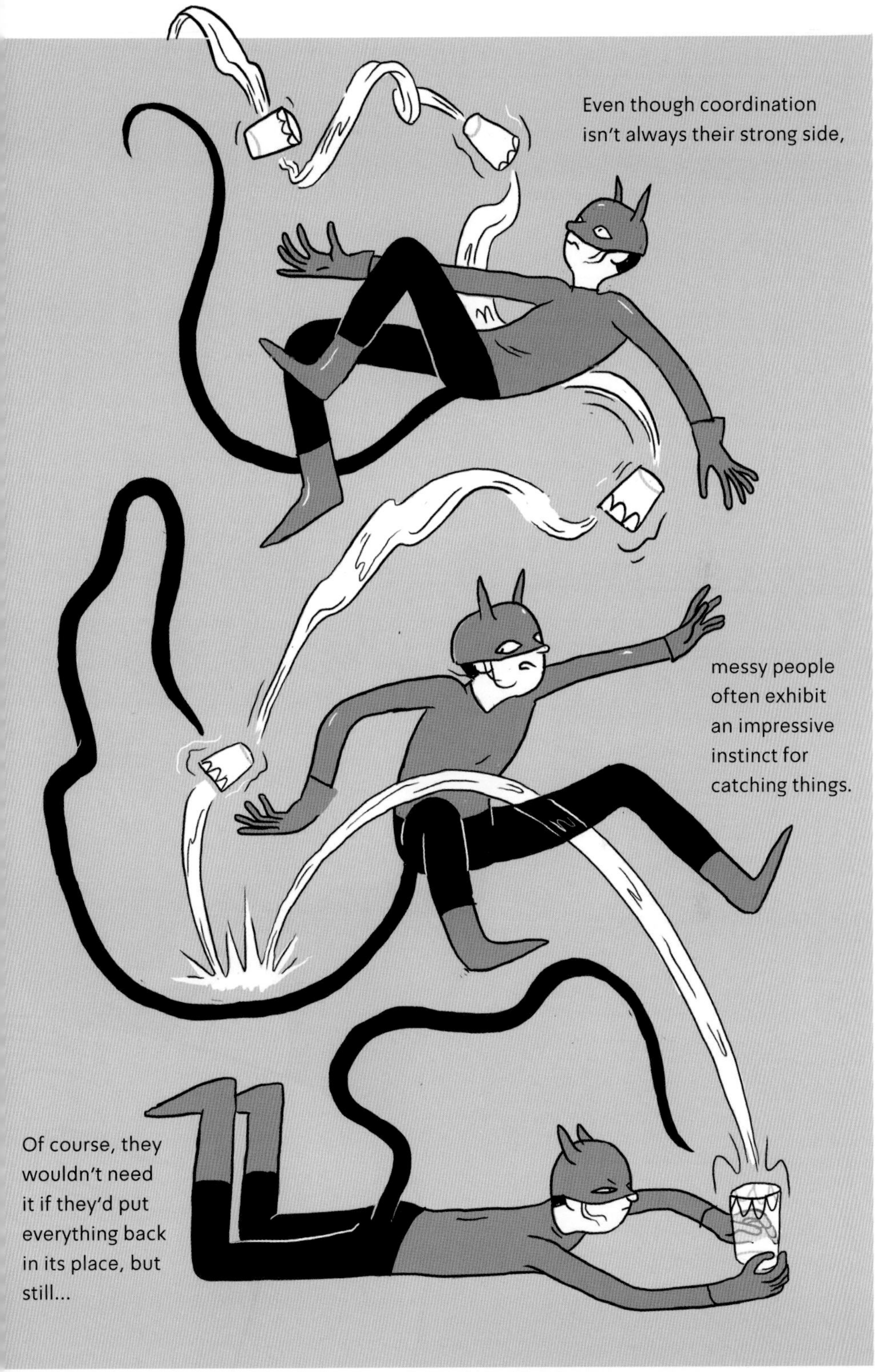
Even though coordination
isn't always their strong side,
messy people
often exhibit
an impressive
instinct for
catching things.
Of course, they
wouldn't need
it if they'd put
everything back
in its place, but
still...

2. The Power to Mentally Go Back in Time

The messy person doesn't have the cognitive ability to put an object back in its place (as I noted before). To make up for this, they've developed the ability to trace and reconstruct the chain of events that have happened since they saw it last. And, no, it's not the same as "just remember where you saw it last" (which is a sentence that never helped anyone).

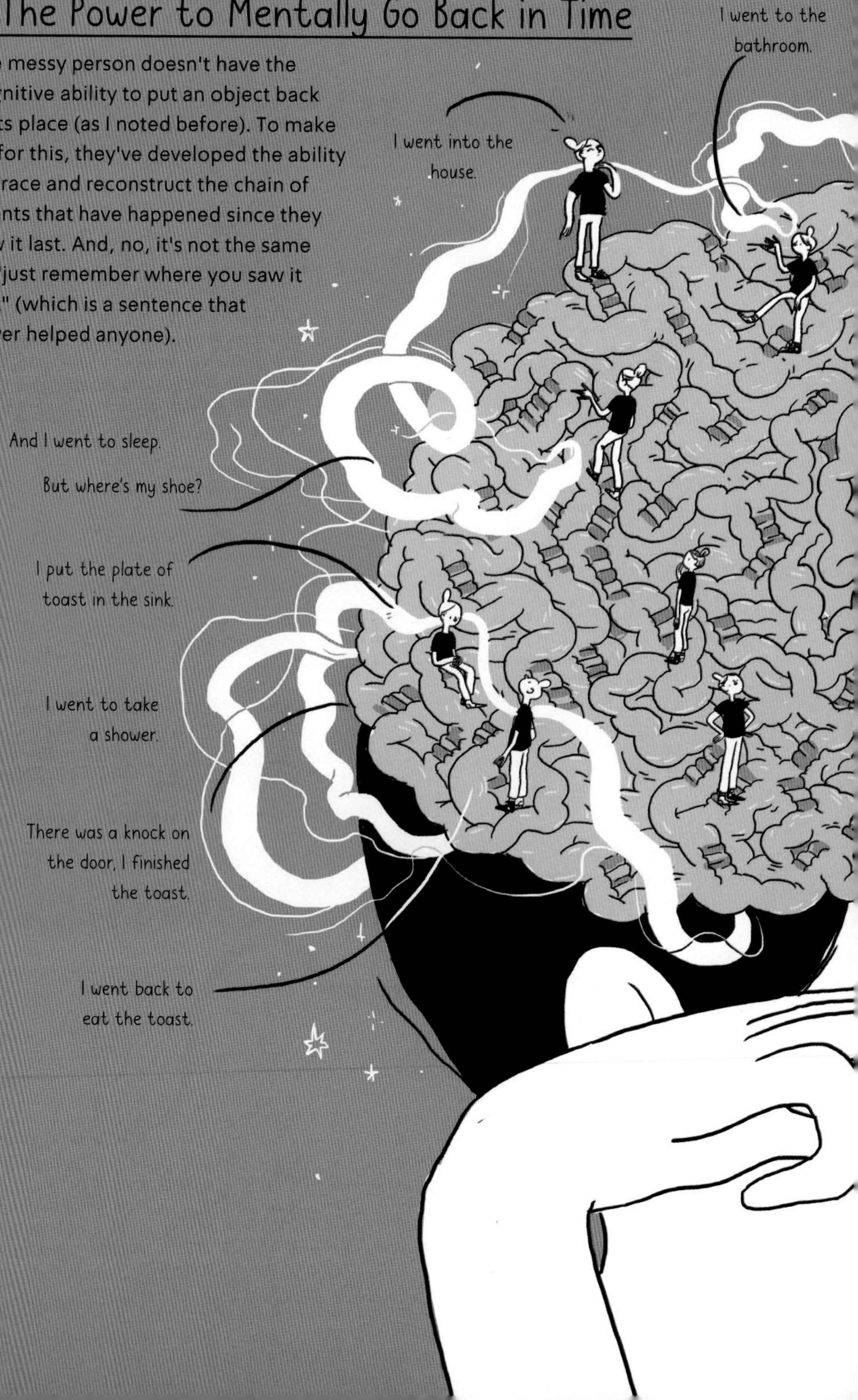
I went to the bathroom.
I went into the house.
And I went to sleep.
But where's my shoe?
I put the plate of toast in the sink.
I went to take a shower.
There was a knock on the door, I finished the toast.
I went back to eat the toast.

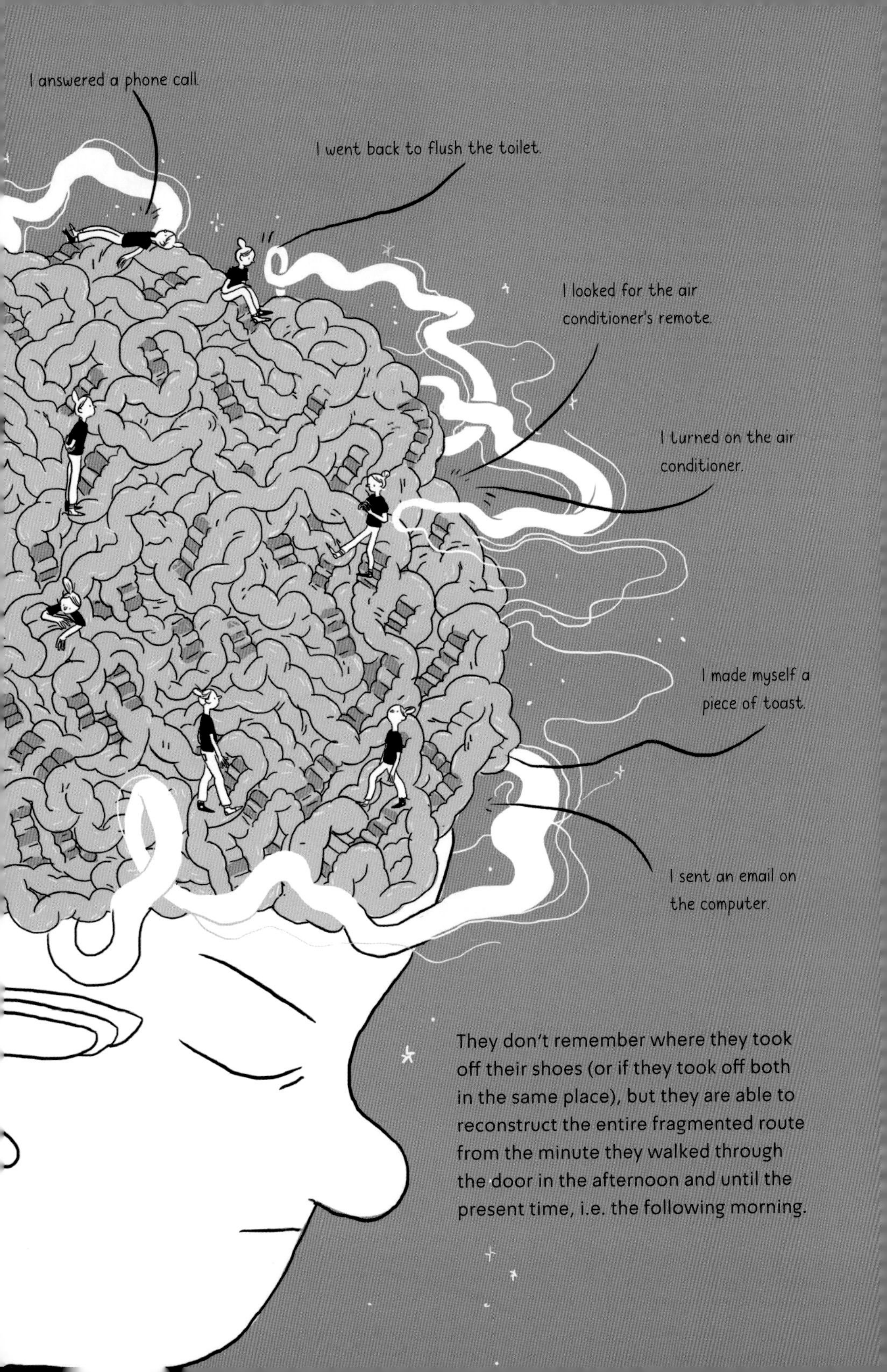
I answered a phone call.
I went back to flush the toilet.
I looked for the air conditioner's remote.
I turned on the air conditioner.
I made myself a piece of toast.
I sent an email on the computer.

They don't remember where they took off their shoes (or if they took off both in the same place), but they are able to reconstruct the entire fragmented route from the minute they walked through the door in the afternoon and until the present time, i.e. the following morning.

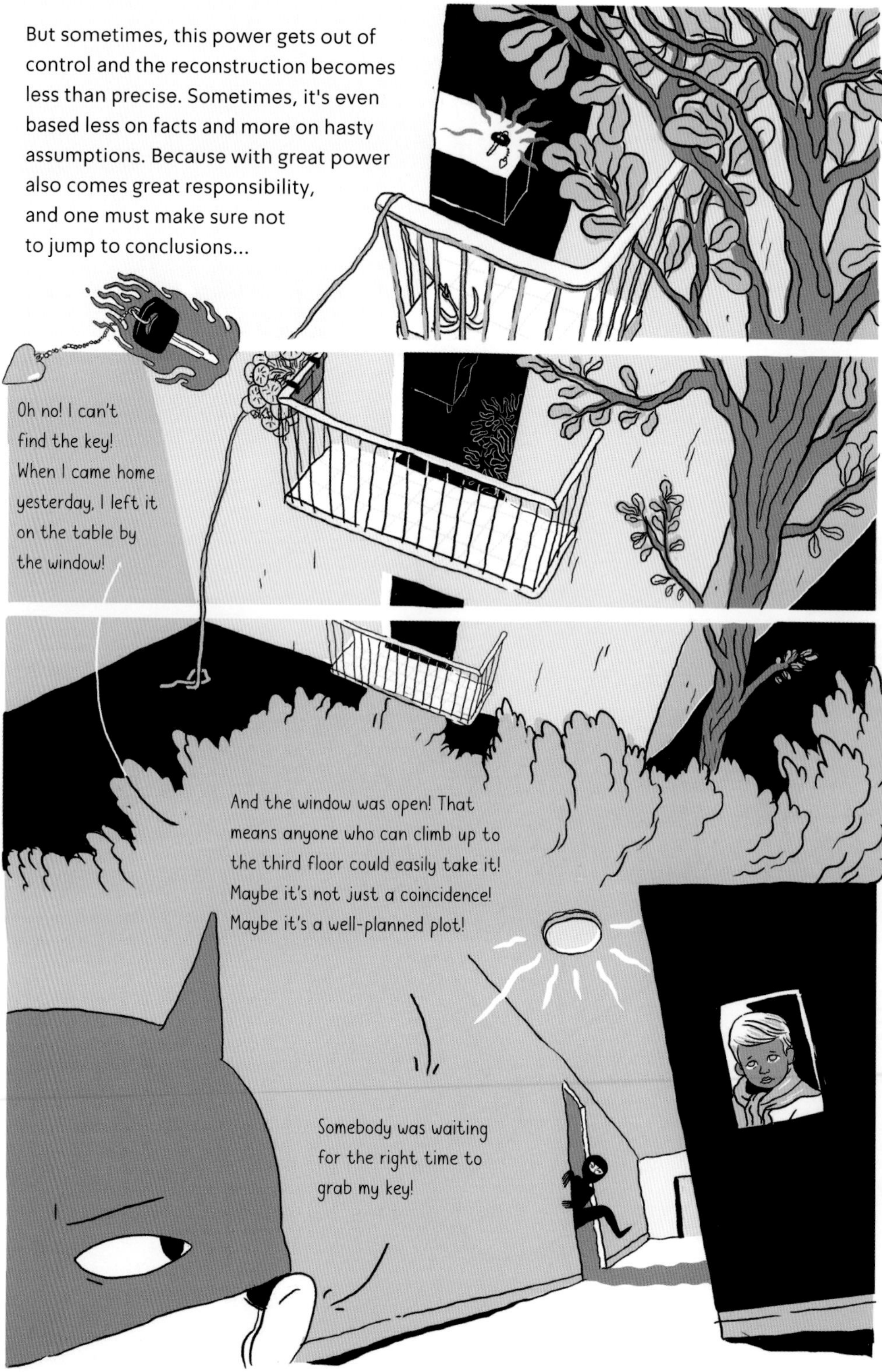

But sometimes, this power gets out of control and the reconstruction becomes less than precise. Sometimes, it's even based less on facts and more on hasty assumptions. Because with great power also comes great responsibility, and one must make sure not to jump to conclusions...
Oh no! I can't find the key! When I came home yesterday, I left it on the table by the window!
And the window was open! That means anyone who can climb up to the third floor could easily take it! Maybe it's not just a coincidence! Maybe it's a well-planned plot!
Somebody was waiting for the right time to grab my key!

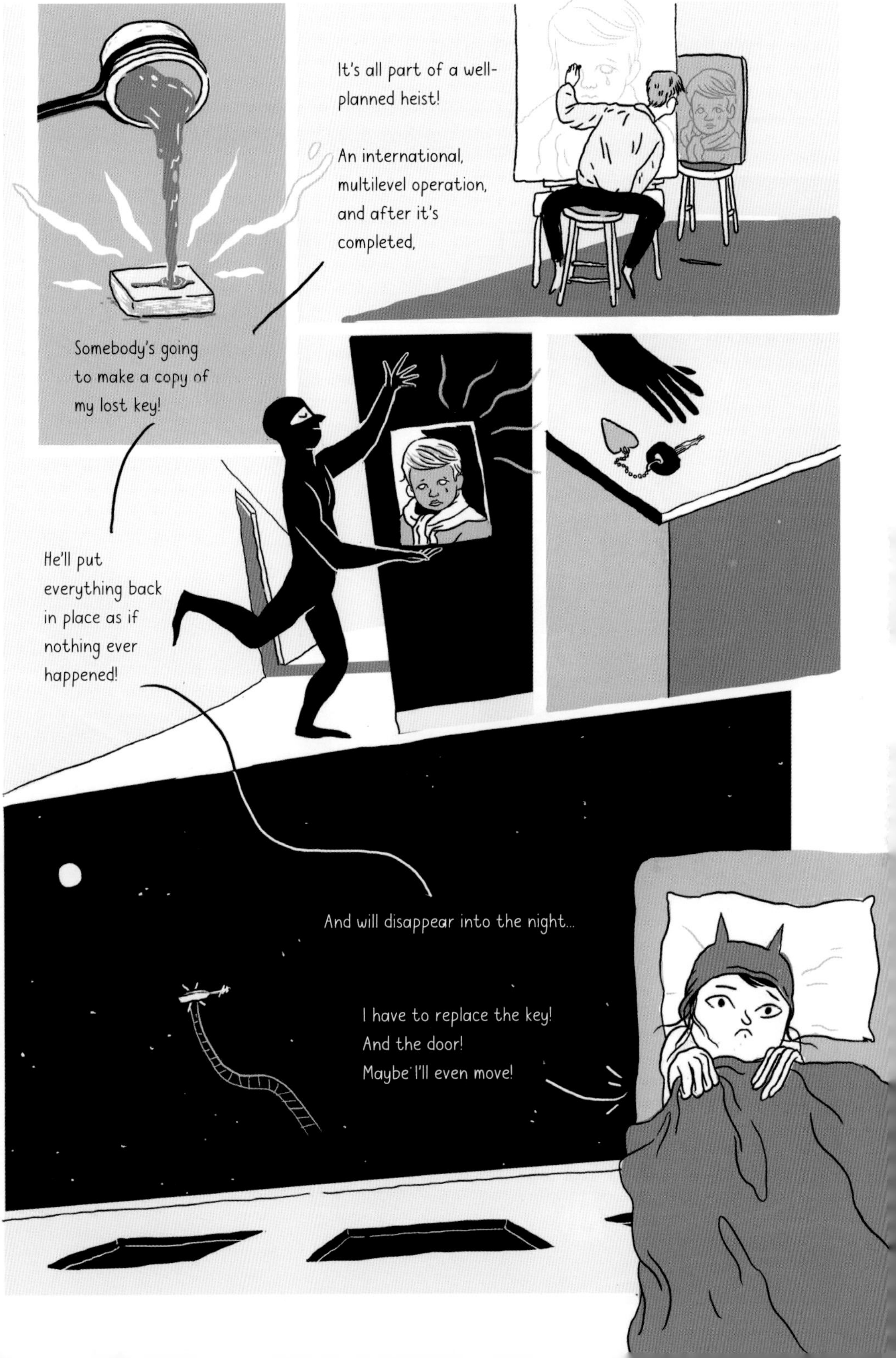
It's all part of a well-planned heist!
An international, multilevel operation, and after it's completed,
Somebody's going to make a copy of my lost key!
He'll put everything back in place as if nothing ever happened!
And will disappear into the night...
I have to replace the key!
And the door!
Maybe I'll even move!

3. The Power to Mentally Going Back in Space

A messy person also has a much more developed visual memory. (This, unfortunately, doesn't work on the gnawing doubt that they locked the door when they left.)

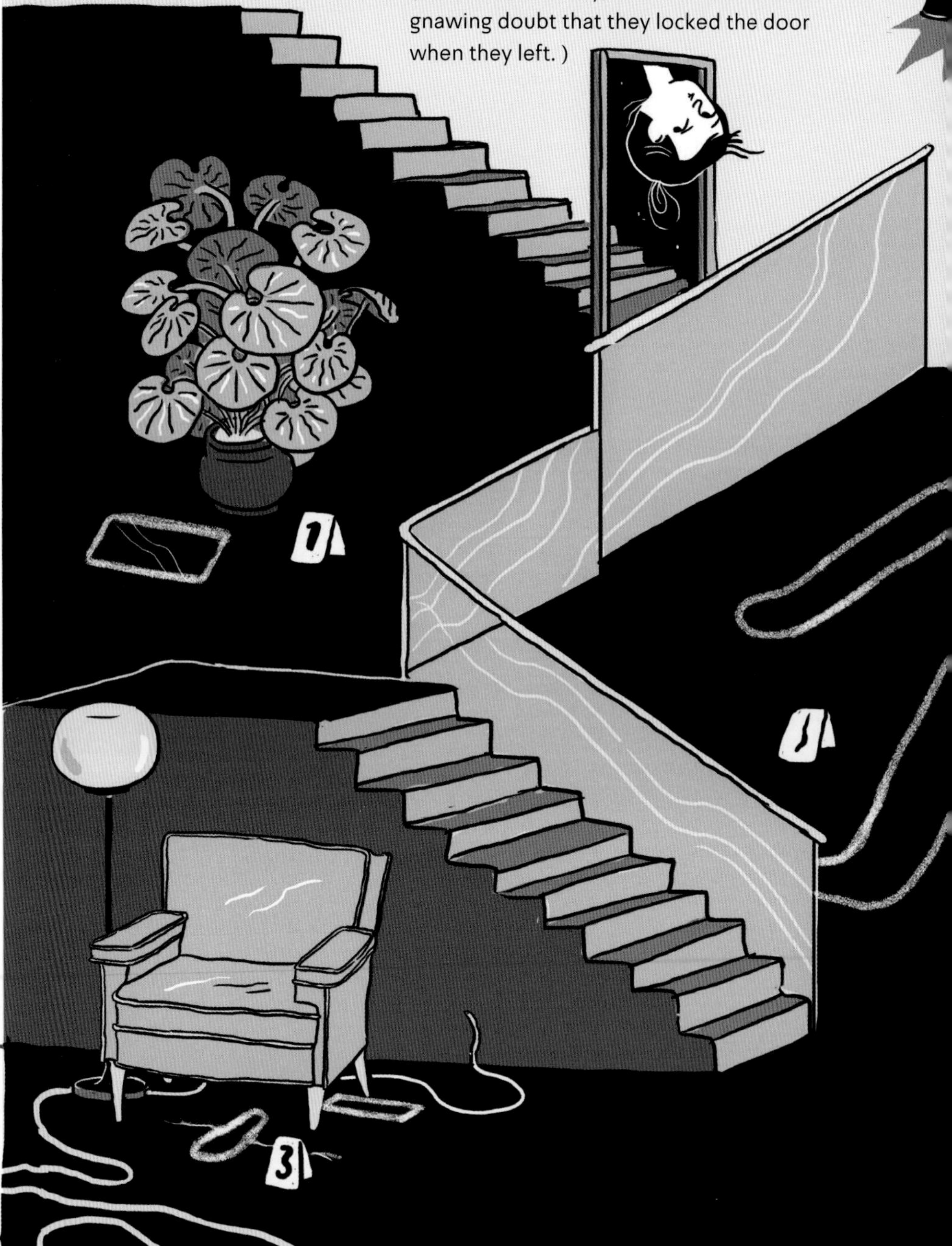

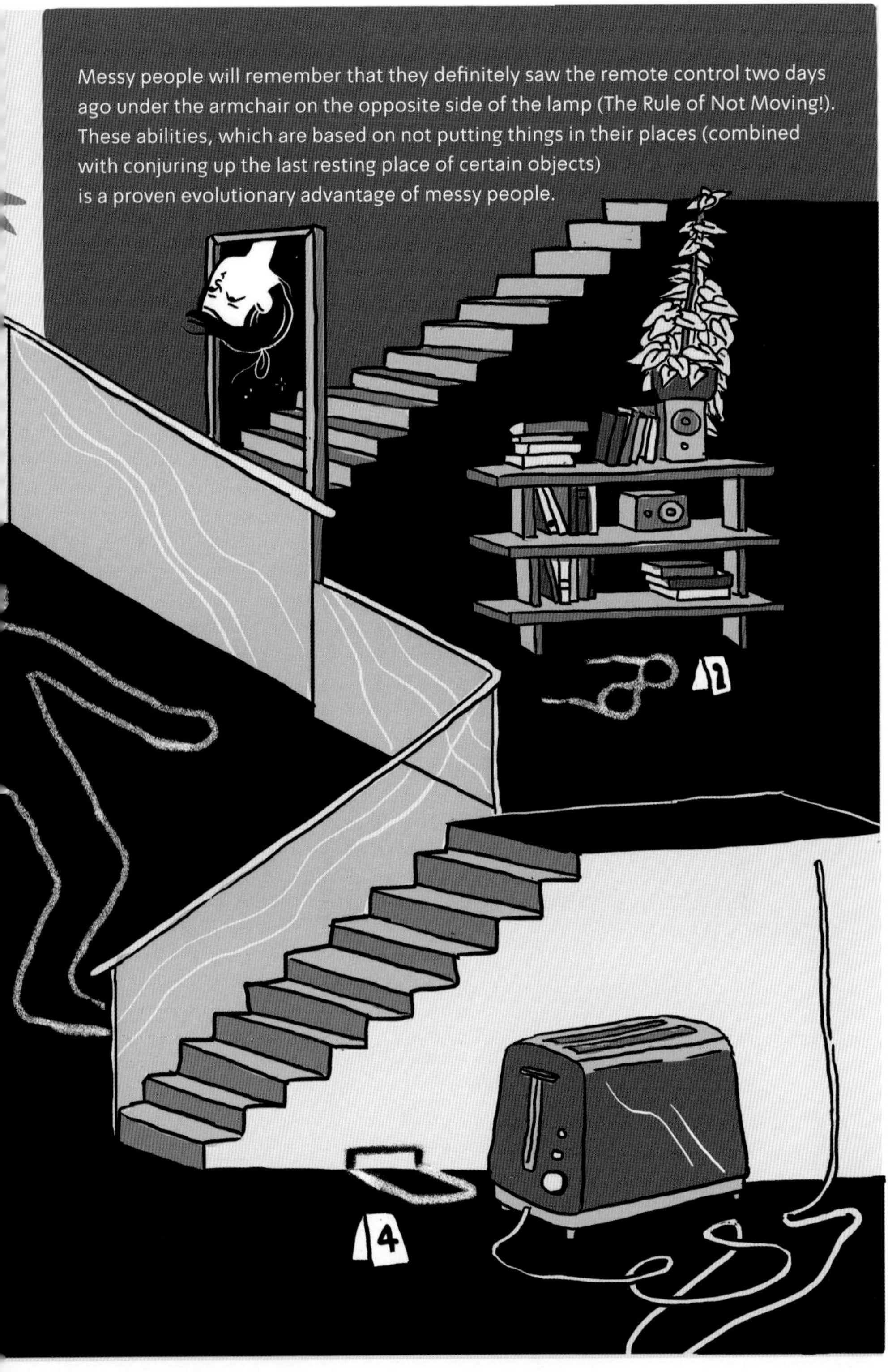
Messy people will remember that they definitely saw the remote control two days ago under the armchair on the opposite side of the lamp (The Rule of Not Moving!). These abilities, which are based on not putting things in their places (combined with conjuring up the last resting place of certain objects) is a proven evolutionary advantage of messy people.
4

This Superpower that also Works in the Dark!

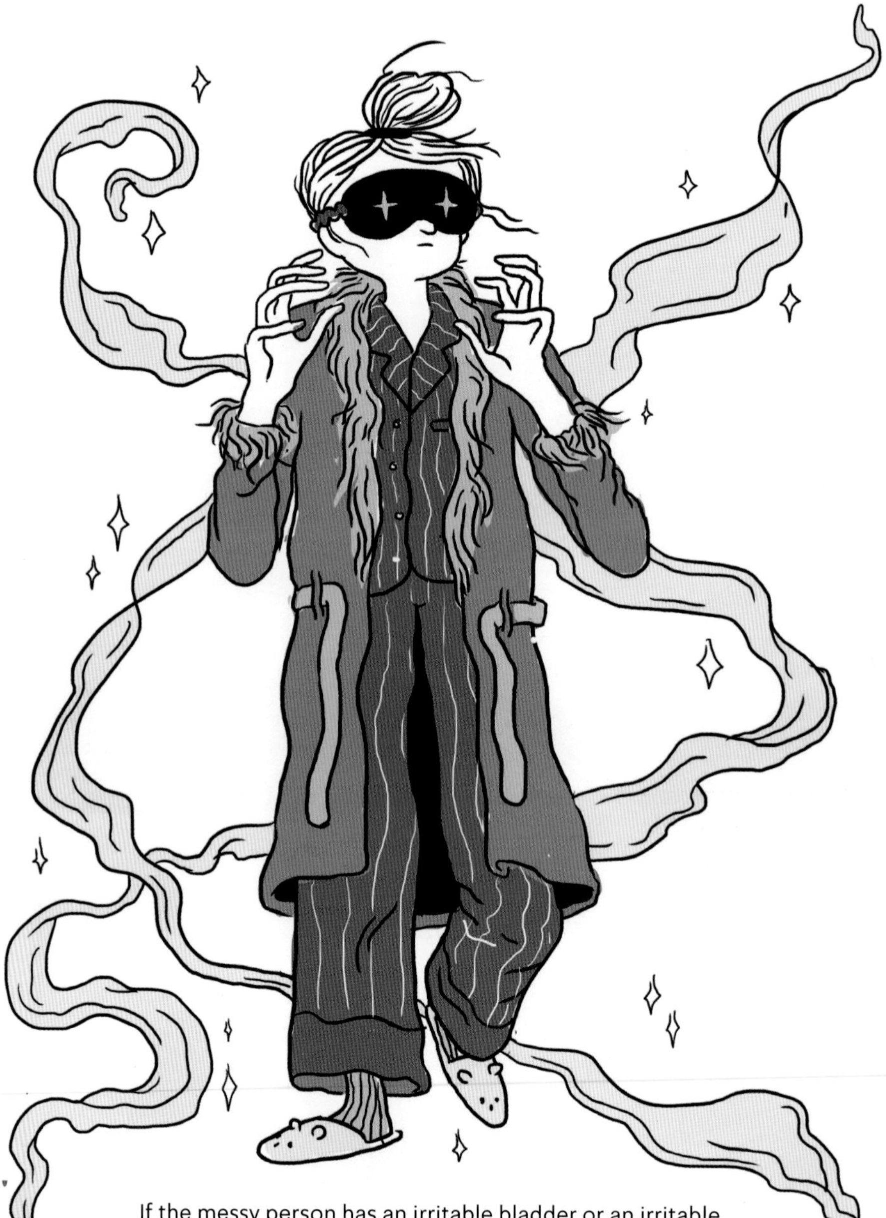

If the messy person has an irritable bladder or an irritable baby, their home could pose a real danger during the night. The phenomenal memory of the way the mess is spread throughout the house helps the messy person find their way in the dark to the bathroom or to the baby, accordingly.

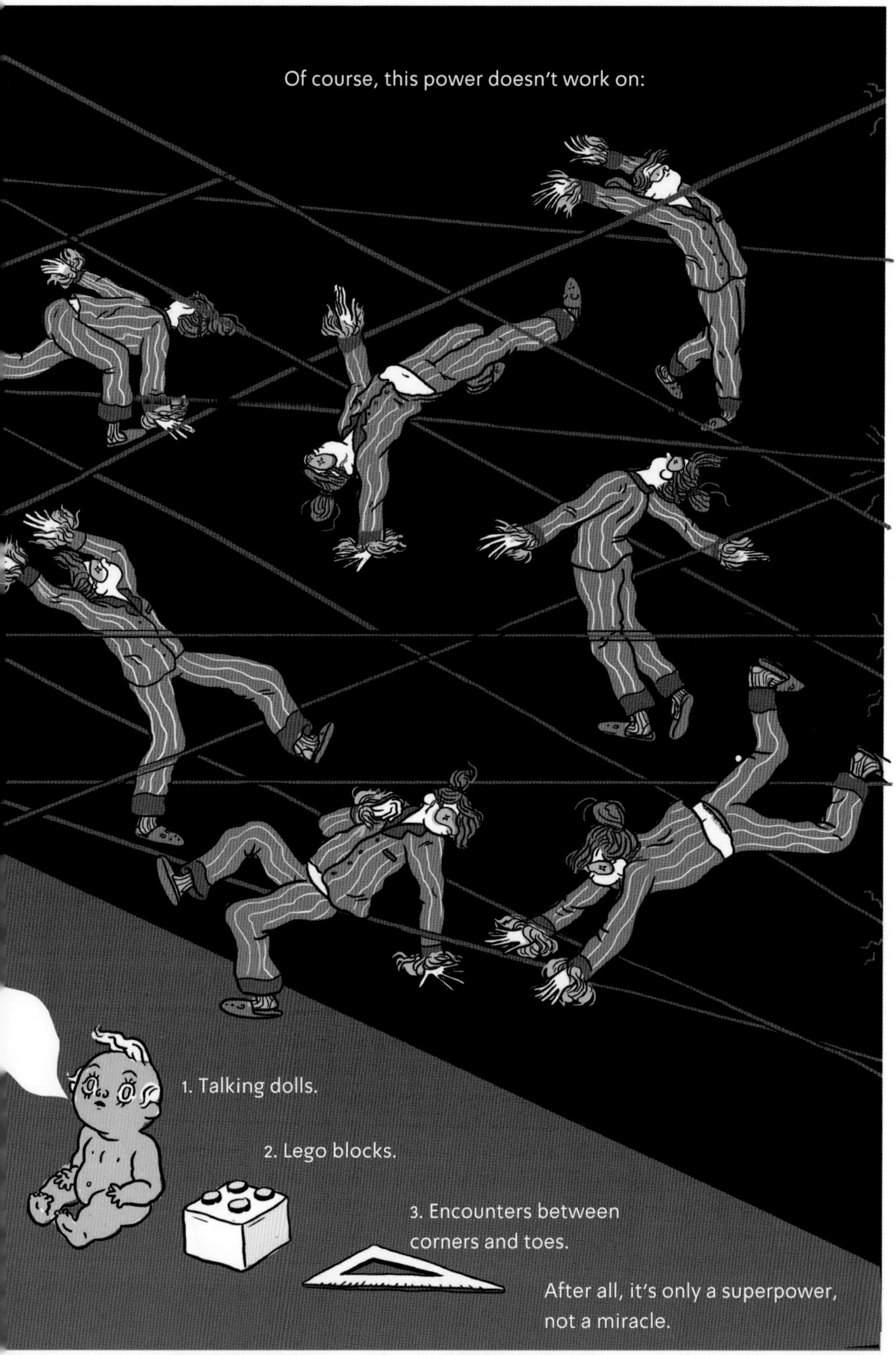
Of course, this power doesn't work on:
1. Talking dolls.
2. Lego blocks.
3. Encounters between corners and toes.
After all, it's only a superpower, not a miracle.

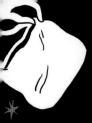

4. The Power of Touch & Tell

This is a sense that enables you to pull things out of a handbag while making the least amount of eye contact with the contents of the bag itself.

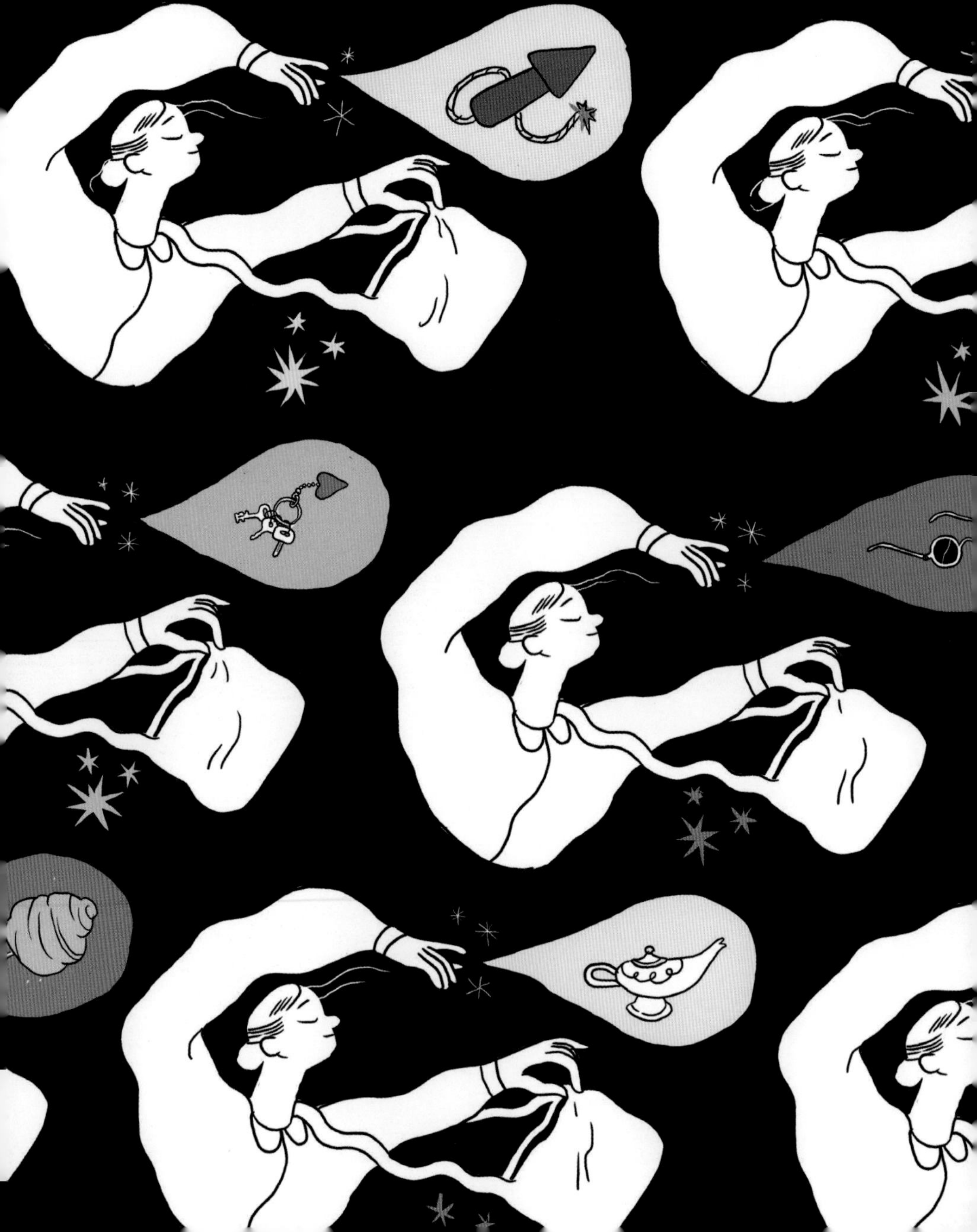

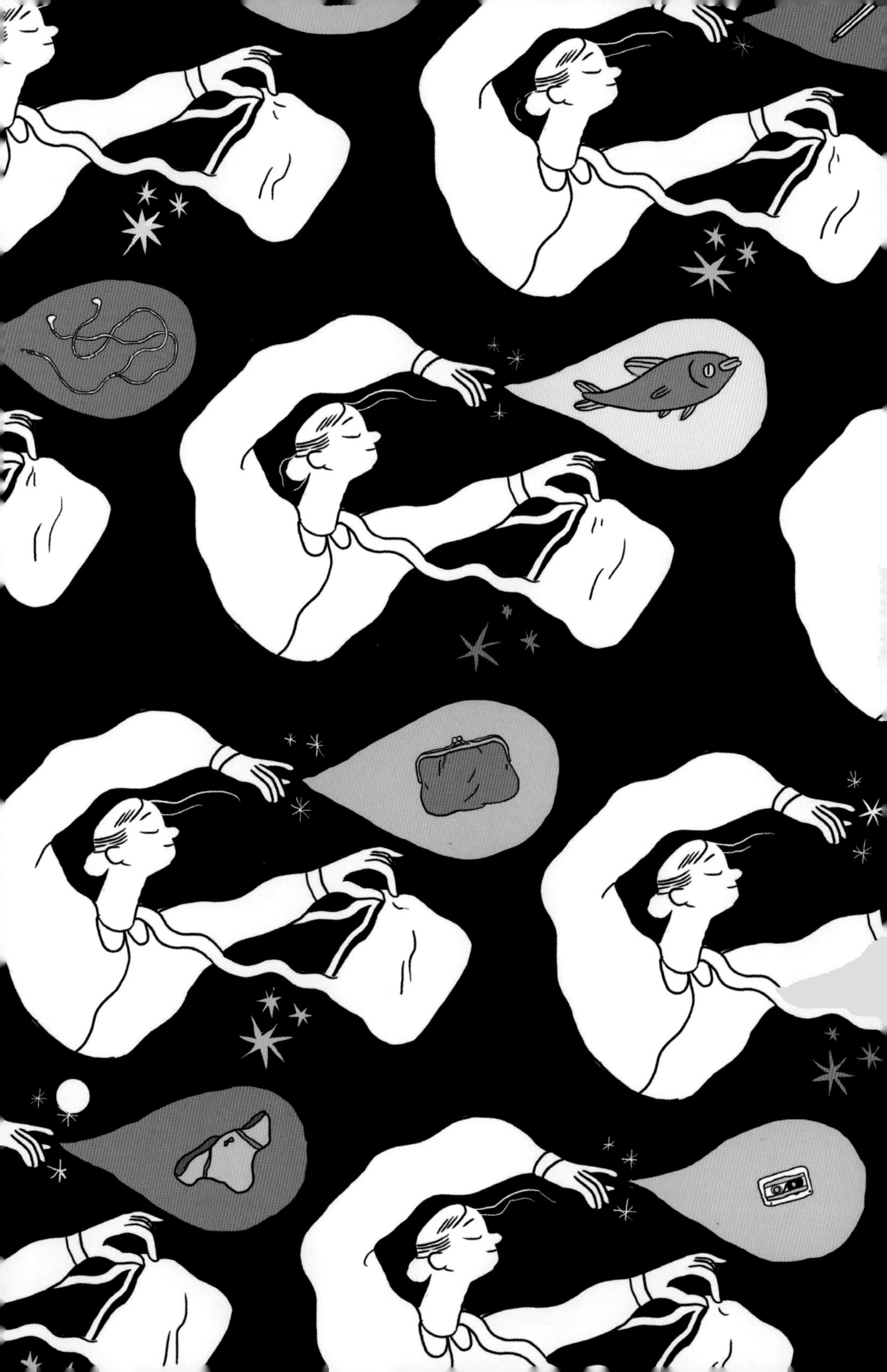

5. The Power of Doesn't-Faze-Me

When something gets lost.
Losing their wallet can ruin an organized person's day. When they can't find the key to the house, the organized person gets really shaken up. They need to collect themselves and summon all their organizational abilities to extract themselves from the unpleasant situation.

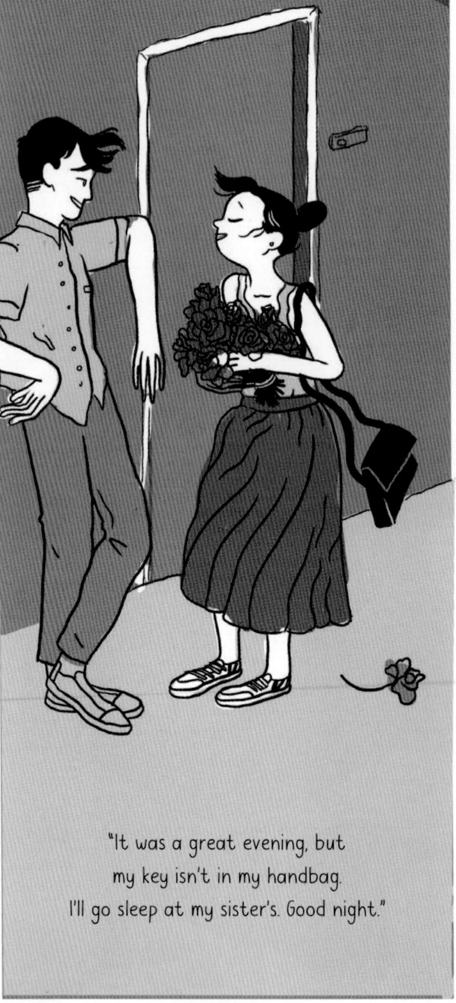
"It was a great evening, but my key isn't in my handbag. I'll go sleep at my sister's. Good night."

For the messy ones, that's just a regular morning. The adult messy people really aren't fazed by it, because it's happened to them millions of times. And also, there's nothing important in the wallet because they never managed to accumulate more than two punch holes on their free coffee membership card.

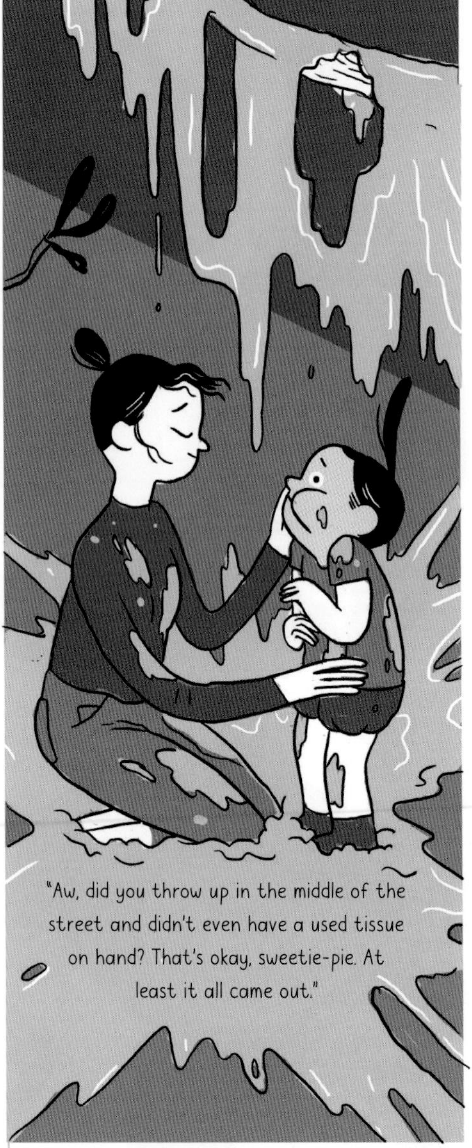
"Aw, did you throw up in the middle of the street and didn't even have a used tissue on hand? That's okay, sweetie-pie. At least it all came out."

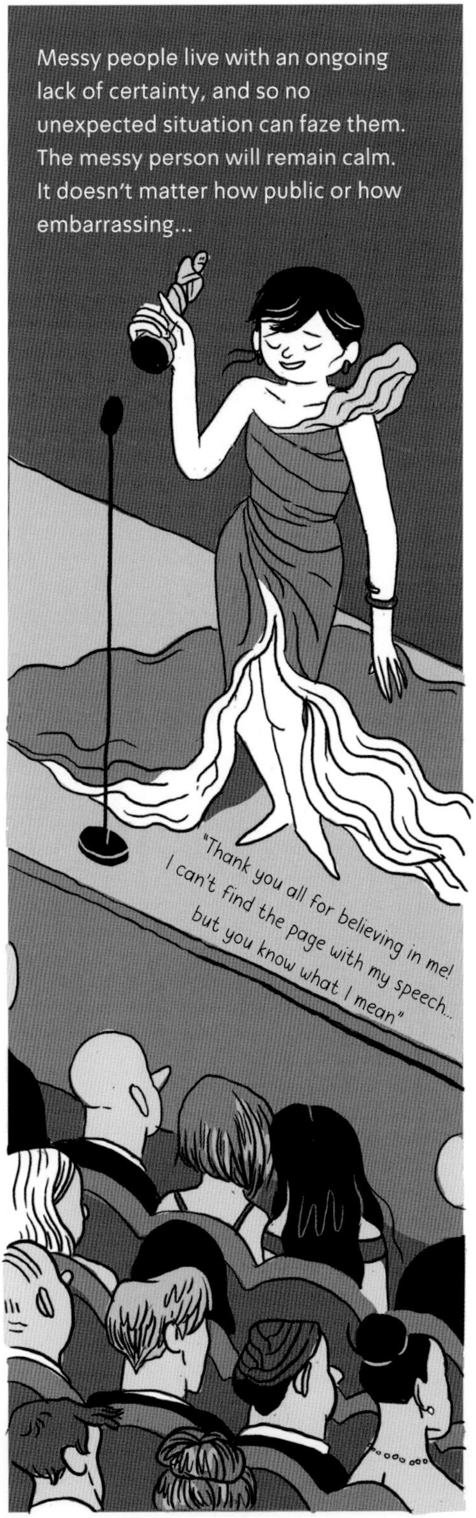
Messy people live with an ongoing lack of certainty, and so no unexpected situation can faze them. The messy person will remain calm. It doesn't matter how public or how embarrassing...
"Thank you all for believing in me! I can't find the page with my speech... but you know what I mean"

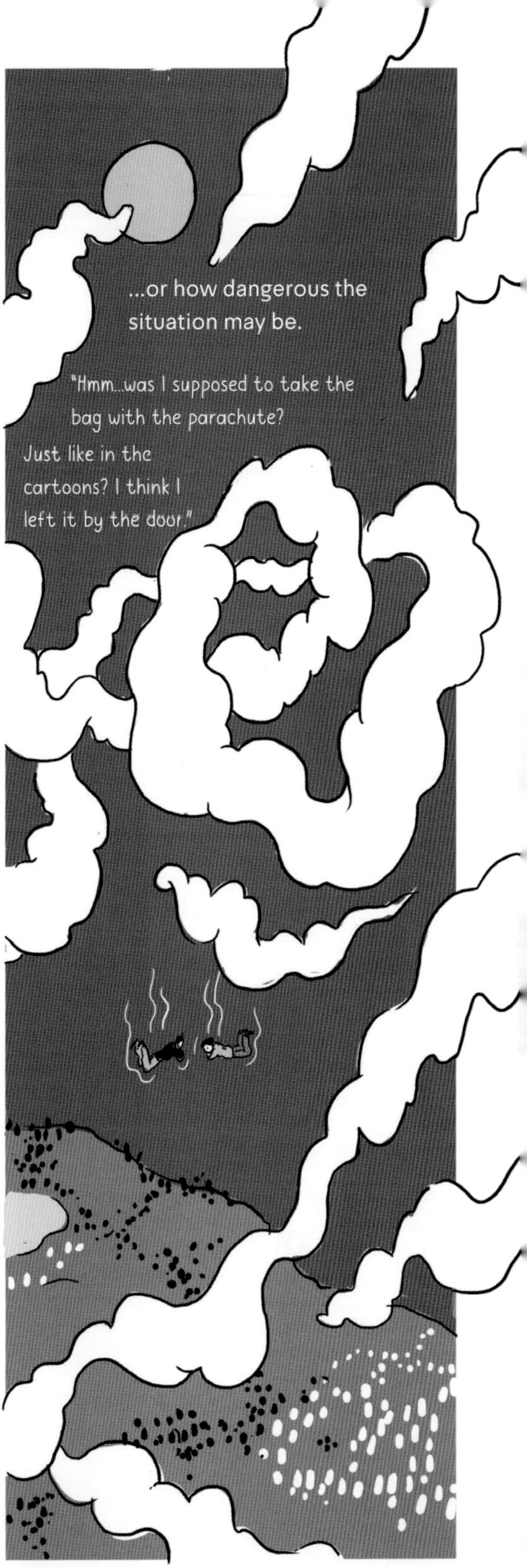
...or how dangerous the situation may be.
"Hmm...was I supposed to take the bag with the parachute? Just like in the cartoons? I think I left it by the door."

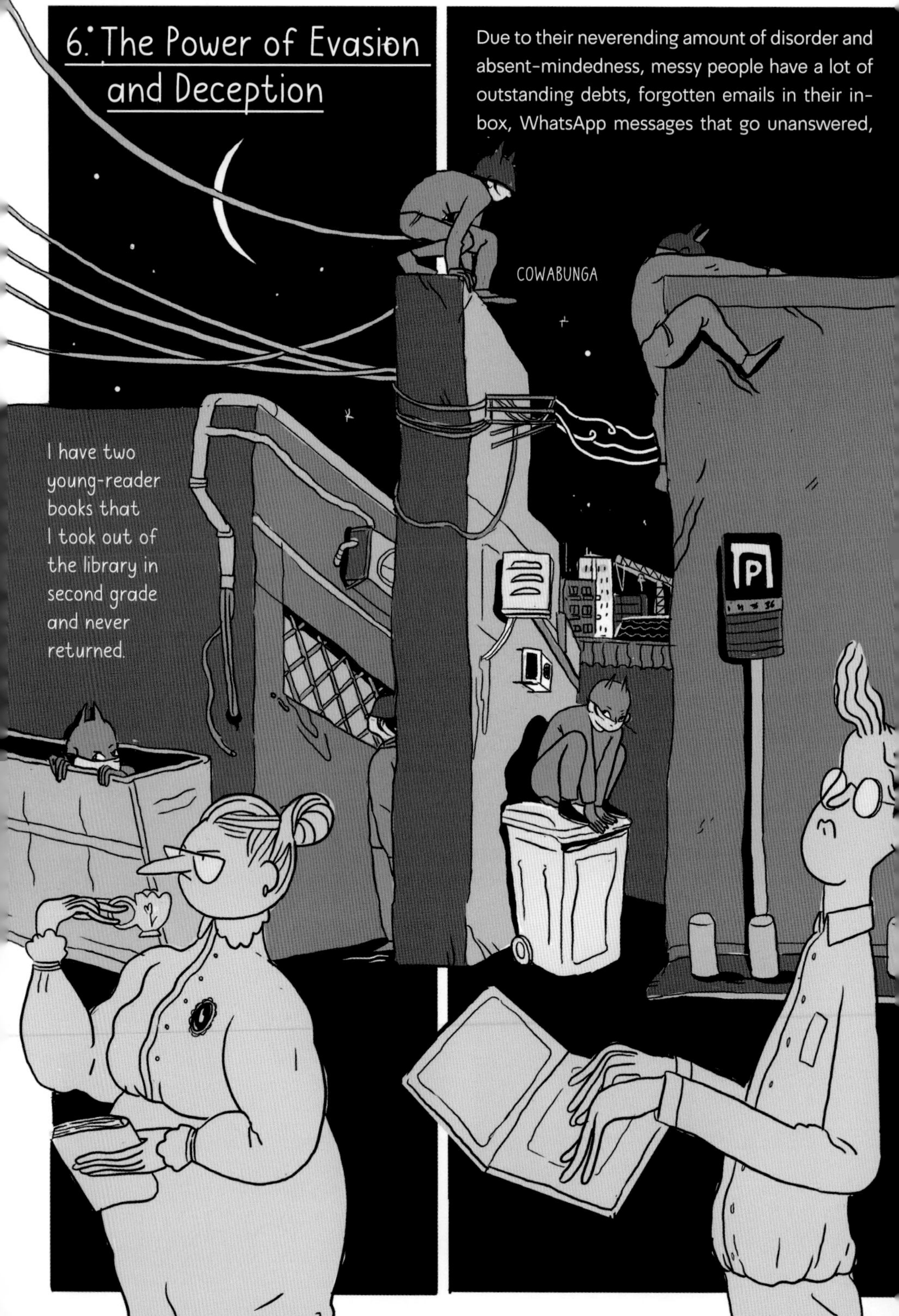
6. The Power of Evasion and Deception
Due to their neverending amount of disorder and absent-mindedness, messy people have a lot of outstanding debts, forgotten emails in their in-box, WhatsApp messages that go unanswered,
COWABUNGA
I have two young-reader books that I took out of the library in second grade and never returned.
P

and library books/company uniforms/ and the neighbor's grater that they forget to return.

. .

There's no doubt that it's healthy to deal with your demons, but sometimes, it's easier to evade them (or to make very weak excuses).

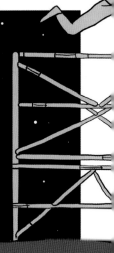

I forgot to give her jeans back (I mean, I didn't really forget – they shrunk in the wash and now, I feel bad).

I forgot to bring a change of pants to nursery school for him

I didn't answer his email (or his reminder email that asked if I received the first email).

I didn't send him the invoices for January-February

I know that these superpowers aren't such a big deal (telekinesis is way better) and don't make it worth being a messy person. But it does offer a bit of consolation and a little bit of stability in the midst of the disorder that is your life and also your living room.

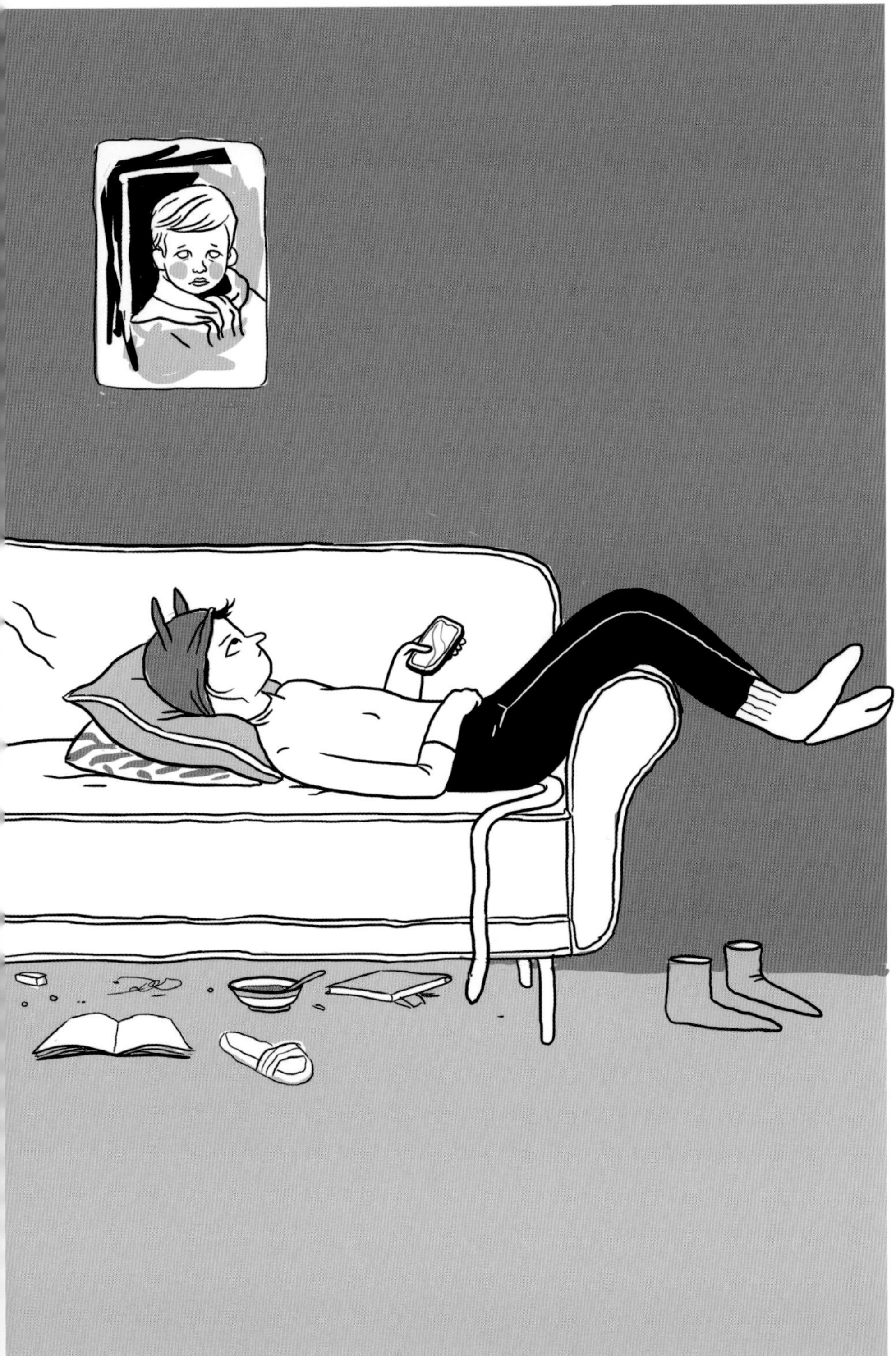

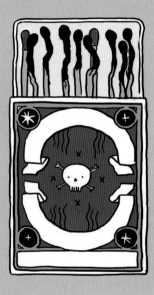

WHEN DO I NEED TO GIVE IN?

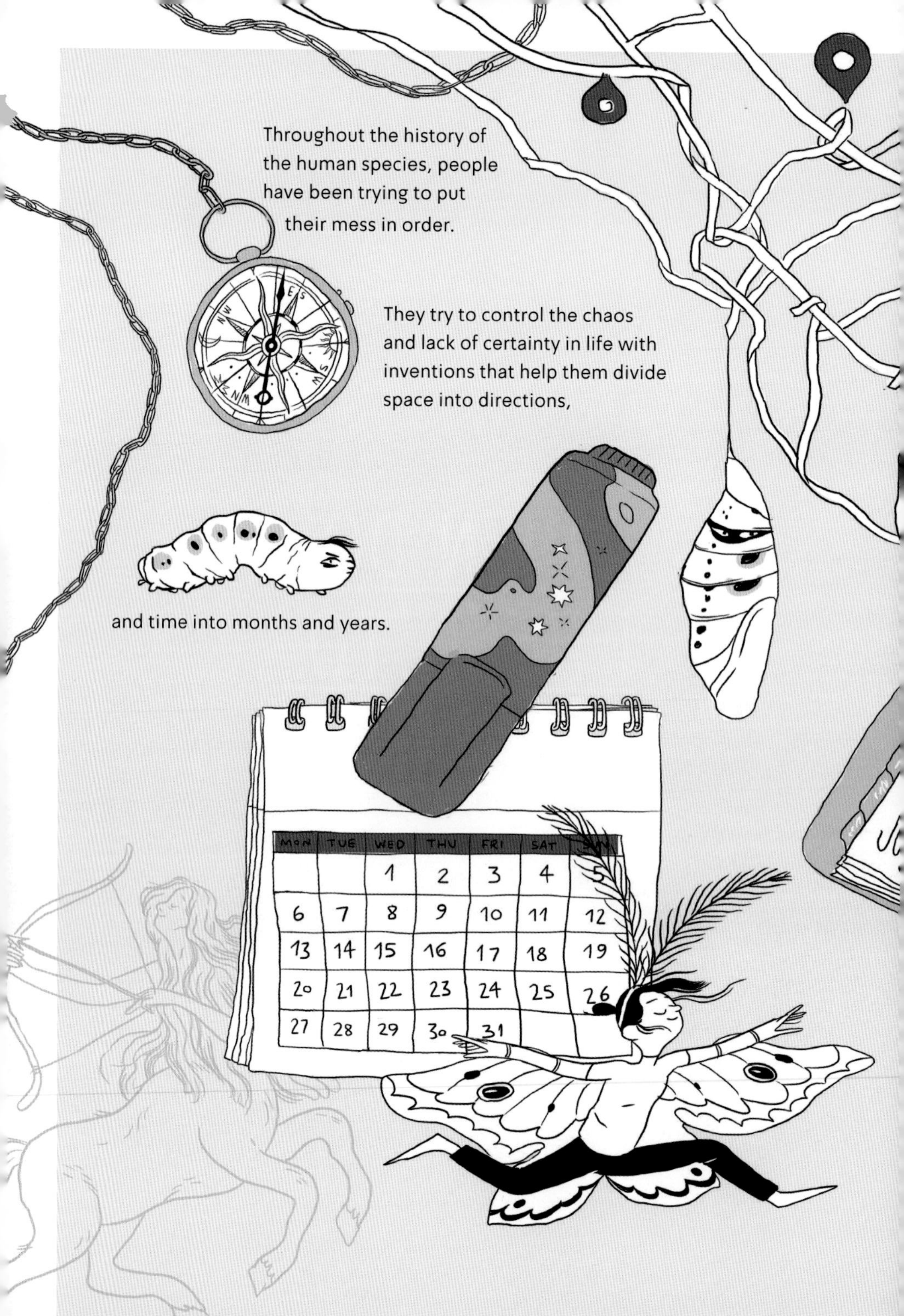

Throughout the history of the human species, people have been trying to put their mess in order.

They try to control the chaos and lack of certainty in life with inventions that help them divide space into directions,

and time into months and years.

MON	TUE	WED	THU	FRI	SAT	SUN
			1	2	3	4
6	7	8	9	10	11	12
13	14	15	16	17	18	19
2o	21	22	23	24	25	26
27	28	29	3o	31		

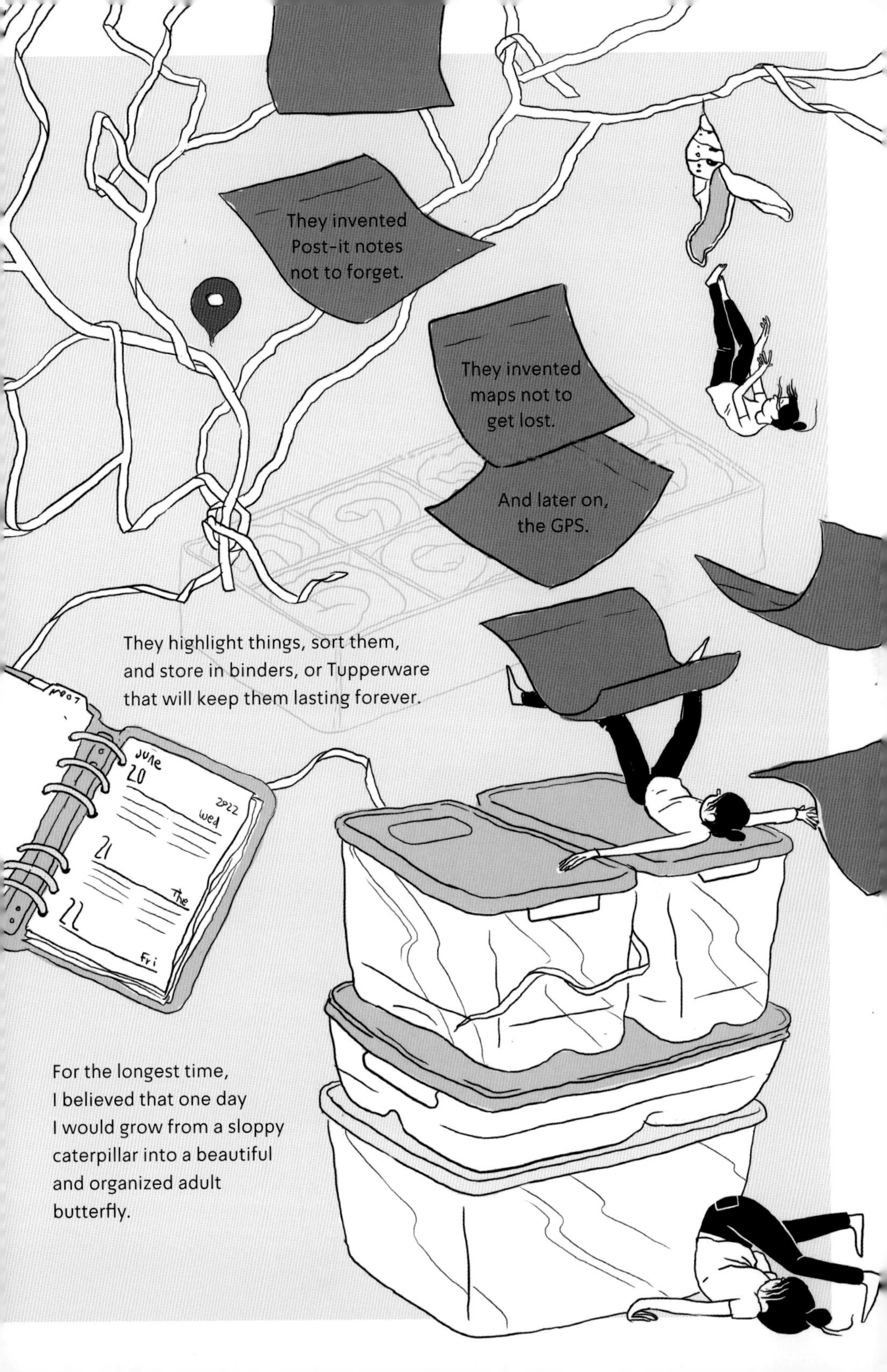
They invented Post-it notes not to forget.
They invented maps not to get lost.
And later on, the GPS.
They highlight things, sort them, and store in binders, or Tupperware that will keep them lasting forever.
June
20
2022
wed
21
22
Fri
For the longest time, I believed that one day I would grow from a sloppy caterpillar into a beautiful and organized adult butterfly.

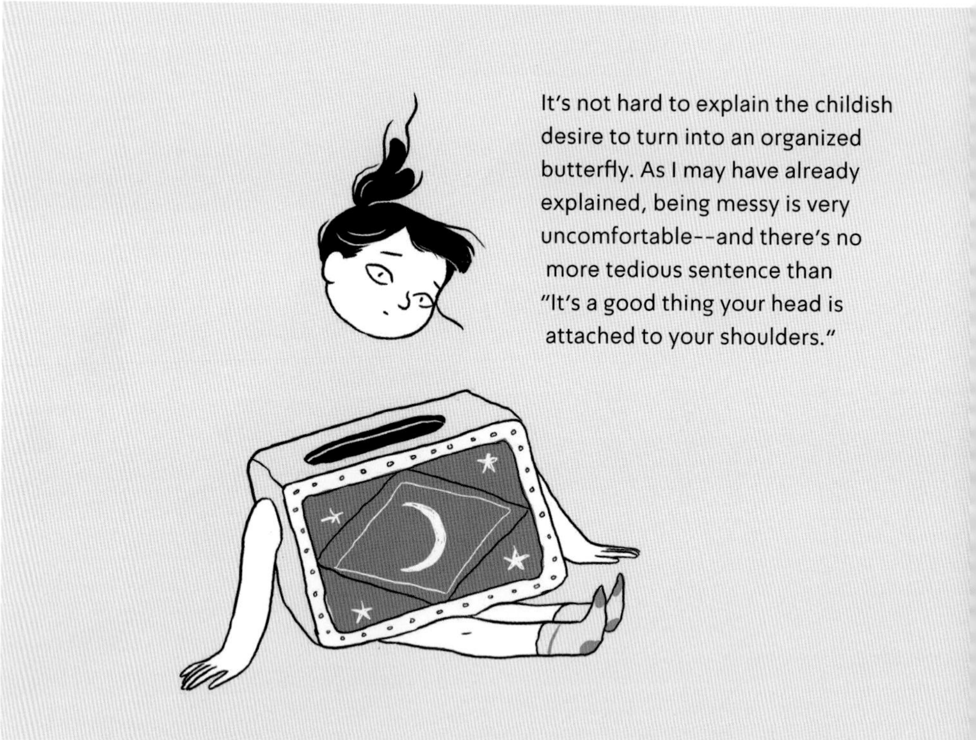
It's not hard to explain the childish desire to turn into an organized butterfly. As I may have already explained, being messy is very uncomfortable--and there's no more tedious sentence than "It's a good thing your head is attached to your shoulders."

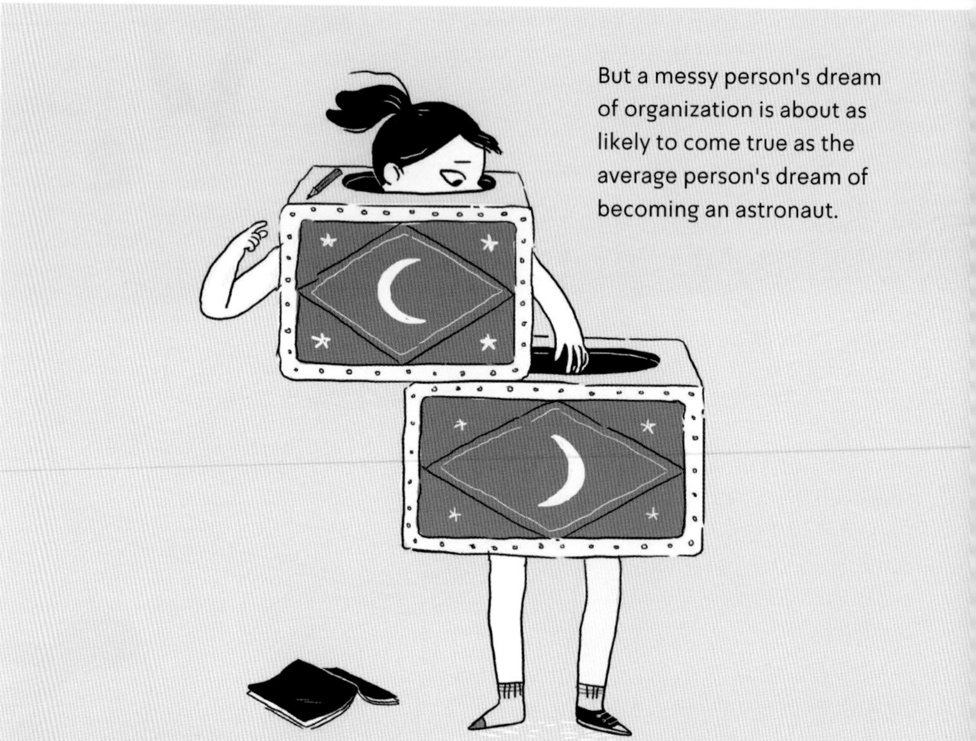
But a messy person's dream of organization is about as likely to come true as the average person's dream of becoming an astronaut.

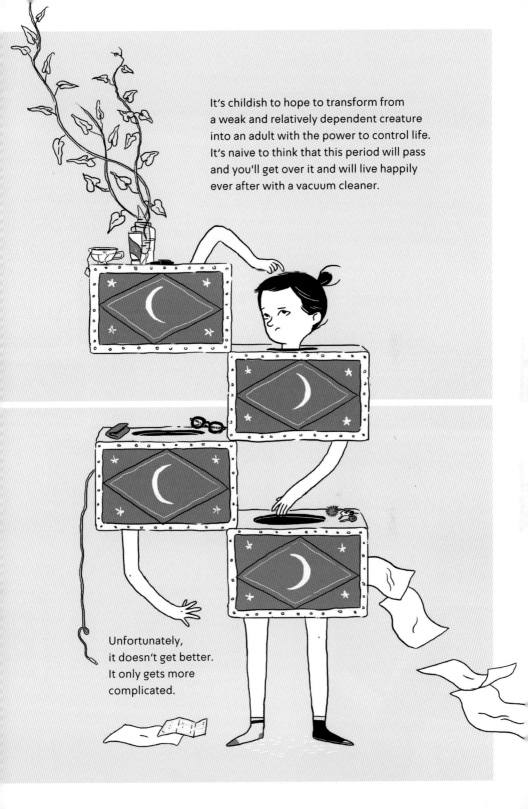

It's childish to hope to transform from a weak and relatively dependent creature into an adult with the power to control life. It's naive to think that this period will pass and you'll get over it and will live happily ever after with a vacuum cleaner.

Unfortunately, it doesn't get better. It only gets more complicated.

You might say that it even gets worse.
Because the life of a modern adult contains myriad tasks and responsiblities, with even more objects that you can misplace. You keep growing and getting more things to lose and meetings to forget and then, you really do have to admit that it's lucky your head is attached to your shoulders.

To continue functioning at this stage, you have to recognize your own boundaries and cut losses. Even though chapter 5 is devoted to how to organize without really organizing, you have to know the things which will inevitably cause you to fail--and you must make peace with them (and know when to give up).

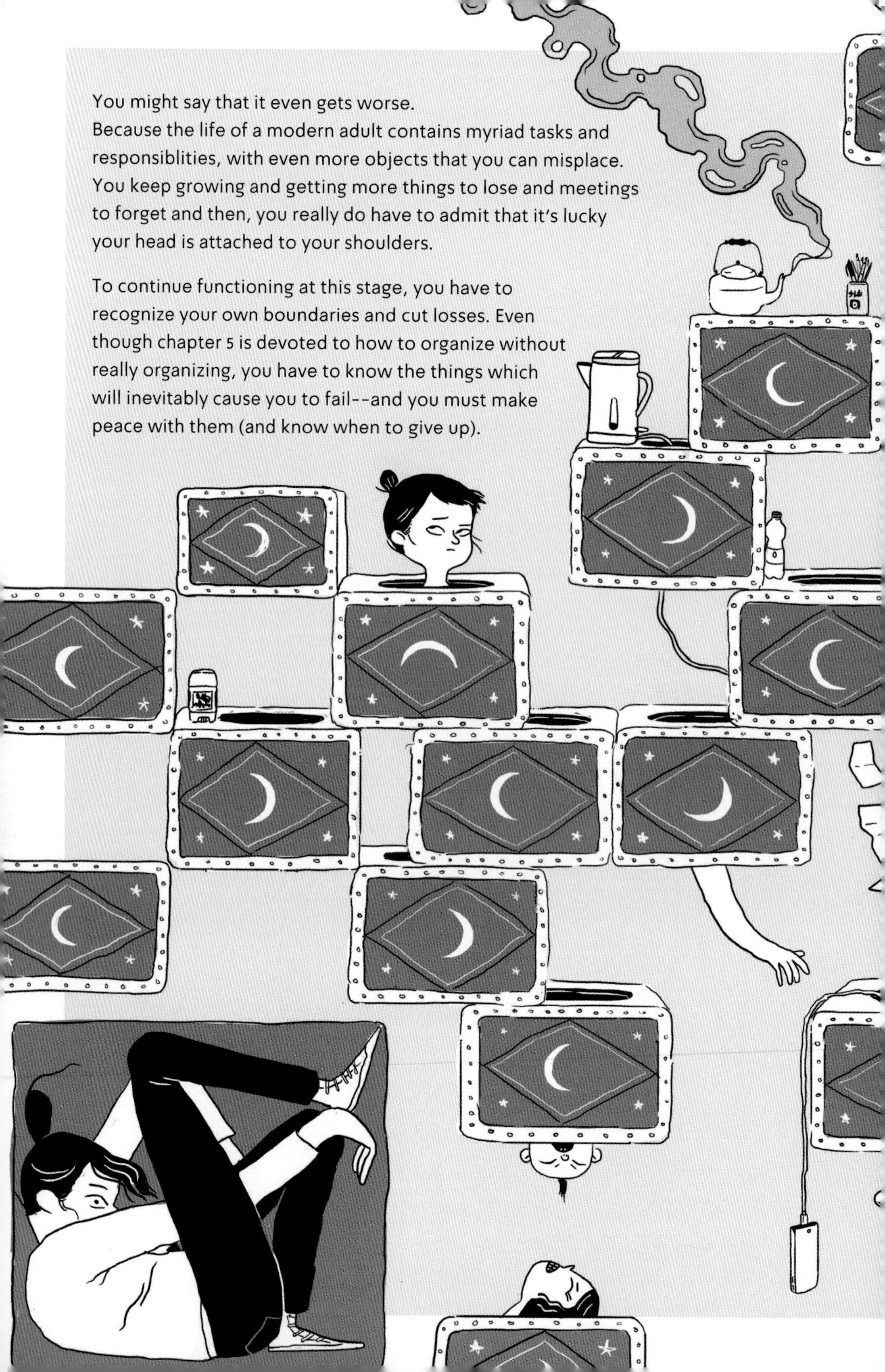

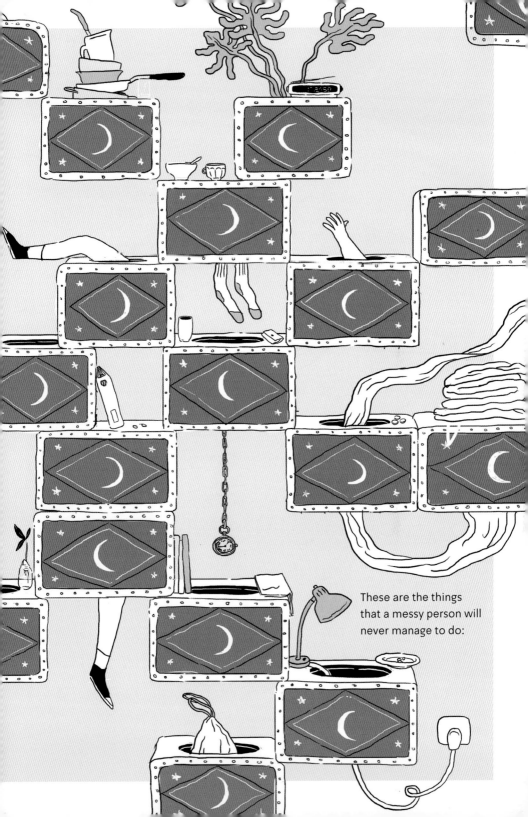

These are the things
that a messy person will
never manage to do:

1. Pay the ticket that's hanging on the refrigerator. Today, it is clear that getting a ticket is sixty percent of the punishment. In the past, public hangings, whipping in the town square, and burning at the stake were popular punishments. Now, you could say that this is an attempt to copy this paradigm, with public self-flagellation and maybe also an attempt at penance.

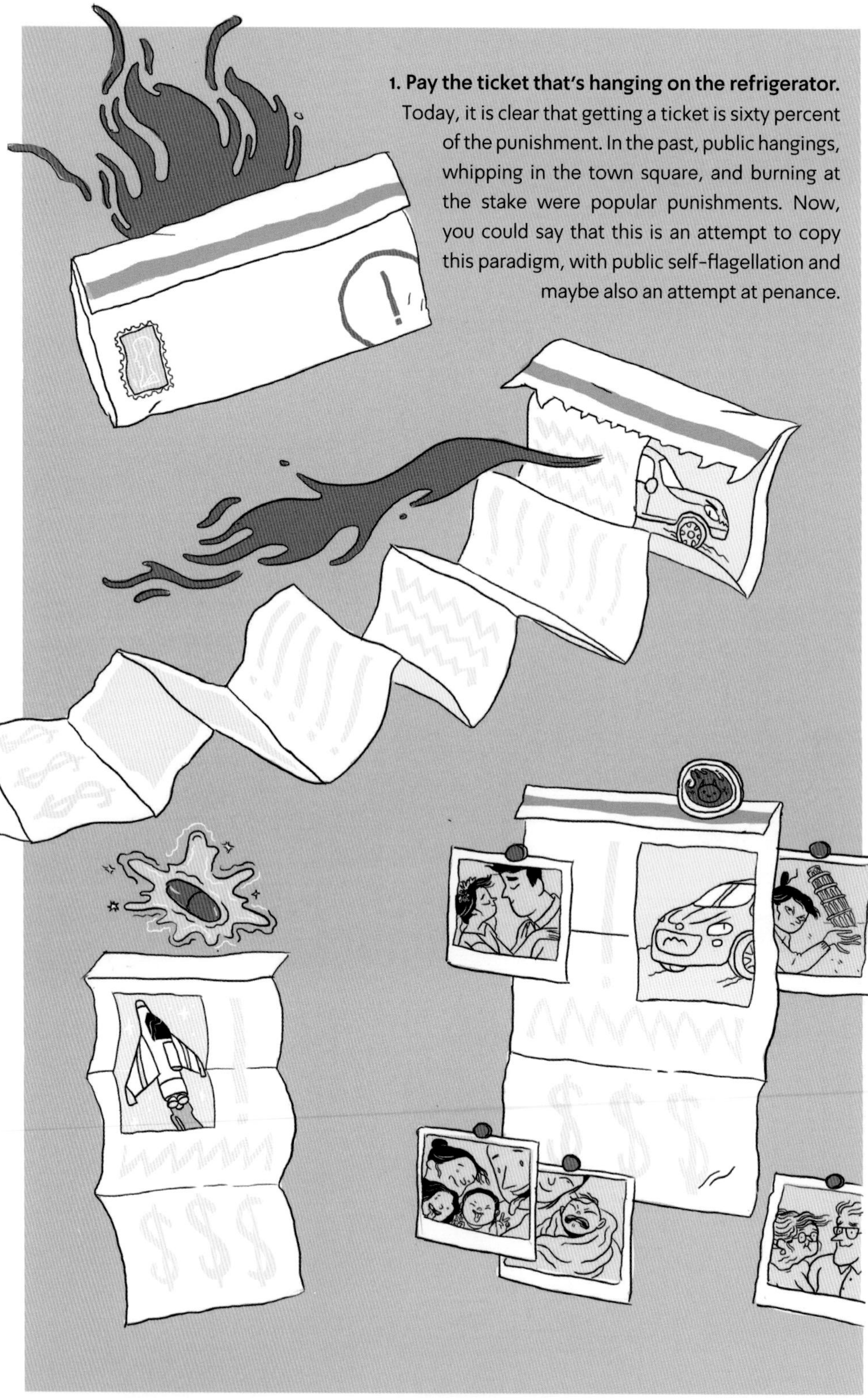

A ticket is a very nerve-wracking thing. But after the initial shock, when you hang something on the refrigerator, it's automatically incorporated into the backdrop of the kitchen and refrigerator. This ticket will never be paid. It will remain on the refrigerator door for eternity, or at least until you move.

I think that, in the future, when human nutrition is entirely provided by futuristic food capsules and refrigerators won't need to exist, people will keep making refrigerators, if only to have a place to hang their tickets.

2. Remember to by a new pack of toilet paper.

When the pack of toilet paper is fresh and new, it seems like it will never get used up. But toilet paper always runs out faster than expected.

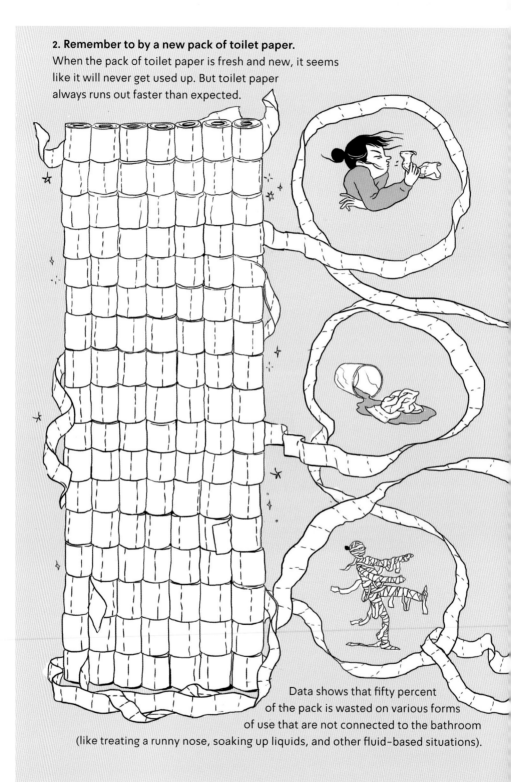

Data shows that fifty percent of the pack is wasted on various forms of use that are not connected to the bathroom (like treating a runny nose, soaking up liquids, and other fluid-based situations).

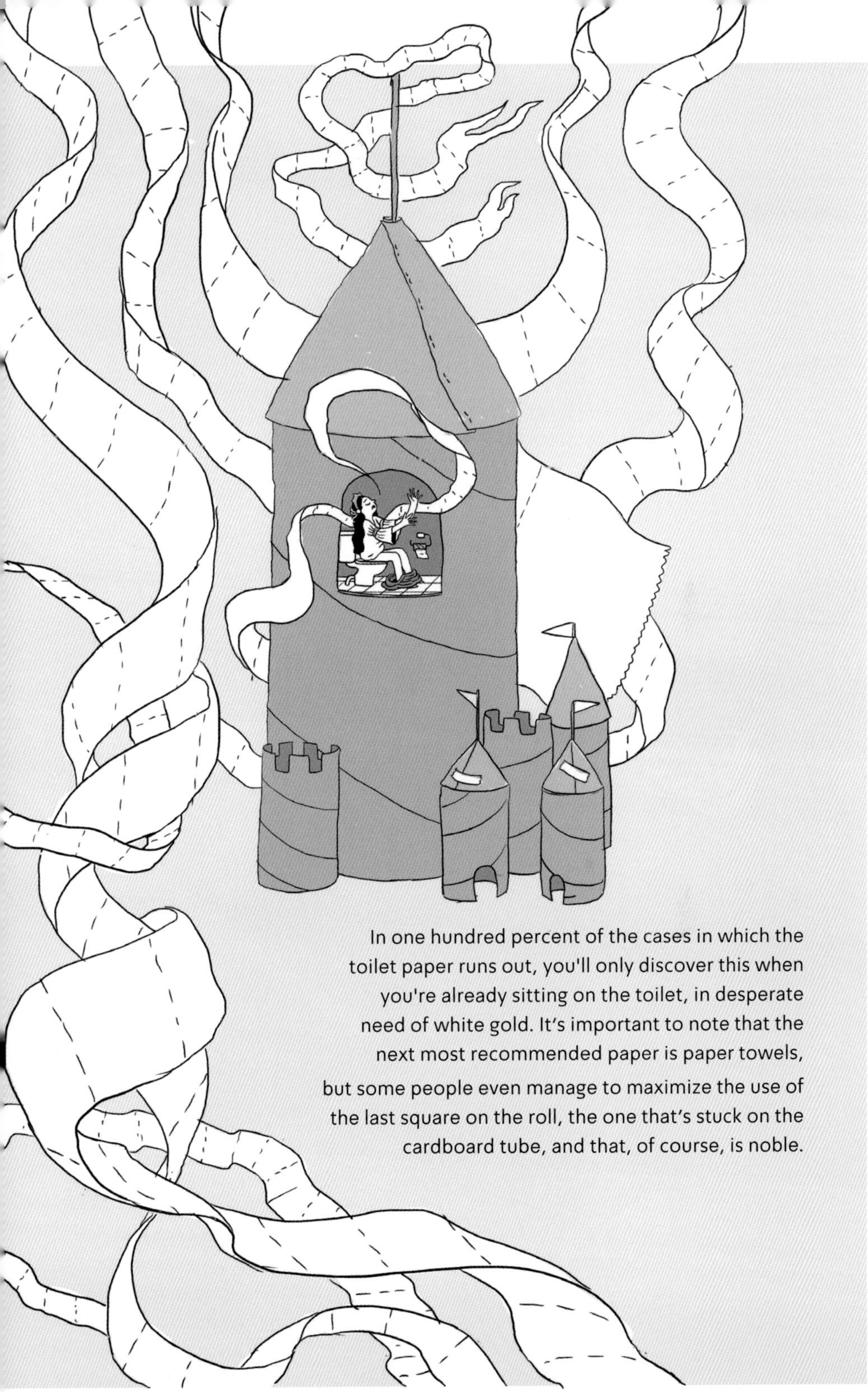

In one hundred percent of the cases in which the toilet paper runs out, you'll only discover this when you're already sitting on the toilet, in desperate need of white gold. It's important to note that the next most recommended paper is paper towels, but some people even manage to maximize the use of the last square on the roll, the one that's stuck on the cardboard tube, and that, of course, is noble.

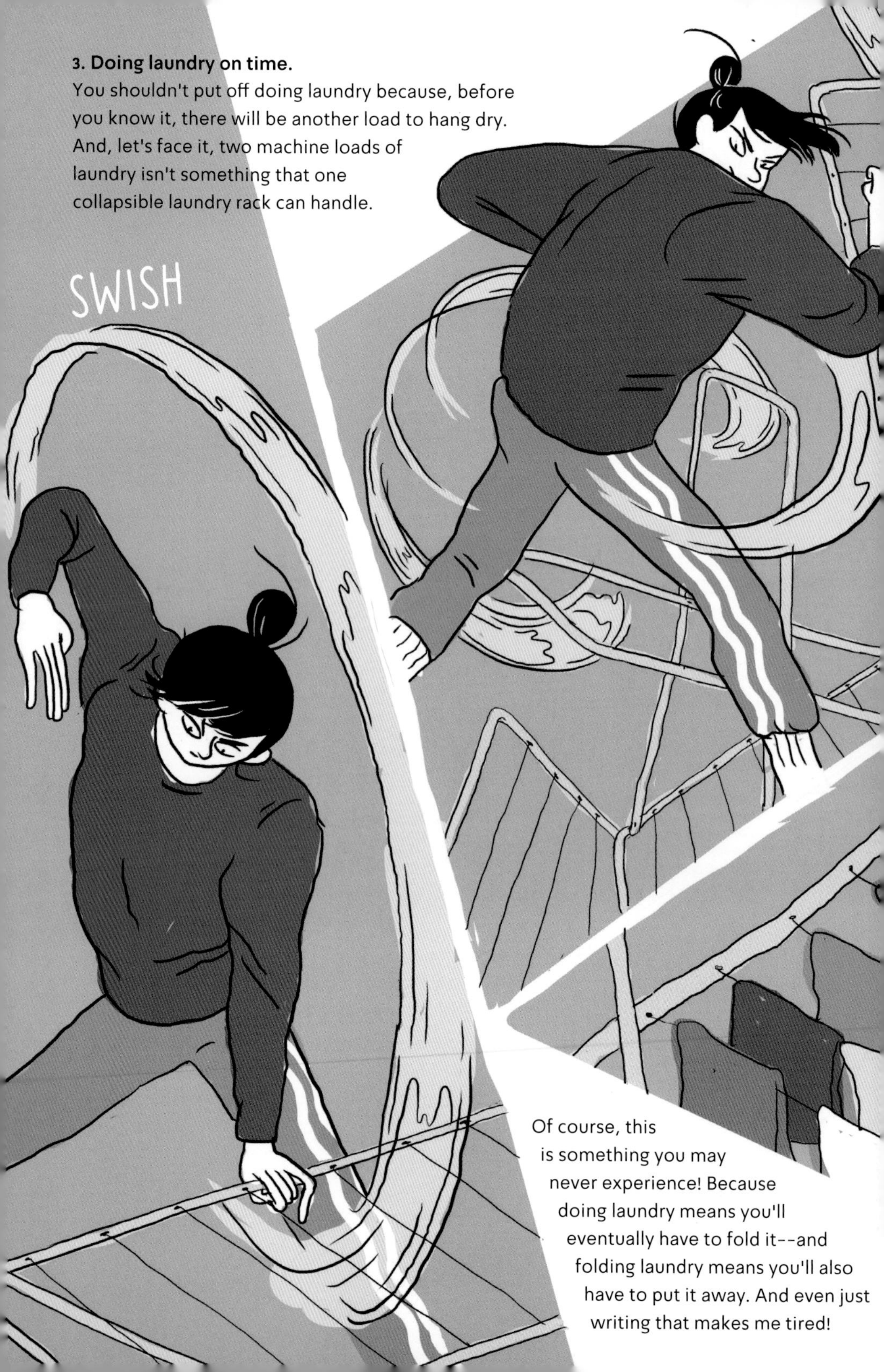
3. Doing laundry on time.
You shouldn't put off doing laundry because, before you know it, there will be another load to hang dry. And, let's face it, two machine loads of laundry isn't something that one collapsible laundry rack can handle.
SWISH
Of course, this is something you may never experience! Because doing laundry means you'll eventually have to fold it--and folding laundry means you'll also have to put it away. And even just writing that makes me tired!

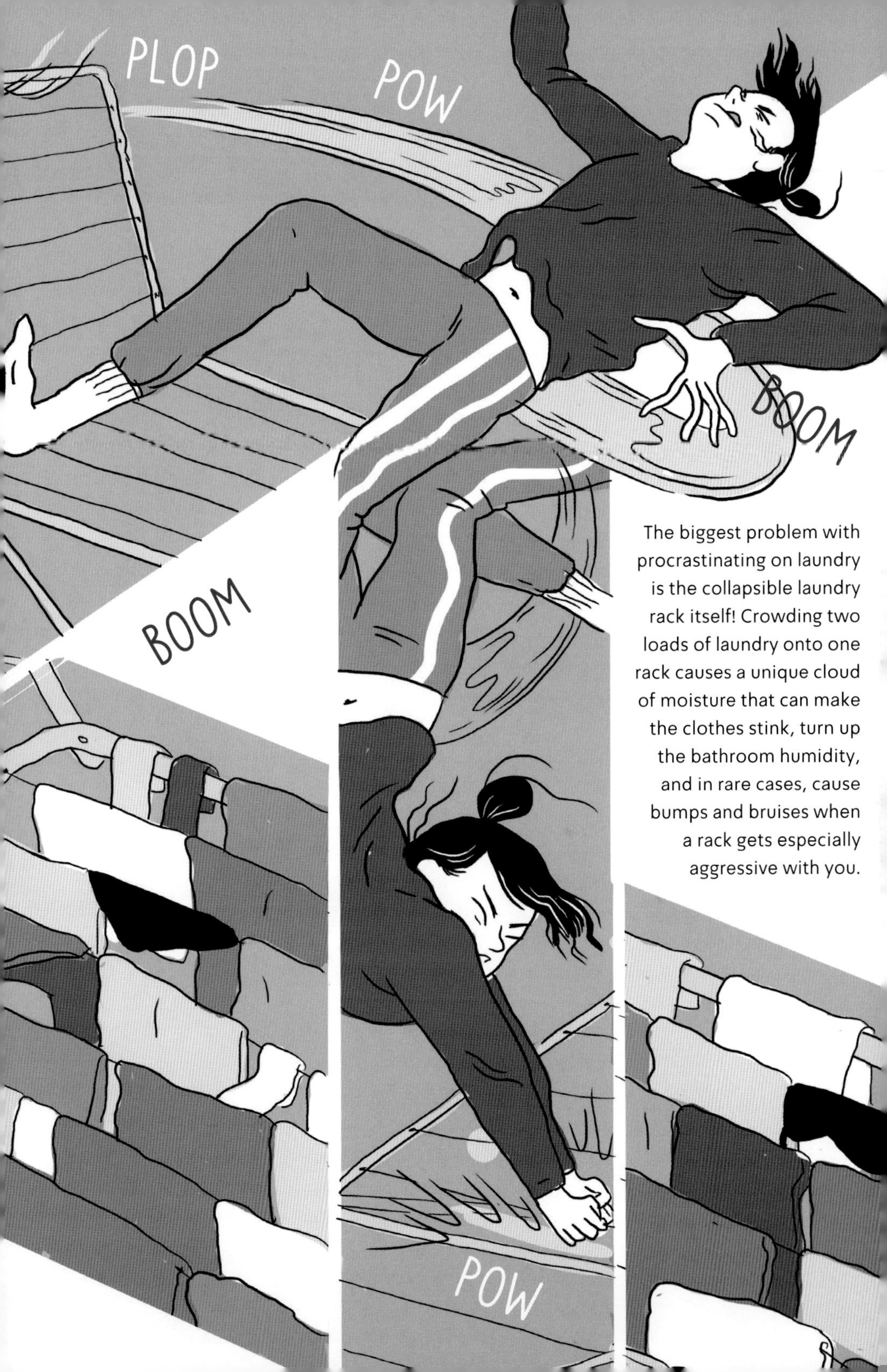
PLOP
POW
BOOM
BOOM
The biggest problem with procrastinating on laundry is the collapsible laundry rack itself! Crowding two loads of laundry onto one rack causes a unique cloud of moisture that can make the clothes stink, turn up the bathroom humidity, and in rare cases, cause bumps and bruises when a rack gets especially aggressive with you.
POW

4. Fit the sheet tightly on the mattress.

I don't feel the need to elaborate. Changing sheets is the most horrifying task in the world. In fact, some people say that's where ghost stories come from (if only to provide a rational and less-terrifying explanation of the phenomenon).

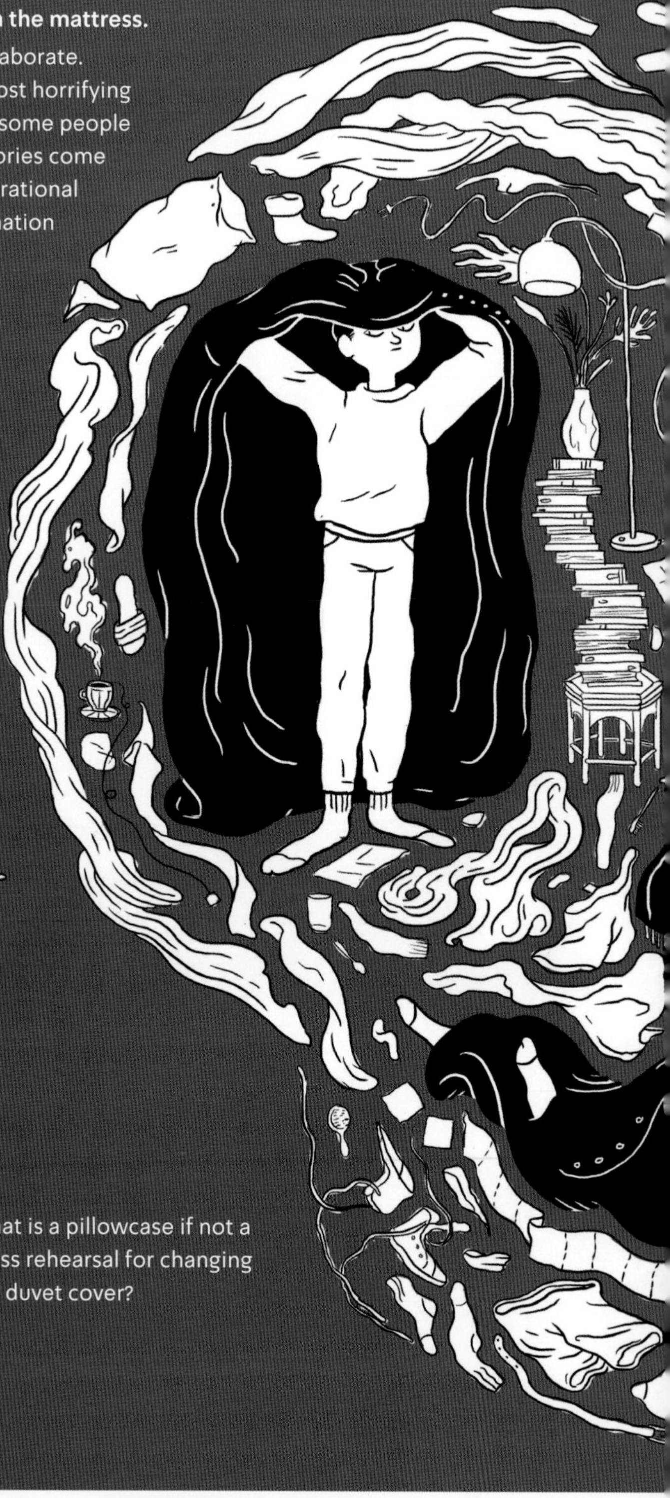

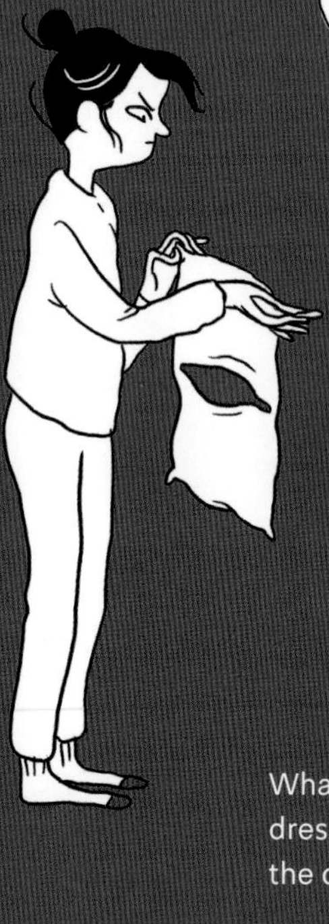

What is a pillowcase if not a dress rehearsal for changing the duvet cover?

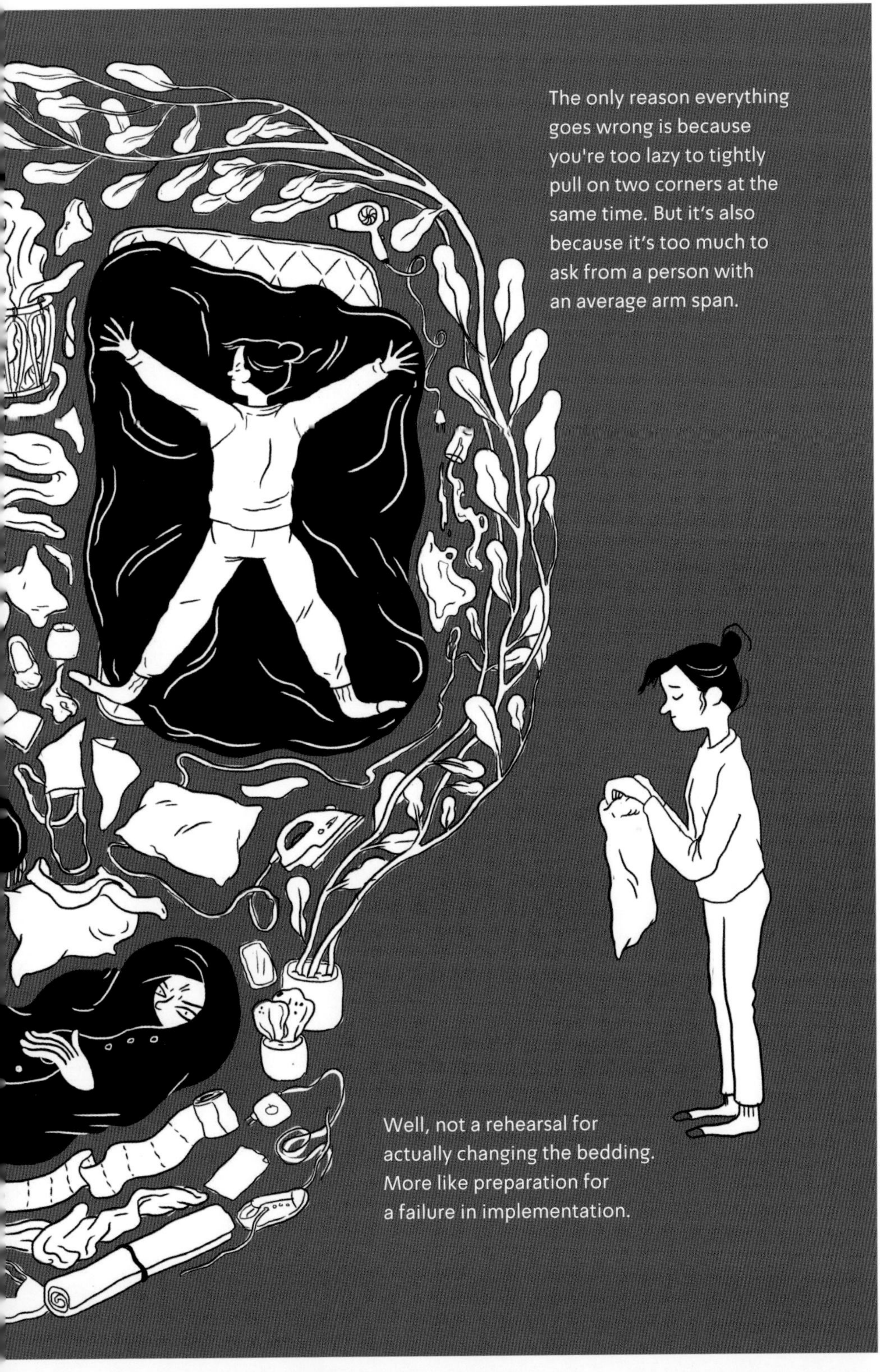
The only reason everything goes wrong is because you're too lazy to tightly pull on two corners at the same time. But it's also because it's too much to ask from a person with an average arm span.
Well, not a rehearsal for actually changing the bedding. More like preparation for a failure in implementation.

5. Clearing out the bottom of the sink.

No one knows the psychological explanation behind it, but sixty percent of all messy people do not clean out the pieces of food that accumulate in the sink's drain cover immediately after they finish washing the dishes. Apparently, this is an ancient reward mechanism: They are so pleased with themselves that they washed the dishes in the first place that they feel that they deserve immunity.

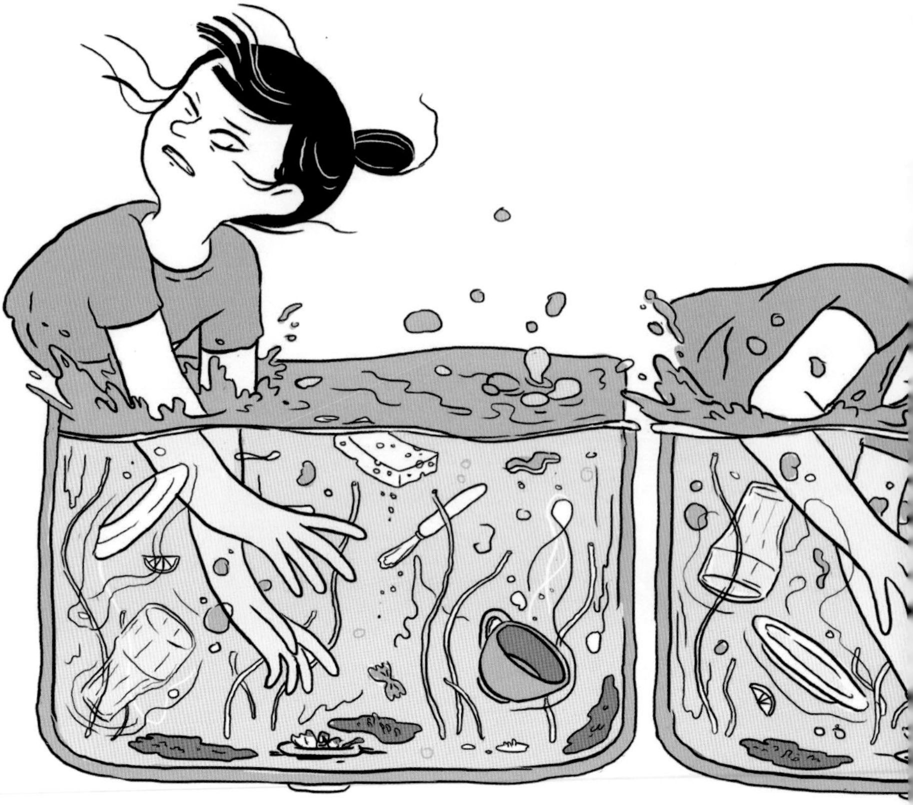

Of course, in just two short days the residue at the
bottom of the sink has transformed into a unique state that
is neither solid nor liquid. Some sort of thick mucus-like
slime. Sometimes, the micro-ecosystem that developed
has a mind of its own and a different moral code as well.

It's important to note that even though letting drain
residue sit in the sink doesn't work, the same tactic
works for the pans you forgot in the oven.

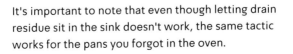

6. Keeping the space underneath the bed clean

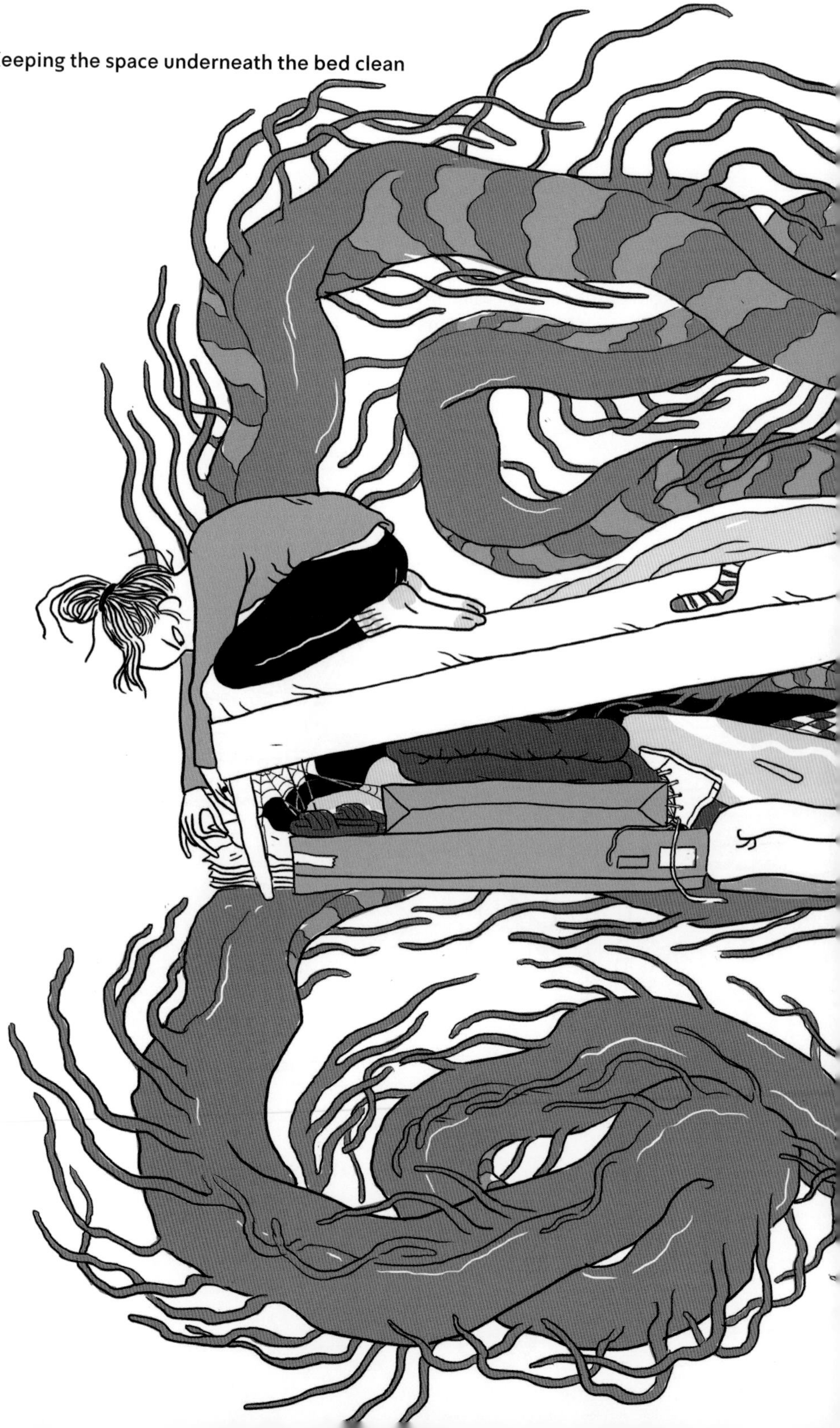

The monsters under the bed when you were little didn't disappearor go to some other child's bedroom. The mess monsters under the bed simply gobbled them up--and still have room for dessert.

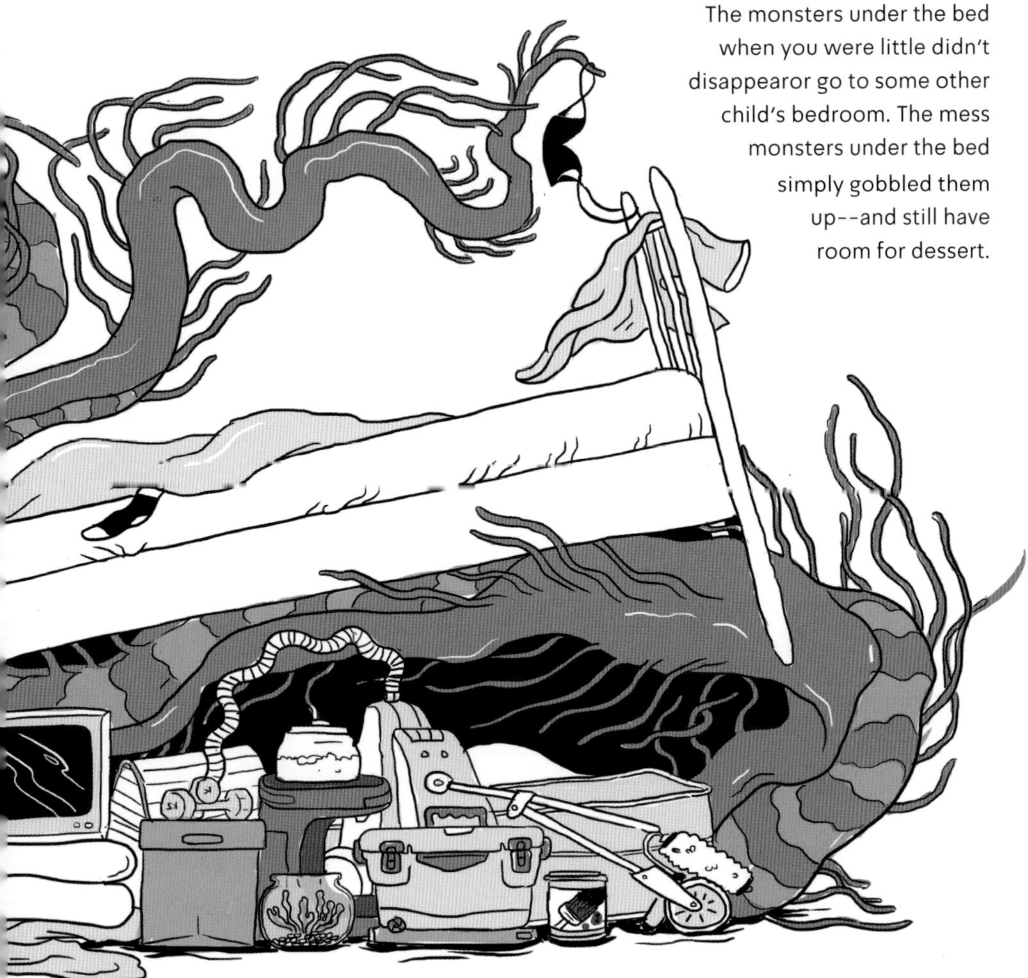

The mess under the bed is one of the most monstrous piles of clutter in existence. A combination of pajama pieces and stray socks and things that were put there purposely and over time turned into a mini vertical warehouse of childhood memories, souvenirs from difficult break-ups, dreams about camping, and more.

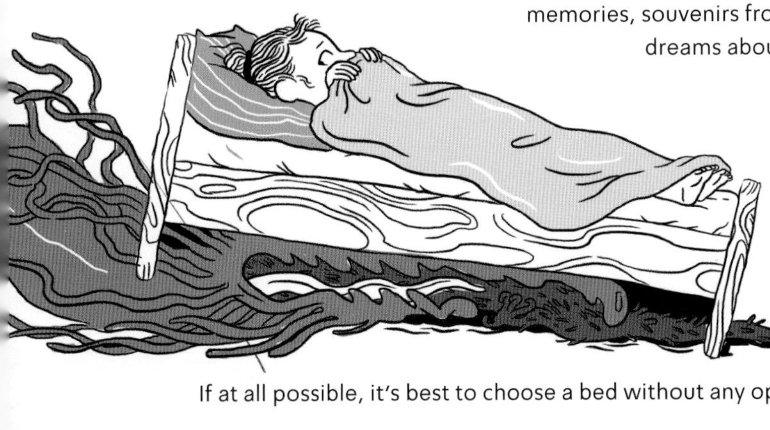

If at all possible, it's best to choose a bed without any open space underneath.

7. Picking up a pack of cotton swabs that fell on the floor.
No one can do that (not even organized people).
If a pack of cotton swabs falls on the floor,
you're just going to have to move.

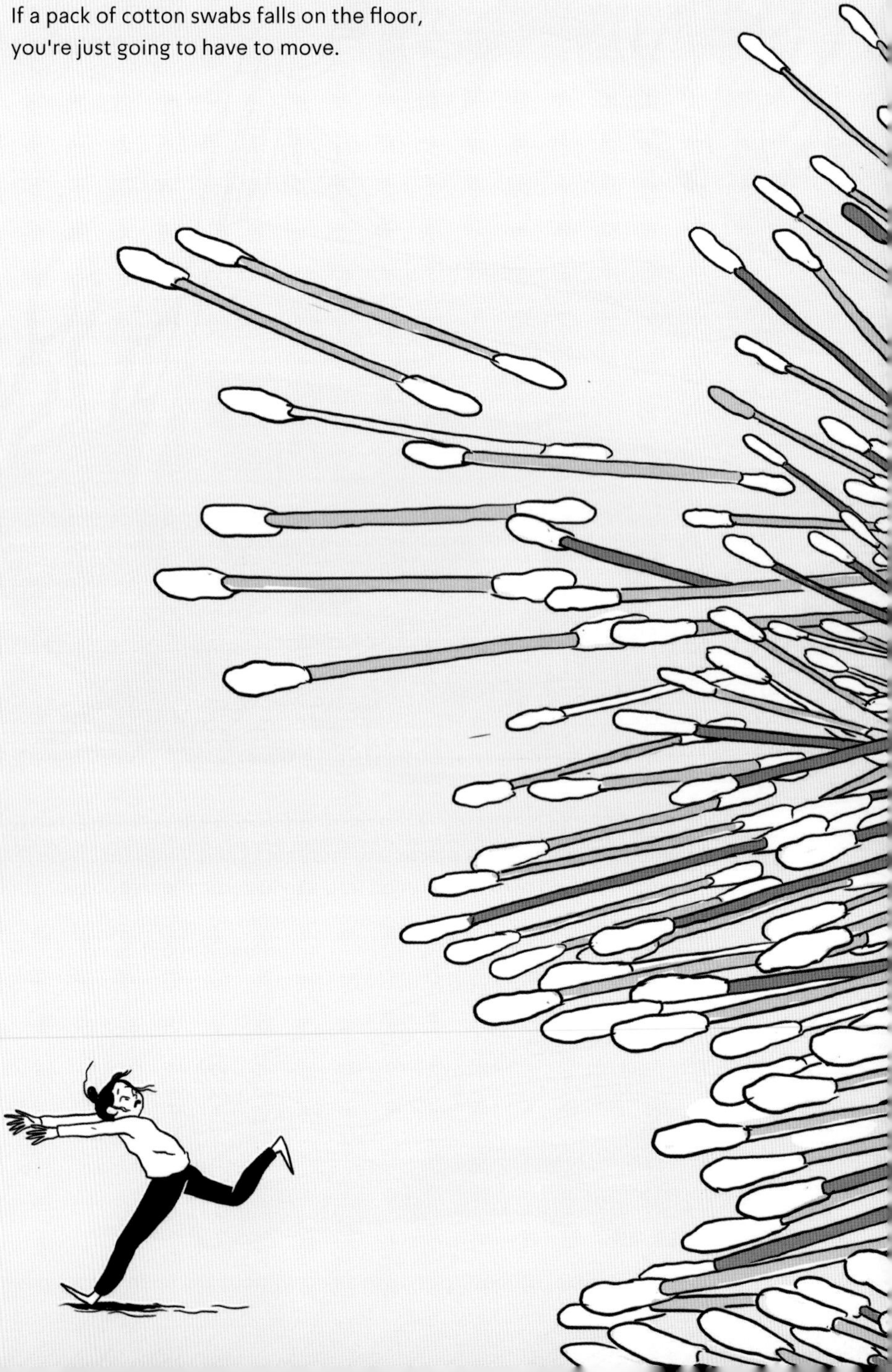

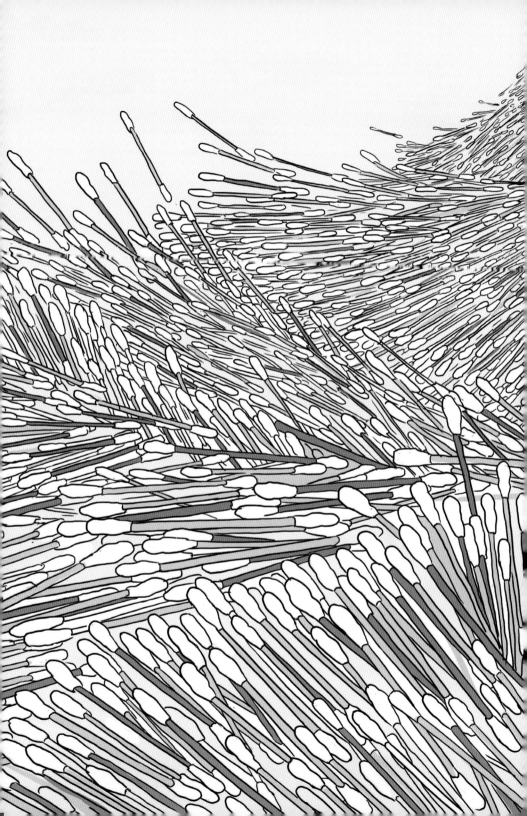

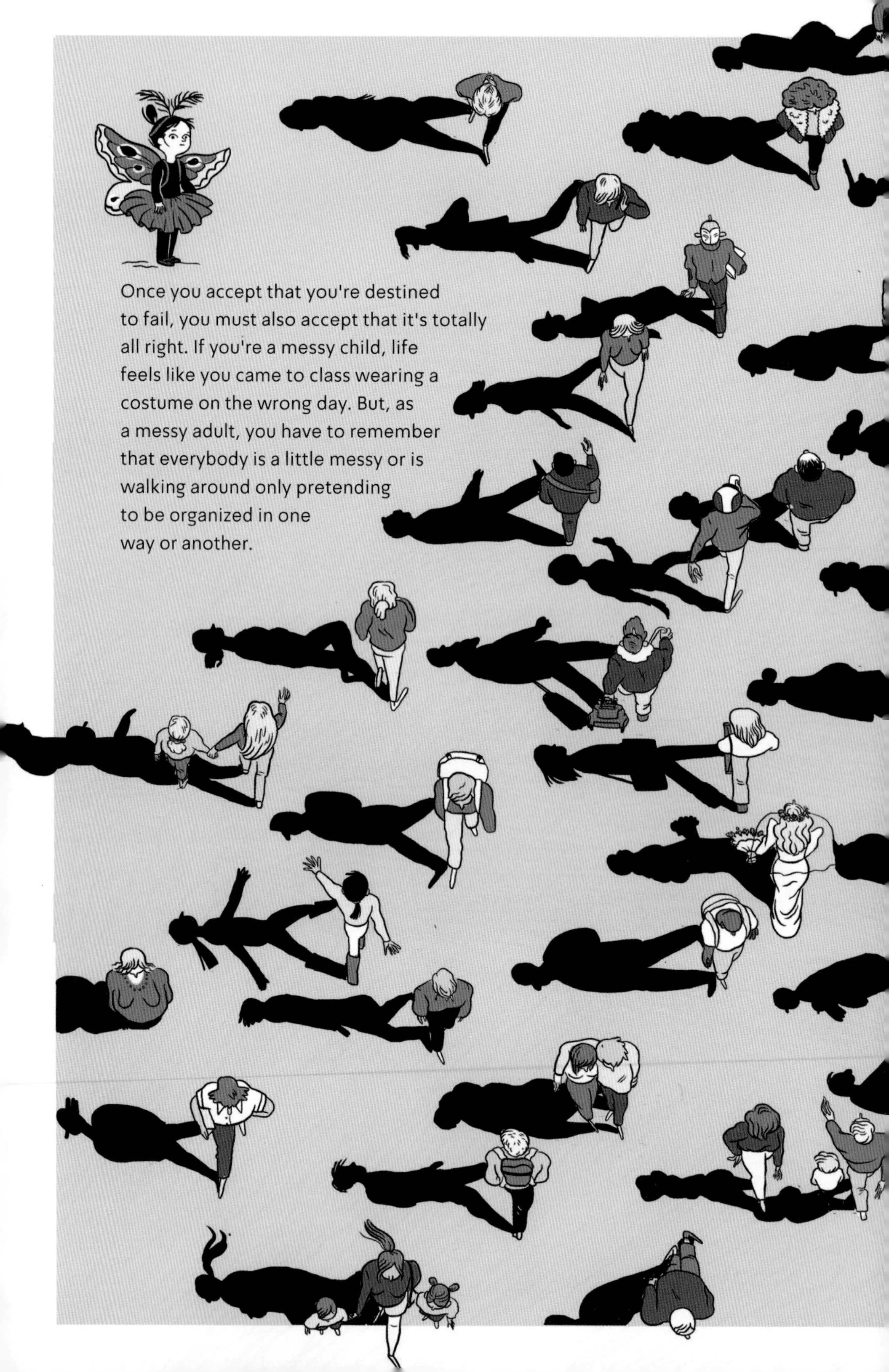

Once you accept that you're destined to fail, you must also accept that it's totally all right. If you're a messy child, life feels like you came to class wearing a costume on the wrong day. But, as a messy adult, you have to remember that everybody is a little messy or is walking around only pretending to be organized in one way or another.

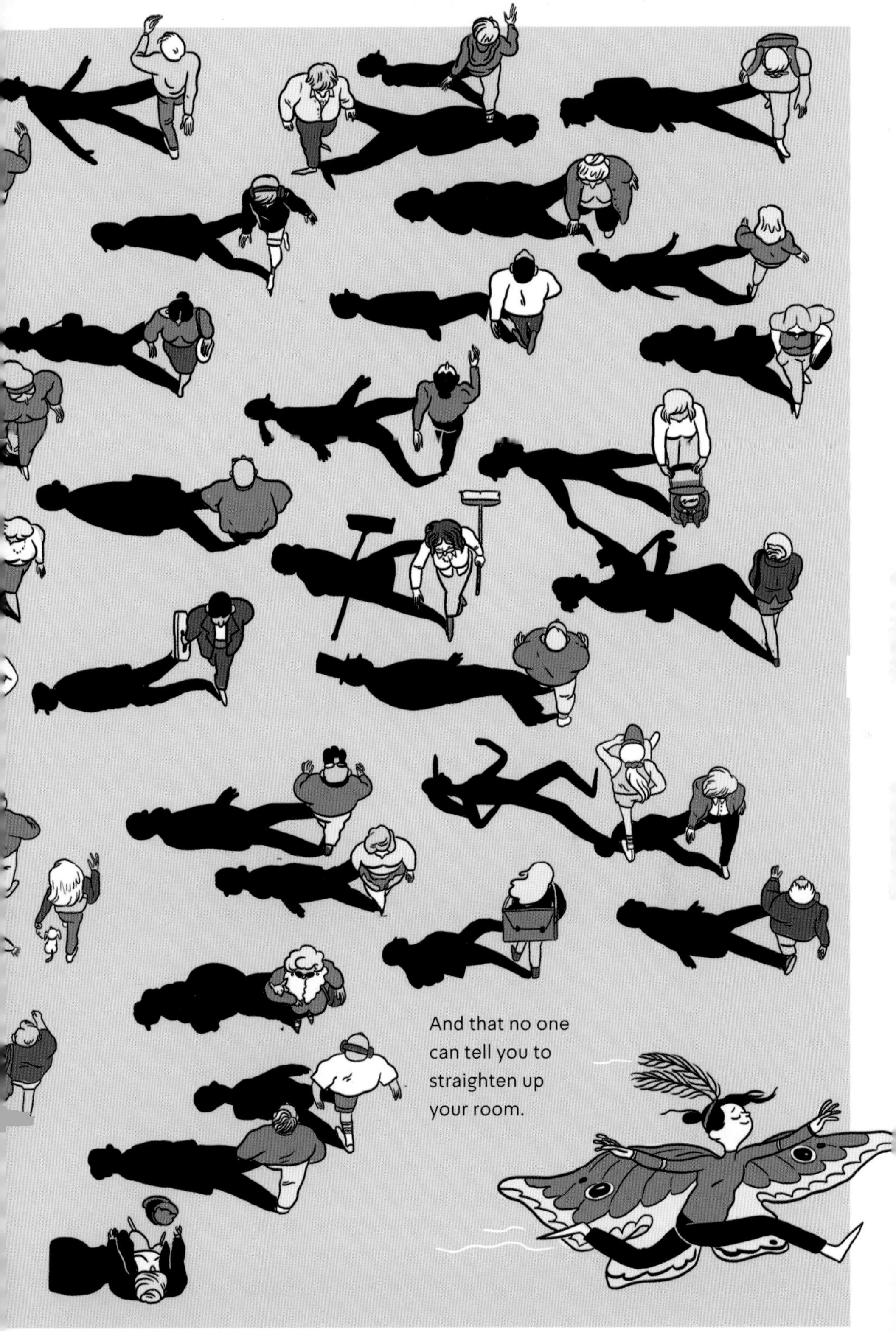
And that no one can tell you to straighten up your room.

SALVATION

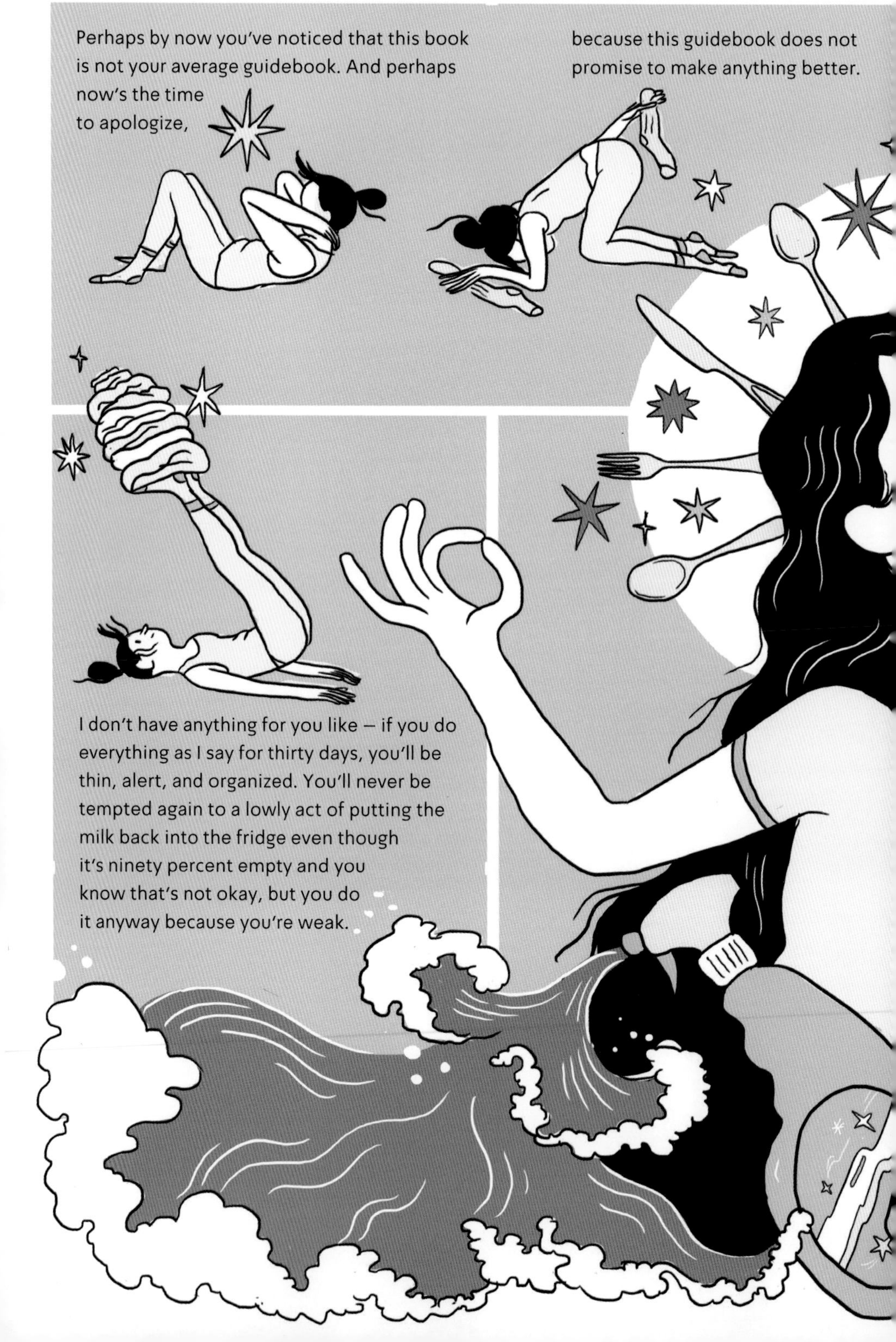
Perhaps by now you've noticed that this book is not your average guidebook. And perhaps now's the time to apologize,
because this guidebook does not promise to make anything better.
I don't have anything for you like – if you do everything as I say for thirty days, you'll be thin, alert, and organized. You'll never be tempted again to a lowly act of putting the milk back into the fridge even though it's ninety percent empty and you know that's not okay, but you do it anyway because you're weak.

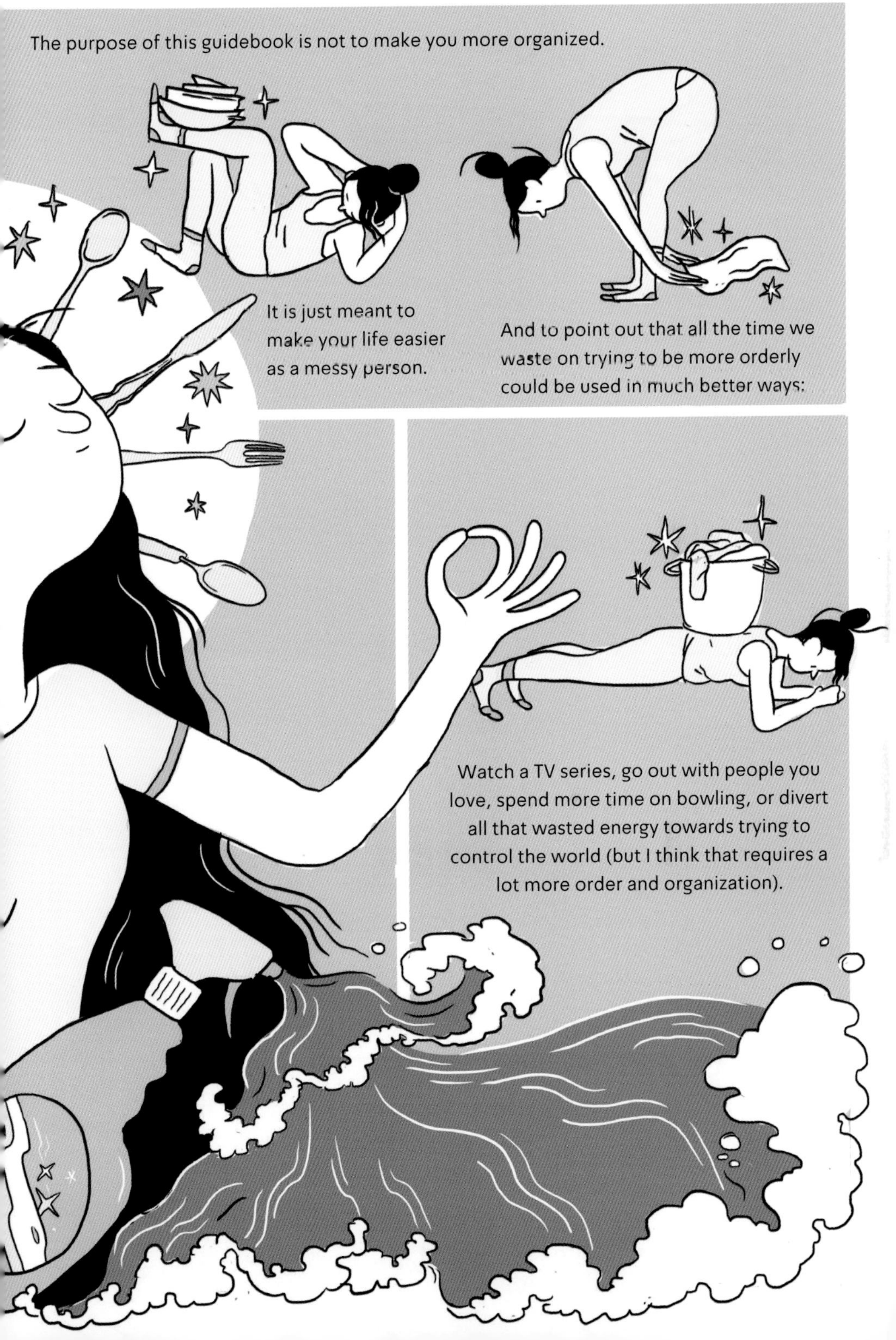

The purpose of this guidebook is not to make you more organized.
It is just meant to make your life easier as a messy person.
And to point out that all the time we waste on trying to be more orderly could be used in much better ways:
Watch a TV series, go out with people you love, spend more time on bowling, or divert all that wasted energy towards trying to control the world (but I think that requires a lot more order and organization).

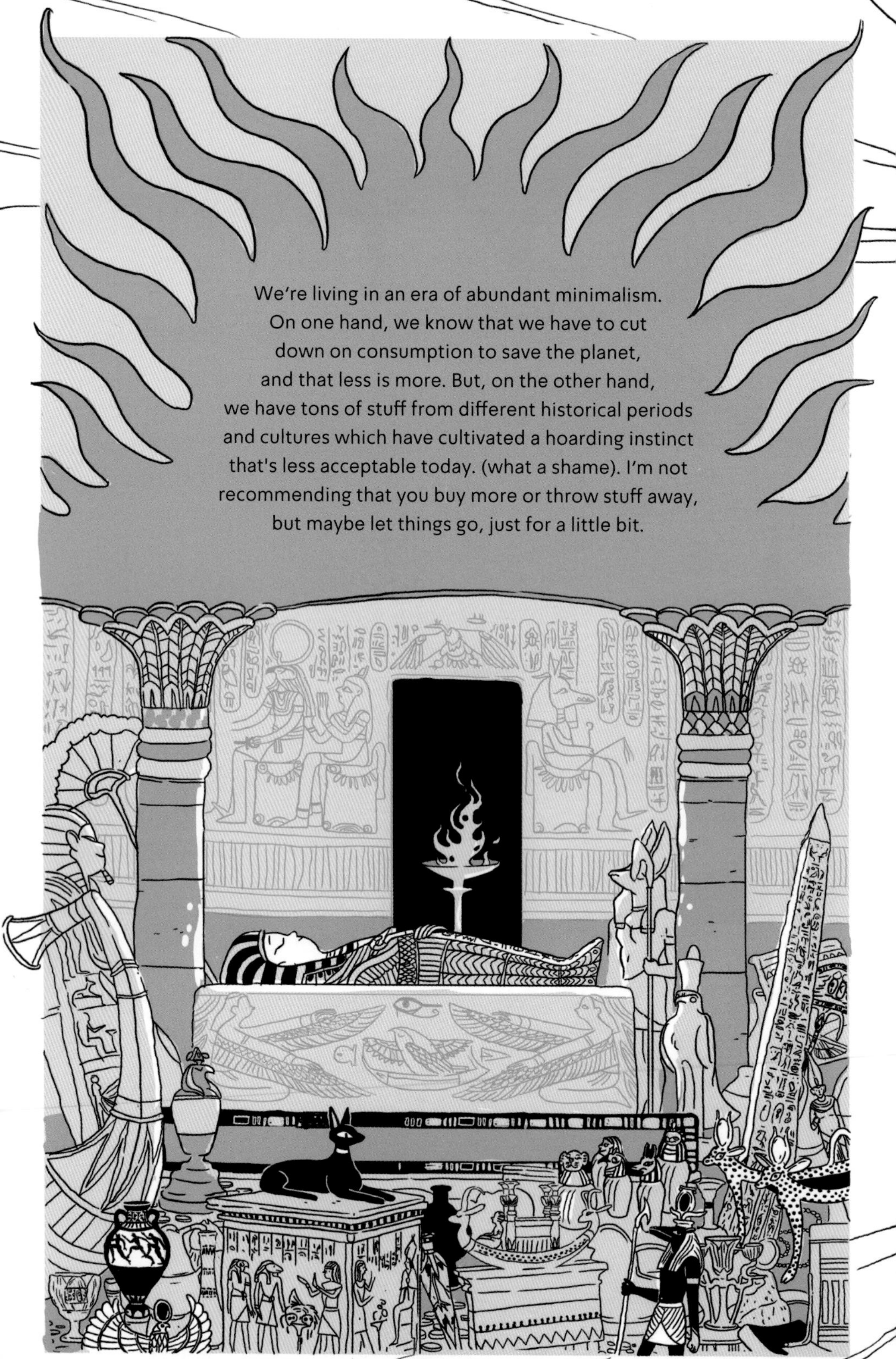
We're living in an era of abundant minimalism. On one hand, we know that we have to cut down on consumption to save the planet, and that less is more. But, on the other hand, we have tons of stuff from different historical periods and cultures which have cultivated a hoarding instinct that's less acceptable today. (what a shame). I'm not recommending that you buy more or throw stuff away, but maybe let things go, just for a little bit.

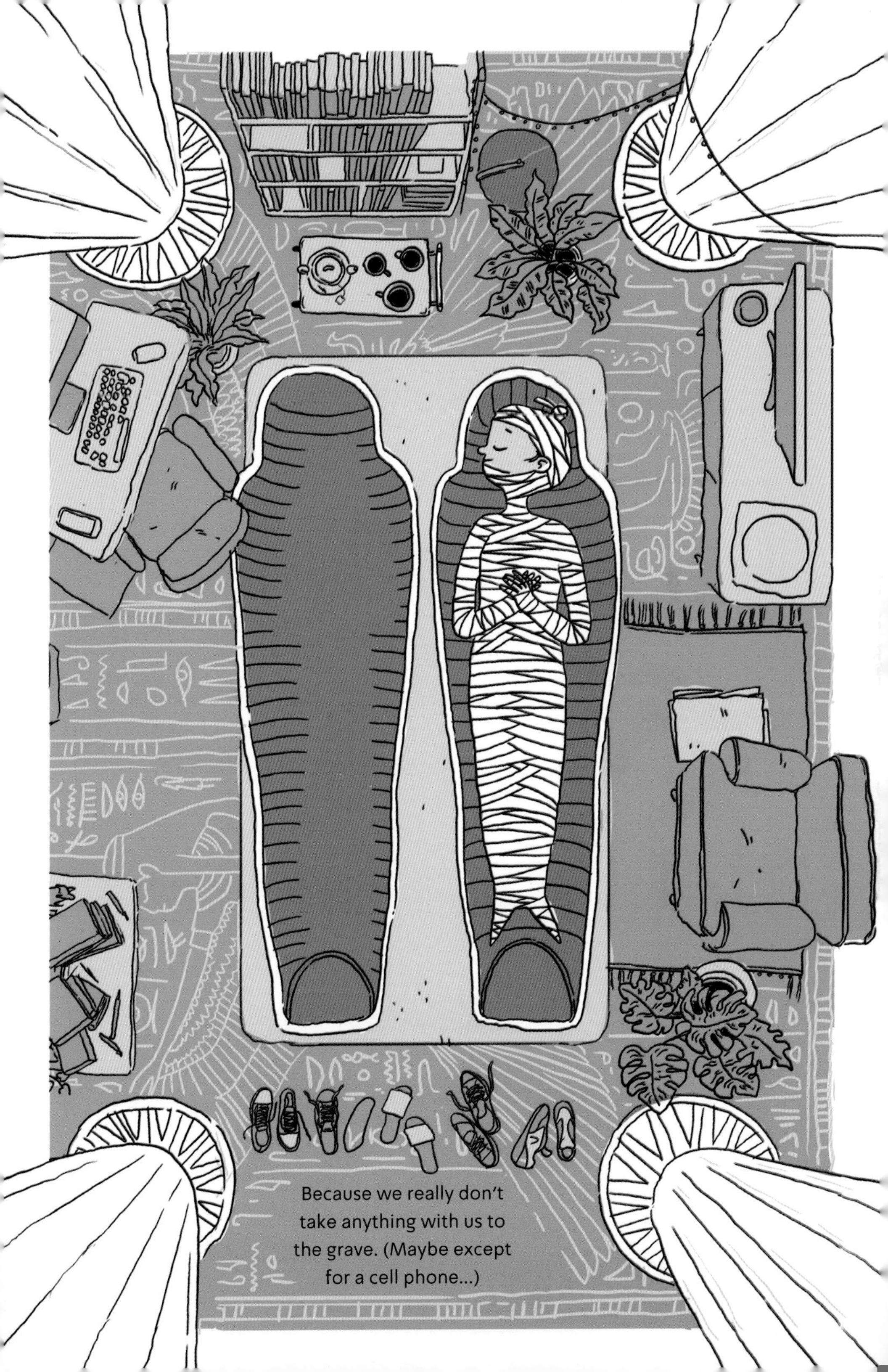
Because we really don't take anything with us to the grave. (Maybe except for a cell phone...)

Don't try so hard and make peace with the fact that mess is just part of life. Even with all its drawbacks, a mess is the secret ingredient that makes the difference between a hotel and a home.

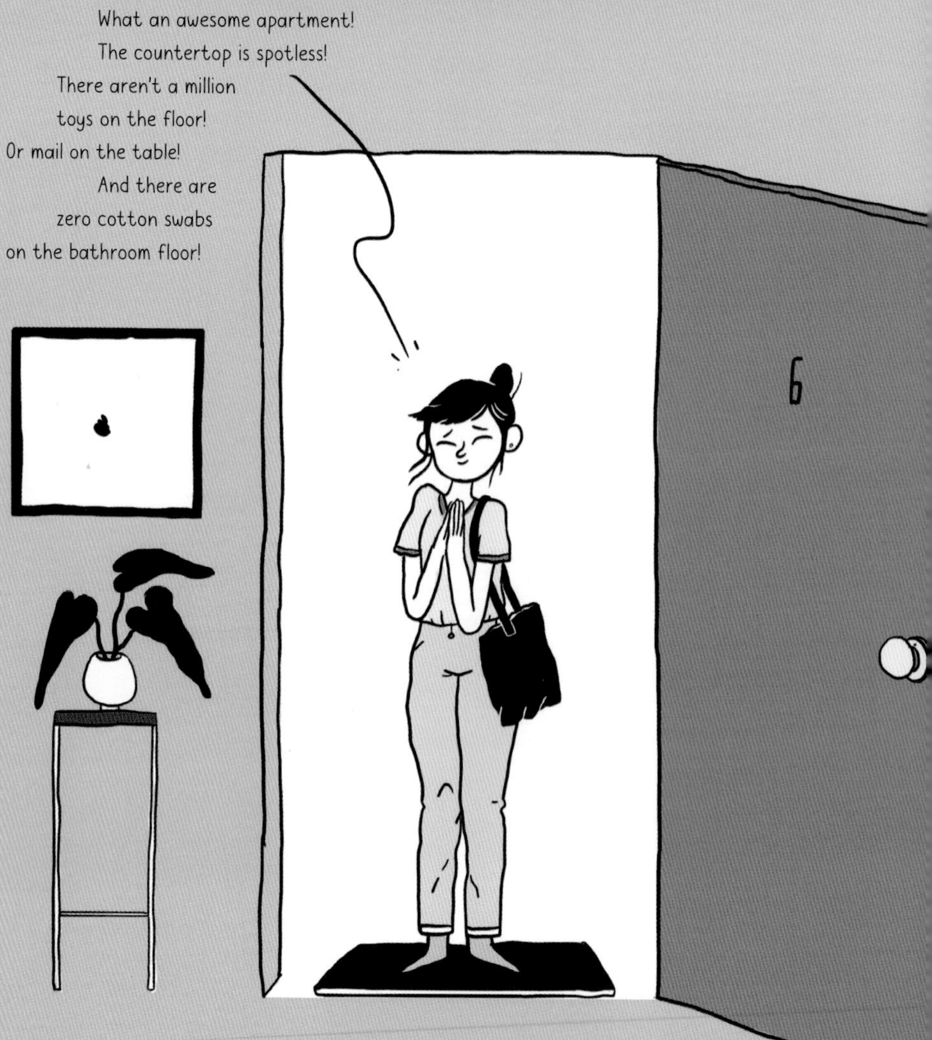
What an awesome apartment!
The countertop is spotless!
There aren't a million toys on the floor!
Or mail on the table!
And there are zero cotton swabs on the bathroom floor!
6

Temporary residences are always more organized.

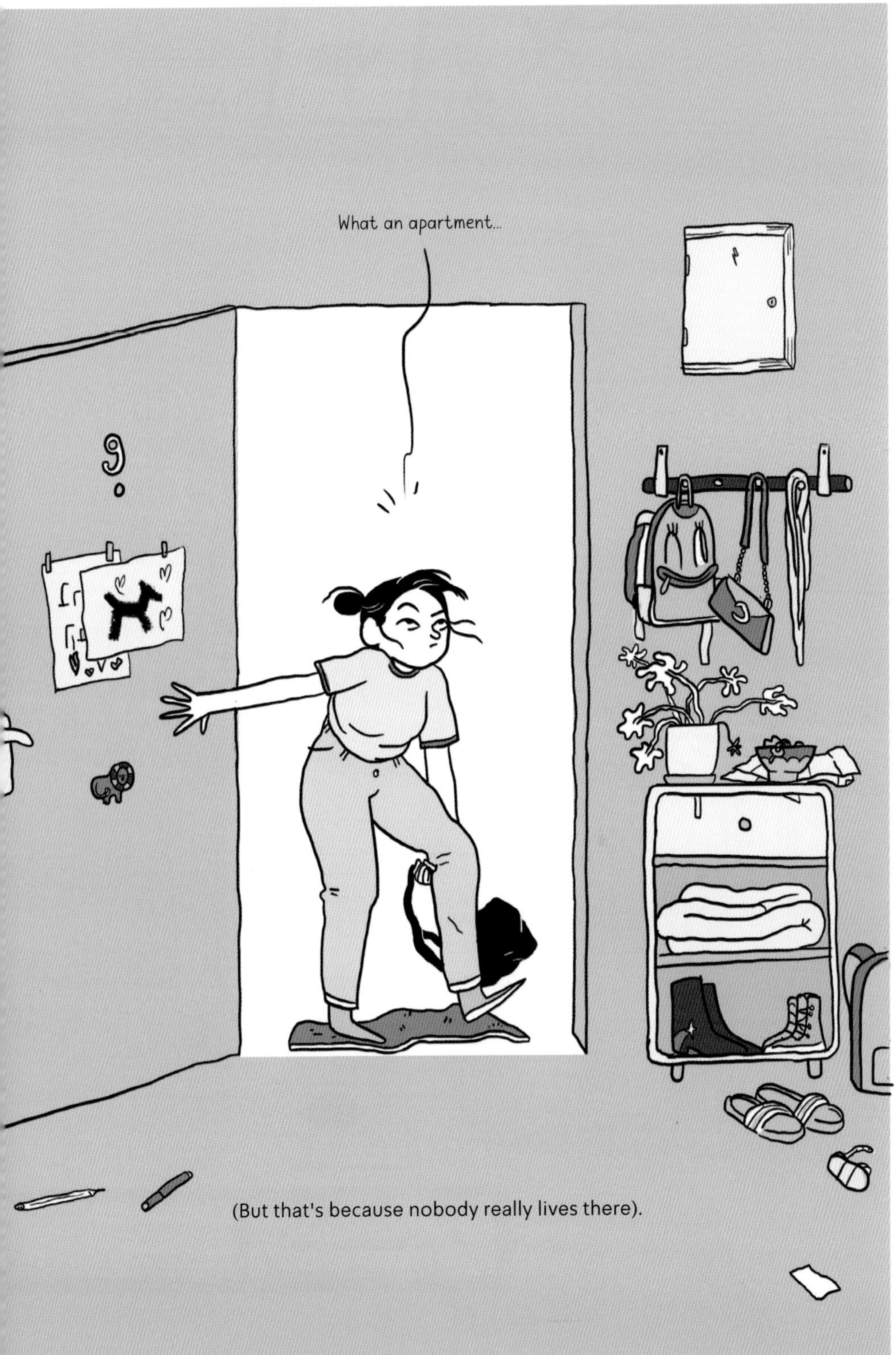
What an apartment...
9
(But that's because nobody really lives there).

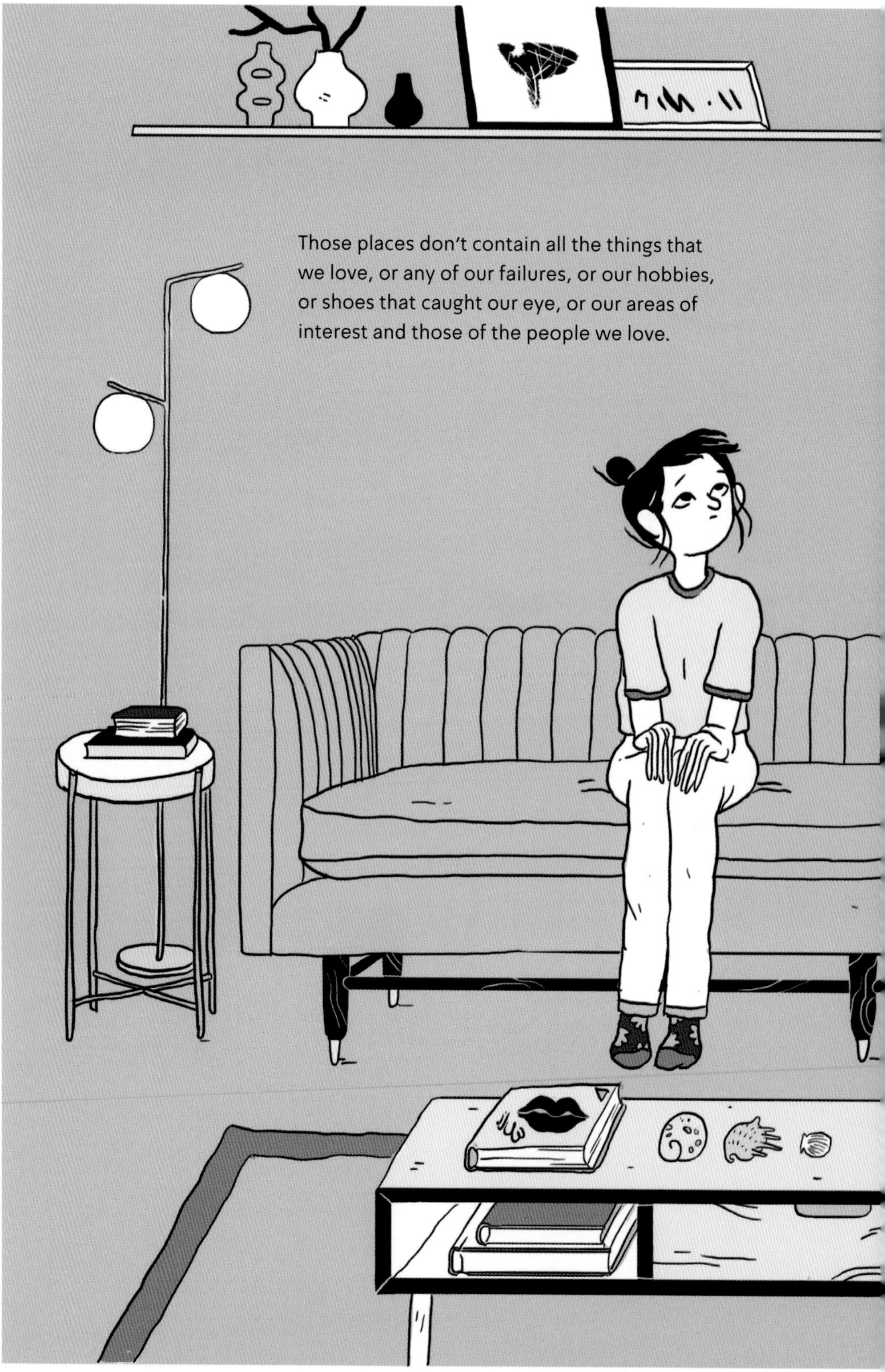
Those places don't contain all the things that we love, or any of our failures, or our hobbies, or shoes that caught our eye, or our areas of interest and those of the people we love.

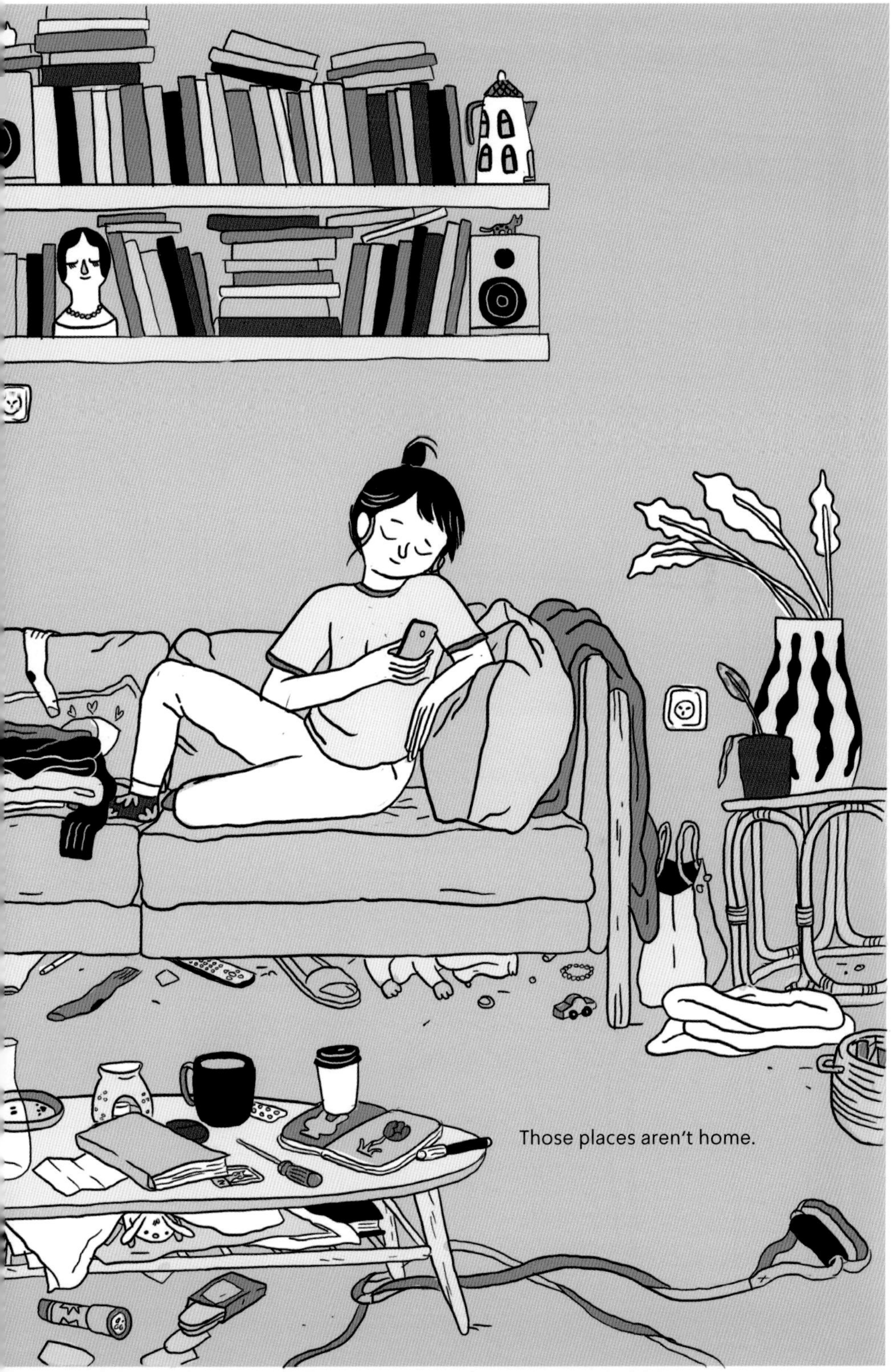
Those places aren't home.

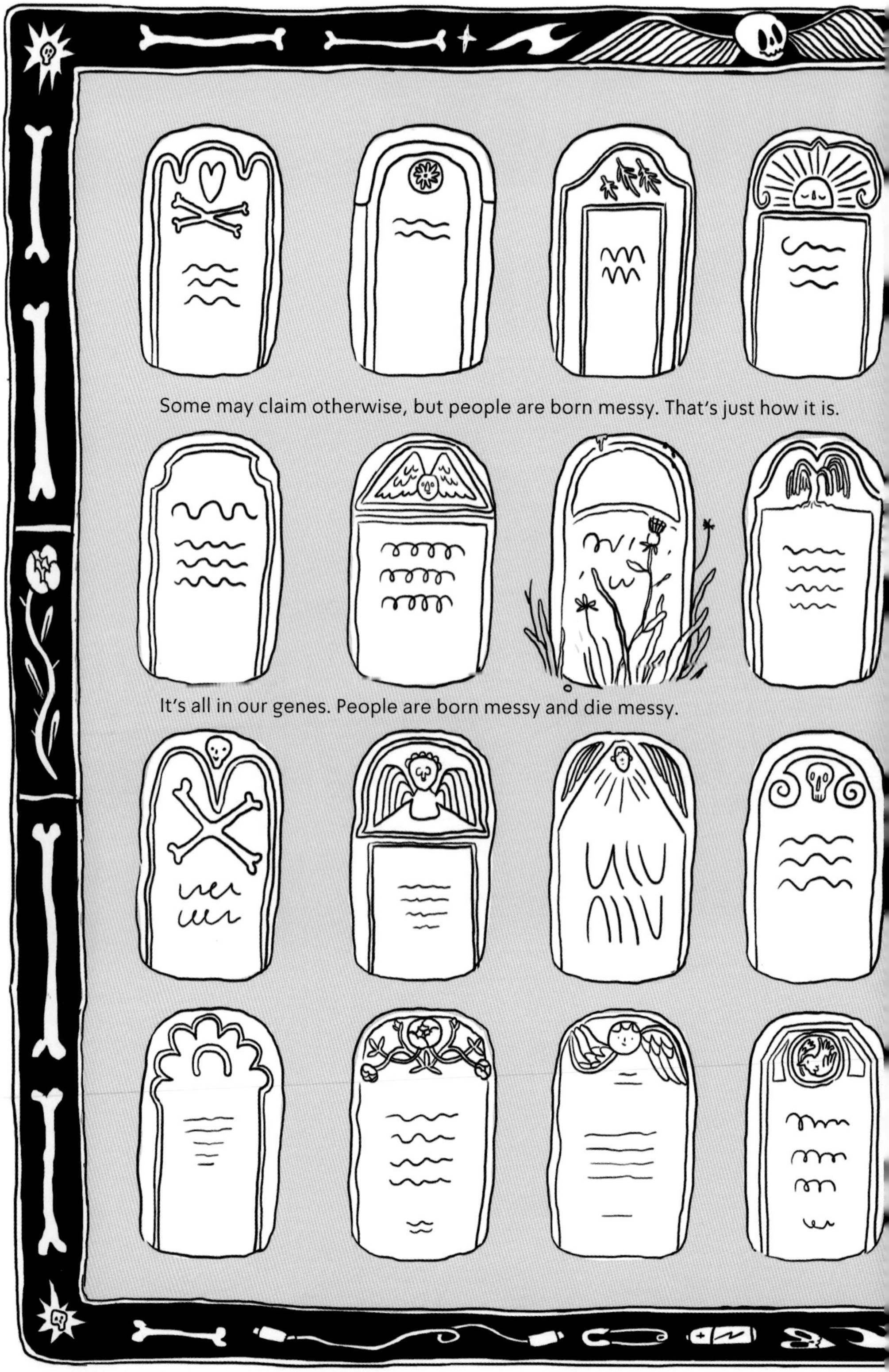
Some may claim otherwise, but people are born messy. That's just how it is.
It's all in our genes. People are born messy and die messy.

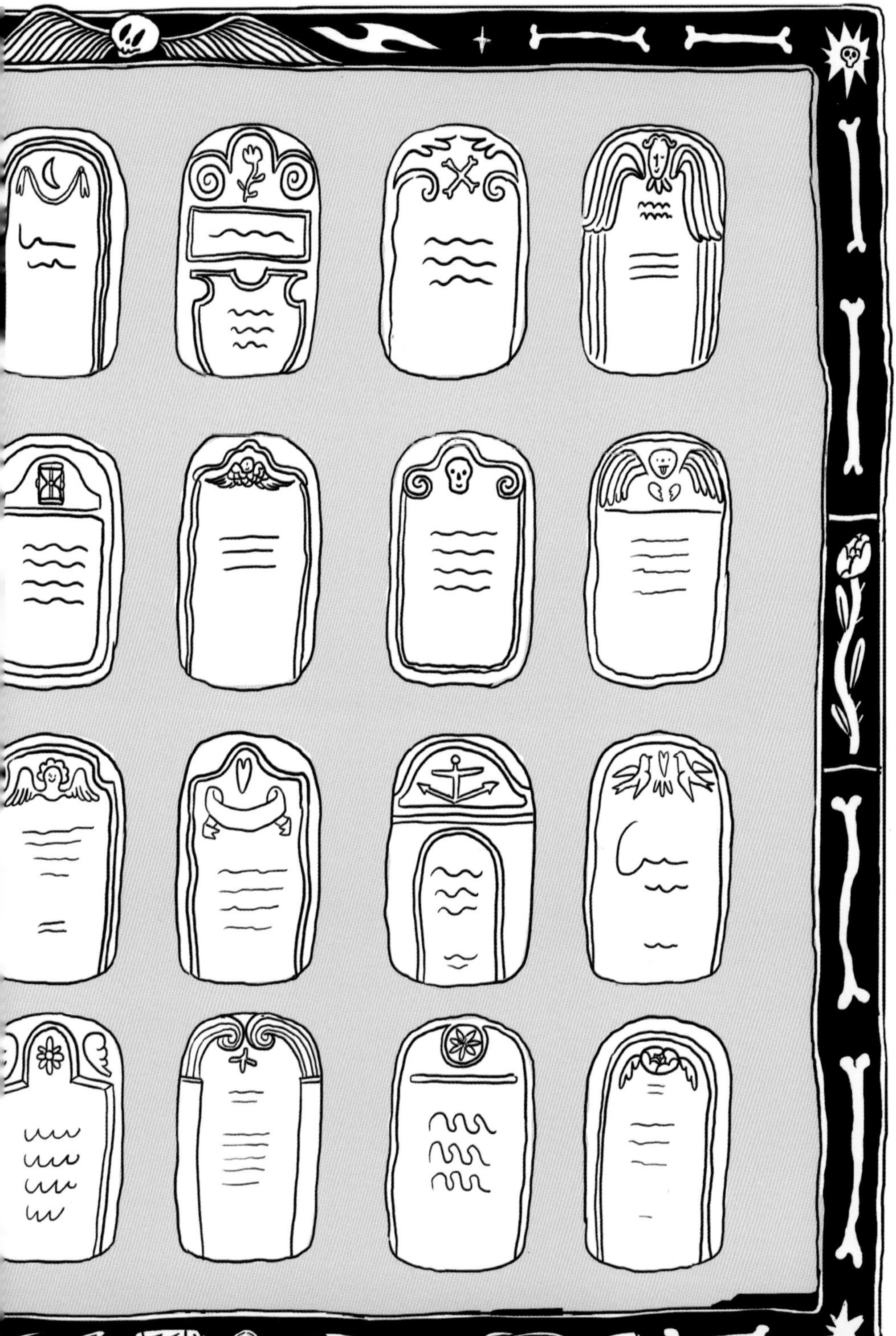

And all we can do is not waste
all the time in between by tidying up.

NOTES